Social Movements
in India

Asia/Pacific/Perspectives

Series Editor: Mark Selden

Social Movements in India

Poverty, Power, and Politics

Edited by
Raka Ray and Mary Fainsod Katzenstein

ROWMAN & LITTLEFIELD PUBLISHERS, INC.
Lanham • Boulder • New York • Toronto • Oxford

ROWMAN & LITTLEFIELD PUBLISHERS, INC.

Published in the United States of America
by Rowman & Littlefield Publishers, Inc.
A wholly owned subsidiary of The Rowman & Littlefield Publishing Group, Inc.
4501 Forbes Boulevard, Suite 200, Lanham, MD 20706
www.rowmanlittlefield.com

P.O. Box 317, Oxford OX2 9RU, UK

British Library Cataloguing in Publication Information Available

Library of Congress Cataloging-in-Publication Data

Social movements in India : poverty, power, and politics / edited by Raka Ray and
Mary Fainsod Katzenstein.
    p. cm. — (Asia/Pacific/Perspectives).
Includes bibliographical references and index.
    ISBN 0-7425-3842-7 (cloth: alk. paper) — ISBN 0-7425-3843-5 (pbk.: alk. paper)
    1. Social movements—India. 2. Poverty—India. 3. Poor—Government policy—
India. 4. India—Politics and government—1947– I. Ray, Raka. II. Katzenstein, Mary
Fainsod, 1945– III. Series.
    HN683.5.S61423 2004
    303.48'4'0954—dc22
                                                                              2004026499

Printed in the United States of America

♾™ The paper used in this publication meets the minimum requirements of
American National Standard for Information Sciences—Permanence of Paper
for Printed Library Materials, ANSI/NISO Z39.48-1992.

Contents

Acknowledgments

This book, like all other collaborative efforts, has a long history. In April 2001, most of the contributors came together for a workshop on *Social Movements and Poverty in India* at the University of California at Berkeley cosponsored by the Center for South Asia at Berkeley and Cornell University's Department of Government and South Asia Program. This book is the result of that conference.

We would like to thank the participants at that workshop, particularly the discussants Michael Burawoy, Indrani Chatterjee, Pradeep Chibber, Lawrence Cohen, Ruth Collier, Louise Fortmann, Ruthie Gilmore, Gillian Hart, Barbara Metcalf, David Meyer, Ellora Shahabuddin and Michael Watts. We also thank the staff of the Center for its organization of the conference and gratefully acknowledge both the University of California, Berkeley, and Cornell University for their generous support of the workshop and this book.

Many friends, colleagues, and students at Cornell and Berkeley contributed to the development and ultimate production of this book, particularly Sarah Tarrow, Matt Baxter, Ruprekha Chowdhury, and Laurie Coon. Finally, we would like to thank our friend and colleague, Mark Selden, series editor at Rowman and Littlefield for his thoughtful comments and advice and Susan McEachern and Jessica Gribble for shepherding this book through to the end.

Introduction

In the Beginning, There Was the Nehruvian State

Raka Ray and Mary Fainsod Katzenstein

My only excuse for taking up poverty as an area of concern so late in my life, despite my knowing that it is a vast and complex subject, is that those who should be concerned about it are moving further away from either diagnosing and analyzing the phenomenon of poverty and the new depths of destitution and untold human suffering to which it has sunk, or providing new thresholds of understanding which can enable the poor themselves to overcome it.

—Rajni Kothari[1]

Not only is the persistence of widespread undernourishment in India—more than in all other regions in the world—quite extraordinary, so is the silence with which it is tolerated, not to mention the smugness with which it is sometimes dismissed. . . .

Given our democratic system, nothing is as important as a clearer understanding of the causes of deprivation and the exact effects of alleged policy remedies that can be used. Public action includes not only what is done for the public by the state, but also what is done by the public for itself. It includes what people can do by demanding remedial action and through making governments accountable. I have argued in favour of a closer scrutiny of the class-specific implications of public policies that cost the earth and yet neglect—and sometimes worsen—the opportunities and interests of the underdogs of society. The case for protesting against the continuation of old disadvantages has been strong enough for a long time, but to that has to be added the further challenge of resisting new afflictions in the form of policies that are allegedly aimed at equity and do much to undermine just that. The case for relating public policy to a close scrutiny

1

of its actual effects is certainly very strong, but the need to protest—to rage, to holler—is not any weaker.

—Amartya Sen[2]

India has long stood out among the newly formed states of the last century as rich in the resources of civic life. Dating from well before the inception of the new nation in 1947, organized societal actors have played a vital role in India. In post-independent India, it would be similarly impossible to account for emerging social identities or critical policy junctures without acknowledging the influence of these organized societal forces, perhaps particularly of social movement organizing: It is hard to imagine, for instance, the 1950s land reforms without the previous decades' Tebhaga and Telengana movement struggles in West Bengal and Andhra Pradesh.[3] It is impossible to contemplate Prime Minister Jawaharlal Nehru's consent to linguistically divided states without attributing a major role to the mass-based agitations around language in Southern India in the late 1950s and mid-1960s.[4] The fiery actions of the Naxalites in the late 1960s and 1970s, the pro- and anti-sati protests after Roop Kanwar's death in Deorala in the 1980s, and the Rath Yatra (the chariot-led processional) that traversed India destined to reach the Ram Temple in Ayodhya, Uttar Pradesh, in the 1990s were epochal events that significantly altered the contours of Indian political, economic and social life.[5] None of these actions was spontaneous. They were all planned or influenced by organizations which had effectively mobilized their constituents—students, farmers, Hindu and Muslim women, youth.

Our purpose in this book, however, is not to argue for the general importance of social movements in India but to consider, rather, the question of whether movement activism has served the constituencies of the least advantaged that movements in India have so strongly over the years claimed to represent. In the age of liberalization and globalization—denigrated in some quarters, celebrated in others—the Nobel Prize–winning economist, Amartya Sen, and political scientist and social activist Rajni Kothari both remind us not to lose sight of the importance of poverty alleviation and other issues of oppression as a standard against which to measure the fast moving economic and political changes of our time. As recently as 2001, the discovery that poor tribals in Orissa had died after consuming the rotted kernels of mangoes sparked a renewed debate about the numbers of Indians who were dying of starvation at a moment when most discussions about the Indian economy concerned the future of the technology sector and the expansion of markets.[6]

The very need for such a reminder is itself a sign in India as in much of the rest of the world of an important shift in political thinking. Global consciousness about the poor appears to have receded to the far reaches of official discussions and policy debates. In the Nehruvian era, from the time of independence to Nehru's death in 1964, "poverty alleviation" was a foundational standard against which policy proposals and political claims were measured. Movement activism was in some sense directly accountable to this discourse. But with the shift from state to market and from reigning ideologies of secularism to credos of religious nationalism of the last several decades, poverty reduction no longer serves its earlier role as a political template against which political or policy initiatives are assessed. Imputed, instead, has been the assumption, largely unspoken, that the unleashing of market forces will improve the livelihood of all.[7]

In this volume, we ask how social movements have responded to these changing times against the background of an assessment of social movements of the previous half century. Did the once social democratic discourse of the Nehruvian period empower the redistributive purposes of social movements or appropriate and deflect their issues? With the decline of the Nehruvian state, have class and poverty concerns lacked legitimation or have the movements become, in some sense, the carriers or "abeyance structures" which continue to keep such concerns alive? As social movements face these new choices and constraints, what conceptual and political strategies have they pursued?

THE BOOK'S APPROACH

The essays in this book are grounded in two premises about social movement politics in India shared by the authors. The first is a core generalization that sees the preponderance of Indian movements as having in the early post-Independence years been accountable to a master frame which required activists to attest to an engagement with issues of class and specifically the poor. The second generalization is that social movements whose thinking and actions were once framed by their rotation in the orbit of the Nehruvian "sun" have had to reinvent themselves. This reinvention has been necessitated by the dramatic swing from the early post-Independence symbiosis of state, party, and movement organized around democratic socialism on the left to its unraveling in the mid 1960s through the 1980s and the ascendance of its institutional mirror image on the right, the similarly synergistic nexus of state, party, and movement now organized, however, around religious nationalism and the market.

Yet even as the state has failed to keep its promises to the poor and the left parties' influence has been relegated to specific regional locales, scholars have increasingly looked to organized civil society as a possible force which can articulate the interests of the poor. But if we are to focus on civil society actors as potential agents in this transformation, then we need to put social movements back into the story. This is particularly the case in India where social movements have been such a long-standing force.

Scholars concerned with the decline of the Nehruvian state and the failure
of its promise to the poor have not paid much attention to social movements
as actors who may buffer, accelerate, ameliorate, and challenge the shifting
agendas of the state. The Marxist argument highlights the significance of the
capturing of state power by dominant societal interests as the decisive issue
determining social outcomes. Thus, Pranab Bardhan, for example, argues
that compromises and conflicts among dominant interests such as industrial
capitalists, rich farmers, and urban white collar and public sector officials
have shaped the political economy in India. This prompted, in his view, an
accommodationist politics which failed to seriously undertake land reform,
and therefore left intact the root of the real issue of poverty. The problem
here is the capture of the state by elite interests.

There is another long tradition in the study of Indian politics that situates
the failure of poverty remediation in the failure of state capacity, in state deinstitutionalization, or in the weak-strong character of state institutions.
Scholars in this tradition such as Atul Kohli focus on issues of governability
and in particular, on the relationship of political parties to the state. Thus the
state's failure to govern and to minister effectively to its poor is, by and large,
a consequence of the post-Nehru decline of the Congress Party.[8] Others, such
as Pratap Mehta and Kanchan Chandra, point to failures of intra-party democracy, which leads to factionalism and ultimately disunity and poor governance.[9] Precisely because the Nehruvian state was interventionist, its role
in development was crucial, and its diminishing effectiveness a cause of great
concern. Failure to deliver services (especially for the poor) due to a failure
of governance, then, is what explains the ultimate downfall of the anti-
poverty commitments of the Nehruvian state. Thus, had the state been sufficiently institutionalized, the picture of Indian politics and Indian poverty
would look very different today. The problem, then, is de-institutionalization.

A third answer, offered by pro-market scholars such as Ashutosh Varshney
and Jagdish Bhagwati, is that the problem of effective poverty alleviation lies
precisely in the excessive democratization of the Indian polity. As Varshney
argues, "democracies by themselves don't remove poverty, economic strategies do."[10] He argues that democratic pressures from below prompt politicians to choose short-term redistributive strategies rather than more effective
indirect long-term poverty alleviation strategies such as trade liberalization.
Varshney concludes, in effect, that the sort of market-driven economic reforms that do best at removing poverty are more likely to be undertaken by
authoritarian than by democratic or populist regimes. Thus in democracies
market reformers need to convince politicians that markets are simply better
in the long run, and this is no easy task. The problem here is the capture of
the state by voters—the excess of democracy.

Finally, a now increasingly popular answer stems from postcolonial scholars such as Ashis Nandy and Partha Chatterjee. In essence, they argue that

the Indian state, arrogating to itself the supreme power of the land, imposed upon the Indian people a nationalism that rode roughshod over all other identities,[11] a secularism that was incompatible with the importance of religion in India,[12] and a socialism which, in its focus on industrial development, excluded most of rural India.[13] The rise of the Hindu Right, then, is a backlash, a reaction to the exclusions and incompatible ideologies of the Nehruvian project. The problem here is cultural incompatibility, or in Sudipta Kaviraj's succinct phrasing, one of "alien provenance."[14]

All four arguments pay attention, in individual ways, to the crucial links between the state and society and grapple with the questions that most haunt India today, the manifest failure of the nation to offer adequate food, shelter, security and respect to its poorest citizens. There is, however, a lurking consensus that unites these four otherwise disparate theoretical approaches and that is that the key actors in the Indian drama are the state, competitors of the state, and economic elites. The role assigned to poor and non-elite sections of society is to be governed and to suffer from poor governance. They vote and are at worst dysfunctional to smooth governance or at best are of crucial importance as voting blocs in a democracy, but no more. They react, in the end, in primordial ways, turning to identities of caste and religion to reject the state and its failure to represent them or to give them what they need.[15] While "dramatic confrontations between the dominant and dominated" have merited attention, few scholars have actually considered these confrontations, and the organizations that do the confronting, as key actors in postcolonial India's political world.[16] Following subaltern studies, more attention has been paid in the recent past to insurgent consciousness and daily acts of resistance, including the observation that while these actions may indeed have constraining effects on authority, they are not necessarily conscious political acts.[17] Thus while resistance on the part of the subaltern has come to be seen as a regular feature of Indian politics,[18] strangely, with a few notable exceptions, the significance of organized political action has been minimized in such analyses.[19]

The role of social movements in India has been documented in numerous individual case studies of ethnic, language, gender, environmental, and other movements. There are, however, surprisingly few studies of social movements in India that range across the political landscape or endeavor to track the changing character of social movement cohorts in relationship to particular issues or institutions over time. One scholar who casts a wide net is Ghanshyam Shah. In his early work, Shah classifies movements by the degree of their transformative intent or consequence, identifying movements as revolts, rebellions, reformist, or revolutionary.[20] However, in later studies, Shah endeavors to build in the possibility of seeing movement activism in more dynamic terms by categorizing movements by their preeminent subject-actors whose organizing efforts may shift over time.[21] This effort to understand changing cohorts of movement actors is taken up also by Gail Omvedt in one of the most compelling analytical overviews to date of the changing character of social movements in India. In *Reinventing Revolution,* Omvedt argues that the most important shift in movement politics has been conceptual: In response to changing governance and ascendant societal shifts, she contends, a class of "new social movements" emerged (in the 1970s) that defined exploitation and oppression in relationship to traditional Marxism ". . . but [had] clear differences with it."[22] The "vanguardship" of the working class was repudiated, she states, in favor of a more plural organizing base located in caste, gender, and other socio-economic identities. At the same time, inequality and oppression were still the reigning ideas driving the organizational momentum.

This book builds on Shah's and Omvedt's analyses to make a more temporally and conceptually comprehensive set of claims. Where Omvedt, writing in 1993, depicts a single landmark shift in social movement strategy and identity, we propose in this volume a periodization of three distinct time frames. The essays here range across three phases (1947–1966; 1967–1988; 1989–the present) which we see as distinct cohorts of movement activism. This framework is based on the importance of social movement response in India to the shifting master frame of the state (from state to market; from secular and social democracy to religious nationalism coupled with liberalization). We build on Shah and Omvedt in arguing also for a broader conceptualization of social movement strategies. The shifting master frame has entailed for social movements not only a choice in what Shah notes as degrees of movement "radicalism" or of what Omvedt[23] speaks of as changing movement conceptualizations—the enlarging out from class conceptualizations to other understandings of movement identities. This shift in master frame has also galvanized the development of a highly variegated set of movement strategies. Indeed, the chapters in this book suggest we identify five quite distinct responses, ranging from the repudiation of the Nehruvian master frame—its repudiation, dilution, adaptation, and reconfiguration—to its adoption/espousal. In the sections that follow, we first delineate the character of the Nehruvian master frame, providing an overview of the movement responses. We then turn to a more detailed description of the three periods of social movement development, and conclude with some observations about what lessons emerge in aggregate from the analyses of the movements since Independence.

THE MASTER FRAME OF DEMOCRATIC SOCIALISM

Whether in India or elsewhere, social movement politics are invariably shaped by master frames. In Germany, for instance, for the 1968 generation, the disassociation from the imprint of fascism was an ideological imperative that reverberated strongly two decades after World War II. In the United States, the master frame of civil rights informed much feminist activism and the organizing of other movements that fought discrimination throughout the 1970s and into the next decades as well. In India, the intersection of the massive mobilization of the nationalist movement under Gandhi's leadership with Nehru's very different visionary commitment to democratic socialism following Independence set the terms of movement politics from the earliest days of post-1947 politics.

In the decades prior to Independence, both communist and socialist activists brought issues of economic justice to the fore of Congress party debates, and Nehru himself, albeit more in his earlier than in later years, made issues of economic subsistence and well-being for India's poor a central part of his writing and speeches. Gandhian populism, central to the nationalist movement, and the leadership of B. R. Ambedkar which gave prominence to the debates over untouchability, propelled issues of equality and social justice into the political limelight. Heated debates among Gandhi, Nehru, Ambedkar, and Ram Manohar Lohia focused on the manifestations and causes of Indian poverty and the policies that would best serve the needs of the most deprived.[24]

During the pre-Independence period and Nehruvian years (from Independence until a few years past Prime Minister Jawaharlal Nehru's death in 1964), the twin discourses of poverty alleviation and development, with its attendant contradictions, came to occupy the status of a dominant social script. The Directive Principles of State policy held out a promise that the state would attempt to maintain a minimum standard of living for all its citizens. Indeed, as Rajni Kothari has argued, poverty removal came to be seen as a political task, and one that was necessary to the development of a healthy democracy.[25] Yet the language of democratic socialism continued to stand in tension with the pressures of capitalist development.[26] Given the tension between building a capitalist, independent economy on the one hand and redistributive equality on the other, though there was much talk about reducing poverty through land reform and progressive taxation, in the first three Five Year Plans it was assumed that "sustained high rates of growth" would be the principal means to alleviate poverty.[27] Rather than undertaking sweeping redistributive changes, the poverty alleviation strategies that were undertaken were piecemeal, and great care was taken to avoid losing the support of the propertied classes. It was thus the bureaucracy which was entrusted with the task of administering redistribution.[28]

During this phase, Nehru and the Congress, the party of independence, of "nationalism," "democracy," and "secularism," spoke in the name of the nation and all interest groups. Despite little actual poverty alleviation, social movements were more or less quiescent. During the period of the Nehruvian state, from 1947 until the mid-1960s, much political activism that sought to represent particular groups emerged in the form of political parties and/or social movements from within the body of the state/Congress party. Thus labor, among other movements, was incorporated within the parent body of Congress, and tamed in the process. This phase coincided with the height of the developmental state and its modernist hubris (dams as the new temples of India). During this period, with the exception of periods of communist activism, distributive movements made few disruptive demands. In the classic formulation about what Rajni Kothari called the Congress Party system, Robert L. Hardgrave writes, "[o]rganized groups emerged from the Congress umbrella as distinct parties [and social movements] but each left within the Congress an ideologically congruent and sympathetic faction. Thus each of the opposition parties, the Jan Sangh, Swatantra, the Socialists, and the Communists—retained access to the Congress that provided it with an influence disproportionate to its size."[29] Despite this influence, it also followed that many of these newly emergent groups expected to work in alliance with the Nehruvian state and continued to take their ideological cues from the priorities of their erstwhile parent.

The one force that stood outside this dominant discourse, that resisted discussion of rights and poverty, and countered it with unity of blood and the importance of the non-material was the early ideology of the Rashtriya Swayamsevak Sangh (RSS), as Tanika Sarkar points out in this volume. It was the one voice, though faint, that was heard outside the Nehruvian social democratic compact.

Within just a few years after Nehru's death in 1964 and through the late 1980s—referred to here as the second phase—the language of class and of poverty amelioration reverted to a mere strategy in the grab bag of populist/electoral resources rather than to a prevailing presumption of official discourse. By the late sixties, the Mahalanobis Commission found no reductions in inequalities of wealth, health, or consumption in the course of two decades of independence. In accordance with a much rehearsed account, by 1967 the Indian state had entered what can arguably be called a crisis of deinstitutionalization. Three years after Nehru's death, the Congress Party lost its majority in eight states in the 1967 elections and secured a bare popular majority in the parliamentary elections. The splits in the Communist Party (1964 and 1969), the other major political force that had highlighted poverty alleviation, led to a decline in their hitherto crucial presence, and their institutional weakness was accompanied by their inability to speak in one voice.[30] By the early seventies, poverty had risen sharply, and development economists and international agencies came to question the idea that macroeconomic factors would solve the problem of growing poverty, advocating instead "direct attack" (e.g. poverty alleviation programs). Prime Minister Indira Gandhi then initiated her famous "garibi hatao" (destroy poverty) scheme to garner popular support in the impending 1971 and 1972 elections, which she used as leverage to concentrate power in her hands.[31] Gandhi recreated the Congress as a more personalistic vehicle, thus destroying the old institutional base of the Congress Party,[32] leading to massive protests against her rule and to the Emergency of 1975. The class populism of Indira Gandhi's Prime Ministership, however, was short lived, giving way to a pluralization of debates (about caste, ethnic, tribal, and gender identities). By the 1990s, the politics of religious nationalism and the ascendance of economic liberalization began to displace the discourse of economic justice within the bureaucratic offices and legislative chambers of national-level politics. Despite this fragmentation of the left and the deinstitutionalization of the Congress, or perhaps because of it, new political formations came into being during the seventies and eighties. With the loss of the legitimacy of the Congress came a decline in confidence in the state. The state could now no longer be trusted to deliver services or to act in good faith.

In this third phase (from the late 1980s to the present), there is a striking change in political discourse with the emergence of the twin forces of the market and religious nationalism from minority to dominant voices. Precipitated by the 1991 foreign-exchange crisis, Indian trade and industrial policies shifted quite dramatically from state-led to market-driven capitalist growth. Key changes include reduction of governmental controls, encouragement of imports, greater autonomy of private investment, and a sharp decline in emphasis on the public sector.[33] Tariffs fell from 300 percent in 1990–1991 to less than 40 percent in 1997–1998. Bureaucratic controls were dismantled: the import licensing scheme for all but some consumer goods was abandoned and the industrial licensing scheme effectively dismantled.[34] The state has withdrawn from many of the previously unquestioned policies of welfare provision such as food and agricultural subsidies and some ration/food programs. Economic liberalization has been accompanied by the massive NGO-ification of civil society arguably crowding out some of the more protest-oriented forms of organizing within the social movement sector. In the eyes of some, as the state has moved to relinquish its responsibilities towards the poor, NGOs increasingly function as no more than "global soup kitchens" of the New World Order.[35]

In terms of poverty alleviation, the reports are mixed: Viewed from the baseline of the 1970s, the percentage of India's population that is poor has declined, literacy has risen, and morbidity and mortality have diminished. But India has not seen the inroads into poverty which much of East and Southeast Asia have witnessed over the last decades. According to a recent report of the World Bank, an institution inclined not to overestimate the incidence of poverty, "every third person in India still lived [in 1993–1994] in conditions of absolute poverty meaning that India had 50% more poor than all of Sub-Saharan Africa."[36] Since the 1990s, as the Bank report citing India's National Sample Survey goes on to observe, there has been only a slight decrease in poverty despite the period of high growth in the mid-1990s.[37]

Alongside these transformative economic changes to a more market-driven economy has been a tectonic shift in governance. Beginning in the late 1980s, Indian politics has seen the sudden rise of the Bharatiya Janata Party (BJP) and the ascendance of a Hindu nationalist ideology. Moving from two to eighty-five parliamentary seats between 1984 and 1989, the Hindu right-wing BJP was catapulted onto the national political map where it remained as the ruling party at the national level until May 2004, and offered the most comprehensive challenge to the Nehruvian state agenda in India's post-Independence history. The BJP envisions a polity based on the commonalities of Hinduness and the incorporation of non-Hindu communities within a unitary political entity displacing the idea of a secular state based on rights. Amrita Basu writes that the BJP's vision of nationhood is "best expressed in the concept of Hindurashtra (nation-state), a term its leadership constantly uses."[38] Whatever may be the meaning to the BJP of a Hindu nation-state, there is no question about the virulent anti-secularism that is at the core of the party ideology. The rise of the BJP and the actions which propelled it to power have been amply documented.[39] As these accounts show, the political issues of the past four years have not revolved around the liberal reforms so quickly put into place or issues of poverty or equity, but, rather, nuclear bombs, wars against Pakistan, pogroms against Muslims in Gujarat, the possibility of finding the remnants of Ram's temple under the Babri Mosque, and the rewriting (Hinduizing) of history textbooks.[40]

In this volume we look at Indian politics and society from the perspective of organized social actors—its political parties, mass organizations, labor unions and non-governmental groups—as well as the social movements that make up an unusually thriving sector of Indian political and social life. We do so because we believe that without a consideration of their role in the making of the nation's successes and failures, the picture is incomplete and distorted. Almost every major Indian policy has been debated, challenged, or supported by a slew of organized groups of constituents. While political parties are often assigned this role in India precisely because they are at the interface of citizens and the state, the role of mobilizing and organizing constituents has been effectively and systematically undertaken by mass based organizations affiliated with parties, mass-based organizations not affiliated with parties, as well as by smaller non-profit organizations and collectives. These organizations range from Maoist groups operating in the countryside to established service providers such as the All India Women's Conference (AIWC), and from the large and messy coalitions around the Narmada Dam issue to the highly organized political party affiliated labor unions.[41] What role have social movements played thus far in the amelioration of poverty, in addressing the needs of its poorest constituents? What has shaped their responses to these issues, and what shifts in focus, discourse, or strategy, in this era of marketization and nationalism, have they been able to adopt?

What does this master frame mean for social movements in India? Social movements, by and large, do not embrace this frame cynically, but neither does this frame determine their agendas in any direct or simple causal form. Rather, their approach towards the poor is negotiated between the ideals (framing norms) and the exigencies of institutional and daily politics. Movements are not blank slates on which master frames are imprinted; master frames, rather, function as a template of accountability to which movements bring their own histories, distinctive constituencies and ideologies. Master frames are broad categories that allow for multiple interpretations; they are thus malleable by interpretation as well as by change. Indeed, they may be transformed in times of crisis or may evolve over time.[42]

Some scholars have argued that social movements in India have seen themselves defined by a commitment to ending inequality and economic injustice, whatever the range of issues they take up. Ramachandra Guha writes, for instance, that unlike its counterpart movement of the West, the "dominant thrust of the environmental movement in India focuses on questions of production and distribution within human society."[43] The concern in India, Guha maintains, is with "the use of the environment and who should benefit from it; not with environmental protection for its own sake."[44] This kind of assertion is a familiar one even outside the domain of environmental politics in India. This is evident in the organizations often held up as exemplifying an archetype of activist politics—as with the widely heralded NGO, SEWA (the Self-Employed Women's Association in Ahmedabad), depicted in one description as an "organization with an Indian soul" whose "vision and language" is itself produced by the poor women who stand to be its organizational beneficiaries.[45] As an overarching framework, poverty alleviation long functioned as a template through which critiques of movement politics were regularly generated. That some group can or cannot speak for the "toiling masses" was the recurrent claim by or charge against a particular organization of rural laborers or peasant farmers or environmental or women's groups. Revealing, too, is the way that even those organizations outside the dominion of "progressive" politics at least into the 1980s insisted on their credentials as the voice of India's poor. In its early years, even the religious nationalist BJP, for instance, in a 1980 "Statement of Commitments" declared, "the ideology of the BJP would be, broadly speaking, that of Gandhian socialism. Bread, freedom and employment are the Gandhian first principles."[46]

The idea that movements should be measured by their accountability to social justice norms is in India broadly thought to be the signatory principle of movement organizing. Whether or not movements have met this standard, there was for many years after Independence wide agreement among both activists and the scholarly community that was itself engaged in what is often termed "progressive" politics, that social movements must serve the foundational imperatives of ameliorating the ravages of poverty and inequality. Even if they have not actually served the needs of the poor, some scholars argue, they gained legitimacy through speaking in their name. Thus in a recent anthology on India's democracy, economist Pranab Bardhan says, "All the lobbies, of course, speak in the name of the poor."[47] Given the change in master discourse, however, this volume asks whether this analysis of social movements is too static. Do all lobbies still speak in the name of the poor? Which social movements still do, and under what circumstances do they do so? If we think of the discourse of poverty alleviation and class as serving the function of a master frame within movement politics in India, what then of the social movements once the master narrative of democratic socialism has faltered and well after the Nehruvian years have come to an end and nationalism in the guise of Hindutva has become the dominant discourse?[48]

PHASE I: SOCIAL MOVEMENTS UNDER NEHRUVIAN SOCIAL DEMOCRACY: DILUTION, COMMITMENT, AND REPUDIATION

In post-Independence India, there has been no period in which the awareness of inequality and commitment to its reduction has been more a matter of state concern than during Nehru's prime ministership; and yet, ironically, in this very period those movements that were most able to advance a strong redistributive agenda were able to do so largely by opposing the state rather than by seeking state sponsorship or alliance. During the period of Nehru's prime ministership, social movement leaders for the most part seemed to have understood the political choices they faced in largely binary terms—as either falling in with or standing outside the class and poverty agenda of the Nehruvian state. As the Guru and Chakravarty chapter of this book shows, the Nehru government overrode Ambedkar's argument that caste was the social basis of poverty in India rather than class. In later decades, social movements pursued a greater plurality of strategic choices seeking out a multiple set of middle options (the reinterpretation of rather than the accommodation to or rejection of the reigning state ideologies, autonomy from but not full repudiation of the state). But in the first decade and a half after Independence, political activism came to be either subsumed by or insistent on a full disassociation from the institutional power of the Nehruvian state, and the ideological lines were also, concomitantly, more sharply drawn. In other words, the discursive repertoire available to social movements were frame commitment—a determination to sustain a movement's redistributive goals; frame dilution—a dilution of a movement's redistributive goals; and frame repudiation—a rejection of redistributive goals.

Three of the movements portrayed in this book capture what was emblematic of this early post-Independence period. Vivek Chibber describes organized labor as allowing its own political agenda to be assimilated by the Congress Party's priorities. Organized labor was in some ways more typical than atypical of much movement politics of the period that saw the independent voices of the women's movement, the cooperative movement, and other activist groups often overpowered by the dominant strength of the state and the Congress party, and their own agendas appropriated and deflected by the discourse of Nehruvian social democracy.

By contrast, Tanika Sarkar's chapter on the Hindu "right" (the RSS and what later came to be called the Sangh Parivar) reveals the ways in which Hindu nationalism, in this period of time, was marginalized by the dominant master narrative, both excluded by as well as self-exiled from the governing ideologies and institutions of the 1950s era.

But perhaps most revealing of all were the "redistributive social struggles" in Kerala about which Patrick Heller writes. In Kerala, the mobilization of a worker-peasant-tenant alliance in the 1950s pushed the social democratic Nehruvian agenda farther to the left than Nehru's Congress Party had ever intended. By opting out institutionally (as did the Hindu nationalist organizations) and remaining outside the Nehruvian umbrella but by adhering to a redistributive agenda (which Hindu nationalists did not), the Kerala movement became a foremost exponent of combating poverty in the early post-Independence period. It was the competitive mobilization in Kerala that fostered this more redistributive movement and party politics—conditions not present in the one-party dominant structure of national politics in the Nehruvian era.

Between Independence and 1964, "the Congress System," named as such by Rajni Kothari,[49] meant that much of the ideological and organizational opposition to the Congress Party operated from within the party itself. Sardar Patel's death in 1950 weakened the chances of the conservative elements within the Congress overtaking Nehru in any contest over leadership. The influence of the left within Congress had, similarly, been diluted by several events—the Communist Party of India's refusal to support the "Quit India" movement against the British (seen by many as deeply disloyal to the nationalist cause,[50] and the 1948 Patel-initiated amendment that prohibited Congress members from also holding membership in another organization (designed to undercut the influence of the socialist membership within the Congress). Gandhi's assassination, in addition, had for the years after Independence fully delegitimized the influence of Hindu forces within the Congress. None of this is to say that conservative or leftist forces were silenced within Congress. Indeed they did counterbalance each other to some degree, with Nehru conceding far more to the conservative forces than advocates of a stronger land reform, collectivist, and redistributive agenda sought and more to the role of government planning and regulation than the business or industrial flank of the Congress Party desired.

The immediate post-Independent period, Vivek Chibber argues in his chapter on organized labor, set the terms for social movement activism for a long time to come. Chibber contends that 1947-1950 was a "critical moment" in which the Industrial Truce Conference, in particular, signified Indian labor willingness to settle for class accommodation rather than compromise, thus weakening itself and its ability to represent the needs and interests of the majority of the working class. This failure, Chibber writes, was due in part to the strength of the employers and their offensive, the state's class bias, and labor's strategic mistakes such as their agreement to demobilize. As a result of this compromise, the industrial relations regime was tilted heavily towards capital, collective bargaining was discouraged, multiple unions hampered plant-level collective action, and unions at the national level were split into warring federations dependent on state patronage. Labor gave up its organizational independence and chose inclusion in policy agencies over mobilization. Thus, even at the moment of formation of the Nehruvian state, perhaps because of the co-occurrence of the state's emergence and the birth of the labor movement, labor became more dependent on than autonomous of state and party interests leading to a future trajectory in which labor was "destined" to remain subordinate.

Chibber's narrative captures the experience of a number of movements of the post-Independence period. Although perspectives on these claims could no doubt be contested, both the cooperative movement and the women's movement could arguably be depicted as having similarly succumbed to the strong hand of the Nehruvian state. In their edited book on the Indian Cooperative Union and its role in the Cooperative Movement, L. C. Jain (the founder along with Kamaladevi Chattopadhyaya of the Indian Cooperative Union) and Karen Coelho record the early struggles between the cooperative movement and the state. "Astoundingly," Jain writes, "the State itself, which had chosen cooperatives to be an important vehicle, became in a sense its rival and competitor."[51] The ICU started, Jain writes, with handloom cooperatives, only to see the government launch its own Handloom Development Corporation. Instead of fostering self-management, the state assigned civil servants to administer the cooperative enterprises. Writing on one of the success stories of the cooperative movement, the Kheda district dairy project, Coelho comments on how the cooperatives' successes relied on the dominant place of the landowning caste of the region and, "contrary to expectation, the landless or the very poor did not figure prominently among the beneficiaries."[52] The goal of the cooperative movement, of freeing the poor from the "local regimes that held them oppressed—from the zamindar, the moneylender and the trader, the clutches of caste, class and communal systems" had to be significantly modified with time.

The experience of the women's movement in this early period reflects, in some similar but also some different ways, the hegemonic place of the Congress Party and the State. The largest women's organization of the period was the All India Women's Conference (AIWC), founded in 1927 at the initiative of Margaret Cousins and with the organizational impetus of a broad cast of leaders. Even from the beginning, the many-layered and regional diversity of the movement including of the AIWC itself makes it difficult to generalize about the movement's strategy and goals, but it is revealing (as Geraldine Forbes reports) that Cousins used her address to the membership in 1936 to invoke Nehru's critique of the movement's superficiality and the need for it to address "root causes."[53] Although, as Forbes writes, some of the local branches had addressed issues of poor women—"supporting peasant women, teaching untouchables, encouraging political involvement"[54]—in general the national level organization did not make class inequalities or poverty central to the development of Conference programs or mobilizational campaigns.[55] Many decades later, it was the women in organizations that had distanced themselves from the Congress and the State—the women of the agrarian Telengana and Tebhaga movements, women who composed the National Federation of Indian Women (NFIW), founded in 1954 and associated with the Communist Party of India, who took on the dual struggle of establishing women's rights within their own organization and prioritizing poverty as an issue affecting women. As with Chibber's argument about the labor movement in the early years of Independence, the close nexus of movement and state probably weakened the radical agenda of the cooperative movement; and while it may have strengthened the attention to poverty of the moderate wing of the women's movement, it still remained the case that those who prioritized class inequalities and poverty remained more distant from Congress and the state.

Although Chibber's discussion of organized labor at the time of Independence and the claim dilution, which he argues followed labor's incorporation within Nehruvian social democracy, is representative of a range of social movements of the time, the chapters in this book on the mobilizational alliance in Kerala and on the growth of Hindu nationalism are distinct cases. Both, however, are in some sense examples of "repudiation"—movements which refused incorporation or even cooperation with the state. Heller's discussion of the Kerala case shows how this autonomy allowed a movement to commit itself to a redistributive agenda, whereas that by Sarkar registers how this institutional autonomy led to a mobilizational practice that had little to do with class equality.

Heller's chapter is instructive as a critical "outlier" case. What has made Kerala a successful example, both by Indian and by global standards, of a region where the interests of the poor are addressed is the particular synergistic relationship between the state and social movement politics. State responsiveness is triggered by mobilized pressures from below, which are in turn fostered by state policies. Kerala's achievements (measured by key social

indicators like literacy and mortality) have been more favorable to the poor because of the post-1947 history in which Kerala has been a highly mobilized society. Social movement activism has kept the state responsive to the needs of
broad sectors of the population, and in turn the state has both delivered goods
and services and has provoked further political involvement. As Heller observes, "There are probably few examples in the world where the causal link
between organized social movements and significant redistributive and social
gains is as strong as in Kerala." If Chibber is right about there being early critical moments that direct movements towards commitment to redistribution
rather than the dilution of these goals, the Kerala case provides an affirmation
of this lesson. Right from the mid-1950s, a tenant-worker-peasant alliance was
mobilized by the Communist Party that stood resolutely outside the Nehruvian
umbrella. Indeed when the Communist Party of India (CPI) won the 1957 state
legislative elections, its ministries were dismissed by Nehru and President's
Rule was imposed for the first time in India. But there is another lesson from
Heller's discussion that is different from the "critical moment" argument advanced by Chibber: What has kept the redistributive process alive in Kerala is
the continuous pattern of popular mobilization. As Heller observes, Kerala's is
a history of "acute conflict and recurrent episodes of social mobilization." In
contrast to, in Heller's words, "Nehruvian high modernism, [where] top-down
planning became the instrument of choice," Kerala has had a history of "pressure from social movements and a vocal civil society for state action."

Tanika Sarkar's chapter on the RSS shows us that there was, even in the
Nehruvian period, at least one organized movement which rejected the anti-
poverty stance of the state. The chapter considers, at the outset, several alternative interpretations of the Hindutva "combine"—which has spoken in
many different voices allowing for apparent simultaneous and contradictory
postures. Hindutva is seen by some as the "fruit of the same womb: of communalism—the byproduct of "zealous nation-worship." For others it is
merely an expression of violence (sometimes seen as the "systematic intimidation of non-Hindus) that is sometimes local in nature, sometimes broader,
arising out of class contradictions. Going beyond this, some see Hindutva as
"basically a bourgeois pathology propped up by global capitalism and
served by an aggressive and militaristic lumpenproletariat." While this last interpretation is basically plausible, it is sometimes understood in too simplistic ways, remaining "mired in the realm of mechanical causality." Sarkar's
own approach is to identify the caste and class interests within the Hindutva
"formation" that oppose the liberal and secular commitments to social equality and to the basic tenets of democratic representation themselves.

The immediate period after Independence was in some sense a "critical
moment" in which claim repudiation comes to define the Jan Sangh's (precursor of the BJP) politics. With the banning of the RSS following the assassination of Gandhi by one of its members, appeals to religiously-based

Hindu identity were temporarily discredited. But the institutional constraints and opportunities shifted with time, as Heller argues. As long as the Nehruvian polity held sway, the Jan Sangh had little chance of winning substantial electoral support and little reason to broaden its support base. With shifts in the political order, the 1964 death of Nehru and the decline of Congress, the opportunity to secure electoral power led the Sangh to think more strategically about appealing in word if not in deed to the large banks of low-caste groups in the electorate. The paradox with which this section began—the less close a movement was to being incorporated within the Nehruvian democratic framework, the more committed it could be to a radically redistributive politics—is not undercut by the narrative of the Sangh. What the post-Independence history of the Sangh does elucidate is that autonomy could also be used to foster a politics that ran counter to the egalitarian pledges of the Nehruvian government.

PHASE II: SOCIAL MOVEMENTS DURING DE-INSTITUTIONALIZATION: STRATEGIC ADAPTATION

Between 1964 and 1984, social movements in India entered what can be considered a transitional phase, one in which the ideological underpinnings of poverty alleviation still reigned supreme, but when the institutional vehicle thus far expected to carry out the project—the Congress—was crumbling. The new movements whose origins post-dated the birth of the nation fostered quite a different movement politics from that of the Nehruvian era. Some saw the collapse of the Congress-dominated state and the dilution of the social democratic Nehruvian idealism as both an opportunity and a reason to seek the full capture of state power. Some movements, such as civil liberties movements, and the women's movement, distrustful of the state, sought to occupy a societal space where they could function more autonomously. The politics of poverty, at least at the beginning of this period, was still the unchallenged master frame, but the conception of and activism around it in this new era was far more differentiated. At a time when institutional strength seemed to be replaced by a personalized power (in the person of Indira Gandhi), social movement politics mushroomed in multiple forms in India's political field.

With the disillusionment with Nehruvian policies of development, fueled in part by growing regional and sectoral inequalities, segments of Indian society came to believe that neither the political parties of the Center nor of the Left adequately represented the interests of all excluded groups. Until this moment in the late 1960s, there had been little effective opposition, except for the movements based on linguistic identity that played a part in the formation of new states between 1947 and 1966. The Communist Party split into the CPI and the Communist Party of India (Marxist), or the CPI(M), largely over the relationship to the national state in 1964, and from within the radical ranks of the CPI(M) burst forth the Naxalite upsurge (1967–1973). Starting with a tribal uprising in Naxalbari, in northern Bengal, and spreading to a number of rural areas around the country, Naxalism was shaped not only by agricultural crisis and drought, but also by the image of China as the revolutionary center, and inspired by New Left uprisings around the world.[56]

Naxalism was a major break with the politics of Nehruvian socialism, asserting instead an aggressive, pro-peasant Maoism. In 1972, the Jharkhand Mukti Morcha, the All-Assam Students Union, the Self-Employed Women's Association, various regional farmers association, the Chipko movement, and the Dalit Panthers were all formed.[57] Civil liberties organizations, people's science movements, and a range of other organizations followed, and a revolution in Indian politics was underway. While these movements may not fit comfortably under the Western European notion of new social movements, given their strongly material agendas, they are new in that they challenged the categories of traditional Marxism, and were populated by groups ignored by it. The organizational vehicles for these groups varied widely. Some were small, autonomous, urban groups, others, mass-based rural groups, and yet others were radical wings of political parties. What needs to be emphasized here is that though these movements were marked by organizational variation and innovation, they retained their connection to the master frame's commitment to the poor.

We call the dominant discursive mode of this period "frame multiplication." The larger movements with a national presence soon came to be represented by groups of many kinds. Both the women's movement and the dalit movement, for example, could count autonomous groups, wings of political parties (in the case of the women's movement), political parties (in the case of dalits), unions, rural mass-based organizations, and social work/service organizations within their fold. Thus there was considerable within-movement variation in attention to the needs of the poor. The papers in this section, Mary John's essay on the women's movement and Guru and Chakravarty's on the dalit movement, show that during this period, despite organizational variation, the language of class could be challenged but not ignored.

In their study of dalits, Guru and Chakravarty argue that dalits have faced unparalleled injustices and failed promises in independent India. The extent and depth of historical and contemporary experiences of poverty and abjection shape the contours of dalit politics today. And yet, dalit politics has taken quite different organizational forms, and these have implications for the extent to which the politics deals with poverty. The loosely organized but militant Dalit Panthers, for example, who emerged in Maharashtra in 1972, articulated powerfully through a predominantly class-based frame the necessity of fighting against dalit poverty and for dignity. This class-based framework, they argue, shifted only in the late eighties when the "Mandal Commission recommendations were resuscitated by V. P. Singh's government at the national level. Caste became an overtly political issue with significant electoral incentives for political parties mobilizing on that basis. Caste questions began to occupy center stage in national debates about modernity and citizenship in India." With this came mobilization in terms of caste identity, and the creation of organizations and electoral strategies based on caste.

While dalit activism was shaped by electoral imperatives, the women's movement was able to act more freely precisely because it lacked that imperative. While some segments of the women's movement (especially the urban groups) came to be easily branded as middle class and westernized, as Mary John's chapter shows, the movement remained anchored to the master frame, even as it modified and embraced alternative frames. Some mass based organizations and unions such as SEWA dedicated themselves explicitly to women of the poorest sections of society. Autonomous women's organizations, formed explicitly to counter the subordination of women's interests to political parties, and which saw themselves as part of an international women's movement, introduced the possibility of an agenda that was not strictly within the master frame, but continued to exist in a complex relationship to inherited categories of Nehruvian socialism.

The women's movement of the seventies and early eighties received considerable attention for its campaigns against dowry and for tougher rape legislation. While these campaigns were carried out in the name of all women, particular attention was nevertheless paid to the needs of poor women. The movement as a whole continued to address itself to the failed promises of the Indian state, and devoted considerable attention not just to newer issues of violence against women but to the spheres in women's work, its measurement, problems of undervaluation, declining work participation rates, grassroots organizing, and so on (John, this volume). The extent to which various organizations made poverty-related claims was not uniform, as particular organizations made their own compromises with the Nehruvian master frame and the other allies and discourses to which they felt accountable. The argument here is not, in fact, that all women's organizations successfully mobilized and represented the poor, but rather that in order to establish themselves as legitimate, they had to explicitly retain a commitment to the poor.

This explicit commitment to the poor was not limited to the women's movement and dalit movements of this time, but indeed extended to other movements such as the environmental movement, as Ram Guha's work and Amita Baviskar's chapter here show. And yet, as we shall see, the grip of the master frame noticeably slips in the late eighties. In this transitional phase, we see the emergence of new frames; but the poverty frame still has a firm grip even as institutional autonomy enables the emergence of alternative frames. But in this transitional period, the power of the frame and the space occupied by movement politics were able to block, at least for a while, the rights framing of the agenda. Up until the mid 1980s, as Gail Omvedt so accurately put it, "all the movements were concerned to stress exploitation and contradiction (some sections of society living off the labor and benefiting from the enslavement or poverty of the rest): they [saw] this as historically created; they projected the possibility of the establishment of a nonexploitative casteless, nonpatriarchal, nonlooting sustainable society. They [all saw] themselves as somehow fighting to create this."[58]

PHASE III: SOCIAL MOVEMENTS IN THE AGE OF THE MARKET AND RELIGIOUS NATIONALISM

Between 1984 and 2000, the twin impulses of Hindu nationalism and neo-liberalism fundamentally altered the face of politics in India. The country witnessed two prime ministerial assassinations, the rise and fall of the V. P. Singh government, as well as several other short-lived governments. Two events marked the first signs of the breakdown of the Nehruvian triumvirate of democracy, secularism, and socialism. The first was the furor over the Muslim Women's Bill (1984), which grew in strength and passion even as the BJP used the bill to appropriate the feminist demand for a uniform civil code. The second, which is worth some consideration in the context of poverty alleviation, was the unexpectedly powerful upper caste protest against V. P. Singh's attempt to implement the findings of the Mandal Commission in 1990 through the reservation of 27 percent of jobs in the public sector for Other Backward Castes. This fierce and public agitation threw into crisis the hitherto unchallenged assumption that affirmative action policies were a legitimate means of improving the lives of those who had historically been discriminated against.

In what is often called the Mandal-Masjid sequence of events, the agitations were followed by the now infamous procession of Rama's chariot (*ratha yatra*) which signaled the ascendance of the BJP and majoritarian Hindu politics. The destruction of the Babri Mosque (1991), the Bombay riots (1992), and the establishment of a BJP-headed coalitional government (1998) soon followed. The BJP emerged as the winner in the multiple attempts to reconstruct India politically following the decline of the congress system[59] and the loss of faith in the Nehruvian master frame. The parties of the left appeared, until the 2004 elections, to be moribund and the associated organizations of the BJP—the Vishwa Hindu Parishad (VHP) and RSS—now reign as the most powerful and energized social movements. The fragmented political field of the seventies and eighties, marked as it was by deinstitutionalization, has been replaced by a new institutionalization, coupled with twin ideologies of market and Hindu nationalism.

Internationally, the global neo-liberal agenda has met with some opposition (the massive anti–World Trade Organization [WTO] rallies in Seattle and beyond), but has generally been undertaken with remarkable rapidity in countries around the world, including India.[60] With the shift towards liberalization accelerated in 1991 but begun earlier, there has been a remarkable ideological transformation for many bureaucrats and some sectors of the "intelligentsia" who have come to place far greater faith in the market, in entrepreneurship, and in the private sector, with a much reduced role for the state. Has a concomitant shift occurred among social movement activists? Does the proliferation of non-governmental organizations reflect a process of decentralization in the movement sphere that parallels the one that is taking place in the market? Has the market come, if not to displace the state, then to occupy a now-competing discourse among activist groups that address the needs of the poor? To what extent has the turn towards the global and the economically liberal pushed social movements away from the poor? Faced with the remarkable ideological swing toward markets and the dismantling of state subsidies and guarantees, with an apparent turn away from the poor, social movements increasingly react in one of three ways—frame reconstitution, frame commitment, and frame replacement.

NGOs in India have consistently adjusted their relationship with the state and to poverty through the three phases, from supporting the state by providing welfare and relief immediately following independence, to a more sharply oppositional role in the second phase, and now to its present "uneasy partnership" as they accept money from both selected state and global sources even as they continue to oppose other parts of the state. Through the case studies of three NGOs in Karnataka, Andhra Pradesh, and West Bengal, Kudva shows that the effectiveness of an NGO in poverty alleviation depends not only on its organizational capacity and flexibility, but also, ironically, on the extent to which the state within which it is located is sympathetic to a pro-poor politics. Thus, while SHARE failed in Tamil Nadu, both because of its lack of flexibility and the absence of a pro-poor alliance in the state, the government-initiated and flexible Mahila Samakhya is partially successful in Karnataka, though blocked by entrenched anti-poor alliances. In West Bengal, where the ruling coalition is not actually sympathetic to NGOs, its pro-poor stance and the efficacy of local institutions enables the Nari Bikash Samiti to flourish.

The dominant sectors of the farmer's and biotechnology movements have reconstituted their claims in keeping with the shift towards markets. The environmental movement has also reconstituted its claims in keeping with its alliances with transnational NGOs. The CPI(M) and the Kerala Sastra Sahity Parishad (KSSP) have renewed commitment to their claims as electoral

imperatives and a highly mobilized populace forces them to continually expand democracy. And finally, the RSS's rejection of Nehruvian ideologies is
now backed by the new institutional structures of neo-liberalism.

For the farmer's movements and the movements around genetically modified organisms (GMOs), as Ron Herring and Gail Omvedt show, farmers are
concerned with their material improvement, and often speak about the poor,
but there has been a remarkable shift in the analysis of poverty. Omvedt argues that between the 1980s, when "the farmers' movement spoke with one
voice, though many accents on the issue of rural poverty and exploitation"
and the 1990s, there emerged competition between two major politically autonomous farmer's organizations which hinged not on whether one group
cared about poor farmers or not, but rather on the sources of and solutions
for farmer poverty. The declared winner, Sharad Joshi's Shetkari Sanghatana,
presents a pro-liberalization and pro-technology view which contrasts
sharply not only with the other farmer organizations, but also with farmer
movements in the past. Farmer poverty is seen as caused by urban elites, and
by the state, which holds on to knowledge and technology while purporting
to protect the farmers. Farmer prosperity will come when farmers have access to technology and knowledge and can keep the surplus in the village.
The farmer is presented as a rational entrepreneur who only needs the government to step out of the way. Thus, in a remarkable reversal of social
movement analysis of the past, the market is the solution and the state is the
problem. The parameters of debate have shifted dramatically.

Ron Herring's essay on the struggle around genetically modified organisms
indicates a similar dynamic. Here, we see the state promoting biotechnology
in the name of the poor, but with little real pro-poor political discourse. At the
same time, there is an ideological division between those who could potentially form a pro-poor rural coalition. Herring explores the tension between
the Karnataka Rajya Raitha Sangha (KRRS)–Shetkari Sanghatana mentioned
by Omvedt, focusing closely on their position toward transgenic seeds. Opposition to transgenic crops is articulated in the name of sovereignty, nature,
and health, while pro-transgenic crop discourse appears to be by and large
an assertion of middle farmer rights to wealth and lower debt. Together, Herring and Omvedt argue that despite the opposition to transgenic seeds and Bt
cotton, and the state's inability to enforce biosafety provision, the farmers
themselves are increasingly embracing these seeds. Thus in the farmer's
movement at least, the market appears to have triumphed.

Amita Baviskar's account of the environmental movement brings to the
fore the role of transnational actors in affecting the possibility of poor people's movements. Her account makes clear that the label of "environmental"
movement is, in fact, quite arbitrary, and has more to do with a) the nature
of capital that a movement confronts and b) the nature of alliances it culti-
vates. While the environmental movement of the seventies did indeed assert

a "red" agenda, in keeping with the master discourse, in the late eighties and nineties, the strength of that discourse has waned. Claims over resources now get reconstituted not as claims about equity but as claims about environmental protection. This form of claim is particularly effective when the issue involves global capital, such as the Sardar Sarovar Dam on the Narmada River, precisely because international financial institutions such as the Word Bank are susceptible to pressure from the transnational actors of the environmental movement.[61] These transnational actors, who inhabit the metropolitan areas of the North, in turn, are stirred by images of indigenous dwellers of the South who are keepers of the earth, rather than by images of poor people who demand their right to a living. Left out in this strategy of claims-making, Baviskar thus eloquently argues, are the poorest of the poor who have no land, and no "indigenous" tradition. Thus the strategy of claim reconstitution may be, in the end, costly for the poor.

The remarkable development in Kerala, of a party-led grassroots movement for democratic and decentralized planning, shows that it is possible to use the discursive shift away from centralization to create a corresponding institutional shift that yet retains a commitment to the poor. The new campaign for decentralization is the latest innovation in this distinctive state-society dynamic. Propelled by the KSSP, a movement within a movement, the state has devolved a large percentage of its development budget on localities, thus "reimbedding the state" again in civil society. What Heller calls the "dense tapestry" of Kerala's civil society combines with a stable competitive electoral dynamic to push the CPI(M) to continually mobilize the masses. In this regard, what distinguishes the CPI(M) ruled state of West Bengal from Kerala may well be that the CPI(M) has governed West Bengal without a break, and with little viable competition, from 1977 to today. In Kerala, on the other hand, the Congress and CPI(M), locked in intense competition, trade off electoral victories, and thus the CPI(M) in Kerala must remain innovative and responsive to its constituents. This in turn makes the social movement elements of the party stronger than the corporatist and political elements of the party, unlike the national labor movement of the Nehruvian period, and unlike the labor movement in West Bengal today. The example of Kerala shows, above all, the most successful strategies for democratization are carried out with twin impulses from above and below.

The changes in discursive and institutional terrain in this period has enabled the RSS to gain in momentum and strength. From the very beginning, the RSS has sought to remain outside of the Nehruvian frame, offering the commonality of blood to counter the new nation's talk of rights, and a critique of materialism to offset discussions of poverty. In this new phase, with political opportunity structure on their side, they have, with renewed energy, repudiated the claims of the Nehruvian state. Those segments of the middle classes who wavered between them and Nehruvian ideals now live in a world where much of that ideal is, as Tanika Sarkar puts it, "dismissed as a failure" whose roots can be traced back to "the philosophy of the public sector." Instead of a critique of class inequality, the RSS offers cultural nationalism with a clear "alien" villain—the Muslim—as the explanation for the ills that befall the nation and its deprived. Thus it appears that the institutions and ideologies have come together to enable the RSS not only to assert their own claims more vigorously, but to now push the BJP government to the right much as the Communists attempted to push the Congress to the left in the early years. However, as Sarkar and other scholars note, there is a tension between the BJP government's wholehearted embrace of liberalization and the RSS concerns with India's economic autonomy. In this regard, the party seems to have the upper hand at present, but an uneasiness remains. In this unease may lie the seeds of a potentially new paradigm shift.

Perhaps the most energized yet complex evolution has occurred in the dalit movement in this phase. The movement has adapted itself in different ways to the twin pressures of Hindu nationalism and neo-liberal globalization. In the state of Uttar Pradesh, the dalit-based Bahujan Samaj Party (BSP) engages in a complex series of negotiations with the Bharatiya Janata Party, sometimes acting as its electoral ally and sometimes as its foe. As identity politics grows in strength, the BSP has access to power for the first time. Historic indeed that a political party whose constituents are dalit should be so close to power in India's largest state. It appears that while the BJP needs the BSP to appear legitimate to all Hindus, not just upper caste Hindus, the BSP needs the BJP to approach the possibility of power. As it enmeshes itself in electoral logic, the BSP focuses increasingly on visible markers of cultural recognition rather than the economic demands. At the same time, this third phase has seen a proliferation of dalit-oriented NGOs who seek poverty amelioration through self-help programs, and who strongly advocate human rights. Many such organizations are linked to transnational antiracist movements, and so bring the question of dalit rights to international attention.

CONCLUSION

The focus of this volume has been on the ways in which state–society relations have shifted as India has moved from the state-led development characteristic of Nehruvian "dirigiste" democracy to the newly emerging market-driven economy and to a polity in which religious nationalism has emerged as a preeminent force. The springboard of this book's analysis is the comment by Ramachandra Guha (1997) in which he described the distinctiveness of (environmental) protest politics characteristic of India and of other nations of the "South" as the insistent combining of the politics of red and green. Ideas and identities about environmental protest, he said, were enmeshed in a committed redistributive politics. This dual accountability—to the norms of redistribution and to the specific (environmental/gender/caste/tribal, etc.) goals of a particular movement politics—was widely accepted by social movement activists as a faithful self-description. Indeed, Gail Omvedt's *Reinventing Revolution* effectively named the post-Nehru 1970s and 1980s as the invention of this dual politics blending class ideology with the identities and issue specificities of social movement activism.

From the vantage point of over a decade later, and seen across three different time periods between Independence and the present, we come in this volume to a different set of emphases.

Through the three-phase periodization that organizes the chapter accounts in this volume, we see that the process of pulling away from a redistributive politics was already well underway during the Nehru era itself. As Chibber's essay notes, the radicalism of labor's goals was diluted through its appropriation by Congress Party hegemony. As Sarkar's essay describes, the forebears of the BJP, rather than conforming to the democratic socialist praxis of mainstream (Congress Party) politics, was long at work creating the ideational foundation of a religious populism. And, as Heller's essay so vividly records, it was only in a situation where party organizations firmly located themselves both to the left of and organizationally outside the Nehruvian Congress umbrella that an undiluted anti-poverty politics was fueled.

The standing-on-two-legs that Guha and Omvedt[62] draw our attention to during the post-Nehruvian period rings true; a number of progressive movements did seek to combine a politics of class with other issues and identities, weaving the dual sets of concerns into their language and practices. But we understand the significance of this mixture of issues in somewhat different terms. Whereas it might have been expected that the forces leading to a dilution of the social movement's redistributive concerns would have accelerated with the death of Nehru in 1964, unleashing in full force the proliferation of movements with concerns that diverged far from the Nehruvian language of democratic socialism, this did not happen. Instead, the 1970s and 1980s became witness to the endurance of an (albeit earlier diluted) class and anti-poverty politics. The Nehruvian master frame endured beyond the lifetime of its "master," leaving the movements at least discursively accountable to redistributive goals.[63] The environmental, women's, and dalit movements persevered throughout the two decades subsequent to Nehru's death, to make claims that invoked the importance of keeping anti-poverty goals in view. They did so in a myriad of different ways which makes any attempt at pronouncing the acceleration or deceleration of an anti-poverty politics a conceptual impossibility. As the John, Baviskar, and Guru and Chakravarty chapters show, the women's, environmental, and caste movements of the late 1960s through the 1980s sought to negotiate their way between material and status concerns, ways of sometimes representing and sometimes involving the poor, calculations about alliances with the state or with an oppositional set of other interests and organizations.

They sometimes adapted, sometimes reconceptualized their objectives to accommodate new constituencies and new electoral imperatives, and even as their claims and practices proliferated, poverty concerns were rarely out of sight or hearing. From the vantage of the present day, what bears emphasizing in this period is that there was in fact less a uniformity of "practice" and more a widely shared "conscience" that social movements took with them out of the early social democratic ethos of Nehruvian state politics.

But by the 1990s (the third phase we describe), there is less adherence to the rhetorical requisites of an anti-poverty politics. The language of anti-poverty has emerged in the media again in the wake of the BJP's startling electoral defeat. Yet it is clear that anti-poverty is no longer seen as the motivator for policy, but rather as a modifier or check on pure market economics. The rationales that social movements utilized to argue for clean air, for trade policies that would admit or bar GMOs, for higher prices for farm products find legitimation in language that is no longer as fully laced with populist, anti-poverty language. The Guha argument can be supported with images of the more equity-focused concerns of the Indian environmental movements and the trope of a strongly benefit/distributive justice–conscious activism. There are still Medha Patkars protesting the displacement of impoverished villagers who practice civil disobedience in the face of the rising waters of the Narmada Dam. But there is also, and with increasing visibility, important movement activism (see Baviskar's and Herring's chapters in this volume) that is reconstituting their demands to accord with changing times in ways that often do not foreground the concerns of the poor. And it bears emphasizing that the more powerful movements of the day, represented by the BJP/RSS, have been able to substitute religious populism for class politics.

The redistributive agenda that emerges from the interaction between social movements and the state in India generally bears little resemblance to the Kerala experience in which competitive party politics and popular mobilization have produced significant land reform and a process of decentralization that has encouraged further popular participation. With the waning influence of Nehruvian democracy, the regular invocation of an anti-poverty politics is no longer routine. But social movement politics, perhaps more than any other institutional space (the courts, the parliament, even party politics) is a domain in which the language of anti-poverty remains extant. Whether these movements can survive as abeyance structures—the holding vessels for the egalitarian conscience of India—remains to be seen.

NOTES

The authors thank Mark Selden for his close reading and guidance as well as Amita Baviskar, Anuradha Chakravarty, Ron Herring, Mary John, and the anonymous reviewers for the press for their helpful comments.

1. Rajni Kothari, *Growing Amnesia. An Essay on Poverty and the Human Consciousness* (New York: Viking, 1993), 1.

2. Amartya Sen, "Hunger: Old Torments, New Blunders," *The Little Magazine* 2, no. 6, Internet edition: http://www.littlemag.com/hunger/aks.html.

3. On Tebhaga, see Asok Majumdar, *Peasant Protest in Indian Politics. Tebhaga Movement in Bengal* (New Delhi: NIB Publishers, 1993); Rabindra Nath Mandal, *The Tebhaga Movement in Kakdwip* (Kolkata: Ratna Prakashan, 2001); Peter Custers, *Women in the Tebhaga Uprising. Rural Poor Women and Revolutionary Leadership (1946-47)* (Calcutta: Naya Prokash XII, 235 S., 1987). On Telengana, see Stree Shakti Sanghatana, *"We Were Making History": Women and the Telengana Uprising* (London: Zed Books, 1989); Carolyn M. Elliott, "Decline of a Patrimonial Regime: The Telengana Rebellion in India, 1946–51," *Journal of Asian Studies* 34, no. 1 (1974): 27–47; and I. Thirumalai, "Peasant Class Assertions in Nalgonda and Warangal Districts of Telengana, 1930–1946," *Indian Economic and Social History Review* 31, no. 2 (1994): 217–38.

4. On language-based movements, see Robert D. King, *Nehru and the Language Politics of India* (Delhi: Oxford University Press, 1977), and Jyotirindra Das Gupta, *Language Conflict and National Development; Group Politics and National Language Policy in India* (Berkeley: University of California Press, 1970).

5. On Naxalism, see Sumanta Banerjee, *In the Wake of Naxalbari: A History of the Naxalite Movement in India* (Calcutta: Subarnarekha, 1980). On Sati, see John Stratton Hawley, ed., *Sati, The Blessing and the Curse: The Burning of Wives in India* (New York: Oxford University Press, 1993). On the Rath Yatra and other related events, see Sarvepalli Gopal, ed., *Anatomy of a Confrontation: The Babri Masjid-Ramjanmabhumi Issue* (London: Zed Books, 1993); Thomas B. Hansen, *The Saffron Wave. Democracy and Hindu Nationalism in Modern India* (Princeton, N. J.: Princeton University Press, 1999); Christophe Jaffrelot, *The Hindu Nationalist Movement and Indian Politics, 1925 to the 1990s* (New York: Columbia University Press, 1998).

6. Rashida Bhagat, "The Spectre of Starvation," *Frontline* 18, no. 21 (13–26 October 2001).

7. While this assumption has suffered a temporary setback with the widely held perception that the BJP's electoral defeat in May 2004 has been due precisely to the failure of the market to improve the lives of most Indians, the general policies set in motion in the past decade are unlikely to change substantially with the new Congress government under the stewardship of Prime Minister Manmohan Singh.

8. Atul Kohli, *The State and Poverty in India: The Politics of Reform* (Cambridge: Cambridge University Press, 1987).

9. Kanchan Chandra, "The Ethnification of the Party System in Uttar Pradesh and Its Consequences," in *Indian Politics and the 1998 Election; Regionalism, Hindutva and State Politics*, ed. Ramashray Roy and Paul Wallace (New Delhi and Thousand Oaks, Calif.: Sage Publications, 1999), 55–104; Devesh Kapur and Pratap Mehta, "India in 1998: The Travails of Political Fragmentation," *Asian Survey* 39, no. 1 (January/February 1999).

10. Ashutosh Varshney, "Democracy and Poverty," *Conference on World Development Report*, 1999.

11. Ashis Nandy, *The Savage Freud and Other Essays on Possible and Retrievable Selves* (New Delhi: Oxford, 1995). Partha Chatterjee, "The Nationalist Resolution of

the Women's Question," in *Recasting Women: Essays in Colonial History*, ed. Kumkum Sanghari and Sudesh Vaid (New Delhi: Kali for Women, 1989).

12. Ashis Nandy, "The Political Culture of the Indian State," in *Politics and the State in India; Readings in Indian Government and Politics*, vol. 3, ed. Zoya Hasan (New Delhi: Sage Publications, 2000).

13. Akhil Gupta, *Postcolonial Developments: Agriculture in the Making of Modern India* (Chapel Hill: Duke University Press, 1998).

14. Sudipta Kaviraj, *Politics in India* (New Delhi: Oxford University Press, 1997).

15. Dipesh Chakrabarty, *Rethinking Working-Class History: Bengal 1890-1940* (Delhi: Oxford University Press, 1989).

16. Douglas Haynes and Gyan Prakash, *Contesting Power: Resistance and Everyday Social Relations in South Asia* (Berkeley: University of California Press, 1992), 1.

17. See the series of Subaltern Studies edited by Ranajit Guha, published by Oxford University Press.

18. Haynes and Prakash, *Contesting Power*, 1.

19. Sumit Sarkar, among others, does indeed pay attention to organized movement politics outside the Congress Party, during the struggle for India's independence. See Sumit Sarkar, *Modern India, 1885–1947* (New York: St. Martin's Press, 1989).

20. Ghanshyam Shah, *Protest Movements in Two Indian States: A Study of the Gujarat and Bihar Movements* (Delhi: Ajanta Publications, 1977).

21. Ghanshyam Shah, *Social Movements in India; A Review of the Literature* (New Delhi: Sage Publications, 1990).

22. Gail Omvedt, *Reinventing Revolution: New Social Movements and the Socialist Tradition in India* (Armonk, N.Y.: M. E. Sharpe, 1993), xv.

23. Omvedt, *Reinventing Revolution*.

24. For a flavor of the debates, see the letters Nehru wrote to Gandhi, countering Gandhi's critique of industrialism with his own critique of capitalism. Sarvepalli Gopal, ed., *Selected Works of Jawaharlal Nehru*, vol. 3 (New Delhi: Orient Longman, 1972), 3–5. Gandhi on trusteeship (the rich should treat their riches as a trust for the people) versus Nehru who thinks it impracticable. In Nehru's own words: "If an industry cannot be run without starving its workers, then the industry must be closed down. If the workers on the land have not had enough to eat, then the intermediaries who deprive them of their full share must go." Jawaharlal Nehru, *India's Freedom* (London: Allen and Unwin, 1962), 15–16.

25. Kothari, *Growing Amnesia*.

26. Francine Frankel, *India's Political Economy, 1947–1977; The Gradual Revolution*. (Princeton, N. J.: Princeton University Press, 1978).

27. A. Vaidyanathan, "Poverty and Development Policy," *Economic and Political Weekly* (26 May 2001): 1807–22.

28. Sudipta Kaviraj, "The Modern State in India," in Hasan, ed., *Politics and the State in India*.

29. Robert L. Hardgrave Jr. and Stanley A. Kochanek, *India: Government and Politics in a Developing Nation*, fifth edition (Fort Worth, Texas: Harcourt Brace College Publishers, 1993), 197.

30. Kaviraj, "The Modern State."

31. Hasan, ed., *Politics and the State in India*, 388.

32. Kohli, *State and Poverty in India*.

33. Hasan, *Politics and the State in India*, 388.

34. Rob Jenkins, *Democratic Politics and Economic Reform in India* (Cambridge: Cambridge University Press, 1999).

35. Alan Fowler, "Capacity Building and NGOs: A Case of Strengthening Ladles for the Global Soup Kitchen?" *Institutional Development* 1, no. 1: 18–24.

36. The comparison is not just with East Asia. According to a World Bank report, the proportion of Indonesia's population living in poverty dropped from 58 percent to 8 percent between 1970 and 1993. "India Shows Mixed Progress in the War Against Poverty," World Bank News Release No. 98/1449SAS, 1997.

37. Though there are many conflicting reports, there seems to be reasonable consensus over the following pattern: Rural poverty rose from perhaps 40 to 56 percent between 1961 and 1973-4, and declined to perhaps 34 percent in 1988–89. See Terence J. Byres, "Introduction," in Byres, ed., *The State, Development Planning and Liberalization in India* (New Delhi: Oxford University Press, 1998), 24–25. For a discussion of estimate methods, see Kaushik Basu, "Has Poverty in India Declined?" *Business Standard* (23 January 2003).

38. David Ludden, ed., *Making India Hindu: Community, Conflict and the Politics of Democracy* (New Delhi: Oxford University Press, 1966).

39. See Ludden, *Making India Hindu*; Yogendra K. Malik and V. B. Singh, *Hindu Nationalists in India. The Rise of the Bharatiya Janata Party* (Boulder, Colo.: Westview Press, 1994); and Jaffrelot, *The Hindu Nationalist Movement and Indian Politics*.

40. On the speed and stealth of economic reforms, see Jenkins, *Democratic Politics*.

41. On women's movements, see Nandita Gandhi and Nandita Shah, *The Issues at Stake: Theory and Practice in the Contemporary Women's Movement in India* (New Delhi: Kali for Women, 1992); Raka Ray, *Fields of Protest: Women's Movements in India* (Minneapolis: University of Minnesota Press, 1999); Radha Kumar, *A History of Doing: An Illustrated Account of Movements for Women's Rights and Feminism in India, 1800-1990* (New Delhi: Kali for Women, 1993). On environmental movements, see Madhav Gadgil and Ramachandra Guha, *This Fissured Land: An Ecological History of India* (New Delhi: Oxford University Press, 1992); Amita Baviskar, *In the Belly of the River: Tribal Conflicts over Development in the Narmada Valley* (New Delhi: Oxford University Press, 1996). On Naxalites, see Sumanta Banerjee, *India's Simmering Revolution: The Naxalite Uprising* (London: Zed Books, 1984); Achin Vanaik, *The Painful Transition: Bourgeois Democracy in India* (London: Verso Books, 1996). On Indian labor unions, see E. A. Ramaswamy, *Worker Consciousness and Trade Union Response* (Delhi: Oxford University Press, 1988).

42. See Rita Noonan's discussion of gender politics in Chile, for example, in Rita K. Noonan, "Women against the State: Political Opportunities and Collective Action Frames in Chile's Transition to Democracy," *Sociological Forum* 10:81–111. The diffusion of human rights norms internationally has also affected the political language with which many countries now speak of minority claims, as Margaret Keck and Kathryn Sikkink explore in *Activists Beyond Borders: Advocacy Networks in International Politics* (Ithaca, N. Y.: Cornell University Press, 1998); see also Julie Stone Peters and Andrea Wolper, eds., *Women's Rights, Human Rights: International Feminist Perspectives* (New York: Routledge, 1995).

43. Ramachandra Guha, "The Environmentalism of the Poor," in *Between Resistance and Revolution; Cultural Politics and Social Protest,* ed. Richard G. Fox and Orin Starn (New Brunswick, N.J.: Rutgers University Press, 1997), 35.

44. Guha, "Environmentalism," citing Anil Agarwal, "Human–Nature Interactions in a Third World Country," *The Environmentalist* 6, no. 3: 167.

45. Kamla Chowdry, "The Frontyards and Backyards of Development: Dissent and the Voluntary Sector," in *A Common Cause: NGOs & Civil Society,* ed. Anuradha Maharishi and Rasna Dhillon (New Delhi: National Foundation for India, 2002), 48.

46. Partha S. Ghosh, *BJP and the Evolution of Hindu Nationalism: From Periphery to Centre* (New Delhi: Manohar Publishers & Distributors, 1999), 280.

47. Pranab Bardhan, "Sharing the Spoils: Group Equity, Development and Democracy," in *The Success of India's Democracy,* ed. Atul Kohli (Cambridge: Cambridge University Press, 2001), 226–241.

48. "Master frames are to movement specific collective action frames as paradigms are to finely tuned theories. Master frames are generic; specific collective action frames are derivative." David Snow and Robert D. Benford, "Master Frames and Cycles of Protest," in *Frontiers of Social Movement Theory,* ed. Aldon Morris and Carol Mueller (New Haven, Conn.: Yale University Press, 1992), 138. See also Erving Goffman, *Frame Analysis* (New York: Harper Colophon, 1974); David Snow and Robert D. Benford, "Ideology, Frame Resonance, and Participant Mobilization," in *International Social Movement Research* 1 (Greenwich, Conn.: JAI Press, 1988), 197–217.

49. Rajni Kothari, *"The Congress 'System' in India," Party System and Election Studies,* Occasional Papers of the Centre for Developing Societies, No. 1 (Bombay: Allied Publishers, 1967).

50. Frankel, *India's Political Economy,* 62.

51. L. C. Jain and Karen Coelho, *In the Wake of Freedom: India's Tryst with Cooperatives* (New Delhi: Concept, 1996), 18.

52. L. C. Jain, citing Shanti George, "Cooperatives and Indian Dairy Policy: More Anand than Pattern," and B. S. Baviskar, "Dairy Cooperatives and Rural Development in Gujarat," in *Who Shares? Cooperatives and Rural Development,* ed. D. W. Attwood and B. S. Baviskar (Delhi: Oxford University Press, 1988).

53. Geraldine Forbes, *Women in Modern India; The New Cambridge History of India,* IV, no. 2 (Cambridge: Cambridge University Press, 1996), 81.

54. Forbes, *Women in Modern India,* 83.

55. On the AIWC, see Aparna Basu and Bharati Ray's *Women's Struggle: A History of the All India Women's Conference, 1927–1990* (New Delhi: South Asia Books, 1990), and Radha Kumar, *The History of Doing: An Illustrated Account of Movements for Women's Rights and Feminism in India, 1800–1990* (Delhi: Kali for Women, 1993). Radha Kumar remarks on the "noticeable presence of women in works' movements" and describes the 1930 conference in Gwalior at which a special session on "labour" questions was held in which resolutions were passed on the needs of factory workers and an inquiry into the conditions of women mine workers was sought (1993, 69–70).

56. Vanaik, *The Painful Transition.*

57. Omvedt, *Reinventing Revolution,* 47.

58. Omvedt, *Reinventing Revolution,* 314.

59. Atul Kohli, *Democracy and Discontent; India's Growing Crisis of Governability* (Cambridge: Cambridge University Press, 1990).

60. While the BJP government has been instrumental in pushing forward economic liberalization, it has not been without opposition from its affiliates, particularly

the RSS. See Baldev Raj Nayar, "The Limits of Economic Nationalism in India: Economic Reforms under the BJP-led Government," *Asian Survey* XL, no. 5 (2000): 792–815.

61. Keck and Sikkink, *Activists beyond Borders.*

62. Guha, "Environmentalism," and Omvedt, *Reinventing Revolution.*

63. Discussing this accountability, Jane Mansbridge writes about the way in which groups that may not be connected by membership or authority structures nevertheless may feel themselves to be beholden to a collective discourse through a shared set of norms and shared language. Jane Mansbridge, "What Is the Feminist Movement?" in *Feminist Organizations; Harvest of the Women's Movement,* ed. Myra Marx Ferree and Patricia Yancey Martin (Philadelphia: Temple University Press, 1995).

1

From Class Compromise to Class Accommodation: Labor's Incorporation into the Indian Political Economy

Vivek Chibber

For labor in the developing world, the process of rapid industrialization over the past five decades or so has been a decidedly mixed bag. On the one hand, it has brought, in many regions, rates of growth that surpass anything witnessed in the nineteenth and early twentieth centuries; on the other hand, this rapid growth has been accompanied by regimes marked by labor's political exclusion or simple, brutal repression. One need only to glance at the experience of Latin America or East Asia during the 1960s and 1970s for the unpleasant record. In this regard, labor in India seems to have fared somewhat better than its counterparts elsewhere. Growth rates in India since decolonization have been consistently higher than those of the colonial era; further, but for a short spell in 1975–1977, the Indian working class has enjoyed the full gamut of democratic rights in this period, now stretching beyond five decades.

This happy conjunction, however, should not obscure some less comforting dimensions of Indian labor's fortunes. Of particular interest to us is the fact that, despite having secured the formal democratic freedoms which have eluded workers for long stretches elsewhere, organized labor in the subcontinent has been, and remains, exceedingly weak in its organizational power. In their relations with employers, unions are constrained by an industrial relations regime which is tilted heavily toward capital. Collective bargaining is discouraged in favor of compulsory arbitration; the rules governing arbitration are such as to make it toothless against employer intransigence; the capacity for plant-level collective action is hampered by the allowance of multiple unions; the capacity for sectoral collective action is crippled by the rarity of peak bargaining.[1] At the level of national politics, unions are split into warring federations, each of which is deeply dependent on state patronage. As a result, unions are typically the wards of political parties, their leaders often appointed or forced into position by party bosses instead of being voted into place by rank and file workers, and labor strategy is often subordinated to the exigencies of party politics.

This has some far-reaching implications for the concerns that animate this collection of essays. First, poverty is quintessentially a class phenomenon, despite the latter category's fall from academic fashion in recent years. Now, it is of course true that, in developing countries, the industrial working class only comprises one part of the laboring poor—a category that also encompasses rural workers, peasants, and the teeming millions in the unorganized, informal sector. Nevertheless, any analysis of the dynamics of poverty and inequality is incomplete without a careful consideration of the reproduction of industrial labor. Second, for this category of labor in particular, improvements in material welfare are centrally bound up with the capacity of collective action—within the workplace and without. Labor makes gains for itself when it becomes a labor *movement*. This being the case, the industrial working class is perhaps the poster-child for analyses which seek to link the dynamics of poverty to social movements.

This essay seeks to explore the roots of the Indian working class's organizational weakness. Now, the structural conditions of a developing country are never favorable to its working class. The ubiquity of a massive reserve army of the unemployed or underemployed, the small size of the organized factory sector, the migratory character of much industrial labor—such factors centrally contribute to labor's weakness relative to capital, and India is no exception to this. But it is also true that the underlying structural conditions can be mitigated by the institutional framework which governs the labor-capital relation. Conversely, an unfriendly set of institutions can function to amplify the weaknesses generated by the underlying structure. There is, depending on the nature of the institutional mediation, a wide diversity of class politics compatible with capitalist economic structures. The fact of the Indian labor movement's weakness cannot, therefore, be "read off" from those features of backward capitalism which it shares with so many other countries. For the same features have produced starkly different political dynamics elsewhere—one need only think of the remarkable resurgence of the labor movement in Brazil and South Africa in the 1980s.[2] To explain why the subcontinental working class has remained organizationally weak, we must, therefore, attend to the manner in which it has been incorporated into the political economy.

Investigating this issue in the Indian case is made somewhat *easier* by the fact that the relevant institutions were installed during one brief "critical juncture"—the years immediately following Independence in 1947. It is made *interesting* by the fact that, at the time, the labor movement was not only very different from that which we witness today—in that it was centrally coordinated and relied on mobilizational strategies—but it also managed to place on the policy agenda a set of proposals which, if enacted, would have amounted to a very different kind of labor politics in India. In fact, in early 1947, perhaps few could have predicted that labor would end up as enfeebled as it eventually did. It seemed at the time that the governing framework for labor-capital relations would be of a solidly social-democratic kind, with labor having considerable power at the level of the plant as well as the state. As I shall show, all indications were that labor would be party to a far-reaching class compromise with employers, complete with legally sanctioned works committees, profit-sharing, and limited co-determination at the firm level, complemented by sectoral bargaining at the meso-level and state representation at the macro-level. In the event, these reforms were either never passed, or did not go beyond the cosmetic. The policies which were passed produced the pattern of class politics which has been characteristic of the subcontinent since, and which was described above.

The distance between initial promise and eventual outcome invites analysis. Its value, however, should not be taken to be of a purely historical sort—as an exercise in excavating a buried past. It is also of some analytical and political interest. The examination of why Indian labor was unable to push through its agenda for postcolonial industrial relations provides insight into two issues that are critical to the contemporary political scene. First, I will argue that a basic constraint on labor's ability to extract greater concessions was the economic project that the state had taken up, which was structured by an alliance between the state and domestic capital. This made state managers view labor's interests as secondary to the imperative of maintaining the goodwill of employers. That is to say, the immediate desideratum of state policy was taken to be the cultivation of investor confidence, with labor's interests viewed as a constraint that had to be *accommodated*, not maximized. Second, given this political environment, labor made crucial strategic mistakes which deprived it of the very resources which had enabled it to put its demands on the immediate agenda. In particular, I shall argue, labor leaders erred in abandoning unions' organizational independence and reliance on mobilization; instead, a considerable segment of the labor movement chose to demobilize, subordinate its independence to a political alliance with the ruling party, and rely on the latter's goodwill. But given the structural pressures on the ruling party, this resulted in an immediate loss of leverage and negotiating power. These factors—the state's political bias and the strategy which it recommends—are, I suggest, still in play decades later. The mistakes of the past therefore still hold lessons for the present.

The relevance of the labor movement's strategic choices during the "critical juncture" of 1947–1950 is highlighted toward the end of the paper, when I close with a discussion of the strikingly different fate of labor in the southwestern state of Kerala. The Kerala working class chose a political strategy quite different from the one adopted by the national labor movement after

Independence. Instead of hitching their wagon to the discretion of state managers, unions in the state protected and built upon their independence. While it is true that the labor movement has been allied with a major political party in the state—the Communist Party of India (Marxist)—the fact that the latter itself has never been able to enjoy a steady monopoly of power in Kerala has meant that the reliance on the *party* has not turned into a reliance on the *state*. Indeed, if anything, it is the CPM that is dependent on its union federation. This organizational independence has provided the means for unions to protect their interests through a steady and rather successful use of mobilization as a strategy, as against the politics of political favors and patronage. As a consequence, not only has Kerala labor been more successful than the national labor movement in averting factory despotism, but it has been able to wrest an impressive *class compromise* from employers. So whereas the promise of a class compromise was glimpsed and then lost at the national level, it came to something approaching fruition in one state. That these contrasting outcomes can be connected to different political strategies adopted by labor is, I believe, highly significant not only for understanding the *past*, but also for devising a politics for the *present*.

THE CONGRESS PREPARES FOR INDEPENDENCE

The central elements of the Indian labor relations system, most of which continue to this day, were put into place within a span of less than four years after 1947. This makes the initial postcolonial juncture of immediate interest; what makes it even more interesting is the fact that, in the immediate aftermath of World War II, there appeared to be a strong possibility that the ultimate political settlement of the "labor question" might be strongly social democratic—with considerable power for labor at the level of the shop floor as well as at higher institutional and political levels. The promise—and for some, the threat—of a kind of class compromise between capital and labor was in the air. Of course, at the end of those four years, the position of unions and organized labor was anything but what its leadership had originally envisioned. So it is not just that, in these four years, the foundations for postwar labor relations were put into place. It is that, in this short interlude, forces came into play which managed to sharply turn the political momentum away from the possibility of a class compromise, toward the kind of statist paternalism that has been the hallmark of the industrial relations system.

As the country emerged from World War II, it was widely recognized that independence from the British was imminent, though its precise time-line still unclear. For the past ten years, the Indian National Congress (INC) had been preparing for taking over the reins of state power, and inaugurating the first government of Independent India. The turning point had come in 1935, when the colonial state passed the Government of India Act, which allowed for competitive elections in several Indian provinces. Led by Nehru, the Congress entered the fray with gusto, winning handily in most all of the major Provinces.[3] With the reins of government now in hand, the Congress High Command moved rapidly toward two ends: first, to cement its somewhat shaky relationship with Indian capitalists, who, until this point, had evinced a decidedly suspicious mien toward the Party.[4] The industrialists' attitude was not without foundation, for the Congress was, in the 1920s and '30s fast transforming itself from an elite lobbying caucus into an organization of mass mobilization, with an increasingly vocal radical wing.[5] But the conferral of state power had a sobering effect on the Congress hotheads. Within a year of the Provincial Ministries' formation, the various governments were moving in tandem to placate Indian capital. On the one hand, the ministries lavished domestic business with government contracts—a mine quarry operation in Madras,[6] an electrification scheme in Gujarat,[7] and a paper mill for the Birlas in Orissa.[8] On the other hand, the ministries took a stern stance against labor militancy in their provinces. After a short spell in 1937 when it dealt somewhat sympathetically with labor, the Party took a decidedly negative view of strikes and independent labor action, passing a law in Bombay which severely curbed the right to strike.[9] These two dimensions of Congress policy—boosting business sales and curbing labor militancy—triggered a sea-change in its relations with domestic capital. While segments of the class continued to harbor doubts about the Party's reliability, most of the prominent industrialists now adopted the INC as their party of choice.

The second step taken by the INC in anticipation of its eventual ascension to power was to establish a body that would draw up the contours of future development policy. In 1939, under the leadership of Jawaharlal Nehru, the Congress High Command convened a National Planning Committee (NPC), which was assigned just this task. Continuing the political tilt described in the previous paragraph, the NPC was heavily dominated by industrialists and Congress-appointed "experts," with only one recognized labor leader (as against five industrialists and seven "experts").[10] The Committee's life was short-lived, lasting scarcely one year, but it managed to make a good bit of progress. Through its deliberations, it was able to effect a consensus around one basic fact: that India's future development would be initiated under the guiding hand of the state, through some kind of national planning, with a focus on rapid industrialization.[11] On this, there was agreement between the Congress leaders, the experts, and industrialists—though there was some considerable disagreement around the *scope* of state regulation of capital.[12]

But equally significant was that on the matter of labor policy, the NPC offered recommendations that were surprisingly radical. Chaired by N. M. Joshi, one of the pioneering leaders of the Indian labor movement, the NPC's subcommittee on labor policy submitted a report that was, from the standpoint of Indian industry, a virtual charter for the rights of labor. It recommended the reduction of the working week to forty-eight hours, the implementation of a child labor law which put the minimum age for factory labor at fifteen; the upgrading, and more importantly, the implementation of health and safety regulations, and the implementation of a minimum wage.[13] But more troubling than any of these recommendations was the final section of the report, entitled "Workers Voice or Control." If the future plans are to succeed, the report argued, workers must be willing to "devote to their work all the intelligence, physical skill, energy, and enthusiasm they possess"; under the present regime, in which capital held unfettered sway over all matters pertaining to the functioning of enterprise, "two of the greatest fears of the workers are that to the extent they improve their efficiency and their production, they stand the risk of unemployment and their wages going down." Hence, it concluded, "in order both to remove their fear about the future and to give them security and also to give them the satisfaction of a higher motive, the workers will be required to be given a voice or control in the conduct of the industrial system." The report refrained from submitting any concrete proposals toward this end, as the committee regarded it as being "too early" to arrive at decisions on these matters; it simply pointed to the need for such machinery if future plans were to succeed.[14] But it was difficult to miss the basic message: future industrial relations in India would have to be structured by a political exchange between labor and capital—a class compromise, if you will.[15]

The recommendations of the Sub-Committee on Labor represented the possibility of a direct challenge to the statist model of development for which Congress leaders were showing a clear preference. The consensus coming out of the rest of the subcommittees was that the direction of future development would be negotiated between the state and domestic capital; this was also evidenced in practice, in the Congress Provincial Ministries, as described above. Labor's welfare and rights would be respected, but there was no indication that it would exercise any real power in the political economy. The idea of a political exchange, however, carried the possibility of extending to labor just such power—at the level of the shop floor and beyond. Of course, these recommendations did not represent the reigning view in the Congress High Command, in which the attitude toward labor ranged from paternalism to outright hostility. But they were in keeping with the opinions of the segment of Congress leadership that was at the front ranks of the labor movement. Furthermore, they did very much reflect the wider consensus among non-Congress labor leaders—in particular, the Communist Party and other left groupings. Which of the two approaches to labor eventually came to reign would depend on the balance of forces within the Party, and within the broader civil society. As long as the labor movement did not gather considerable independent momentum, the Congress High Command would be able to ward off ideas such as those expressed by the subcommittee. But of course, if the movement did career out of control, it would be a different matter altogether.

THE POSTWAR LABOR UPSURGE

The course of the war in India changed the political equation rather drastically. For some, the war had been an opportunity for enormous windfall gains in income. Industry and merchants groups benefited tremendously, as operations in India were financed through enormous deficits, and hence inflation.[16] The steady rise in prices afforded splendid opportunities for profit to local business, while a thriving black market for goods under controlled distribution gave a boost to merchant groups who were able to corner those items in short supply.[17] On the other hand, wages, though increasing in money terms, failed to keep up with the price rise and hence declined in real terms. Throughout the war years and in the immediate aftermath of it, Indian labor suffered a declining real wage, which did not stabilize to prewar levels until 1950.[18] In 1945–47, the real wage hovered at between 80 and 90 percent of its prewar level. This should be considered while keeping in mind that the 1939 wage levels were hardly adequate to begin with.[19]

The Indian labor movement was led at this time by two labor federations—the All-India Trade Union Congress (AITUC) and the Indian Federation of Labor (IFL). AITUC was the oldest of the labor organizations in India, founded in 1920 and with a strong base in the industrial centers. In the first two decades of its history, AITUC had had a strong Congress presence in its leadership: its very first president was the Congressman Lala Lajpat Rai, and in the years that followed AITUC worked closely with the INC. But the two organizations never established formal links, despite some considerable effort by the Congress Left in the mid-1930s to secure functional representation for unions within the High Command.[20] The Congress's formal links with labor therefore remained limited to Gandhi's HMSS, a kind of volunteer service for labor which, while it took part in labor actions, never really assumed the role of a full union. The IFL was a younger organization, founded in 1941 as a break-away faction from AITUC. It was led by followers of M. N. Roy, one of the founders of the Indian Communist movement, and renowned for his debate with Lenin in the Second Congress of the Communist International. Roy led his colleagues out of AITUC in 1941 over the issue of nonparticipation in the war, arguing against the Congress's position of abstaining until Britain conceded more favorable terms for Indian self-rule; he founded the Radical Democratic Party (one step in his rapid move away from communism) and the IFL was its offshoot.

Hence, as the war came to an end and negotiations around the issue of Independence went into full swing, the INC found itself confronted with two labor organizations, both of which were out of its control, both of which were led by leftist parties, and hence opposed to the continuing upward redistribution of income due to inflation and business malfeasance. The result was that, starting in late 1945, the level of strike activity and labor actions in India exploded. The new militant mood within the Indian working class was of course dangerous in itself, but more so because it was being harnessed by political grouping which the Congress neither controlled nor trusted. Of course, this was exactly the circumstance which could catapult the notions of a "political exchange" between labor and capital into prominence. The strike wave itself would have been enough to embolden unions to question the elite pact that Congress leaders preferred as a foundation for future development; but the fact that this upsurge came with Independence within sight gave labor leaders added motivation to push through their agenda, since so much was clearly at stake.

Business, for its part, responded with a steady stream of pleas to the public and the new government to take measures to quell the labor unrest. Significantly—and the importance of this point will emerge particularly sharply below—while business complained unrelentingly about the strike wave, one searches in vain for public calls emanating from this class for economic concessions to labor. Instead, the typical tactic was to point to the strikes and demands as signs of labor's narrow self-interest,[21] the proper response to which was to remind labor of the need for sacrifice in order to build the nation.[22]

By early 1947 it was clear that there was no end in sight to the industrial conflict. And now the idea of a political exchange, long buried in the proceedings of the National Planning Committee, came once again to the fore. With the pleas from employers and the Congress for industrial peace having little to no effect, the new government reached for an institutional solution. By Spring of that year, Nehru began to float the idea that there ought to be a conference to bring together the two sides in order to reach an agreement—a truce—so that production could be brought back to normal levels.[23] Nehru thus explicitly called for a class compromise between labor and capital, to be brokered by the state. Both unions and employers saw this as a welcome opportunity to break the impasse, and hence arrangements were quickly made for the affair. India achieved its independence on August 15, 1947, and four months to the day after that was held the tripartite conference to end the class hostilities.

THE INDUSTRIAL TRUCE CONFERENCE

The Industrial Truce Conference was held in New Delhi on December 15–18, 1947, a massive affair with almost 150 listed participants representing government, labor, and industry. Its immediate aim was to negotiate a truce, ostensibly for three years, between labor and capital; its more ambitious design, however, was to lay out the terms on which both parties would agree to the construction of institutions appropriate to long-term planning.[24] The conference was thus intended to hammer out a class compromise between labor and capital, and to then point to the institutions which would cement this compromise for the long term.

As a first and immediate measure, both labor and capital agreed to bring to an end all strikes and lock-outs for three years. But more importantly, recognizing that this was in large part a concession by labor,[25] particular measures were agreed to which would give workers both economic security and greater participation in economic decision-making. These were codified in the notorious Resolution 9, which became the focus of employer criticism the moment it was introduced. Some of its components were innocent enough, like the call for adequate safety and health conditions at the workplace. But in addition to this, the Resolution called for measures which amounted to nothing less than a revival of the idea of a class compromise. Starting with the announcement that workers were entitled to a "fair wage,"[26] it went on to call, even more audaciously, for:

- the prevention of excessive profits, through taxation and other redistributive measures;
- the redistribution of excessive profits through a means of profit-sharing of such profits between labor and capital;
- methods for the involvement of labor "in all matters concerning industrial production," through such bodies as "central, regional, and unit production committees," as well as works committees.[27]

These components of the Resolution were geared, explicitly, to hammer out a compromise with regard to labor's distributive interests (profit sharing, fair wages), as well as its participatory interests (works committees and regional production committees).

In addition to the terms of the compromise between labor and capital, the Conference also laid down the framework for immediate and future industrial policy in India. For the immediate measures, the Conference agreed to a number of technical and operational issues which government was enjoined to tackle: the procurement of raw materials, the provision of adequate technicians in high-skill industries, the provision of adequate credit and foreign exchange to firms, the provision of adequate transport, and the like.[28] But in addition to this immediate role, the Conference also agreed that the state should undertake measures to initiate *long-term* planning,[29] for which the following conditions were agreed to:

- a separate planning commission or planning board devoted exclusively to planning;

- the division of industries into three groups: state owned, jointly owned and managed by the state and private capital, and privately owned/managed;
- measures to ensure that the spread of industry would be centrally controlled, so as to ensure a fair regional dispersion of industry;
- measures to ensure that industrial policy would be guided by the constraints of equity and social justice.[30]

Taken together, these resolutions pointed to a framework that was, or could have been, a pioneering attempt at a labor-inclusive developmental state—a type, if you will, of a social democratic developmental state. On the one hand, it granted labor an enormous role in the planning process, at every relevant level; on the other hand, it also granted the state considerable discretionary power with respect to capital. Private property itself was not threatened; its prerogatives, however, were to be severely constrained. Business itself wanted planning of some sort, so the Congress could reasonably be optimistic. As for the agreements on labor issues, capital was not happy with them, but labor was simply too strong to ignore or simply dismiss. Further, measures such as those proposed and agreed to in the Conference were being implemented across Europe with some success, and without threatening the rule of private capital. If they were being used as a means of achieving industrial peace elsewhere, perhaps Indian capital could be persuaded to learn to live with them at home. In any case, they had agreed to it, and if it could be made to succeed in the first few years, if profits could be stabilized and normal conditions restored, there was good reason to believe that the compromise would stabilize.

But the compromise would not stabilize. As we shall see in the next section, the resolutions of the Truce began to break down almost as soon as they were agreed to. The institutions which the Truce envisioned guiding Indian industrial policy, for the most part, never materialized—or if they did, it was in a form which rendered them largely ineffectual. There were two basic reasons why the promise of the industrial truce conference was not realized: first, the INC had already moved to demobilize and weaken labor. Congress leaders were wedded to a vision of development policy which would basically revolve around a partnership between the state and the business class; and active labor voice was regarded as too disruptive. Second, employers themselves had no intention of sticking by the agreement. Given the weakened labor movement and an unsympathetic ruling regime, it was little surprise that the employer offensive was successful in scuttling the agreements of the conference.

THE DEMOBILIZATION OF LABOR

The demobilization of labor[31] occurred in two steps, both of which *preceded* the convening of the industrial truce conference. The first was a legislative package aimed at increasing the presence and latitude of the state—as opposed to the unions—in the industrial relations regime. At the core of this strategy was the Industrial Disputes Act of 1947, which drastically reduced the scope for collective bargaining between unions and employers. First, all strikes or lockouts were to be resorted to only after providing a notification of at least fourteen days. But more importantly, in the case of public utilities, government was given the power to compel the parties to resort to an arbitrator if it saw fit. This immediately foisted compulsory arbitration onto workers in the postal service, the railroads, and power industry. But the Act also gave state governments the power to declare *any* industry a public utility for a period of six months; this meant that compulsory arbitration could now be extended to virtually all sectors of industry.

The combined effect of these two aspects of labor law was this: when faced with an intransigent management, labor was forced to contemplate a strike only if it provided a two-week notice to the appropriate government. But the moment it got a whiff of any such impending action, the government could simply intervene and refer the dispute to an arbitrator. Further, while the law provided for compulsory arbitration, it did nothing to ensure rapid delivery of a verdict. Management was left with the ability to drag out the proceedings for months, even years.[32] This meant that under the new dispensation, collective bargaining held little value for employers, as their recalcitrance was only likely to deliver the parties to a conciliator or arbitrator, and in such a case, the whole matter would turn on which of the parties would give in first. And with immeasurably greater resources at its command, the odds always favored management.

To complete the circle, legislation was passed so that matters which are normally the objects of deliberation between labor and capital—conditions of employment, promotion, wage scales, safety, leave and holidays, discipline, etc.—were now covered by a new legislation, most prominently the Industrial Employment (Standing Orders) Act and the Factories Act. Together, these defined the conditions of employment to which employers with establishments above a nominal size now had to adhere. Nominally, these orders and conditions were to be drafted through consultation with unions, to insert a semblance of mutuality into what would otherwise seem a blatantly authoritarian series of measures; but the authority rested firmly with the state.

The new laws crippling labor's place in collective bargaining were accompanied by the creation of a new national union, programmatically committed to arbitration and labor peace. The key here was to wrest control of the labor movement away from the Communist-dominated AITUC and bring it under the broad carapace of the INC leadership. In May 1947, three months after the Industrial Disputes Act was passed, Congress labor leaders and the HMSS called a meeting to launch a new national labor federation, one that was explicitly committed to the party's labor policy. The idea had wide support within the party, from the Right as well as from much of the Left (with the exception of the Socialists).[33] The new federation was called the Indian National Trade Union Congress (INTUC) and was fashioned to be the arm of the party, disclaimers notwithstanding. The INTUC constitution made it clear that its strategy was to be "in harmony with the ideas and resolutions of the Indian National Congress."[34] Specifically, this entailed a commitment to the arbitration regime and a disavowal of militancy.

The creation of INTUC created a split within the labor movement from which it never recovered. Moreover, with the backing of the party in state power, the proportion of the national unions which came under the Congress influence could only grow with time. Indeed, within just a few years, INTUC did in fact become the largest labor federation in the country, ensuring that the bulk of the labor movement was now demobilized and programmatically committed to industrial peace. When conjoined with the new labor legislation, this move cemented the INC's attempts to tame what appeared to be an unruly and unpredictable ally, clearing the way for some kind of compact with capital.

What made this whole project a contradictory one, as we shall see presently, was that the Congress failed to appreciate the difference between industrial peace attained through a genuine class compromise, and one achieved through the kind of statist measures that it favored. Nehru and other (though not all) members of the Left within the Party continued to labor with the conviction that the mechanisms used for the latter could take the place of those required for the former: instead of resting social democracy on the independent power of unions, it could be developed by bringing a tamed labor leadership into the institutions of the state, where it would bargain with capital under the watchful eye of bureaucrats and party leaders. But events were to prove otherwise, and in a rather drastic fashion. We turn now to examining how the steps taken by the Congress prior to the Industrial Truce Conference, when conjoined with the employer reaction to the Conference's resolutions, scuttled the nascent class compromise.

THE EMPLOYER OFFENSIVE AND THE FATE OF THE INDUSTRIAL TRUCE

The immediate effect of the Truce was in fact what the concerned parties had hoped for. Despite the new divisions, unions did by and large attempt to scale down the strike activity of previous years, and did so more or less immediately.[35] The drop-off in industrial conflict was not, however, complete, and this is somewhat significant. It signified the continuing suspicion among labor leaders that employers were not serious about their commitment to the truce,[36] and indeed, as we shall see, this suspicion came to be confirmed. Moreover, the intransigence of the employers was coupled with the persistent lag in wages behind the unceasing rise in prices. Recall that it was not until 1950 that the real wage began to approximate prewar levels. Given these conditions, it is perhaps remarkable that unions were able to contain labor unrest at all.

While the actions of the Congress weakened labor, the escalating industrial conflict of the past two years and the danger of the Congress Left served to bring together the disparate elements of the business class. This unity was only galvanized by the content of the Truce Conference's resolutions, which, despite the friendly show of hands by the Congress, were regarded as a series of major concessions by employers. Far from taking the actions of the past year as signs that the Congress leadership could be trusted with a labor-friendly industrial policy, as the latter had in fact hoped, employers took the events and the resulting scenario as an opportunity to escalate their attacks against the strategy.

The resolutions of the Industrial Truce Conference pertaining to labor had, it will be recalled, focused on several objectives. We may group these together into two broad clusters, embodying different aspects of labor's interests:

1. *Distributive interests*: These are interests related directly to issues of wages and remuneration. The measures central to these interests were the call for minimum wages and, most ambitiously, the recommendation of profit-sharing.
2. *Participatory interests*: These are interests pertaining to the degree of voice that labor might have in economic decision-making, both at plant-level and on a larger scale. These interests were embodied in the proposals for works committees and, more ambitiously, for co-determination. They also extended into proposals for labor representation in governmental and bureaucratic bodies presiding over industrial issues.

The striking aspect of the business response to these proposed measures is not just that it was unhappy with them, but that it opposed them *in toto*, and the opposition *was across the board*. The Congress had hoped, even expected, that the "lead segment" of Indian business, like Birla, Tata, and Kasturbhai Lalbhai, would back the measures proposed in the Truce. But such support was nowhere on the horizon. These elements were either loudly denouncing the proposed measures regarding labor (like G. D. Birla), or remained silent (like Lala Shri Ram). Indeed, one searches the available sources in vain for any defense of the measures within the business class. The attack on the agreements of the Industrial Truce Conference was universal.

LABOR'S DISTRIBUTIVE INTERESTS

The main focus of criticism from business was the proposal for profit-sharing and its attendant measures. As it stood, the proposal as stated in the Resolution gave the impression that profit-sharing was to mean that all profits above a certain minimum would be shared between labor and capital:

> The system of remuneration to capital as well as to labour must be so devised that while in the interests of the consumers and the primary producers excessive profits should be prevented by suitable measures of taxation and otherwise *both will share in the product of their common effort after making provision for payment of fair wages to labour, a fair return on capital employed in the industry and reasonable reserves for the maintenance and expansion of the undertaking.*[37]

Thus, the first charge on revenues would be the "fair" remuneration to labor and capital, after which the remainder would be shared between them. To employers, the whole proposal was objectionable, from top to bottom. The dilemma was that they had agreed to it, and it was on the basis of the agreements embodied in the Resolutions adopted at the conference that labor was carrying through on its promise to scale back strikes. It is therefore worthy of notice that, despite an initial hesitation in some quarters, employers nonetheless went forward with a vigorous attack on the proposed scheme.[38]

The fundamental issue for employers was, as Planning Member Ardishir Dalal put it, that the proposal gave labor the claim to the surplus "as a matter of right," rather than as conditional upon performance.[39] They were of the view that the central problem plaguing Indian industry at the time was lagging labor productivity, which had been further exacerbated by the radicalization of the postwar years and the increasing recourse to strikes. Implementing the profit-sharing scheme, employers argued, would only add to the problem. If it was ever going to be acceptable, profit-sharing would have to be more directly tied to labor's productivity—if the latter increased, those revenues arising as a consequence could be passed on to labor.[40]

A second issue to which employers objected, again on principle, was the implication in the profit-sharing scheme that labor and capital were to be regarded as partners in enterprise. But if labor was to be granted all the advantages of partnership, in that it would share in excess profits, it ought also share in the risks. "Profit sharing in this form," the Federation of Indian Chambers of Congress and Industry (FICCI) wrote to the Industry Minister S. P. Mookerji, "seeks to give labour a partnership in industry without the liabilities and obligations attendant upon partnership."[41] It is not clear what was meant by the insistence that labor ought to share in the risks of enterprise; presumably this referred to something over and above the loss of livelihood that typically accompanies the closure of uncompetitive units. But if so, what? It was a part of the scheme that in lean years labor would of course have no claim to "excess profits," since there would be none. There was therefore no implication that *all* profits would be shared, regardless of the condition of the enterprise.[42] It seems more likely that this latter point was a rhetorical lead-up to the more substantive demand industry was striving to make: if profit-sharing was to be premised on a ceiling on profits, with the excess being shared between labor and capital, then the latter ought to be remunerated by the state in years with less than normal profits. In other words, if profits were going to be regulated, then they should also be *guaranteed*.[43] Hence, if labor was a partner in industry, sharing in its spoils, then the state, as custodian of labor's interests, should step in to compensate for losses.

While it ratcheted upwards the conditions which would have to be met if profit-sharing was to see light of day, thereby making it increasingly remote, industry recommended in its stead another proposal, more consistent with the concerns it had raised thus far—and that was a policy of remuneration through a production bonus.[44] The distinction between profit-sharing and a bonus system is not entirely clear, and it was unclear to industry's interlocutors as well.[45] After all, the former was to be instituted in such a manner that the extra remuneration would flow to labor only in years with excess profits, much as it would in a bonus system. And a bonus is, as most commentators recognize, a subtle form of profit-sharing, as it is disbursed in periods of above-normal profits. What appear to have been the motivation behind this preference were two factors: first, in the scheme visualized by employers, the bonus would be expressed as a percentage of excess *production*, and not of excess *profits*. A production target would be set by management at the beginning of the period and if production exceeded that target, workers would be given a bonus proportional to the excess.[46] Second, the bonus system would operate at an enterprise level, as opposed to the profit-sharing scheme, which was likely to rest on a sectoral pooling of profits, which would then be distributed to workers in that sector. Employers were fiercely committed to blocking any scheme that pooled resources in such a manner.[47] The bonus scheme would thus, in the view of industrialists', not only tie extra payments to labor productivity, but would also tie it to the performance of the particular firm. A natural consequence would be a less solidaristic labor movement. Lastly, this system would leave a great deal more leeway to employer discretion and power. Bonuses would accrue only after they exceeded production targets, and those targets were to be set by management.

Where capital stood firmly and resolutely opposed to all talk of profit-sharing—its acceptance of the proposal at the Truce Conference notwithstanding—it soon became clear that labor, for its part, did not meet the challenge with a correspondingly committed stance in the proposal's favor. This is not to say that profit-sharing had entirely fallen out of favor with the latter.

But in the Left unions—AITUC, the IFL and Hind Mazdoor Sabha (HMS)—the measure was regarded as a second-best means of meeting workers' economic interests, after the more preferable route of a guaranteed fair wage and employment policy. There was a concern among the unions that the profit-sharing scheme was being considered as the sole means to extend a fair remuneration to labor, rather than as part of a larger package; being aware of the fierce opposition to the scheme by the business class, union leaders regarded this possibility with some alarm.[48] Further, they were uncertain of the political ramifications of the proposal, since it carried the possibility that it would further weaken the organizational capacity of unions, who would no longer play any real role in the setting of wages and payments to labor.[49] Hence the unions moved to insure that the focus of the negotiations did not lose sight of the necessity for adequate wage legislation as the first concern, with profit sharing playing a subsidiary role.[50]

The support for profit-sharing among the Left unions was thus lukewarm. It was, nonetheless, real, for reasons that did not bear directly on labor's economic interests: unions saw the scheme as a means to increase the democratization of the workplace. Having lost the battle on collective bargaining, unions were keenly aware that the prospect for their influence on firm-level decision making was rapidly receding. If the state was serious about the profit-sharing proposal, then this provided an avenue to continue the fight. For the proposal, if it was to work without descending into endless squabbles about actual profits and fair disbursement, would have to carry in train significant powers for unions in the managerial domain. Profit sharing could thus provide a bridge to codetermination.[51]

The decision to focus on the need for adequate wage legislation was perhaps understandable, but to publicly announce its priority turned out to be a tactical mistake. In contrast to labor's equivocation, business stood firmly united in its stand. The apex organizations like the Federation of Indian Chambers of Commerce and Industry and the Indian Merchants Chamber took the lead in making certain that the resistance was not only concerted but also coordinated, with correspondence flowing back and forth and member firms adroitly coached on appropriate public positions.[52] The strategy worked. As the business community's resistance to profit sharing continued to be unshakable, negotiations on the mechanics of the measure soon became bogged down in matters of detail. The tripartite body appointed to facilitate a modus vivendi between capital and labor, the Central Labor Advisory Council, had its first two meetings end in a fast deadlock;[53] even the expert committee convened to produce a report on the matter submitted a document in which, of the seven non-official members (i.e., members who were not representatives of government), six submitted dissenting notes.[54] The deadlock was apparent and seemed irredeemable. It was resolved by two factors, one a testimony to business's adroit maneuvering and the other a fallout of labor's dithering. With respect to the former, as the deadlock wore on and the investment slowdown continued, business increasingly took the line that any measure that further dampened the investment climate or did not contribute toward its amelioration was not desirable—and profit sharing seemed a glowing example of such a measure.[55] In this context, labor's stated lack of enthusiasm provided the INC with an easy way out of the dilemma. Rather than push capital into accepting the proposal, the government let it die a quiet death, and it never passed into legislation.[56] Instead, remuneration reflecting excess profits was to be decided through the channel that had been pushed by employers all along—an annual production bonus.

With profit sharing a dead letter by late 1950, labor's economic interests came to rest squarely on wage legislation and the bonus system. An examination of the mechanics of these measures, however, will have to be put off for a short spell, as it will be best understood in the wider discussion of the fate of the labor ministry, which will be dealt with in the final section of the paper. Before that, let us examine the struggle around the other axis of contention, viz. labor's participatory interests.

LABOR'S PARTICIPATORY INTERESTS

The measures to democratize economic decision-making were to rest in labor's direct voice through the works committee and codetermination, as well as through its place on tripartite policy committees appointed by the state. The first casualty of the post-truce dispensation was the initiative toward codetermination. The resolution of the Truce Conference had called for instituting "methods for the association of labour *in all matters concerning industrial production*," and had suggested as examples "the formation of Central, Regional, and Unit production committees."[57] The production committee was to be supplemented by the works committees, and both of these would in turn be bolstered by the powers that would flow from the profit-sharing measures.

The success of this scheme would depend centrally on the development of an institutional environment that would conduce to the adequate functioning of these bodies, once they were instituted. But events had already conspired to render any such prospects distressingly remote. First, Congress's measures to undermine collective bargaining dealt a preemptive and decisive blow to the prospects of a proper setting for micro-level comanagement. The recourse to a system of compulsory arbitration virtually ensured that labor and capital would be perennially locked in disputes over wages and conditions of work, so that the typical relation between the management and workers in any given firm would be fiercely hostile and mutually suspicious. In such circumstances, the prospects for a genuine participation by labor in matters pertaining to production were greatly reduced. Further, with the labor movement itself split between several and competing unions, the animosity between the rivals would simply get reflected onto the committees themselves. This was only exacerbated by the conspicuous links between INTUC and the INC, which made competing unions suspect that governmental and bureaucratic partiality would militate against the prospects of their getting adequate representation of the committees. Lastly, despite the pleas of labor leaders like Guruswamy and N. M. Joshi, legislation to protect such committees from employer manipulation was never set up, and union suspicion of its vulnerability to abuse was thus never allayed.

The lack of progress on this front was conditioned strongly, as suggested above, by the shrill opposition by business to the granting of further powers to labor. The Industrial Disputes Act was passed not simply to tackle conflict around wages, but in a manner which assuaged employers' concerns. Its collateral effects on measures pertaining to labor participation could have been taken as signals for its appropriate revision. But again, the Congress leadership decided in favor of jettisoning another component of the Truce, as employers continued with their opposition to it. Hence, despite the fact that a small number of such committees were set up in firms across the country, they tended to remain a dead letter. Worse yet, given the weak institutional backing, the success of the employer offensive in making increased production the *sine qua non* of any policy tended to subordinate any autonomy that the committees may have had to the authority of management. As one student of the subject, himself a former labor administrator in the civil service, observes:

> [In] the early days of mental [*sic*] participation in management, there were serious expectations that there would be legislation giving labour an adequate share in management. . . . [But] labour leaders whose visions were restricted to the possibilities close at hand were quite disturbed when *participation* was in turn reduced first to *cooperation* and then to *consultation*.[58]

The same author concludes, after a study of the Indian experience with works committees, that:

> Joint consultation can be a success only in a climate of satisfactory adjustment of labour-management disputes and differences. . . . So one of the important prerequisites to joint consultation is the existence of a well-organized and well-conducted trade union, recognized by management, for the purpose of collective bargaining. The settlement of terms and conditions of employment in a satisfactory and acceptable manner is the foundation of all joint consultation.[59]

Throughout the debate on profit sharing, employers had steadfastly maintained their opposition to the implication that labour would come to enjoy the status of a partner in production. The INC seemed to be laboring under the illusion that capital's animosity toward such schemes could be reduced if union autonomy was sufficiently circumscribed by governmental control. What it failed to see was that employers were opposed to workers' participation on *principle*. As the power of the labor movement to force the issue was reduced, employers took the route of simply ignoring the committees or extracting their subordination to decisions already arrived at. Though some committees continued to function in various sectors, they remained, like many other products of Indian labor legislation, ornamental.

What the labor movement was left with in the end was the following: its *distributive* interests were to be met through legislation laying down appropriate wage levels, to be administered through wage boards and provincial governments, and through a system of bonus payments, which would be adjudicated through labor tribunals and courts; its *participatory* interests were now to be filtered through governmental tripartite bodies and through its input into policy through the ties between unions and parties. For both, labor was now by and large completely dependent on official patronage and succor. The capacity to force legislation more conducive to its autonomous development was greatly reduced by the splits that occurred in 1947; this was reinforced by the ties that INTUC enjoyed with the INC, which generated an incentive for the new organization to maintain its distinct identity on the one hand, and to support the state's control over so many matters pertaining to labor's interests on the other.

With labor split and demobilized, and a significant segment programmatically committed to political quiescence, the fortunes of the remaining parts of the Truce now came to rest in large measure on the willingness of the Indian state to take up the cause.

FROM INDUSTRIAL PARTNERSHIP TO INDUSTRIAL RELATIONS

It had been assumed by the more pliant union leaders, particularly those in INTUC, that their retreat on the more ambitious measures would be rewarded by a degree of indulgence by employers and the state on the basic issues of minimum wages and industrial welfare. But the offensive launched by business against profit sharing and codetermination also extended into these seemingly less controversial demands. Throughout the years following the war, employers continued to hammer away against the idea of mandated minimum wages,[60] insisting that wages should be pegged according to industry's ability to pay, and that industry was in no such position. But here, unlike with the measures for profit sharing and codetermination, the case was more difficult to make. Business during the war had made enormous profits, and was continuing to do well in the postwar inflationary scene. Further, the miserable condition of most of Indian labor made it more difficult still to argue in principle against wage legislation. Those elements of the business class involved in negotiations on labor policy therefore had to show a concessive face on wage issues.[61] They agreed in principle to wage legislation, but argued that it ought to be implemented in a manner that took cognizance of the dismal economic situation and the peculiarities of an underdeveloped economy.[62] Given the enormous regional and sectoral differences in economic development, any standardization of wages would have to proceed with extreme caution, so as not to increase the panic within industry.

The overall effect of this strategy—to rail against the foolishness of wage policy in public forums while counseling caution in private—was to drive policy makers to the view that if wage policy was going to be implemented, it would have to wait for the development of an apparatus adequate to meet industrialists' worries, so that production would not be disturbed. Since such an apparatus was not in view, wage legislation could be passed, but its implementation would have to wait; a corollary to this was that those sections of the state which were pushing for speedier movement on labor policy increasingly found themselves losing power and status. The most concrete expression of this was the changing fortune of the Labor Ministry.

The Labor Ministry had been the primary fount for the formulation and implementation of labor policy throughout the immediate postcolonial years. It had drawn up the ambitious five-year plan for labor policy in early 1947, had been the main mover behind the labor-inclusive parts of the Industrial Truce, and continued to be that part of the state that was in closest touch with unions.[63] With the proposals for profit sharing and codetermination in cold storage after the first two years following independence, the ministry was pushing in 1950 for a speedy implementation of the remaining wage legislation. But this brought it into direct conflict with those ministries in closest touch with industry and involved in devising industrial policy, for by mid-1950, it was becoming clear that even on the issue of minimum wage policy, government had decided to adopt a "go slow" strategy.[64]

Policy makers in the labor ministry now found that the state's initial enthusiasm for labor policy had subsided considerably. Far from pushing ahead with the remaining agenda, state managers now came to regard these matters with a considerable measure of skepticism. By 1950, the rising star on the policy-making horizon was the nascent Planning Commission, and the attention of the Congress leadership was riveted to the formulation of the first five-year plan. If the plan was to succeed, the first priority would have to be given to mobilizing private capital in the required quantum and direction; given the latter's views on wage policy, it would have to wait for more propitious times. Hence, as the year wore on, the labor ministry even found itself excluded from the inter-ministerial discussions on industrial and labor policy.[65] Increasingly, the responsibility for the formulation of labor policy shifted to the Planning Commission and other economic ministries, and the views of planners were far less congenial to the agenda that had been laid in the Industrial Truce. Labor policy now was placed firmly behind industrial policy, and the labor ministry's efforts on such matters as wage legislation, employee insurance, and broader welfare issues were rebuffed, as their "added cost to the employer would be burdensome and would discourage industrial expansion and production."[66]

The result of this change was twofold. First, the labor ministry was no longer the central node for the formulation of labor policy. That had shifted to the Planning Commission.[67] Indeed, with the transfer of policy-making initiative to the latter, labor policy itself as a distinct concern rapidly faded, becoming incorporated into the broader fold of industrial planning. Second, the ministry was apparently reduced mainly to the implementation of policy, but even here it would have to wait for the signal from other ministries. Legislation that had been passed would be implemented only if it did not interfere with plans, and since plans depended centrally on the participation of private capital, the implementation of labor legislation came to be influenced heavily by the demands of Indian business. The latter, for their part, increasingly questioned the right of the labor ministry's activity in such matters, insisting that they fell under the purview of the planning bodies.[68] The immediate expression of this new dynamic was the successful delay by the planning commission in the implementation of the Minimum Wages Act of 1948 and the Employees State Insurance Act of 1951.[69] The Labor's Ministry's role fell from formulation of policy to its implementation, and, given the veto power of other ministries even in this dimension, from *power* over implementation to what can only be called an *allowance* to administer.

For labor, the most concrete effect of this development with regard to its distributive interests was a ten-year delay in the setting up of the wage boards that were to administer minimum wage legislation. Despite the fact that the law was passed in 1948, it was not until the late 1950's that the wage boards were in fact set up.[70] During this time, wage policy came to be driven by the tribunals and courts set up by the arbitration system.[71] Thus this last vestige of the Industrial Truce, while not jettisoned altogether, was put into cold storage for over a decade.

A more important long-term effect was this: not only was the initial idea of a class compromise radically undermined, but the institutional infrastructure that might have sustained such a development in the future was never developed. While capital had the capacity as well as the institutions to develop and articulate its economic and political interests, labor—now split into competing unions and utterly dependent on the state—did not. It would enjoy a presence on governmental bodies and study teams, but the meso and micro level organization that could give such a presence meaning was drastically undermined. Labor representatives would thus not only lack the authority to actually represent labor interests—since labor was split into competing organizations—but the lack of organizational coherence made it a remote possibility that the representatives would even be able to *formulate* the interests.[72] Governmental bodies would thus become deliberative machines for representatives of industry and a labor bureaucracy that was increasingly remote from the concerns of its constituents.

CONCLUSION

By 1950, the basic lineaments of the Indian political economy were in place, at least as regards labor's incorporation into it. In that sense, these years were the "critical juncture" at which the institutional mediation of labor's interests was settled. There are two axes on which the outcome can be understood: one which seeks to make sense of the overall nature of the settlement and another which points to the conditions that might have brought about another possibility from the menu of choices. In the current literature on Indian labor, there is scant attention paid to either of these issues, for while it is realized that the immediate post-Independence years were critical, the actual class dynamics of these years have rarely been brought under scrutiny. Indeed, the Industrial Truce Conference, which was the lodestone for virtually all debates on the Indian future at the time, barely even registers in the current historiography of the period. It is not altogether surprising, therefore, that the possibility of other political settlements is not even examined, since the occasion at which such possibilities were inscribed into the political agenda has been lost from sight. But now that we have rediscovered it, there is some merit in pondering its significance and the conditions which might have facilitated the realization of its promise.

How are we to understand the nature of the settlement? The possibility that was ruled out from the outset was that of an *exclusionary* regime—one in which the labor question would be dealt with through basically coercive mechanisms. While employers may not have been averse to such an outcome, it would have been difficult to force through, given the balance of forces; but it was ruled out by a more fundamental condition, which was the INC's commitment to basic democratic rights for labor, a commitment which even the conservative elements held steadfastly.[73] As far as the rights of labor are concerned, there was only one framework on the agenda, viz. an inclusive one. But what this essay has shown is that *within* the rubric of an inclusive political regime, there were two further possibilities as to what the final outcome would be. One possibility was that the capital-labor relation would be governed by some kind of *class compromise*, in which labor would promise industrial peace in exchange for some concessions from employers on the shop floor and on distributive issues. This is what some of the Congress Left hoped for, and what most of the Socialists and Communists were demanding. The ultimate outcome, however, was in the direction of the second possibility within an inclusive regime—one in which labor's interests were merely *accommodated*, and not maximized. Put another way, labor was not strong enough to push through a class compromise, but it was strong enough to ensure that its interests would have to be accommodated.[74]

These two kinds of settlements differ in the place they grant specific class interests. Unions and the Left were pushing for a system in which the furtherance of capital's interests would be *conditional*—on, for example, capital's willingness to concede certain prerogatives to labor and the broader national community. Profits would be respected, in other words, if capital submitted to discipline. In this system, it was labor's interests that would be the immediate maximand of state policy, and capital's interests that would be taken as a constraint. Hence, the importance of the business climate and investor confidence would be recognized, but only as a constraint, as a condition that had to be met in order to further other goals. This has been the strategic vision of left-wing social democracy in more developed countries, especially in its most well-known avatars, such as Sweden of the late 1960s and 1970s. Opposing this vision was one which reversed the order of importance with regard to class interests: on this view, it was *labor's* interests that would be taken as a *constraint*, and the interests of investors that would be given first priority. This was the immediate preference of employers, one which they did their utmost to bring to life, despite having agreed to the class compromise embodied in Resolution 9 of the Truce Conference.

The treatment of labor's interests as a constraint instead of a maximand was also the preferred option of the Indian state and the INC. This is the final piece in the puzzle, which is crucial not only for understanding the nature of the political economy that emerged, but also for appreciating the strategic orientation that labor would have had to adopt for bringing about a class compromise. For the Party had a project of its own, common to so many political elites in developing countries, viz. to launch upon a program of rapid industrialization. As shown in this paper, the mechanism that Congress leaders sought to secure this program was an alliance with domestic capital, which was in evidence as early as 1937, in the Provincial Ministries. For the top leaders of the Congress, including Nehru, this meant that, while they were in principle sympathetic to labor's interests, they had to give the highest priority to employers and their willingness to undertake the warranted investments.[75] But since employers insisted that a condition for their making such investment was the imposition of labor discipline, the new state could not but see an autonomous, organizationally strong, and potentially

militant labor movement as an unjustifiable disruption *to the development process itself.*
Which brings us to the issue of strategy. If two critical factors leading to the dissolution of the class compromise were the employer offensive and the state's class bias, the third was labor's decision to agree to demobilization. Even the Communist-led AITUC scaled down their strike activity after the Truce conference; for the unions affiliated with the new Congress labor federation, INTUC, the decision was made on the assumption that direct action could now be replaced by participation in the bodies put in charge of labor administration and policy. It seems difficult to escape the conclusion that this was a crucial strategic miscalculation. That the matter of a possible class compromise was put on the agenda at all was because of the upsurge in strike activity after the war; it was not something to which the INC was programmatically committed. It was, in other words, direct class pressure that brought the issue to the fore. Its abandonment for committee membership simply allowed the more basic structural pressures on the state to now gain ascendance, forcing state managers to attend to the matter of business confidence as their first priority. This is not to say that labor should have foresworn participation in policy-making—it is difficult to imagine a class compromise stabilizing without some state support. The mistake, rather, was to see inclusion in the policy agencies as a *substitute* for mobilization.

Interestingly, an example of a development strategy based on a class compromise, or at least something approximating such a compromise, is at hand in India itself. Though it probably does not warrant the designation of a "model," the experience in the Southwestern state of Kerala might offer a vision of an alternative, which, if the INC had so chosen, it could have pursued. Kerala is typically pointed to as proof positive of the virtues of significant redistribution, and the provision of basic state services.[76] But recent work has pointed to another component of the state's development strategy, which is its quite successful forging of a class compromise between labor and capital.[77] The turning point in its history was the coming to power of the Communist Party in 1957, which initiated its development program as one based on agrarian reform but which has gradually incorporated a mobilizational approach to industrial relations as well.

The strategy adopted by the Communist Party of India (Marxist) (CPM) and its union federation, the Confederation of Indian Trade Unions (CITU), bears an interesting contrast with that of the larger Indian labor movement. Crucially, whereas since its demobilization after Independence Indian labor has largely relied on the patronage of employers or local political bosses, unions in Kerala have relied instead on an explicit strategy of political mobilization around class interests. Just as importantly, they have found a political ally in the Communist Party of India (Marxist) which, unlike the INC in 1947, has used this mobilizational strategy to further empower unions in their bargaining with employers. Knowing that they could not rely on a sympathetic state government (as long as the CPM was in power), employers had to reach agreements with labor around basic issues of wages, work conditions, tenure, etc.—again, in contrast to the rest of the country, where work relations tend to be straightforwardly despotic. In turn, this has closed off many "low road" strategies of accumulation, which in turn has forced employers to give greater attention to innovating and upgrading plant and equipment.[78] Patrick Heller has called this the "democratic developmental state" model of development, though it would probably be more accurate to refer to it as the "*social democratic* developmental state." Of course, the comparison is more suggestive than definitive; to cast the experience of one state onto the larger canvas requires a heroic imagination. Nevertheless, the Kerala experience highlights the fact that development strategies need not be different varieties of top-down arrangements, with labor necessarily a marginal force.

NOTES

1. E. A. Ramaswamy and Uma Ramaswamy, *Industry and Labour: An Introduction* (Oxford: Oxford University Press, 1981), and E. A. Ramaswamy, *Power and Justice: The State in Industrial Relations* (Oxford: Oxford University Press: 1984).

2. For an illuminating analysis of this very pair, see Gay Seidman, *Manufacturing Militance: Workers' Movements in Brazil and South Africa, 1970–1985* (Berkeley: University of California Press, 1994).

3. The victories were in the United Provinces, Bihar, Orissa, Bombay, Madras, the Central Provinces, the Northwest Frontier Provinces, and Assam.

4. The fullest account of the relations between the INC and Indian capitalists in these years is Claude Markovits, *Indian Business and Nationalist Politics, 1931–1939* (Cambridge: Cambridge University Press, 1985).

5. The best overview of the INC in these years is still Sumit Sarkar's *Modern India: 1880–1947* (London: Macmillan, 1983).

6. Markovits, *Indian Business and Nationalist Politics*, 170.

7. Markovits, *Indian Business and Nationalist Politics*, 170.

8. W. H. Lewis (Governer of Orissa) to Viceroy Linlithgow, November 14, 1942 (Document #8) in *Quit India Movement: British Secret Documents, Vol. II*, ed. P. N. Chopra (Delhi: Interprint Publishers, 1990).

9. C. Revri, *The Indian Trade Union Movement: An Historical Outline 1880–1947* (Delhi: Orient Longman, 1972), 220–30.

10. Raghabendra Chattopadhyay, *The Idea of Planning in India, 1930–1950* (Ph.D. diss., Australian National University, 1985), 96. What is even more significant, perhaps, than the small presence of labor leaders is the virtual absence of any real representatives of rural interests—lordly or peasant.

11. Chattopadhyay, *The Idea of Planning*, chapters 3–4.

12. For this, see V. Chibber, *Locked in Place: State-Building and Late Industrialization in India, 1940–1970* (Princeton, N. J.: Princeton University Press, 2003), chapter 4.

13. *National Planning Committee: Report of the Subcommittee on Labour*, paragraphs 1–19.

14. *National Planning Committee: Report of the Subcommittee on Labour*, paragraph 84.

15. The concept of "political exchange" is taken from Marino Regini, *Uncertain Boundaries: The Social and Political Construction of European Economies* (New York: Cambridge University Press, 1995).

16. Historians have just about entirely ignored the war years as a subject of study, so the contemporary researcher is forced to fall back on the works published contemporaneously with the events. Among these, see, inter alia, Gadgil and Sovani, 1945 for an analysis of wartime inflation.

17. It was not only merchants who thrived thus in the black market. Industrialists too worked to limit supplies to the market so as to divert them to the black market. See the various articles in the *Harijan* during this period for accounts of this.

18. For the most thorough analysis, see Shreekant Palekar, *Real Wages in India, 1939–1950* (London: Asia Publishing House: 1962).

19. Palekar, *Real Wages in India*.

20. The attempt by the Congress Left to secure functional representation of labor in the INC is examined by D. A. Low, in "Congress and 'Mass Contacts' 1936–1937," chapter 5 in his *Rearguard Action: Selected Essays on Late Colonial Indian History* (New Delhi: Sterling Publishers, 1996).

21. See the articles in *Capital*, one of the main organs of the business community, in 1946–1947. In particular, see *Capital*, January 10, 1946, p. 44; "Ditcher's Diary," July 25, 1946, p. 145; "The Present Wave of Industrial Unrest," August 1, 1946; and "The Steel Industry in Britain and India," September 12, 1946, p. 337. The attitude to concessions is also reflected in the business criticisms of calls to shorten the working day to forty-eight hours. See the speech by Homi Mody to the Employers Federation of India in *Capital*, January 3, 1946, p. 2.

22. Another line sometimes taken by business was to concede that there may be some legitimacy to the idea that labor was in a bad way, but that these were being distorted and illegitimately amplified by "outside elements," i.e., Communists. See the speech by M. A. Master, President of the Federation of Indian Chambers of Commerce and Industry, July 9, 1947, in File 336, PT Papers, NMML.

23. Master recalls this in his speech, referred to in the previous footnote.

24. See the "Draft Agenda" as sent out to the participants, in File 336, PT Papers, NMML.

25. This was a concession by labor because the abrogation of the strike weapon in a period of stagnant or declining wages would leave their living standards to the whim of employers.

26. Appendix to *Conference on Industrial Development in India* (Delhi: 1947).

27. *Conference on Industrial Development in India*.

28. These are covered in Resolutions 1, 3, 4, 5, 6, in *Conference on Industrial Development in India*.

29. *Conference on Industrial Development in India*, Resolution 1, paragraph IV.

30. This list is in Resolution 2, *Conference on Industrial Development in India*.

31. This section summarizes chapter 5 of Chibber, *Locked in Place*.

32. See the discussion in Ramaswamy, *Industry and Labour*, 44–48.

33. Pant, the Premier of the United Provinces, considered it an "urgent matter" that the Congress have a "close-knit labour organization" of its own. See G. B. Pant to Patel, September 23, 1947, Patel Papers, Reel 48, NAI.

34. Quoted in Harold Crouch, *The Indian Trade Union Movement* (Bombay: Asia Publishing House, 1966), 83. In a pamphlet issued later that same month, Nanda took the high road, omitting all mention to arbitration and relying instead on the generic anti-Communism that was to become the stock of much of the Congress Left: "It is obvious that the Communists are the perpetual enemy of any established authority in this country and that they will seek to keep the country in a disturbed state in order to suit the international aims of a foreign power. . . . Whenever and wherever we associate ourselves with the Communists we incur loss or liability for ourselves. Therefore, the need for creating a separate Central Organization of Labour is immediate and imperative." Gulzarilal Nanda, *Future of Indian Labour*, May 1947, 7–8. This pamphlet can be found in File 123, Jayprakash Narayan Papers, Inst. II, NMML.

35. See the *Indian Labour Yearbook*, 1948.

36. See the comments by Rajani Mukherji of the IFL in Donavan to Secy. of State, December 23, 1947, 845.5043/12-2347, RG 59, DSR; also, see the discussion of the Truce in "Summary of the Proceedings of the Ninth Session of the Indian Labour Conference held in New Delhi from 19th to 21st April, 1948," File 291, AITUC Papers, NMML. See the comments by the industrialist H. Mody in Donavan to Secy. of State, December 23, 1947, 845.5043/12-2347, RG 59, DSR.

37. Resolution #9, in the Appendix, *Conference on Industrial Development in India: Proceedings* (New Delhi: 1947). Emphasis added.

38. Lala Shri Ram was one such example. When initially contacted by the Indian Employers Federation to join the attack on profit-sharing, he demurred, complaining that the organization had "declared war" on the scheme, despite the fact that employers had committed to it in the Truce Conference. But Shri Ram did not remain on the fence for long, becoming an active votary for industry's cause through much of 1948–49. The letter is contained in File LSR/IFC-5, Lala Shri Ram Archives, New Delhi. Unfortunately, I have lost the exact reference to the dates of the correspondence.

39. Dalal's comments in "Proceedings of the Ninth Session of the Indian Labour Conference, held in New Delhi from the 19th to 21st April, 1948," File 291, AITUC Papers, NMML. Dalal was present at the conference as a delegate of the Employers Federation of India.

40. For complaints against declining labor productivity, see the proceedings of the Industrial Truce Conference; for linking the extra remuneration to labor productivity, see the testimony of K. D. Jalan and M. Birla in "Minutes to the evidence tendered by representatives of the Federation of Indian Chambers of Commerce and Industry to the expert committee on the Determination of a fair return to capital and profit-sharing, Monday, June 28th, 1948," File 1236, IMC Papers, NMML.

41. The Federation of Indian Chambers of Commerce and Industry, memorandum submitted to Mookerji, May 27, 1948, File 1236, IMC Papers, NMML.

42. Employers did at times interpret the proposal in this less generous fashion. For one such instance, and the clarification by government representatives, see the "Minutes to the evidence tendered by representatives of the Federation of Indian Chambers of Commerce and Industry to the expert committee on the Determination of a fair return to capital and profit-sharing, Monday, June 28th, 1948," File 1236, IMC Papers, NMML.

43. This was first demanded by G. D. Birla in the Industrial Truce Conference: "You will be perfectly entitled to put a check on profits provided you also put a check on losses," *Proceedings*, 41. See also the memorandum submitted by the Federation of Indian Chambers of Commerce and Industry to the expert committee on fair return to capital and profit-sharing on June 28th, contained in File 1236, IMC Papers, NMML: "If one were to concede the principle of returns being limited, naturally the state will have to undertake the obligation to make good losses in lean years."(5).

44. See "Proceedings of the Ninth Session of the Indian Labour Conference, held in New Delhi from the 19th to 21st April, 1948," File 291, AITUC Papers, NMML; the "Memorandum submitted by the Federation of Indian Chambers of Commerce and Industry to the expert committee on fair return to capital and profit-sharing on June 28th," contained in File 1236, IMC Papers, NMML; "Proceedings of the subcommittee to formulate a scheme of profit-sharing linking labour's share with increased production" (All-India Organization of Industrial Employers), May 27, 1949, File 180, WH Papers, NMML; report on the proceedings of the Central Advisory Council of Labor, held at Lucknow, November 19th–21st, 1948, File 180, WH Papers, NMML.

45. For government's attempts to understand the distinction, see the discussion between them and the industry representatives in "Minutes to the evidence tendered by representatives of the Federation of Indian Chambers of Commerce and Industry to the expert committee on the Determination of a fair return to capital and profit-sharing, Monday, June 28th, 1948," File 1236, IMC Papers, NMML.

46. "Minutes to the evidence tendered," IMC Papers, NMML.

47. Memorandum by president of the Indian Colliery Owners Association to Secretary, Indian Merchants Chamber, December 4, 1948, File 1236, IMC Papers, NMML; See also the comments by K. D. Jalan in the minutes to the "Proceedings of the subcommittee to formulate a scheme of profit-sharing linking labour's share with increased production" (All-India Organization of Industrial Employers), May 27, 1949, File 180, WH Papers, NMML.

48. "Profit Sharing and Living Wage," memorandum by Peter Alvares, May 8, 1948, JP Papers, File 220.

49. This is enunciated in the "Memorandum of the IFL on the Fixation of fair return to capital and labour's share of surplus profits," File 294, AITUC Papers, NMML.

50. The priority of wage legislation figures in all the Left unions' position papers. In addition to the ones in the above two footnotes, see also the AITUC memorandum to B. B. Saksena, Industry Ministry, June 13, 1948, AITUC Papers, NMML; HMS memorandum to committee of experts, June 25, 1948, File 220, JP Papers, NMML.

51. See memoranda by AITUC, HMS, and especially the IFL referred to above. The latter in particular spells out the logic with admirable clarity.

52. See the correspondence between the Federation of Indian Chambers of Commerce and Industry and the Indian Merchants chamber in File 1236, IMC Papers, and File 180, WH Papers, both in NMML. For an instance of the coaching referred to in the text, see the circular sent out by the Federation to its member bodies on June 3, 1948, on the eve of the deliberations of the expert committee on profit sharing. The circular was sent with attachments providing the conclusions reached by a committee appointed by the Federation to consider the matter, and the Secretary G. L Bansal expressed his hope that "the Member-Bodies will not only support these views, as

expressed by the Federation Sub-committee, at every stage, but will also impress
upon their representatives, who may be asked to tender oral evidence before the Expert Committee, to adhere to these views"; FICCI circular, File 180, WH Papers,
NMML.
  53. See the report by Donovan to Secretary of State, September 2, 1949, 845.504/9-
249, DSR, RG 59.
  54. *Report of the Committee on Profit-Sharing* (Delhi: 1951).
  55. This was a tactic that seemed to have been crucially dependent on the time factor. In mid-1948, when it was first suggested in secret business confabulations, it was
shot down by the majority. But by late 1949, it became the public position of the
class. For the former, see the report of the preliminary meeting of employers leading
up to the first meeting of the Central Advisory Council of Labour, contained in the All-
India Organization of Industrial Employers circular, File 180, WH Papers, NMML; for
the latter, see the minutes to the meeting of the AIOIE subcommittee in the circular
of May 26, 1949, and the report on the Central Advisory Council's second meeting in
File 180, WH Papers, NMML.
  56. See the story carried by *The Times of India*, 11/30/50. See also Deimel to Department of State, #1255, 891.19/12-450, RG 59, DSR. Deimel reported that officials from the
Industry and Supply Ministry had admitted to him that "it was the intention of [the gov-
ernment] to resist any attempt that may be made to revive the idea of profit-sharing."
  57. Resolution IX, paragraph (b), Appendix, *Proceedings* . . . (emphasis added).
  58. K. N. Subramanian, *Labour-Management Relations in India* (Bombay: Asia
Publishing House, 1967), 343.
  59. Subramanian, *Labour-Management Relations*, 346.
  60. A good source for business views on this issue is the weekly *Capital*, which
not only editorialized freely, but also published speeches and addresses by prominent businessmen. On wages, see for example the speech by S. S. H. Sitwell to the
Indian Engineering Association, April 4, 1946; speech by J. Latimer, president of the
Indian Mining Association, in the April 3, 1947 issue; speech by G.D. Birla at the annual meeting of the United Commercial Bank, in April 24, 1947, issue; editorial, 993,
June 11, 1947; editorial, 1095–96, June 26, 1947.
  61. "Report in brief on the proceedings of the first meeting of the Central Advisory
Council of Labour, held at Lucknow, 19th–21st November 1948," File 180, WH Papers,
NMML; All-India Organization of Industrial Employers circular, "Second meeting of the
Central Advisory Council of Labour," July 26, 1949, File 180, WH Papers, NMML.
  62. "Summary of the Proceedings of the Indian Industrial Committee on Cotton
Textiles held in New Delhi, January 12–14, 1948," File 285, AITUC Papers, NMML.
  63. The five-year agenda for labor relations can be found in "Program of Work
During the Next Five Years," File 278, AITUC Papers, NMML.
  64. "Memorandum of conversation with Sadashiya Prasad, deputy secretary to the
Ministry of Labour," November 27, 1950, 891.06/11-2750, RG 59, DSR.
  65. Steere to Secretary of State, May 24, 1951, 891.06/5-2451, RG 59, DSR.
  66. Steere to Secretary of State, May 10, 1951. 891.06/5-1051, RG 59, DSR.
  67. Ironically, while the Commission overshadowed the Labor Ministry on these issues, planners themselves had little power in the policy apparatus relative to other
economic ministries. See chapters 6 and 7, Chibber, *Locked in Place*.

68. See the report on the Eleventh Session of the Indian Labor Conference, Held on August 11–12, 1951, in Drumright to Secretary of State, September 12, 1951, 891.06/9-1251, RG 59, DSR.

69. Wilkins to Secretary of State, August 30, 1951, 891.06/5-2451, RG 59, DSR; Drumright to Secretary of State, September 12, 1951, 891.06/9-2151, RG 59, DSR.

70. Even so, in 1950, only three wage boards were in existence—in cotton textiles, sugar, and cement. See the ILO, "Report to the Government of India on Labour-Management Relations and Some Aspects of Wage Policy" (Geneva, 1960), 33.

71. Subramanian, *Labour-Management Relations*, 413–14.

72. For a discussion of this and related theoretical issues, see Claus Offe and Helmut Wisenthal, "The Two Logics of Collective Action," in *Disorganized Capitalism,* ed. Claus Offe (Cambridge: MIT Press: 1985).

73. This commitment was mediated for many Congress leaders, however, by an attenuated conception of citizenship. In particular, the abuse of the rights of Muslims was, for these more communal leaders, within the bounds of reason, since it was not clear that Muslims were "Indians." Interestingly, while the political marginalization was openly mooted by Congress leaders, the extension of this principle to labor was not.

74. Erik Wright has recently made a distinction, which I basically follow, between positive and negative class compromise. I have used "class accommodation" instead of the term "negative class compromise," because it seems a more felicitous way of expressing the treatment of class interests in such a settlement. See Erik Olin Wright, "Worker's Organization and Capitalist Class Interests," *American Journal of Sociology* (March 2000).

75. Just how far the new state went to accommodate itself to this imperative is examined in chapter 6 of Chibber, *Locked in Place.*

76. The work of Amartya Kumar Sen and Jean Drèze has been particularly important in heralding the region's achievements. See, inter alia, their book, *India: Economic Development and Social Opportunity* (Delhi: Oxford University Press, 1995).

77. Patrick Heller, *The Labor of Development: Workers and the Transformation of Capitalism in Kerala, India* (Ithaca, N.Y.: Cornell University Press, 1999).

78. Heller, *Labor of Development*, chapter 7.

2

Problems of Social Power and the Discourses of the Hindu Right

Tanika Sarkar

On May 13, 2004, in a historic reversal of Indian electoral fortunes, the National Democratic Alliance was dislodged from power. The Alliance had been led by the Bharatiya Janata Party, an electoral wing of the Rashtriya Swayam-sevak Sangh (RSS): an organization inspired by and teaching the ideology of militaristic Hindu extremism in its daily training schedules or *shakhas*.

Commenting on the event, the *Wall Street Journal* wondered if India was really suited for "competitive electoral politics" (read: democracy). It suggested that the verdict of the Indian people went against the mandate of another electorate that was no less decisive: the opinion of global investors.[1] The preference of global investors, or of multinational capital, for a chauvinistic, anti-Christian political force—a force which cashes in on its resistance to western values—may seem paradoxical. It requires of us an exploration into the symbiotic links between cultural nationalism and western imperialism. The task is enormously complicated as the RSS and its interlocking combine of mass fronts—electoral, religious, cultural, trade union, educational—speak in many different, even contradictory voices to address many mutually opposed constituencies. I will merely point out a few clues in this direction which have not been picked up in the frameworks of analysis for the Hindu Right movements or Hindutva politics.

The Bharatiya Janata Party, the electoral wing of the Rashtriya Swayamsevak Sangh, was the dominant partner in the coalition that, until very recently, ruled the Central Government in India. It was also the party that rules Gujarat, the scene of prolonged anti-Muslim pogroms that lashed the state in 2002. Advocates of a militaristic and nuclearized India, the party claims to embody the purest essence of Indian nationalism. Its economic policies, when it was in power, paradoxically, followed the International Monetary Fund-World

Bank–driven liberalization regime faithfully. India was opened up to foreign investments on easy terms, the public sector was folded back, a newly created Ministry of Disinvestment sold off profitable public sector industries,[2] and a hire-and-fire labor policy was sought to be imposed on a labor force that knows no safety net or security of livelihood and survival.[3] Farmers' subsidies were reduced or canceled, and ecologically unsafe big dam projects were developed which drove out masses of rural and tribal people from their habitat with no prospects of rehabilitation. Public welfare investments were reduced in favor of the development of new information technology projects. In the election manifestos, the entire economic package was celebrated as "India Shining" under BJP guidance. The mass media did not question the government's claims. Some of the more secularist journalists, in fact, welcomed this alignment to the larger world as a sign of overcoming the closed mindset that characterizes the RSS. They hoped that the accent on economic development indicated that the party had matured enough to turn away from its policies of Hindu extremism. In the meantime, in Andhra Pradesh, thousands of farmers were taking their own lives in the throes of extreme distress,[4] and the rural landscape was a bleak one without power and water. The savings of pensioners and lower middle classes were wiped out by the reduction of interest rates on small savings, and many urban laborers were thrown out on the streets as the public sector industries faced closure. It was a classic case of the emperor's new clothes: nobody could actually see the splendor, but everybody said that the clothes were shining brightly.[5]

It is easy enough to explain the cultural, anti-western nationalism of the RSS as a compensation for the bartering away of economic sovereignty. However, the roots of this relationship between economic imperialism and cultural closures and chauvinism lie in an older past. Born in 1925, the RSS had steadfastly avoided all engagement with anticolonial movements. In its place, it developed an agenda of a Hindu nation-state which would deny the equality of all religions, thus refusing Muslims and Christians the status of full citizens. If western political and economic domination lay outside its concerns during colonial rule, it nonetheless developed a coherent opposition to several universalizable values such as equality, social justice, and democracy, all of which, it said, were of foreign origin and thus illegitimate aspirations for India and its Hindu culture. At the same time, while contestations of social power were made into foreign and illicit concepts, the RSS also denied that there were any significant exploitative power relations within the Hindu bloc. Not only was this body of ideas systematized, but the RSS founded an elaborate and intricate network of institutions—religious, educational, cultural, leisure- and entertainment-oriented, and philanthropic—that systematically inserted these ideas into the very pores of civil society.

The RSS started operating from the 1920s. But the ideological formation began to engross scholarly and media attention only from the beginning of the 1990s. The immediate occasion was the Ramjanambhoomi agitation that unfolded through widening circles of anti-Muslim pogroms and that culminated in the demolition of the historic Babri Mosque at Ayodhya in 1992. Political observers were taken unawares. What had earlier seemed to be a little known, lunatic-fringe organization called the Vishwa Hindu Parishad (VHP) suddenly emerged as the leader of huge urban crowds, with some toehold among upper castes in North and Western Indian rural areas. It also commanded a formidable tribal following. The Bharatiya Janata Party, with which even the Left had been allied against the Congress Party in the very recent past, and which was generally regarded as a conservative wing of mainstream nationalism, now theatrically displayed itself as a major component of the Hindutva forces.[6] And, behind apparently disjunct organizations and institutions, with increasing clarity appeared the master figure of an erstwhile shadowy Rashtriya Swayamsevak Sangh whose daily training centers and myriad affiliates and subaffiliates taught and calibrated the ideology of violent communalism.[7] As the entire script and a novel dramatis personae gradually came into focus, it was still difficult to discover the connections between the growing occasions of local communal conflicts and the single overarching narrative of the Ramjanambhoomi campaigns. There was the need also to explore the linkages of both local riots and the all-India campaign with the systemic production of ideology, the historical beginnings of which go back to the mid-1920s when the RSS had been founded.[8] It was even more difficult to conceive of an intricate apparatus with mass fronts, ecclesiastical fronts, and an electoral wing that interconnected and overlapped under a single chain of command. The ramifications still need to be precisely charted. The very self-proliferation of the interlinked combine allows it to speak in many different voices and strike contradictory postures at the same time, so that the multiphonality also allows for extremely varied self-definitions and self-descriptions.

Hindutva discourses, read practically for the first time by people outside or opposed to the formation, were mined hastily from 1990 for whatever they would tell us about its communal agenda. For it suddenly struck scholars and political observers alike that histories of Indian sectarian violence have neglected this prominent field of production of communal concepts and violence, even though the RSS has a history that is more than seventy years old.[9] The consequent focus on the anti-Muslim lineages of the Sangh combine, therefore, overwhelmed all other possible trajectories of exploration.[10]

Simultaneously, there appeared a number of broad characterizations of religious violence and pogroms that dissolved the identity of religious extremists into something external to it, something that is an abstract idea rather than a concrete historical entity. At times, communal violence was attached to an amorphous category called Hindu nationalism. In this definition, communalism was a byproduct of a zealous nation-worship that—unlike other variants of nationalism—insisted on conceptualizing the nation as Hindu in its cultural essence rather than as multi-cultural. Left secular nationalism deplored its exclusivism, its worship of past traditions. Non-communal critics of modern secularism, on the other hand, saw it as a fallout of the same process of modernity that tore India out of her moorings in sacred traditions and produced a new, pathologized understanding of religion. In this reading, secularism and communalism are fruits of the same womb, displaying strong family features.[11] In somewhat different kinds of readings, communal violence is dissolved into the abstract and undifferentiated category of violence: either local in nature, arising out of strictly local class contradictions, or an existential category, an independent figure that stalks the land and initiates action as autonomous agent.[12]

Modernity, nationalism, or an abstract will to violence—Hindutva is merged and dissolved into these larger contexts to such an extent that it is sometimes hard even to recuperate its communal content adequately. A recent incisive study has reminded us that such foster homes in other, different ideologies and discourses mask its ideological identity: there is a constitutive unsayable at the heart of communalism that is articulated in its own words and name only at crucial moments, for communalists themselves always refuse the nomenclature of communalism.[13] Having delineated communalism as an ideology that is autonomous and free-standing, and that survives through an organizational apparatus, we need to go further: is communalization of the national identity through a systematic intimidation of non-Hindus the heart of the Hindutva enterprise? If that is so, what drives this compulsion, since religious minorities in India are in no position to make a bid for effective social, political, and cultural power? Moreover, what explains the continuous, systematic, if less strongly articulated, critique of the politics of equality and rights even within Hinduism? To an extent, then, the focus on its proclivity for great violence has obscured other aspects, no less vital to the RSS agenda.

There is an Indian Left critique of Hindutva that goes beyond this.[14] With some noted exceptions, however, the Left understanding provides an incomplete answer. Hindutva is described as basically a bourgeois pathology which is propped up by global capitalism and which is served by an aggressive and militaristic lumpenproletariat. There are some differences among Leftists about whether or not it forms an Indian variant of fascism. Insofar as the critique leads us into the realms of social interests and agendas, it probably provides the most relevant rubric for our discussion. The problem, however, is that the critique often remains mired in the realm of a mechanical causality: If such is the state of class formation and perspectives, then such will be the nature of the ideological structure. Specific historical conjunctures are rarely explored, except as symptoms of laws of historical necessity. The critique does not differentiate among bourgeois ideologies, nor does it take care to relate Hindutva self-display to possible strategies of state power or capitalist requirements. The aspects of Brahmanical caste-gender norms to which the Sangh is, at bottom, deeply committed, are not aligned in Left analysis to the picture of capitalism-driven Hindutva. Moreover, the focus is on the BJP rather than on the Sangh combine as a whole. The basic line of argument about the economic necessities of a class dismisses all other gestures and discourses rather too easily as mere rhetoric.

I would suggest a more connected and integrated description of communalism and of the class basis and strategies of the combine as a whole. Given the very delicate and subtle doublespeak in Hindutva discourses which enables it to be a politics for all seasons and something to everybody, I would prefer to locate its basic drives in specific historical conjunctures rather than derive them from rhetorical strategies alone. I would approach the problem through a delineation of four crucial moments in its history: its inception in the 1920s, its spread and self-proliferation between the thirties and fifties, the phase of the mass campaigns around Ramjanambhoomi, and its present status as the dominant partner in a coalition government. It is important to remember that no fixed, essential, monolithic agenda got articulated through the decades, accomplishing a teleological self-actualization. There were, rather, certain fairly constant interests and motives that adjusted continuously with changing political and economic opportunities and predicaments.

THE BIRTH OF THE RSS

The Rashtriya Swayamsevak Sangh was founded in 1925 at Nagpur with five educated Maharashtrian Brahman men from middle-class families. It emerged at a moment when the political horizon had been rendered radically unstable through a number of experiments that had stretched the limits of the possible. The Congress-Khilafat movements solicited tribal-peasant participation in anticolonial politics, and the response was overwhelming. The interweaving between elite nationalism and mass upsurges to an extent regulated subaltern militancy along pre-selected channels. At the same time, however, the solicitation had its own logic that exceeded simple elite manipulation. It decisively expanded subaltern bargaining power and self-esteem. Moreover, the movement was based on Hindu-Muslim unity on a scale that was unique since 1857. Outside the Congress movements, women's organizations had already made a mark with their demands for larger gender justice and for a right to franchise. Left movements, taking coherent shape from the twenties, worried the colonial state at times far more than the Congress movements did, commanding trade unions and launching widespread strike waves in Bombay, Calcutta, and Kanpur. What was perhaps most worrisome for Hindu social leadership was the upsurge in low-caste, dalit movements in western and south India. In different ways, all these diverse and some-times mutually acrimonious struggles underscored the emergence of new political norms and values: that of self-determination and of equal rights, among nations, races, sexes, and classes.[15]

V. D. Savarkar, the political guru of the Hindu Right, developed very different concepts of primary political conflicts and contradictions. An erstwhile revolutionary terrorist who had spent long years in the Andaman prisons, he published a text in 1923 that moved away entirely from the problem of colo-nialism or of social, caste, and class conflict. He wrote that the chief point of contention was between Indians who were Hindus in their religio-cultural orientation, and "non-Indians" whose fatherland, land of action, and land of holy places were not within the boundaries of Bharat. In other words, it was necessary to classify Muslims and Christians as non- and anti-Indian since their places of worship fell outside India. Class asymmetries were not recog-nized as a problem area in this text, but the very silence indicated deep anx-ieties, especially about caste. And caste was inseparably interlinked with class, since labor arrangements by and large followed caste lines.

Savarkar said that lower castes were the survivors of aboriginal people whom Aryan upper caste invaders had annexed. However, over the cen-turies, miscegenation had mixed up blood across caste and racial lines, re-sulting in a complete fusion, cross-caste kinship ties, and a mixed but unified Hindu family. Shared blood, therefore, admitted asymmetries but in the same move negated their significance, overshadowing social differences with common blood ties.

Savarkar provided an ideological blueprint for a politics that countered the emancipatory dimensions of anticolonial and other radical movements, and that provided a justification for an exclusively communalized cultural politics.[16]

Dr. Hegdewar, who founded the first RSS *shakha* or daily training center for boys in 1925, tried to provide an organizational focus that would con-cretize the message. Especially disturbed by the social consequences of the Gandhian movements, he wrote at length about "the evils in social life that the movement had generated," referring specifically to "Brahman–non-Brahman conflicts" and to "yavana snakes reared on the milk of Non–Cooperation."[17] His Sangh tried to draw youth of pure caste and afflu-ent class away from the anticolonial wave to the RSS alternative, which pro-vided youth with training in anti-Muslim sentiments. Within two years of its foundation, the Sangh proved its mettle by provoking a riot against Muslims in Nagpur.[18] By 1940, the Nagpur-based *shakhas* began to acquire an all-In-dia character. If we look at the chronology of its spread, we find a striking coincidence between moments of rapid growth and the peaking of commu-nal violence. It was founded in 1925, in the middle of the first wave of coun-try-wide communal strife. The next major spurt, which took it beyond the western-central India confines, was between 1937 and 1940 when strife was in the air again. This time, contact had been made with Punjab, Delhi, the United Provinces and Bihar, Tamil Nadu, and Karnataka regions. *Shakhas* now totaled about four hundred, with approximately 100,000 members in all.[19]

Recruitment in the 1940s was confined to the same castes and classes as in the 1920s, albeit in larger proportions: urban students, traders and shop-keepers, and the junior members of the bureaucracy.[20] The RSS clearly rested on a petite bourgeois class-base, made up largely of a vernacular elite: urban educated men, trained in local, vernacular-medium institutions in non-metropolitan places and deeply resentful of the metropolitan cultural influences, as well as of the Urdu courtly culture of the North Indian Muslim gentry. They were also affluent, upper-caste people with deeply conservative, Brahmanical habits and values, fearful of low-caste or womens' movements, and of class struggles.

The RSS, now under the dynamic ideological and organizational control of M. S. Golwalkar, brought to these people the vision of the moral leadership of Hindu society which would be unified under a new orientation, with anticolonials Hindi and Sanskrit as the national and sacred languages of all Hindus.[21] Golwalkar visualized an upper caste–middle class hegemony, based on a modified version of Brahmanical *samskaras* or dispositions, where inherited powers would be substituted with acquired virtues and training in leadership qualities. The vanguard would then fan out among wider social circles, acquiring mass bases through some amount of welfare, relief, and charitable works. Mobilization, however, would be secured, above all, through communal ideology and its institutionalized transmission through the daily *shakha* sessions which would insist on an already-achieved Hindu unity whose internal divisions were of no significance, given the alleged threat from Muslims.[22]

In 1946–1947, when the partition of India produced its own version of the holocaust, the communal assertions proved to be a self-fulfilling prophecy. The country was physically partitioned between warring communities even before the formal territorial division came through. This is not to say that the RSS was responsible for all or most of the violence,[23] but it did benefit enormously from it. The violence seemed to confirm its assertions about a unified Hindu community pitted against Muslims. The memories of the holocaust also proved a valuable asset, recasting the future in terms of the past. RSS cadres were very active in relief work among Hindu and Sikh refugees from West Punjab. The relief work gave them a strong base among the refugees.

Before the assassination of Gandhi by a man who had earlier trained with the RSS, their organizational activities were already in a state of fine health. Unlike the Congress or the Communist Party of India, it did not have to face colonial repression, bans, or a precarious underground existence for long stretches of time. Its resources remained intact and indeed flourished. Just before the Second World War began and praise of Nazi Germany became contraband in British India, Golwalkar published a highly significant text in 1938 where he described the Jewish policies of the Nazis as the ideal model for the treatment of minorities in India.[24] Gandhi's assassination led to a brief ban on the organization, and a high degree of popular anger. It retired to a brief period of purely constructive work: it started a chain of schools to be run on RSS principles.[25]

If Partition aided the wider acceptance of the Sangh, the Constitution of independent India created enormous problems. For the first time, universal adult franchise and representative democracy made the political choices of the majority of Indians the key player in politics; and the real majority in India have always been the poor, low-caste laboring men and women.

In his articles of the late forties, Golwalkar railed against the constitutional provisions.

"Democracy will poison the peace and tranquility of the human mind and disrupt mutual harmony of individuals in society. . . . Not equality but harmony . . . monarchy was found to be a highly beneficial institution, continuing for thousands of years, showering peace and prosperity on the whole of our people." He found the idea of universal literacy and education troublesome for it might lead people to question the notion of social harmony.[26] And what should be the basis of social harmony which is incompatible with equality, parliamentary democracy, or even universal education? He cited the Purushasukta verse from the *Rig Veda* that propounds the theological basis of caste:

> From His mouth came brahmans, from His arms the *Kshatriyas*
> From His thighs appeared *Vaishyas*, and *Shudras* came out of His feet.[27]

He strongly reiterated that the Constitution was a disaster and demanded that it be amended. He argued that if it was no longer possible for India to go back to monarchical tranquility, then at the very least parliamentary democracy should be replaced by the election of representatives from only respectable professions.[28] In other words, the electorate should only elect professionals who would, by definition in a country like India, come from upper castes and middle classes, and, further, be mostly males. The Sangh itself, he openly declared, is not made up of "all kinds of people from the lower strata of social life where people act together like crows flocking together for a piece of flesh."[29]

We should remind ourselves about how extraordinarily tenacious this doctrine has remained in RSS history. As soon as the BJP-led government came to power at the Centre, they renewed the critique of the Constitution and they set up a commission to suggest possible revisions. A recent draft Constitution, produced in the name of the RSS students' wing and thinktank, the Akhil

Bharatiya Vidyarthi Parishad, suggests that the Lok Sabha be guided by a transcendent Gurusabha, largely composed of upper-caste Hindu teachers. It should be chosen by an electorate where each teacher would have thirty votes. The Gurusabha's command would prevail against the mandate of the Lok Sabha, which is elected on the basis of universal adult franchise. Under this draft, franchise becomes weighted, and the teeth drawn out of universal franchise by having an elite body that can countermand its decisions.[30]

The contestation of democracy relied profoundly on arguments of a closed cultural nationalism. The critique of democracy was founded on its supposedly alien origin. Golwalkar identified both equality and democracy as western "materialist" and "individualist" values inappropriate for Indians, for they taught people the notion of equal individual rights, which would destroy the social fabric, unleash competition and struggle for power, and may even lead us anticolonials to the great evil of social equality, socialism. Concepts such as equality and democracy bred conflict between "the labour and the industrialist."[31] So, "Purge Present Perversions," he thundered, and bring back "ancient *samskaras*" prescribed by *varnavyavastha*, the sacred institution of caste.

It in fact served as "a great bond of social cohesion" and prevented the stimulation of unhealthy "caste ego," which the present state machinery encourages. India, minus the constitutional order and democracy, will be a land of born-again Hindus who will keep each caste in its place and call it social peace and harmony.[32] This, I suggest, remains the cornerstone of the Sangh moral vision.

LEADING UP TO THE RAMJANAMBHOOMI AGITATION

Tragically for itself, the Sangh had to live in a democratic India, and were thus compelled to start an electoral wing—the Bharatiya Jan Sangh, ancestor of the present BJP. Self-determination, democracy, and even a formal and verbal commitment to equality had emerged as deeply ingrained values in the political sphere. So hegemonic were these in the immediate post-independence period, that any overt and explicit refutation would have been suicidal for a political front that aspired anticolonials to political authority and social power. Contrary to what the Sangh said, democracy was not an alien and superficial grafting, but had tenacious roots in very recent and powerful experiences of mass struggles against factory owners, upper castes, landlords, and, above all, the colonial state. A softer articulation of Sangh desires was, therefore, an urgent necessity. The Sangh combine and its electoral front required discursive strategies that would affirm parliamentary norms and yet surround and overwhelm them by social values that went back to peace and harmony purchased with the hierarchies of caste, class, and gender.

Deen Dayal Upadhyaya, founder of BJS, gave a series of lectures in 1965, which were published as a book called *Integral Humanism*. It did without the customary abuse of Muslims and even repeated Congress promises about full employment and free education. It did not, however, provide a single clue as to how this would be achieved, nor to what caused their absence. It did not talk about Indian poverty but notably repeated Golwalkar's strictures against the materialistic individualism of the capitalist path as well as against the materialist tyranny of the socialist bloc. In fact, it preferred to do without much engagement with material need and interests, for that seemed be a realm that spiritually minded Indians should do without. The logic immediately precludes critical analyses of Indian poverty, the class character of the state, or the contradictions within civil society. We have instead a social order not founded on a social compact but on an organic growth where the structure is born, not made. It is an organ of interrelated and mutually sustaining parts. Since it is born that way, it would be unnatural to transform the asymmetrical arrangements of class and caste, for that would be violently disruptive to the organism. Asymmetries are then fated to remain so, unless we are unduly fond of social chaos and anarchy. Neither the individual nor a group should have aspirations to move beyond the predestined order, and a liberal capitalist democracy and socialism are both equally dangerous.

Upadhyaya brought in another significant argument against social strife, against any addressing of caste-class issues. He insisted that the BJS would be opposed to the essential and indivisible unity of the Indian "soul" that falls apart under references to difference. It amounts, to put it somewhat differently, to a sort of social partition. The threat of social separatism was a powerful weapon. It carried dreadful resonances for a country which had lived with the horrors of a territorial one. Through such valences, gradually, discourses of poverty, class, and inequality were sought to be unraveled and disallowed.

The relatively quietistic cadences of Sangh conservatism began to falter in the seventies and eighties.[33] There were massive dalit upsurges in Gujarat, and the Sangh and the BJP were drawn into battle as ferocious champions of upper castes. There were political formations of low-caste parties who were extremely critical of the Manusamhita, the ancient prescriptive order of brahmanical patriarchy. There were secessionist movements in the border zones where Hindus did not predominate. Above all, BJP fortunes in Parliament remained weak. By the 1980s, the tone of sweet reasonableness that Upadhyaya had professed began to be discarded in favor of a mass-based Right-wing movement, guided by upper-caste Hindus and funded primarily by Non Resident Indians (NRIs).[34]

Middle-class NRIs in Britain and the United States and Canada in particular, have been a vitally important addition to the Sangh orbit of influence and resources. Affluent, highly successful professional people with considerable lo-

cal clout in their countries of adoption, these Hindus nonetheless experience
a certain degree of lack of cultural recognition in the west. To align their cultural status to their socioeconomic one, they require a vision of Indian traditions that corresponds to the recent BJP slogan: India Shining. They seek their
lineage in a glorious ancestry and appear to be suspicious of versions of India's past and traditions that may dim that luster with references to caste,
class, and gender oppression within the Hindu world. Living far away from
India, they can afford to forget harsh realities of the present and the cruelties
of a past that has bred them. The VHP and the RSS cultivated close links with
them through lecture tours, temple building, and youth-counseling activities.
They reassured conservative parents abroad, worried about the breakup of
caste and kinship forms in a different cultural and social environment, about
mixed marriages and rebellious progeny. They also reassured the vulnerable
egos of successful but racially marginalized Indians, uncertain of their heritage and self-esteem in white-dominated societies.[35] At the same time, while
this class of people reveled in their imagined tradition, and basked in the conviction of superiority to the west where they lived, few took part in the antiracist movements in the Anglo-Saxon worlds. The NRIs were politically docile
and self-contained, thus gaining the approval of local governments. The mul-
ticultural politics of these western countries usually rely on classifying Indians
into monolithic and conservative religious communities, living according to
ancient custom and ruled, invariably, by orthodox leaders. Orientalist habits
die hard. Therefore, the VHP proudly tells us, much local official patronage
has come their way, and they have gained important positions in local governance as safe and authentic representatives of their communities.[36] Their
political clout and economic solvency made them cherished allies in the Ramjanambhoomi agitation of the late eighties and early nineties.

FROM RAMJANAMBHOOMI TO THE GOVERNMENT OF INDIA

The Ramjanambhoomi movement to demolish the Babri Mosque at Ayodhya
began quietly. The anti-Muslim pogroms at Meerut and Maliana and Bhagalpur
in the mid- and late eighties were generally ascribed to purely local tensions and
rather less to the VHP's *shilanyas* and *shilapujan* ceremonies at Ayodhya. At
times, sections of dalits could be pressed into action against Muslims, as at Old
Delhi in 1986, and at Nizamuddin in South Delhi in 1990. The logic of Sanskrit-
isation prevailed: camaraderie, even leadership in communal violence, was the
kind of emulation of pure caste conduct that knitted the despised castes more
closely to the Hindu community. It gave them access to a measure of self-esteem
and community-belonging that their caste situation otherwise precluded.
     The Ramjanambhoomi campaigns were masterminded by the ecclesiasti-
cal or religious wing of the RSS—the Vishwa Hindu Parishad. The Parishad

had made great strides among the NRIs as well as among the monastic sects and temple authorities of major religious sites. They had thus seized the mantle of ritual authority: by founding temples and by patronizing *sadhus*.[37] Founded in 1964 to combat Christianity in the Northeast, it turned against the Muslims from 1981, in the wake of the mass conversions of dalits at Meenakshipuram. The critique of conversion is, once again, tied to a critique of social justice. The exit option that conversion provides for the most exploited sections needed to be sealed off. The VHP had, since then, orchestrated considerable violence against Christians and Muslims. Freed from electoral compulsions and the constraints that a parliamentary party needs to reckon with, and not always directly connected with the RSS by the media, it could indulge itself recklessly in open solicitation of violence to an extent which was not possible for other wings of the Sangh.

The logic of a Sangh-driven Hindu unity, founded on communal violence—a unity that can bypass themes of social inequality among Hindus—broke down with the United Front Government's endorsement of the Mandal Commission recommendations which proposed the extension of job reservations to Other Backward Castes in 1990. The Brahmanical face of the RSS was unveiled as its paper, *The Organiser*, invoked Manu in despair and railed openly against a "*shudra* revolution." Abuse of low castes, once carefully excised from its public vocabulary, resurfaced with naked force.[38]

In 1994, writer and journalist M. V. Kamath counseled sobriety and pacification through an extension of hegemonic exercises among low castes: "There is urgent need to build up moral and spiritual forces to counter any fallout from the expected *Shudra* revolution. Already one smells violence in the air."[39] In 1996, the RSS adopted schemes in villages to contact lower castes and to promote "social assimilation and harmony."[40] Co-opted low-caste leaders such as Uma Bharti (the present Chief Minister of Madhya Pradesh) and Bangaru Laxman began to be visibilized and artfully displayed.

As with women and lower castes, the mobilization of workers too proceeded simultaneously with a reinforced critique of social justice: society needed to be hierarchical, and the general Hindu will to violence would provide social cementing. A leader of the Bharatiya Mazdoor Sangh (BMS), the RSS trade union at the Bokaro Steel plant, told us that labor strikes are "anti-national . . . Rashtrahit first, mazdoorhit second," as though the nation were distinct from workers.[41] The BMS leader, Dattopant Thengde, similarly castigated the notion of equality and rights in the case of gender.[42]

THE POWER OF THE STATE

We have seen that through a masterly calibration of collective, trans-class, trans-caste, and non-gendered acts of violence with a conceptual apparatus that stigmatized the politics of rights, the Sangh evolved something like a moral economy of communalism. In 1998 the BJP came into power at the Center, but only as a dominant partner in a coalition. To achieve even this, it had to qualify its policy of co-optation of underprivileged groups in favor of tactical alliances with parties with low-caste bases. Their class basis remained stagnant at best, even though the BJP did funnel governmental funds for relief and charity through party organizations to buy support from people in need of relief.[43]

At the same time, while the primary support base has not changed and as the class-caste composition of the cadre base remains intact, its electoral fortunes in 1998 indicated that a secondary range of electoral support has been created among the upper and middle classes in metropolitan cities and big towns. The stance of the English-language metropolitan media reflects this change. Cases of notorious atrocities like the Staines murder or the Babri Mosque demolition or the Gujarat carnage do invite sharp reactions even now, but such opposition soon wavers when it comes to the economic policies of the BJP-led government. If the Sangh combine grew up as a vernacular elite, then why and how have its aspirations found a resonance in the far more exalted circles of metropolitan elites or big business, connected to multinationals and obeying World Bank–IMF commands? How complete is its integration with the interests of global capitalism in this contemporary moment, and what are the possible fault lines? What, above all, were the implications of this new phase for the victims of Structural Adjustment policies?

Here we need to address certain very profound and long-term reorientations in mainstream, middle-class social thinking. Since colonial times, Indian nationalism had represented the country as desperately poor, and founded its critique of colonialism on the poverty and economic backwardness of India. Post-colonial regimes continued that characterization, albeit with a great deal of optimism for the future. They adhered to a vision of complete economic sovereignty and independent capitalist development under a planned economy that would accept a model of development that would also provide some basic services to the poor and the illiterate. Also, they accepted the principle of affirmative action for dalits. A relatively large public sector provided some social security to its workers and farming was subsidized. Most of these policies remained solely on paper, while the poor continued to live their lives without the protection of any safety net whatsoever. Nonetheless, the tenacity of certain principles cleared a space for the contestation of poverty and class exploitation. Rights and equality were given the status of absolute goods, of desirable norms.

The economic changes of the last two decades have rapidly shifted the basis of earlier self-perception. The entire post-colonial phase is, in this present moment, dismissed as a failure and the roots of the presumed failure are traced to the earlier goals of economic self-determination and to the philosophy of the public welfare. Indian capitalism is eager to participate in the global markets primarily as a consumer, and the state, in this phase of capitalism, is equally eager to buy national and international financial support with a policy of compliance. Above all, the Indian middle class—led by the media—has become notably disinclined to dwell upon poverty. Its tunnel vision sees little beyond what it considers signs of the nation's greatness: Pokhran, Kargil, the IT technological progress and the consumer boom, the dazzle of commodities. It was easy to consolidate the feel-good factor. In this situation, the NDA acquired political power at the Center and made its historic compromise with the forces of national and international capital. All had an investment in markets and constituencies that coveted the goods of the world. All distrusted the philosophy of subaltern rights that might upset the apple cart.

In 2001, the budget speech of the Union Finance Minister suggested drastic revisions in existing labor laws. So far, all retrenchment in factories that employ less than a hundred workers had been conditional on governmental approval. Now, factories employing fewer than a thousand workers—an overwhelming majority of all workplaces—could retrench at will. The formal sector, moreover, was going to be reduced considerably with the unrestricted outsourcing of production in all sectors of employment where workers used to enjoy a modicum of job security. Even the BJP labor union, Bharatiya Mazdoor Sangh, vigorously opposed this.[44] The budget of 2002 was so much more spectacularly anti-poor, even anti-middle class in terms of fiscal and pricing policies, that the BJP had to acknowledge that it played a major role in electoral reverses in several states and municipalities.

This phase of capitalism and dominant economic philosophy is becoming increasingly incompatible with democracy, however non-substantive and formal. As the 2004 elections have just shown, poor voters' response to the erosion of livelihood and survival issues still retain the capability of throwing the governments out, even if they cannot achieve more responsible governance. And even though popular mass movements like the Narmada Bachao Andolan were defeated by the state, there is no guarantee that things are fated to remain so. The visibility of social movements the world over, the World Social Forum that was held at Mumbai in January 2004, made their slogan "Another World Is Possible," something more than rhetorical flourish.

We come back to the Wall Street statement on Indian elections. The BJP proved its worth to the capitalist world, not just because it pushed the new liberalization regime more ruthlessly than previous governments. Its predecessors had also moved in the same direction, without, perhaps, the same ruthlessness. Most importantly, alone of all other political groups, it had provided a coherent and explicit critique of the principle of equality and of rights—of democracy, without naming it as such. More, it has provided a substitute for material welfare for classes that its policies victimize: certain equality in communal violence, a shared vision of the Hindu nation.

It became clear on May 13 that its moral economy lost the Indian majority that exceeds the media and the middle-class consumer once every five years. It was equally clear that it gained the other electorate that Wall Street referred to.

NOTES

1. Cited by P. Sainath in *The Hindu*, June 1, 2004.
2. See the official website of the ministry for more information: http://divest.nic.in/.
3. The new government is less sympathetic to this policy. See "CMP rejects 'hire and fire' labour policy," *Deccan Herald*, May 28, 2004.
4. See, for example, Amy Waldman's reportage on this issue in the *New York Times* on May 14, 2004, and June 7, 2004.
5. For a review of the economic policies, see Jayati Ghosh, "Perceptions of Difference: The Economic Underpinnings," in *The Concerned Indian's Guide to Communalism*, ed. K. N. Panikkar (Delhi: Viking, 1999).
6. Thus in October 1990 the then president of the BJP, L. K Advani, undertook a "rathyatra," a masquerade with a chariot driven by a Toyota car, whipping up frenzy for an attack on the Babri Mosque.
7. One of the first studies that linked up and delineated the entire multifaceted structure in its fullness was Tapan Basu et al., *Khaki Shorts and Saffron Flags: A Critique of the Hindu Right* (Delhi: Orient Longman, 1993).
8. One of the earliest writings that did make the connection was Achin Vanaik's "The Enemy Within," *The Times of India Sunday Review*, December 16, 1990.
9. Gyan Pandey's very well-known and much-cited work on communalisn in colonial North India, for instance, does not even mention the RSS. See his *The Construction of Communalism in North India* (Delhi: Oxford University Press, 1990).
10. Eventually, a very rich crop of studies appeared, especially on communal politics and on the RSS-BJP. See for instance, among many others, Sarvepalli Gopal, ed., *Anatomy of a Confrontation: The Babri Masjid-Ramjanambhoomi Issue* (Delhi: Penguin, 1991); Bruce Graham, *Hindu Nationalism and Indian Politics: The Origins and Development of the Bharatiya Jana Sangh* (Cambridge and New York: Cambridge University Press, 1993); Thomas Blom Hansen, *The Saffron Wave: Democracy and Hindu Nationalism in Modern India* (Princeton, N.J.: Princeton University Press, 1999); Christophe Jaffrelot, *The Hindu Nationalist Movement and Indian Politics, 1925 to the 1990s: Strategies of Nation Building, Implementation and Mobilisation* (London: Hurst Press, 1996); Thomas Blom Hansen and Christophe Jaffrelot, eds., *The BJP and the Compulsions of Politics in India* (Delhi: Oxford University Press, 1998); Tanika Sarkar and Urvashi Butalia, eds., *Women and the Hindu Right* (Delhi: Kali for Women, 1995). For an older study, fairly sympathetic to the Sangh, see Walter K. Anderson and Shridar D. Damle, *The Brotherhood in Saffron: The Rashtriya Swayamsevak Sangh and Hindu Revivalism* (Boulder: Westview Press, 1987).
11. See, for instance, T. N. Madan, *Modern Myths, Locked Minds: Secularism and Fundamentalism in India* (New Delhi: Oxford University Press, 1997); see also Ashis Nandy, "An Anti Secularist Manifesto," *Seminar* 314 (October 1985): 1–12.

12. See Veena Das, "The Anthropological Discourse on India: Reason and Its Other," in *Critical Events: An Anthropological Perspective on Contemporary India,* ed. Veena Das (Delhi: Oxford University Press, 1995).

13. Pradip Kumar Dutta, *Carving Blocks: Communal Ideology in Early Twentieth Century Bengal* (Delhi: Oxford University Press, 1999).

14. See, for instance, Achin Vanaik, *The Furies of Indian Communalism: Religion, Modernity and Secularisation* (London: Verso Press, 1997); Sumit Sarkar, "The Fascism of the Sangh Parivar," *Economic and Political Weekly,* January 30, 1993.

15. For a concise account of this period, see Sumit Sarkar, *Modern India* (Delhi and London: Macmillan, 1983).

16. V. D. Savarkar, *Hindutva: Who Is a Hindu?* 6th ed. (Delhi: Bharti Sahitya Sadan, 1989). See also Jyotirmaya Sharma, *Hindutva: Exploring the Idea of Hindu Nationalism* (New Delhi: Penguin, 2003). For an excellent study of Hindutva ideology in general, see Chetan Bhatt, *Hindu Nationalism: Origins, Ideologies and Modern Myths* (Oxford and New York: Berg, 2001).

17. Cited in C. P. Bhishikar, *Keshub Sanohnirmata.* Pune, 1979. Hindi translation, Delhi, 1980, 7.

18. See Basu, *Khaki Shorts,* 18–20.

19. Basu, *Khaki Shorts.*

20. See J. A. Curran, *Militant Hinduism in Indian Politics: A Study of the RSS* (New York: Institute of Public Relations, 1951): 18–19.

21. Basu, *Khaki Shorts.*

22. That orientation remains unchanged. In fact, the RSS has little more to offer that would carry its own distinctive stamp. See, for instance, a documentary based on a *shakha* for infants in Nagpur City, Lalit Vachani's *The Boy in the Branch,* Channel Four, 1991.

23. Although it did accomplish a lot more than we know, as the archival documents collected by the *Anticolonials Freedom* volumes on those years bear out. Significantly, the BJP Human Resources Minister has forbidden the publication of those volumes.

24. M. S. Golwalkar, *We or Our Nationhood Defined* (Nagpur: Bharat Publication, 1939), 27. Significantly, the passage praising Nazi anti-Semitism was retained in the third edition in 1945, even after the full horrors of Hitler's Final Solution had become known world-wide.

25. Tanika Sarkar, "Educating the Children of the Hindurashtra: Notes on RSS Schools," in *Religion, Religiosity and Communalism,* ed. Praful Bidwai, Harbans Mukhia, and Achin Vanaik (Delhi: Manohar, 1996).

26. "Challenge of the Times" (1949), included in M. S. Golwalkar, *Bunch of Thoughts* (Bangalore: Jagarana Prakashna, 1960), 24–26.

27. "Challenge," 36.

28. "Challenge," 26.

29. "Challenge," 49.

30. This (Akhil Bharatiya Vidyarthi Parishad) was a pamphlet that circulated in 1999–2000 in Delhi University circles. I am grateful to Aditya Nigam for providing me with a copy.

31. Akhil Bharatiya Vidyarthi Parishad, 40–41.

32. Akhil Bharatiya Vidyarthi Parishad, 110–16.

33. For a standard RSS hagiographical account, see C. P. Bhishikar, in *Pandit Deen Dayal Upadhyaya: Ideology and Perception*, Part V (Delhi: Suruchi Prakashan, 1991).

34. On Sangh work in the West, see Parita Mukta and Chetan Bhatt, eds., "Hindutva Movements in the West: Resurgent Hinduism and the Politics of Diaspora," *Ethnic and Racial Studies* 23, no. 3 (May 2000).

35. See H. V. Sheshadri, K. S. Sudarshan, K. Surya Narayan Rao, and Balraj Madhok, *Why Hindu Rashtra?* (Delhi: Suruchi Prakashan, 1990).

36. Sheshadri et al., *Why Hindu Rashtra?*

37. Lise McKean, *Divine Enterprise: Gurus and the Hindu Nationalist Movement* (Chicago: University of Chicago Press, 1996).

38. See *Organiser*, August 26, 1996.

39. Cited in *Organiser*, May 1, 1994.

40. See Hansen and Jaffrelot, *The BJP and the Compulsions of Politics in India.* See also Eri Kakuta, "Hindu Nationalist Views on Rural Development: A Case Study of the Deendayal Research Institute's Chitrakoot Project," in *Journal of the Japanese Association for South Asian Studies* 15 (2003).

41. Interview with S. K. Verma, April 4, 1990. Cited in Basir, *Khaki Shorts.*

42. Cited in T. Sarkar, "The Gender Predicament of the Hindu Right." In *The Concerned Indian's Guide to Communalism*, ed. K. N. Panikkar (Delhi: Viking Press, 1999).

43. See Kakuta, "Hindu Nationalist Views on Rural Development."

44. *The Hindu*, 4 March 2001.

3

Reinventing Public Power in the Age of Globalization

Decentralization and the Transformation of Movement Politics in Kerala

Patrick Heller

Class-based social movements have traditionally been concerned with capturing the state and wielding the instrumentalities of bureaucratic power to compensate for the inequities of market distributions. Redistributive goals have been pursued through a range of centrally coordinated interventions that have included wage support, direct transfers, universal service provision, labor market regulation, and progressive taxation. Both the class politics and policy regimes associated with social democracy have been played out at the national level. Kerala represents an important case of a subnational trajectory of social-democratic development marked by a distinctive history of class-based mobilizations and redistributive social policies.

Globally and locally, however, the effectiveness and viability of this trajectory, and of redistributive strategies of development more generally, is increasingly in doubt. The most obvious problem is that globalization in its neo-liberal form has significantly reduced the nation state's latitude in using traditional instruments of redistribution. Just as critically has been increasing concern, born of the failures of planned development, about the ability of the institutional forms of the modern state—representative democracy and techno-bureaucratic administration—to promote equity.[1] If such doubts first emerged as part of a post-materialist politics in advanced capitalist societies, with in particular the rise of "new" social movements that extended the traditional left critique of market commodification to a critique of state bureaucratization, a similar shift can be discerned in many late developing countries. Thus a wide range of subaltern movements have challenged the post-colonial hegemony of the developmental state. But far from being anti-development, or representing a wholesale rejection of the modernist project of citizenship (as Escobar and other post-colonial theorists argue), many of these movements remain centrally concerned with expanding the role of public powers to underwrite social citizenship. What makes these movements "new" is that they have challenged the high modernist hubris that imparts the state and its technocrats with the vision and capacity for social transformation to the virtual exclusion of civil society.[2] The continuity that marks these movements (as opposed to the rupture presumed in the post-modernist reading) with the past (or "old" social movements) is that they are animated by a political project of expanding social citizenship and are, as such, strategically concerned with engaging the state. The rejection of bureaucratic modes of emancipation (and the attendant political emphasis on capturing the commanding heights of the state) has been accompanied by calls for transforming the very nature of the state and of representative politics, and specifically for deepening democracy through greater participation. These movements have taken a wide range of forms, and as a whole account for the flourishing of civil society that commentators have detected in Latin America, Africa, and South Asia. Of the many political projects that have emerged as a result, none has been more critical than the demand for decentralizing state functions and capacities to levels at which popular movements and organizations can play a more direct role in shaping public investment. The old social movement logic of redistribution from above has in other words been superceded (though not replaced outright) by calls for redistribution from below.

The potential implications of this strategic shift are difficult to exaggerate. On the one hand, democratic decentralization has the potential of leveling the playing field for effective political participation and creating new institutional spaces for civil society activism. On the other hand, given the significant role the state plays as a source of accumulation in much of the developing world—and notably in India—reconfiguring the state and how and where it deploys its resources can have a potentially dramatic distributive effects. The debate and struggle over decentralization looms even larger when one considers that a critical policy tool of neo-liberal economic reforms has been a variant of decentralization that effectively emasculates the role of the public sector. The capacity of social movements as such to reclaim the logic and discourses of decentralization as a vision and strategy of democratic empowerment and expansion of public decision-making emerges as a critical contested terrain of the second great transformation.

There are probably few examples in the world where the causal link between organized social movements and significant redistributive and social gains is as strong as in Kerala. Briefly put, a long history of social mobilization with roots in the late nineteenth century generated an upsurge of caste reform movements and peasant uprisings in the 1920–1940 period then crystallized into a lower class movement under the organizational umbrella of a the communist party which captured power in 1957. Repeated spells in power by the communists combined with an almost continuous process of militant mass mobilization exerted unrelenting pressure on the state to expand social programs, regulate labor markets, and implement land reforms. Despite a two-decade period (1970–1990) of virtual economic stagnation, social indicators have continued to climb, and poverty rates have continued to fall. There is little doubt that no other state has been more consistently pro-poor or successfully redistributive than in all of India, and possibly anywhere in the developing world.[3]

Which makes the launching in 1996 by a CPM-led government of the "People's Campaign for Decentralized Planning" rather intriguing. Widely regarded as the most far reaching and radical experiment in decentralization ever undertaken in India, the campaign's political project has been nothing less than a frontal assault on the bureaucratic fiefdoms of the state and the patronage networks of the political system. The paradox here, in the words of the campaign's key architect, is that "a state government launched a movement to force its own hand to radically restructure the mode of governance. Why should any state embark upon such a mission?"[4]

Though this question, as we shall see, overstates the agency of the state, it certainly calls for an answer. That answer, I shall argue, lies in a profound reconfiguration of the relationship of social movements in Kerala to political parties and the state marked by a dramatic shift from traditional state-oriented distributive struggles to a mode of movement politics deeply embedded in civil society. This shift is inflected with both an important rupture and key continuities that link these two political moments in Kerala's developmental trajectory. The rupture emerges from the fact that the redistributive project was predicated on building a centralized, commandist, and top-heavy state apparatus, linked to a highly disciplined political party and its mass organizations through quasi-corporatist structures. These structures more or less bypassed civil society, and equated lower class power with party control of the state. In contrast, the decentralization project seeks not only to devolve bureaucratic and political power, but to re-embed the state in civil society by promoting participatory democracy. The continuities relate to the dynamics of what has been a steady, if uneven, process of democratic deepening. The process has been driven by iterated engagements between social movements and state institutions centered primarily on issues of social citizenship, the most important political effect of which has been the differentiation of civil society from social structures. A second continuity has been with the CPM itself, and in particular its history as a social movement party.

MOVEMENTS AND DEVELOPMENT IN KERALA

Kerala's achievements on the social front are well known. On all the key social indicators it has dramatically outperformed all other Indian states and even compares favorably with developed countries. Literacy is over 90 percent and life expectancy has reached 72. Between 1957–1958 and 1990–1991, Kerala experienced the most rapid decline in poverty of any major state, including the Punjab and Haryana, India's capitalist growth success stories.[5] Many factors have contributed to these successes, including historically higher levels of literacy and remittances from Kerala's migrant workers. But structural and institutional reforms have been the most important. Lands reforms in the 1970s virtually abolished landlordism and transformed poor tenants into small property owners. Labor market reforms and high levels of unionization leveraged the bargaining power of wage earners to the point that even informal sector workers have seen their wages rise rapidly. Social protection schemes now cover a significant share of the population, and an extensive network of subsidized food shops has practically wiped out malnutrition. Extensive health care and primary education systems have achieved almost universal coverage.[6]

Because Kerala's economy remains backward and growth rates have been, until very recently, modest at best, most observers have attributed these successes to state actions. Whether the task at hand has been getting teachers to teach, children to stay in school, landlords to surrender land, or mediating and enforcing wage rates and work conditions for over two million agricultural workers, the state has consistently delivered. These efforts, moreover, have been sustained over time and regardless of the political party in power. No major public service or redistributive program has ever been reversed, and this despite an increasingly precarious fiscal situation and a decline in Centre financial support. Sustained state intervention has moreover survived a history of fragile multi-party coalition governments. If we consider that Kerala's successes stand in sharp contrast to the overall failure of state intervention in the rest of the country, yet that it shares the same basic institutional, financial, and state structures, and has more often than not been ruled by the same Congress party that has done so little in other states, it is clear that the difference in the state's effectiveness lies not so much in the character of the state itself—as Kohli argues for the case of West Bengal—but in the nature of its engagement with society.[7]

By all accounts, Kerala has a vibrant, plural, and activist civil society. A wide range of NGOs, unions, and associations continually organize and articulate interests and exercise constant pressure on the state and its agencies. But much the same could be said of the rest of India. Between an Anglo-Saxon–style liberal constitutional order that has encouraged pluralism over corporatism and a dynamic and powerful repertoire of contention inherited from a prolonged liberation struggle, India has a long and storied history of voluntarism and popular forms of collective action. Why then has associationalism in Kerala produced a responsive state, whereas the rest of the country governments are better known for their benign neglect of needy citizens at best, and their predatory behavior at worst?

To answer this question, we have to unbundle the idea of civil society and recognize that not all forms of associationalism have democracy-enhancing effects. In contrast to the currently fashionable trend of viewing civil society as by definition good for democracy, it is important to recall that early theorists of civil society—notably Hegel and Marx—viewed civil society as the realm of the self-interested and the particular. If the right and propensity to associate is certainly a necessary part of democracy, it does not follow (as is often assumed) that all forms of voluntary action are good for democracy. Forms of association that are exclusionary, based on traditional hierarchies of authority or geared to securing rents or perpetuating privileges, certainly do not have democracy-deepening effects. For this reason it becomes critical to distinguish associative orders that favor encompassing rather than narrow interests and programmatic reforms rather than group patronage and rent-seeking.

At the risk of making a generalization that inevitably vulgarizes the complexity of the Indian picture, at both the national level and in most states (which for many reasons is the much more appropriate level of analysis for social movements in India), forms of association and demand articulation based on narrow groups or sectoral identities / interests have more or less crowded out more encompassing expressions of political life.[8] With respect to the general configuration of organized interests, upper class and upper caste interests tend to be more effectively organized, and even though the poor have significant opportunities in the political arena, the effective exercise of citizenship for millions of Indians at the lower end of the social order is circumscribed by the persistence of traditional forms of social control and acute forms of material dependency. Certainly, movements emerge and are vocal but tend to be either limited to narrowly defined constituencies or sectors, or simply lack the scope and scaled-up capacity to be politically effective. Most notably, very few social movements have developed synergistic relationships with political parties.[9] With the decline of the Congress Party's hegemony as a catchall party, these fissures have been translated to the political system, which is now increasingly dominated by re-essentialized identities of caste, religious community, and ethnicity (subnationalism). While it is certainly the case, as Guha argues,[10] that the thrust of much subaltern activism in India is distributive (as opposed to the post-materialist logic of "new" social movements), the fragmented and issue-based character of movements has rarely (with the exception of farmer movements) in recent times translated into actionable redistributive policies. Thus while civil society remains vibrant, associational life strong, and movements lively, in the absence of programmatic parties and a state capable of insulating itself from rent-seeking pressures, the remobilization of primary identities over the past two decades has triggered a frantic and zero-sum scramble for preferential treatment that Pranah Bardhan has aptly described as "equal-opportunity plundering by all interest groups."[11] In this scramble, the interests of the poor are rarely heard and the politics of social citizenship are conspicuous by their absence.[12] In this vicious cycle, the failure of the developmental state gives rise to "movements of rage" and the reassertion of primary identities.

In Kerala, civil society is certainly as noisy, but not as cacophonic as the Indian norm. Patterns of association are more likely to be horizontal, cutting across primary identities of caste and communities. Rural life in Kerala is characterized by a dense tapestry of cooperative societies, self-help groups, child care associations, and NGOs. The extensiveness and depth of the institutional infrastructure of civil society—that is, the reach of public legality and the presence of basic differentiated institutions of governance and socialization— have decisively shifted the locus of authority from traditional structures to rational-legal structures.[13] Thus Kerala has the highest levels of unionization in the country, and unlike the national pattern, unionization and social protection schemes also encompass significant segments of the informal sector. The reach of authoritative state institutions and the extent to which basic social rights of citizenship have been institutionalized are most trenchantly reflected in basic indicators: 94 percent of births in Kerala are attended by trained health care personnel (compared to 34 percent in India) and 91 percent of rural females between the ages of 10 and 14 attend school (compared to 42 percent).[14] Finally, political life has been dominated by a fairly stable electoral distribution between class-based parties, rather than the continuous and opportunistic realignments of communal and caste alliances that have become the hallmark of Indian electoral politics. This explains not only why the politics of social citizenship have commanded center stage in Kerala, but also why Kerala has been spared the caste and sectarian violence that has gripped the rest of the country in the past two decades.[15]

The particular modalities (programmatic parties, horizontal forms of association) and the overall intensity of citizen engagement with the state and its institutions in Kerala cannot, as is the case with most neo-Durkheimian theories of social capital, be explained with reference to long-term processes of socialization. If anything, pre-Independence society in Kerala was marked by a degree of caste segmentation and feudal dependency that was acute even by Indian standards. What distinguishes civil society in Kerala is not a particular culture that predisposes individuals to trust each other but rather the extent to which civil society—as a discrete realm of social life—has become differentiated from pre-democratic social structures, which in turn has given free reign to rights-based forms of political participation. This process of differentiation has not been one of linear and evolutionary modernization, but rather the political product of a history of acute conflict and recurrent episodes of social mobilization. That history has been treated extensively elsewhere but can be briefly summarized.[16] The first third of the century saw the rise of three distinct movements: a socioreligious anticaste reform movement, the anticolonial movement, and contentious but disorganized instances of agrarian protest. None of these movements, taken alone, was unique to Kerala. But to the extent that they converged both ideologically and organizationally under the political leadership of a programmatic cadre-based communist party (the CPI), they generated a socially transformative dynamic that has taken Kerala down a very different path from that of the rest of the country. Thus, in sharp contrast to the dominant nationalist Congress Party politics that sought to accommodate rural elites and downplayed class and redistributive issues, the Communists in Kerala explicitly tied colonial rule to the injustices of the caste system and the inequities of the agrarian system. The struggle against British imperialism became a struggle against the social and economic power of Kerala's landed upper caste agrarian elites. From the outset of mass politics, democratic rights in Kerala were about social rights.

This mobilizational trajectory reached an electoral watershed when the CPI won Kerala's first elections in 1957. Unlike in West Bengal, the Communists and their allies have never achieved a stable electoral majority, and have consequently been in and out of power. This, coupled with the fact that they have always remained suspicious of "parliamentary democracy"—having in fact been twice evicted from power by the central government—more than anything else explains why the Party has continually had to reinvent itself and build its mobilizational capacity. As a key party theorist notes, "[T]he Left does not have faith in the autonomous transformative power of the state government, which is only part of the overall bourgeois-landlord Indian state. Therefore, while in power or outside, they continue to mobilize the masses in support of the demands. The constant pressure from below is important in understanding the responsiveness of the state machinery."[17] Adding to this has been the bandwagon effect of other political parties embracing mass-mobilizational politics. Nowhere in India has the contentious repertoire of social movements become such an intrinsic part of routine politics.

The most demonstrable effect of continuous lower class mobilization has been the building of the most socialized economy and developed welfare state in the region. But as the state has responded to demands for social rights, it has also extended the reach of public legality, weakening the material and social hold of traditional dependencies. Thus an equally important effect of Kerala's history of social movements has been the deepening of democracy through a double movement of institution-building and civil society differentiation.

THE CAMPAIGN

By the mid-1980s it had become clear that Kerala's redistributive trajectory of development was in trouble. In both agriculture and industry, growth was stagnant, and unemployment was climbing. The organized left in Kerala responded by abandoning militant class struggle in favor of a social-democratic strategy of class compromise. Industrial militancy fell dramatically and Left Democratic Front (LDF) governments made a series of strategic concessions to capital. In the 1990s, Kerala's economy did out-perform the national economy.[18] But high unemployment levels have persisted, and liberalization has had a particularly acute impact on Kerala's economy, first with the reduction of Centre subsidies (most notably for the Public [food] Distribution System) and second with falling commodity prices (especially rubber) that have come with import liberalization. The resulting fiscal crisis of the state combined with ever more acute inter-state competition for foreign and domestic capital has only increased the pressure to relax labor laws, curtail social protection, and in general downsize the role of the state, in particular its developmental and planning role. If such pressures have seen a marked reduction in social commitments in other states, in Kerala powerful and well-entrenched unions and a political equation, marked by broad-based working and middle-class support for the welfare state, have ruled out downsizing. Addressing the structural crisis of the redistributive-developmental state has required an entirely different strategy. What has emerged has been a project to strengthen the public sector by devolving the responsibility of service provision and development to local governments.

In 1996, a CPM-led LDF government launched the "People's Campaign for Decentralized Planning." The institutional details of the campaign have been explored in detail.[19] Widely acknowledged to be the most ambitious effort at decentralization ever undertaken in India, the scope and depth of institutional reconfiguration has been remarkable.[20] During the five years of the LDF government (1996–2001), the nature of public authority has been transformed along four axes. First, there has been fiscal decentralization: 35–40 percent of all plan expenditures have been allocated directly to 1,214 local, block, and district *panchayats* and municipalities. Under the previous Congress-led government, *panchayats* received Rs. 477 million in grants-in-aid in 1995–1996. In 1996–97 the grants-in-aid jumped three-fold to Rs. 1,770 million and nearly ten times the pre-campaign figure, to Rs. 5,107 million in 1997–98.[21] Second, there has been significant administrative decentralization. Local governments have been given new functions and powers of decision-making, and officials from many line departments have been brought under the authority of *Panchayats* and muncipalities. Third, there has been political decentralization. Thousands of locally elected officials who were little more than agents of centrally or state-sponsored schemes now enjoy the authoritative decision-making power and the budgetary discretion to make and implement development policy. Fourth, planning and budgeting for local development takes place through a series of nested participatory institutions that begin with ward-level popular assemblies (*grama sabhas*) and finish with task forces of local officials and activists that design specific development projects.[22] The scale of participation has been of movement proportions: in the first round of *grama sabhas* of the campaign in August-September 1996, around 2.5 million people participated with an average of 180 persons per *grama sabha,* representing 6.97 percent of the population, or roughly one out of every five households. In the second year, participation increased to 7.16 percent of the rural population.[23] Over three hundred thousand people participated in development seminars that prepared extensive development reports for every local *panchayat* and municipality, and task forces of some twelve thousand produced over one hundred thousand projects.[24]

Though the institutionalization of the campaign remains an open question, particularly in light of the LDF's defeat in the 2001 legislative elections,[25] there is little doubt that the reforms achieved to date represent a significant deepening of participatory democracy. First, by having devolved planning and implementation functions to local arenas, the campaign has for the first time in India meaningfully empowered local governments and communities to directly control local development. The entire planning cycle—which begins with the collection of local data and ends with the formulation of a comprehensive local plan that consists of hundreds of projects—is basically an extended exercise in participatory problem-solving, budgeting, and implementation. Second, both the institutional and the political logic of the campaign have been centrally concerned with levelling the playing field. The devolution of authority and resources to local governments has significantly reduced the transaction costs of participation, and the knowledge and capacity gap that has traditionally excluded ordinary citizens from playing an effective role in governance has been considerably narrowed by mass training programs, the active mobilization of civil society expertise, and concerted efforts to mobilize women, dalits, and *adivasis.*

Whether or not the campaign has produced efficiency gains in developmental expenditures is a question that calls for more detailed research.[26] The principal concern here is, however, not to evaluate the effects of the campaign, but rather to explore the conditions under which such an ambitious project of transforming the role of the state in development was undertaken.

EXPLAINING THE ORIGINS OF THE CAMPAIGN

If the rise of redistributive coalitions in the developing world has been the exception to the rule, so have successful cases of decentralization. India is a case in point. Despite the fact that the idea of empowered local governments has long been a staple of India's Gandhian heritage, from Nehru's Community Development Program to national and sub-national efforts to empower

India's *panchayats,* the history of decentralization, much like land reform, has been one of broken promises, slow political deaths, bureaucratic obfuscation, and hollow legislation.[27] Where local governments have been given some measure of power, they have more often than not been captured by local elites and transformed into instruments of patronage. Regional variations notwithstanding, the balance sheet is clear: with the well-documented exception of West Bengal, the process of shaping and implementing developmental initiatives, including the most basic of day-to-day public services, remains a top-down affair dominated by the bureaucratic and political elites of state capitals and their intermediaries, brokers, and fixers. As EMS Namboodiripad, party patriarch and patron-saint of the Campaign, once put it: "at the level of centre-state relations the constitution gave us democracy. At the level of state-*panchayat* relations, the constitution gave us bureaucracy."[28]

Kerala, one might have thought, should have been an exception, with its long history of grassroots activism and the comparative weakness of local dominant elites (the prime culprits in the subversion of democratic decentralization). Yet the state in Kerala is an institutional replicate of its developmentalist Indian parent, born as it was at the intersection of an imperial bureaucracy and Soviet-inspired visions of planned transformation, and deeply imbued with a high modernist ethos of top-down development. As Sudipta Kaviraj notes of the India state, "By the mid-1950s such an over-rationalistic doctrine became a settled part of the ideology of planning and therefore of the Indian state. 'The state,' or whoever could usurp this title for the time being, rather than the people themselves, was to be the initiator and, more dangerously, the evaluator of the development process."[29] Without falling into the asocial and reductionist public choice view that sees a voracious, self-seeking predator in every bureaucrat and politician, the accumulation of such powers, exercised with little accountability from below, has inevitably produced interests and networks of privilege that have nothing to gain and everything to lose from a devolution of powers. The political solidity of this institutional configuration finds its class logic in the rental havens that the dominant proprietary classes—including bureaucrats and politicians—have all carved out for themselves.[30]

In its demonstrated capacity to deliver social programs and its much higher degree of public accountability, the state in Kerala is a far cry from the proto-predatory states of North India. But the difference is more in the demand side of the equation—pressure from social movements and a vocal civil society for state action—than in the supply side, as the state in Kerala has not been spared the entrenchment and ossification of rent-seeking interests. The size and power of such interests, moreover, is in no small part a product of Kerala's redistributive project, and specifically the exponential growth of the service bureaucracy and the proliferation of (mostly unprofitable) public sector enterprises.

The political party equation in Kerala has also been unfavorable to any serious efforts at state reform. Because the Congress Party has fairly weak grassroots structures compared to the CPM, it has had little interest in empowering *panchayats.* The CPM's historical commitment to decentralization has not been much better. Though there has always been a strong grassroots democratic tendency in the party (what I call the social movement tendency), the party's historical roots in organized class struggles produced a hierarchical internal command structure and a fairly orthodox state-led and top-down vision of development borrowed in large part from Soviet planning.[31] The CPM, moreover, has a direct stake in the bureaucratic state. The CPM's organizational heart is the CITU (Congress of Indian Trade Unions), its labor federation. Composed primarily of industrial workers employed in the public sector and government employees, many of its unions have gained significant control over state agencies through which they command important patronage resources and can exert centralized control over their membership. Having become power bases unto themselves, many have hardened, Olsonian-like, into narrow distributional coalitions.

To explain why the CPM—or at least key elements of the party—has now embraced decentralization and accepted a more independent role for civil society, three developments have to be singled out. First, the party has come to recognize the limits of its electoral appeal, and in a context of competitive party politics has identified democratic decentralization—with its attendant principles of non-partisanship, de-bureaucratized government, and sustainable development—as the key to appealing to new social formations. Second, the embrace of decentralization marks a tacit recognition that the redistributive capacities of the developmental state have exhausted themselves. The broad-based social movements that saw the expansion of social citizenship have been displaced by more narrow and sectoral interests. These distributional coalitions have captured significant rents (the bulk of non-plan expenditures goes to propping up grossly inefficient public enterprises and paying the salaries of an under-performing state bureaucracy), but have also blocked necessary state reform (and indeed remain quite hostile to the campaign). If a strong, centralized, and interventionist state did secure many of the benefits associated with the Kerala model (high levels of social development, extensive public infrastructure, basic institutional reforms), the second generation social development challenges Kerala faces (the quality, rather than the quantity of public services) call for a fundamentally different mode of governance. The fiscal logic of the campaign is revealing: by reducing rents and leakage through greater accountability, more can be done within existing constraints. Third, for all its successes in mobilizing broad segments of the working class, including wage workers in agriculture and other unorganized sectors, the CPM has largely failed to make inroads into some of Kerala's poorest communities, including *adivasis,* fishworkers and Muslims. Fourth, despite a growth spurt in the early 1990s, Kerala's continued economic problems—in particular the lack of dynamism in commodity-producing sectors—has underscored the failures of the dirigist state, and has prompted calls for developing more flexible and decentralized forms of state intervention designed to nurture rather than to control economic activity.

All of these factors in turn have helped strengthen the political position of the social movement tendency in the party. This tendency has always coexisted with the corporatist and centralizing elements of the party. But in contrast to the CPI, the CPM in Kerala has always remained critical of the transformative capacity of the bourgeois-democratic state and has emphasized the political necessity of direct, mobilized forms of democracy.[32] In the intensely competitive environment of Kerala's electoral politics (where outcomes generally hinge on marginal percentage shifts), the CPM's comparative advantage has always been its activist and mobilizational capacities, an advantage honed from periodic stints in the opposition. Tendencies towards organizational sclerosis and machine politics have thus been kept in check by recurrent episodes of rank and file militancy. The contrast with the West Bengal CPM, which has been in continuous power for over two decades and has developed pronounced oligarchical tendencies, is highly illustrative.[33]

Marked as they are by cross-cutting alignments and constant repositioning, the exact boundaries of the corporatist and social movement tendencies are difficult to identify. The divisions do however roughly parallel the oft noted, if often exaggerated, difference between old and new social movements.[34] The corporatist faction (known locally as the CITU faction) has its power base in the larger industrial and public employees' unions and subscribes to the view that popular struggles can be advanced only through the party's disciplined organizational structures. The strategic thrust remains state capture, with corporatist structures securing significant shares of the social surplus for organized elements of the working class. In contrast to the narrow economism of many labor movements (e.g., the myopic character of Indian labor federations), the CITU faction has stubbornly defended broad-based entitlement programs. But while it has in the tradition of Marxist movements developed a class critique of the state (i.e., as an instrument of dominant class interests) it has not developed a critique of the organizational power of the state and of rent-seeking as a form of surplus extraction. Finally, the corporatist tendency remains deeply suspicious of civil society activity that is not subject to party discipline.

The social movement tendency of the CPM can be distinguished from new social movements in its explicit concern with redistributive goals. Moreover, in sharp contrast to what Bardhan in the Indian context has dubbed the anarcho-communitarian view of decentralization,[35] the tendency is also committed to strengthening the state, albeit through new institutional articulations of the local and central state. But in keeping with what might be labeled a neo-class (if not post-class) movement logic, it recognizes other sources of domination and exclusion, including patriarchal and bureaucratic power, that go beyond the traditional labor-capital conflict. The social movement tendency has extensive ties with civil society organizations, including significant cross-cutting membership with the grassroots "people's science movement," the Kerala Sastra Sahitya Parishad (KSSP). The resulting discursive shift is evident in the increasing but cautious introduction of the language of civil society (a term traditionally associated in party language for its "bourgeois" origins)—including non-partisanship, accountability, participation, and decentralization—into party thinking and even cadre training. For the social movement tendency, the significance of democracy is located less in the concept of working class power and its organizational expressions (party and state) than in the nurturing of democratic practices, both through institutional reform (making the state more responsive) and by capacitating citizens (enabling participation and empowerment at all levels of governance). It is in this sense that its project has become one of reinventing public power.

These political shifts, it should be emphasized, have taken place against a backdrop of economic and social developments that have significantly weakened, if not marginalized, the corporatist tendency. The social basis of the organized left has been transformed by the long-term stagnation of the manufacturing sector and the growing size of an educated middle class, itself the product of the welfare state. But the most palpable and devastating blow to the corporatist vision of state-directed development has come from the widely perceived deterioration of public services. In comparative terms, the quality of Kerala's public health and educational services remains decades ahead of any other Indian state. But by local standards, and specifically those of a literate and increasingly middle class society, even a marginal decline in the quality of provision has produced widespread public disaffection, including carefully researched critiques by social movements.[36] Though blamed in large part on an unaccountable bureaucracy, the deterioration of the public sector has also been explicitly tied to the commodifying logic of globalization and the cost-cutting imperatives of neo-liberalism. To quote Planning Board member and CPM leader Shreedharan Namboodiripad:

> The state is withdrawing from social sectors—education, health and other services. Despite advances, educational and health institutions, especially at local level, are facing severe crises because of the resource crunch. This can be overcome only if it is planned at the local level and that all maintenance and other support work is done locally. Thus a major portion of devolved funds are going to the improvement of educational and heath services. They [*panchayats*] are also mobilizing voluntary resources in the form of labor and contribution. The point is that both rich and poor have a common interest to contribute to improve these institutions. . . . The WB/IMF [World Bank/International Monetary Fund] have committed to the retreat of the state. Here, we are trying to make the

state more active at the local level of the economy and social services. Decentralization is our answer to the IMF/World Bank globalization agenda. It is the most integral part of our resistance.[37]

Faced with these threats to the sustainability of Kerala's social democratic developmental trajectory, the crises of a state bloated by excessive commitments and beleaguered by vested interests, the CPM leadership seized on the democratic Left's critique of bureaucratization and developmentalism and endorsed democratic decentralization as the centerpiece of its political platform in the 1996 election.

MOVING THE STATE

Genuine democratic decentralization is synonymous with a fundamental reconfiguration of institutional and political power, and necessarily invites resistance from entrenched bureaucratic and political interests. That this deadlock has been broken in Kerala must be attributed to two key developments from above. The first was the fact that the social movement tendency within the party received the full support of the party high command. The second was that this tendency could operate from the vantage point of a highly autonomous though strategically embedded state agency, the State Planning Board (SPB). When the CPM came to power in 1996, the board was given the institutional status of a supra-ministry, and all its ranking members were appointed from the social movement faction. Five of the six board members were in fact from the KSSP. They in turn recruited a cell of roughly thirty officials redeployed from various departments, the majority of whom were also KSSP members. The board enjoyed the full support of the chief minister, and maybe most importantly the party patriarch, EMS Namboodiripad (who passed away in 1999). The board became the platform from which reformers could orchestrate their decentralization project independent of the power and influence of the corporatist political bosses.

Institutionally empowered and politically protected, the board administered a home-grown brand of shock therapy. It rammed through a legislative budget amendment that in a single stroke devolved 40 percent of plan allocations from line departments to *panchayats*. When members of legislative assembly and some ministers protested their loss of control over developmental (read patronage) funds, they were publicly rebuked by Namboodiripad. A Leninist party being what it is, the Members of the Legislative Assembly (MLAs) quietly fell into line (though the CPI Ministers remained reluctant partners).

The board simultaneously launched a massive publicity campaign in the press and party forums denouncing what it called "the corrupt bureaucratic-politician nexus." A first round of state-wide ward-level *grama sabhas* were held. By the time financial resources began to flow into local government coffers, the political costs of opposing decentralization had become too high. In a classic pincer movement, the board effectively isolated the patronage elements of the party and state bureaucracy by aligning itself directly with grassroots activists and a newly empowered political constituency of some 14,173 elected *panchayat* officials.[38]

If movements in Kerala in the past rallied against exploitation by dominant caste groups, or propertied interests, the campaign has built support by attacking the predations and inefficiencies of the bureaucracy and politicians. In doing so, it has tapped into a very palpable strain of discontent that cuts across class lines and has offered the movement powerful frames of contention. Across the political spectrum, NGO activists, CPM theorists, academics, and journalists, as well as a large number of reformist bureaucrats, all point to the patronage interests of state-level politicians, the centralized power of ministries and their line departments, and the power of some public employees' unions as being at the heart of the crisis of the Kerala model of development. At opening presentations of *grama sabhas,* a favorite theme was to critique the existing process of planning as alienated from the people, overly bureaucratic, and incapable of delivering the goods. Songs and street plays from the campaign "vilified and caricatured development bureaucrats."[39] These criticisms are not of state power or state intervention as such, but rather of the insulated and narrowly technocratic character of the high-modernist state. The committee that designed much of the campaign's legal and regulatory architecture summed up the institutional logic of the campaign succinctly: "In participatory governance patronage has no place."[40] The call is for democratization of state power and specifically the devolution of planned development. Indeed, the campaign is popularly know as *Janakeeya Aasoothranam*—people's planning with its connotations of deliberation—rather than decentralization.

The specific criticisms leveled against the bureaucracy are familiar ones. On the one hand, it is viewed as being fundamentally undemocratic and unresponsive. In the uncompromising words of the Committee on the Decentralisation of Powers: "At present offices and systems, including those under the control of the Local Self Government Institutions (LSGIs) are not people-friendly. A thick veil of secrecy hides inefficiencies, arbitrariness, corruption and nepotism from public gaze."[41] On the other hand, it is accused of being overly centralized as well as balkanized, and as such incapable of taking up the new developmental challenges that Kerala faces. Vertically organized line departments have created a culture of departmentalism in which local officials are more concerned with fulfilling scheme quotas than with meeting local needs. The problem of fragmentation is acute: a former director of agriculture estimated that more than thirty different departments work in the agricultural sector, making it virtually impossible to coordinate inputs such as credit, irrigation, seeds, and agro-machinery.

But the attack on the command-and-control state has gone beyond a critique of its inefficiency and has also taken a distinctly redistributive tone. High-level officials and CPM leaders routinely claim that up to 50 percent of all public expenditures are siphoned off by the "corrupt politician-bureaucrat-contractor nexus" and that only a determined struggle against "development as patronage" can restore these "rents" to the people.[42] Speaking of MLAs, who have traditionally exercised direct power of plan allocations in their districts, a key CPM leader explained the party's "new thinking":

> In Kerala primitive accumulation has taken the form of corruption. The Party has taken the view that they [MLAs] should have no say in development activities and that their functions should be legislating. We want to destroy the politics of patronage. When decisions are made at the grama sabha level, patronage will be exposed. The only way to undermine patronage is through popular participation.[43]

But what marks the campaign as distinct from most state-led reforms is that in challenging bureaucratic and political fiefdoms and responding to the threat posed to Kerala's social compact by globalization, the state has explicitly resorted to creating new mobilizational spaces.[44] The campaign's official literature and the writings of its key architects explicitly argue for tapping into the transformative capacity of civil society organizations. For one Planning Board member the logic is simple: "Politicians and bureaucrats want to hold onto power and the only way to dislodge them is through a social movement."[45] Making his case for democratic decentralization, especially with respect to Kerala's crisis of accumulation, Thomas Isaac writes that "Defending the public infrastructure in education, health and other sectors is no longer possible without improving the quality of their services. All these necessitate a reorientation of the mass movements towards *direct intervention in the development process* in order to improve productivity or improve the quality of services."[46] A permanently mobilized civil society thus emerges as the primary goal of the campaign, and in stark contrast to the technocratic and neo-liberal view of transformation, planning becomes "an instrument of social mobilization" and specifically a means of re-engaging citizens in the process of public decision making:

> The bureaucratic departmental approach to development has to give way to an integrated, democratic vision. . . . The extremely sectarian bipartisan division and clientelism is a major impediment in the development process. In short, the objective of the People's Campaign for Decentralized Planning is not simply to draw up a plan from below. The very process of planning is such as to bring about a transformation in the attitudes of the participants themselves. Such a transformation cannot be secured through government orders alone. It requires the *creativity and the social logic of a movement.*[47]

The fact of the state exhorting the masses to participate is hardly notable or especially democratic in itself. What is notable is that in this instance the state has actually reduced the transaction costs of collective action by decoupling significant resources and authoritative decision-making power from traditional centers of power and devolving them to the grassroots. Budgetary allocations by *panchayats* are now the end product of a long, open process of multi-layered deliberation which has, if nothing else, significantly raised the costs of political capture and rent-seeking. Equally telling, and revealing of the extent to which the CPM—or at least of faction of it—has come to accept the autonomy of civil society, is that mobilization has not been orchestrated through party structures, but has rather been nurtured by creating new and largely non-political (though not a-political) associational spaces. The CPM has explicitly instructed its local branches (which historically have directly controlled CPM-led *panchayats*) not to interfere with the new deliberative structures of local budgeting and has banned local party structures from discussing beneficiary lists for local development projects. Of course, local political equations can often subvert the most carefully designed procedures, but the pattern of resistance to the new institutions underscores the stakes of reform. Just how dramatically the campaign challenges old political habits is captured by the lament of one local CPM official at odds with the campaign: "What kind of party are we if we can't decide who gets a cow?" Traditional networks of privilege—MLA's, some public service unions, a range of bureaucrats (most notably state engineers) and parties with weak grassroots structures (including the CPI) have openly resisted the campaign. And ultra-leftist elements within the CPM itself, no doubt threatened by the shift away from the party's traditional state-centric position, have even accused the campaign of being a Western-inspired and funded plot to weaken the left in Kerala.[48]

THE ROLE OF MOVEMENTS

A sustained process of social transformation, and in particular one that involves significant institutional realignments, requires an "ecology of actors" that answer to different but complementary organizational logics.[49] Because democratic decentralization threatens existing patronage networks and introduces significant uncertainties, political parties are most likely to support reform only when the internal balance of power shifts from traditional party brokers to more grassroots factions. Social movements can play a critical role in occasioning such a shift not only by mobilizing public support for reform, but also by popularizing more participatory institutions and processes through prefigurative actions. Moreover, because democratic decentralization goes beyond legislative acts and resource reallocations, its effectiveness and most importantly its sustainability require far more than the capacities of the state. Civil society organizations and social movements have a critical role to play in making the state more democratic. First, the associational networks of civic organizations and movements can provide vital information about social needs as well as the mobilizational infrastructure that makes continuous and meaningful participation possible. Second, civil society organizations, be they rotating credit schemes or contentious social movements, help develop and nurture the democratic and technical capacities of individuals, and often promote forms of demand-making that are far more deliberative than those of more hierarchical organizations.

In Kerala, the political opening for decentralization was created from above, but it is civil society that provided the critical informational and mobilizational resources. This is most evident in both the ideological repertoires of the campaign and in its policy tools. To attack state-led development and "departmentalism" and to celebrate autonomy, local initiative, transparency, and accountability, is to speak the language of social movements, not technocrats or Leninists.[50] Most of the techniques and favored projects of the campaign—rapid rural appraisal, local resource mapping, community water management, rotating credit schemes, self-help associations—come from a repertoire of practices that NGOs and some of the more proactive *panchayats* have been developing for years.[51] These pilot projects have not only popularized grassroots planning and sustainable development strategies, but have also provided much of the practical knowledge that went into designing the campaign. As early as 1978, the KSSP had created about six hundred rural science fora that functioned as informal *panchayat* planning boards, and during the 1990s the KSSP sponsored twenty-five model *panchayat* projects, experimenting with grassroots planning and sustainable development strategies that served as templates for the campaign. Other NGOs and quasi-governmental institutions have been experimenting with low-cost housing, smokeless *chulas,* watershed management techniques, e-government, and horticulture.

The role of the KSSP and its forty-eight thousand members has been critical. Although an autonomous association, the KSSP which has its roots in the educational community has always shared the mass mobilizational and democratic empowerment politics of the CPM's social movement wing. It has not, however, shared the CPM's growth-centered vision of development or its democratic centralism. The KSSP first came to prominence in the mid 1970s, when it successfully challenged a government project (which had CPM support) to construct a dam in Silent Valley. It has consistently argued for more decentralized and sustainable development, and has focused the bulk of its activities on democratizing knowledge (through the publication and dissemination of literature that brings "science to the people") and promoting grassroots planning. Its organizational structure is quintessentially of the new social movement variety, marked by strong local branches, rotating leaders, the absence of any permanent staff, and a workstyle known locally as *parishattikata* and characterized "by informality, simplicity, frankness, friendship and the absence of rigid hierarchical structures."[52] And though the KSSP has consistently maintained its autonomy, refusing to endorse political parties and rejecting all offers of outside funding, it has also successfully partnered with government, providing for example the bulk of the activists for the Kerala government's Total Literacy Project in 1991.

It is precisely this willingness to engage the state and political organizations that has underscored the KSSP's most significant contribution to the campaign—the creation of a policy reform network that has bridged the CPM/state and civil society and served as the incubator of the campaign. Membership in the KSSP has provided an arena in which CPM cadres could experiment with ideas outside the somewhat doctrinaire straitjacket of the party itself. The reform networks among activists also included educational and research institutions, most notably the Centre for Development Studies and the Centre for Earth Sciences Studies. Over the past few years, these institutes have sponsored a series of seminars and conferences that helped crystallize thinking on decentralization and expanded the policy circle. This not only drew in critical segments of the academic and professional communities, but also helped create a public policy debate outside the highly charged and acrimonious arena of party politics. In building the basic architecture of the campaign, the planning board could draw on a wide and diverse body of knowledge and experience and has sustained synergistic linkages with civil society. Local level experiments have been scaled up and consolidated. New intermediate planning institutions, interactive training seminars, and systematic procedures for aggregating local plans at higher levels have created a dynamic feedback loop. The continuous institutional fine-tuning that has marked the campaign has been made possible by the active engagement of a core group of activist officials (in particular senior Indian Administrative Service [IAS] officers in the Local Government and Finance Departments) who have blurred the line between state and society by developing direct lines of communication with grassroots actors. Diffusion and learning has been facilitated by dense networks of activists and in particular the symbiosis between the KSSP and the SPB. In drawing on KSSP activists to run the campaign the SPB plugged into the KSSPs associational networks and also profoundly changed the work culture of the board. The KSSP cell in the board in effect transformed a 9 to 5 bureaucracy into a round-the-clock operation. Cell officials spend the majority of their time attending meetings in the field and problem-solving on the ground. In their disposition, energy, and commitment they are far more akin to social movement entrepreneurs than to bureaucrats.

The mobilizational resources civil society has provided have been equally critical. Much of the initial publicity for the campaign came from *Janadhikara Kalajathas,* science and arts theatrical processions presented by over one thousand artists and organized around KSSP repertoires of critiquing "current development processes" and "exhorting the people to approach the *grama sabhas* to chalk out a new path."[53] The campaign has involved a massive amount of institution and capacity building, as local actors have had to learn how to design projects, evaluate costs, manage finances, gather data, and implement programs. Though department personnel have been redeployed, they have often been recalcitrant partners. Elected officials have thus had to rely substantially on the input of trained volunteers. With the help of KSSP activists and volunteer experts and a number of academic faculty (all working without pay) the campaign has provided training to over one hundred thousand elected representatives, officials, and ordinary citizens four years running. As is true of many social movements, the campaign's mobilizational success is rooted in exiting activist networks: 70 percent of state-level volunteer key resource persons and 66 percent of district resource persons (who have played the critical role of facilitating the participation) had prior experience in literacy campaigns.[54] Though training has been given a formal character by linking different sectoral programs to a range of educational and government institutions (e.g., Kerala Agricultural University and Institute of Local Administration), civil society inputs remain crucial. Most training in project design takes place through a form of horizontally networked learning in which innovative *panchayats* organize and hold organized district and state-level seminars in areas in which they have achieved notable successes.[55]

In response to resistance from the bureaucracy, and in particular engineers charged with reviewing the technical viability of local projects, the Planning Board also mobilized a Voluntary Technical Corps (VTC). To recruit what one planner called "this wedge against the bureaucracy" the Planning Board launched a publicity campaign using the slogan, "life doesn't end at fifty-five," to get skilled retired professionals to volunteer their expertise. Over five thousand engineers, accountants, agronomists, and doctors joined the VTC. In a manner that closely resembles Judith Tendler's (1997) description of how the state government of Cerea in Brazil created a core of committed government workers and community activists, the Planning Board has actively worked to instill a sense of mission in the VTCs and local resource persons by distributing awards, publicizing achievements, and in general lauding the contributions of these volunteers.

Beyond qualitative assessments of how civil society has shaped participation, there is also robust quantitative evidence of how movement activities have transformed the social configuration of participation. Data from the Planning Board show that participation in *grama sabhas* was stable in the first two years of the campaign.[56] But a disaggregated analysis of the social profile of participation reveals dramatic changes. In 1996, Scheduled Caste/Scheduled Tribe (SC/STs) were only half as likely to participate as the population at large. Similarly, the participation ratio of women to men was only 0.4, and overall women represented only 28 percent of total participants. But by the second year of the campaign, participation rates for both groups had grown dramatically. In 1997, SC/STs were almost one and half times more likely to participate than the population at large. The participation ratio of women to men climbed to 0.68, representing 41 percent of participants. These gains were, moreover, geographically widespread. In 1997, the level of SC/ST participation exceeded the overall level of participation in 760 *panchayats,* compared to 267 in 1996. And whereas in 1996 women out-participated men in only ten *panchayats,* by 1997 the number grew to 155 *panchayats.* Overall, 786 *panchayats* experienced an increase in women's participation.

While it is difficult to isolate the determinants of this social deepening of participation, the effect of social movements on associational crowding-in is clear. In the first year of the campaign, the SPB and the KSSP were openly critical of the low levels of subordinate group participation. The SPB enlisted women's groups to provide targeted training, and the KSSP stepped up its efforts to form neighborhood groups (*ayalkutangal*) of twenty-five to fifty families at the sub-ward level as well as women's credit and savings self-help groups. Recognizing the higher social costs to participation that subordinate groups face, the neighborhood groups were designed to act as prefigurative forms of participatory planning ("a place to practice face to face democracy"), preparing residents, and in particular women, for more active and informed involvement in the planning process.[57] The mobilizational effects have been well documented in a number of cases. In local case studies, researchers directly attribute increased levels of participation in the second year to the associational spillover from neighborhood groups and self-help groups.[58]

CONCLUSION

Social movements are by nature cyclical, and patterns can be cumulative or discontinuous. Shifts in the political opportunity structure shape not only movement strength, but also movement success. Movement cycles in Kerala have been particularly sharp, marked by peaks of mobilization that translated directly into political and institutional transformation (class formation in the 1940s, electoral success in 1957, land reform in 1970, labor market reform in the 1970s). But movement pressure has also been continuous, generating the demand-side dynamic that has underwritten Kerala's redistributive path of development. This institutionalization of contentiousness can most readily be explained by a highly competitive polarized political party system that has put a premium on mobilization, and in particular a mass-based political party whose oligarchical tendencies have been kept in check by its own electoral shortcomings. But it is the existence of a differentiated civil society—both an effect and a cause of movements—more than anything else that explains the cumulative and in particular democratizing impact of social movements in Kerala. The resurgence of movement activity that has marked the campaign flows directly from a political project that was backed by the state. Breaking through the logjam of political and bureaucratic interests opposed to decentralization required the political initiative of a programmatic party and the instrumentalities of a pilot agency that could successfully circumvent traditional power brokers and build direct political ties with local forces. But the working template itself was the product of multiple inputs from civil society, and institutional reform has been shaped by a continuous process of learning and feedback made possible by policy networks that have blurred the boundaries between state and society. Because of its movement character, the campaign has benefited from constant negotiation and re-negotiation of methods and goals, and has thus captured many of the synergies that can result from blending the institutional capacities of the state and the associational resources of civil society.

The movement associated with the campaign defies simple categorization. It is certainly more diverse, more loosely organized, more decentralized, less hierarchical, and concerned with a wider range of social issues than its class-based predecessors. Yet the continuity with the project politics of the past is significant. First, the movements associated with the campaign have maintained a central concern with redistributive issues that have been extended to include broader definitions of social exclusion, including patriarchy and bureaucratic domination. Second, engagement with the state, and the expansion of public authority, are strategic movement goals. But rather than capture a singular state as an instrument of social transformation, the campaign represents an effort to transform the state into a set of more localized, accountable institutions that can serve as the permanent basis of participation—which leads to a last and more general point. As movements necessarily oscillate between the politics of mobilization and institutionalization, sustaining a transformative trajectory depends on delicate equilibria of actors and institutions. There is little doubt that the crystallization of lower class organized interests and the increase in state intervention that has defined Kerala's redistributive developmental trajectory certainly produced its share of entrenched interests and institutional ossification. This has not, however, produced the political sclerosis that public-choice and neoliberal views of participatory democracy would predict. In the context of a differentiated civil society and an electoral system based on competitive mobilization, there is always the possibility of political reconfiguration. And what makes such reconfiguration possible is precisely what a participatory democracy has most to offer: the dynamic tension between the contestatory logic of social movements and the interest aggregation of political parties.

NOTES

I would like to thank Mary Katzenstein, Raka Ray, Michael Watts, and Gillian Hart for their extensive and extremely useful comments.

1. See the introductory essay in A. Fung and E. O. Wright, *Deepening Democracy: Institutional Innovations in Empowered Participatory Governance* (London: Verso, 2003).

2. See James Scott for an extended discussion of high modernism (*Seeing Like a State: How Certain Schemes to Improve the Human Condition Have Failed* (New Haven, Conn.: Yale University Press, 1998).

3. For the most explicit comparative assessments internationally, see Jean Drèze and Amartya Sen, *Hunger and Public Action* (Oxford: Clarendon Press, 1989). For comparisons across Indian states, see Jean Drèze and Amartya Sen, *India: Economic Development and Social Opportunity* (Delhi: Oxford University Press, 1995).

4. T. M. Thomas Isaac and Richard Franke, *Local Democracy and Development: People's Campaign for Decentralised Planning in Kerala* (New Delhi: LeftWord Books, 2000), 316.

5. The annual decline was 2.26 percent on the headcount index and 3.93 percent on the poverty gap index (Guarav Datt and Martin Ravallion, "Why Have Some Indian States Done Better Than Others at Reducing Poverty?" Policy Research Working Paper No. 1594, World Bank, Washington D. C., 1996, 30).

6. For detailed reviews of the data, see V. K. Ramachandran, "On Kerala's Development Achievements," in *Indian Development*, ed. Jean Drèze and Amartya Sen (Delhi: Oxford University Press, 1996), 205–356, and K. P. Kannan, "Poverty Alleviation as Advancing Basic Human Capabilities: Kerala's Achievements Compared," Working Paper No. 294, Centre for Development Studies, Trivandrum, 1999. For a discussion of the informal sector, see Patrick Heller, *The Labor of Development: Workers in the Transformation of Capitalism in Kerala, India* (Ithaca, N. Y.: Cornell University Press, 1999).

7. Atul Kohli, *The State and Poverty in India* (Cambridge: Cambridge University Press, 1987) attributes West Bengal's relatively strong performance in poverty alleviation to the regime characteristics that derive from the CPM's programmatic, cohesive, and pro-poor character.

8. This is the central theme in the Rudolphs' seminal overview of Indian politics (Lloyd I. Rudolph and Susan Hoeber Rudolph, *In Pursuit of Lakshmi: The Political Economy of the Indian State* [Chicago: University of Chicago Press, 1987]).

9. The exception of course is the Hindutva triad of the BJP, RSS, and VHP. These are, however, by definition communal movements built on social exclusions which are moreover internally dominated by traditional hierarchies of patriarchy and caste. They are on both counts reactive movements (Manuel Castells, *The Power of Identity* [Oxford: Blackwell Publishers, 1997]) opposed to the project of social citizenship. At the other end of the spectrum, the CPM has nurtured mass movements. But despite its programmatic commitment to social citizenship, the organizational primacy of electoral politics, "democratic centralism," and a resilient patriarchal culture have often resulted in the subordination of movement demands and identities to party control. For the case of the women's movement, see Amrita Basu, *Two Faces*

of Protest: Contrasting Modes of Women's Activism in India (Berkeley: University of California Press, 1992).

10. See the introductory chapter in this volume.

11. Pranab Bardhan, "Sharing the Spoils: Group Equity, Development, and Democracy," Unpublished paper, University of California, Berkeley, 1997, 16.

12. Pratap Mehta ("India: Fragmentation Amid Consensus," *Journal of Democracy* 8, no. 1 [1997]: 56–69) makes this point forcefully.

13. A survey conducted by the Confederation of Indian Industries found that Kerala ranks first among all states—including far more urbanized states—on the rule of law indicator (Bibek Debroy, Laveesh Bhandari, and Nilanjuan Banik, "How Are the States Doing," Rajiv Gandhi Institute for Contemporary Studies and Confederation of Indian Industry, 2000). For a more qualitative assessment of reach of public legality that explores the degree to which a wide range of material conflicts are mediated and adjudicated through formal rational-legal institutions, see Patrick Heller, "Degrees of Democracy: Some Comparative Lessons from India," *World Politics* 52 (July 2000): 484–519.

14. Kannan, "Poverty Alleviation," 12 and 20.

15. There has been a notable rise in recent years in political violence, especially in the northern districts of Kerala. This violence has, however, been strictly between party activists (most often between CPM and BJP cadres).

16. See Heller, *The Labor of Development*; Ronald Herring, *Land to the Tiller: The Political Economy of Agrarian Reform in South Asia* (New Haven, Conn.: Yale University Press, 1983); K. P. Kannan, *Of Rural Proletarian Struggles: Mobilization and Organization of Rural Workers in South-West India* (Delhi: Oxford University Press, 1988); and Dilip Menon, *Caste, Nationalism and Communism in South India: Malabar 1900-1948* (New Delhi: Cambridge University Press, 1994).

17. Thomas Isaac and Franke, *Local Democracy and Development*, 141–42.

18. In contrast to dire predictions that the Kerala model has become economically unsustainable because of an assumed direct trade-off between social and economic investment, Kerala's per capita gross state domestic product grew at an annual 4.52 percent between 1991-1997 compared to 4.02 percent at the national level (Montek S. Ahluwalia, "Economic Performance of States in Post-Reform Period," *Economic and Political Weekly*, May 6, 2000, 1638). See also K. N. Harilal and K. J. Joseph, "Stagnation and Revival of Kerala Economy: An Open Economy Perspective," Working Paper No. 305, Centre for Development Studies, Trivandrum, 2000.

19. World Bank, "Volume I: Overview of Rural Decentralization in India" and Volume II: Approaches to Rural Decentralization in Seven States," September 27, 2000; R. Véron, "The 'New' Kerala Model: Lessons for Sustainable Development," *World Development* 29, no. 4 (2001): 601-17; Thomas Isaac and Franke, *Local Democracy and Development*; T. M. Thomas Isaac and P. Heller, "Democracy and Development: Decentralized Planning in Kerala," in *Deepening Democracy: Institutional Innovations in Empowering Participatory Governance,* ed. A. Fung and E. O. Wright (London: Verso, 2003); and S. M. Vijayanand, "Issues Related to Administrative Decentralisation and the Administering of Decentralisation," paper presented at the Workshop on Decentralisation organized by the Institute for Social and Economic Change at Bangalore, May 31 and June 1, 2001.

20. A World Bank report on the impact of the 1993 Panchayati Raj constitutional amendments in 1993 found that Kerala has the greatest degree of local expenditure

autonomy and is the most fiscally decentralized state in India, and second only to Colombia in the developing world (2000: vol. I, 28–29).

21. In 1998–1999 the figure was Rs. 6,061 million and Rs. 7,279 million the next year. See World Bank (2000), Vol. II, 130, table 9.

22. There are 990 village *Panchayats* and 58 municipalities in Kerala with an average population of 29,580. Each *panchayat* has 10–12 wards, with a single elected councilor for each ward.

23. These figures are from the State Planning Board which collected attendance figures (based on registration of participants) from every *grama sabha*. A 7 percent participation rate equals roughly 10 percent of the electorate and amounts to approximately one participant for every 3.5 households (Shubham Chaudhuri and Patrick Heller, "The Plasticity of Participation," Working Paper, Columbia University, 2002). Comparisons are by definition problematic, but there is little doubt that this represents the highest level of participation in any Indian state (World Bank, 2000) and compares favorably with the city of Porto Alegre and the province of Rio Grande do Sul in Brazil, the most celebrated and carefully documented case of direct participation in budgeting (Gianpaolo Biaocci, "Participation, Activism, and Politics: The Porto Allegre Experiment," in *Deepening Democracy: Institutional Innovations in Empowered Participatory Governance*, ed. A. Fung and E. O. Wright [London: Verso, 2003]).

24. Government of Kerala (GOK), *People's Planning: Towards a Handbook,* Kerala State Planning Board, 1999, 20–23.

25. Though the Congress-led United Democratic Front government has shown far less enthusiasm for the campaign, it is publicly committed to preserving decentralized planning and has, under significant public pressure, maintained the same relative terms of fiscal devolution.

26. The preliminary review of data collected from seventy-two randomly selected *panchayats* indicates that local level planning has generated significant gains. Key respondents from a cross-section of government and civil society (n = 838) judged the campaign to have significantly improved upon the delivery of basic services and development projects, including assistance to the poor (S. Chaudhuri, K. N. Harilal, and P. Heller, "Does Decentralization Make a Difference? The People Campaign for Decentralized Planning in the India State of Kerala," New Delhi, Report submitted to the Ford Foundation, 2004).

27. Even the latest flurry of decentralization initiatives triggered by the 1993 constitutional amendments does not appear to have produced significant institutional change (World Bank, 2000).

28. As cited by V. K. Ramachandran at the International Conference on Democratic Decentralisation, Trivandrum, May 27, 2000.

29. Sudipta Kaviraj, "Critique of the Passive Revolution," in *State and Politics in India,* ed. Partha Chaterjee (Delhi: Oxford University Press, 1998), 62.

30. Pranab Bardhan (*The Political Economy of Development in India* [New York: Basil Blackwell Inc.,1984]; Bardhan, "Sharing the Spoils") has provided the most influential general theory of this class-based subsidy regime. For a fascinating account of how the rent machine penetrates down to the local level, see R. Wade, "The Market for Public Office: Why the Indian State Is Not Better at Development," *World Development* 13, no. 4 (1995): 467–97.

31. Party officials proclaim their long-standing commitment to decentralized development. But this has certainly not been the party practice historically. As E. M. S.

Namboodiripad, the CPM's most influential figure and leading proponent of the campaign, remarks about his experience as Chief Minister in 1967 with respect to the District Council Bill: "It was revelation to me that no member of the Council of Ministers except the *Panchayat* minster and myself was prepared to transfer power to district councils and *Panchayats*. Neither the bureaucrat nor the political leader who is supposed to control him was prepared to part with power" (cited in K. Nagaraj, "Decentralisation in Kerala: A Note," Discussion Paper No. 2, June, Kerala Research Programme on Local Level Development, Centre for Development Studies, Thiruvananthapuram, 1999, 2).

32. When the CPI split in 1965, the most of the party's rank and file joined the CPM. The CPI has relied largely on its ties to the bureaucracy to maintain its influence, while the CPM has built its support through local level organs, most notably the agricultural laborers' union, the KSKTU. The CPIs support for the campaign has been lukewarm at best.

33. According to one political commentator, critics of the campaign from within the CPM argued that the party is losing its discipline and becoming a social democratic party. They argue that the West Bengal model of decentralization—in which *panchayats* have been given significant implementation responsibilities but no independent planning functions—would be the more appropriate model (Interview, Madhavan Kutty, August 16, 1999).

34. Olle Tornquist ("Making Democratisation Work: From Civil Society and Social Capital to Political Inclusion and Politicisation: Theoretical Reflections on Concrete Cases in Indonesia, Kerala, and the Philippines," Research Programme on Popular Movements, Development and Democratisation, University of Oslo, 1997) draws a similar distinction between "state-modernizers" and "popular developmentalists" and has developed the most extended analysis of the evolution of these tendencies.

35. Described as "the diverse array of social thinkers (from postmodernist cultural anthropologists to grassroots environmental activists and supporters of the cause of indigenous people and technologies) who are both anti-market and anti-(centralized) state" (P. Bardman, "Decentralized Development," *Indian Economic Review*, 31 [1996]: 2, 139–56).

36. The KSSP commissioned and published an extensive study of Kerala's rural health care system and, having documented the general decline in the use of public sector facilities, called for going from quantity to quality provision (K. Kannan et al., *Health and Development in Rural Kerala* [Trivandrum: Kerala Sastra Sahitya Prishad, 1991], 151).

37. Interview, August 16, 1997, Thiruvananthapuram.

38. Judith Tendler argues that a similar top-bottom alliance was critical to the success of decentralization in the Brazilian state of Cerea (Tendler, *Good Government in the Tropics* [Baltimore: Johns Hopkins University Press, 1997]).

39. Thomas Isaac and Franke, *Local Democracy and Development*, 145.

40. Government of Kerala (GOK), Committee on Decentralisation of Powers: Final Report: V. 1, part A and B, December 23, 1997, 3.

41. GOK, 1997, 46.

42. The Committee on the Decentralisation of Powers reports that an informal opinion survey among *panchayat* presidents found that 40 percent of funds spent on road construction (an expenditure preferred for its skimming returns) "do not go into the work for various reasons" (GOK, 1997, 46). The committee also added that the

blatant manipulation of beneficiary committees (required for all public works) was "an insult to the literate and politically aware public of the State" (46).

43. Interview with CPM official, 16 August 1997.

44. This basic idea here of creating "autonomous arenas of popular power" has been at the heart of the Brazilian PT (Workers Party) experiments in popular budgeting, most famously in the city of Porto Alegre. The parallel is of interest not only because the PT's support for creating decentralized budgetary processes evolved out of an explicit critique of the patronage politics of Brazilian cities, but also because the PT is the social movement party *par excellence*. Having said this, the PT's thinking on the question of civil society autonomy has a longer history, and is articulated more explicitly than in Kerala. Most notable is the fact that in Porto Alegre—where grassroots popular budgeting has been the norm for over a decade—the PT has never institutionalized the process on the grounds that rule-making power and initiatives must be left to Porto Alegre's neighborhood assemblies (interview with Tarso Genro, Mayor of Porto Alegre, December 16, 2001). For a comparative discussion of decentralization in Kerala, Brazil, and South Africa, see Patrick Heller, "Moving the State: The Politics of Decentralization in Kerala, South Africa and Porto Alegre," *Politics and Society* 29, no. 1 (2001): 131–63.

45. Interview, E. M. Shreedharan Namboodiripad, 13 August 1997.

46. Thomas Isaac and Franke, *Local Democracy and Development*, 45, emphasis mine.

47. Thomas Isaac and Franke, *Local Democracy and Development*, 1, emphasis mine.

48. In 2002 a party intellectual, M. N. Vijayan, published an article in an obscure Malayalam language journal called *Patdam*, claiming that the campaign had been inspired by the World Bank and the CIA. The accusations were gleefully given full coverage in the mainstream Malayalam press (which has a long-standing antipathy to the CPM) triggering a series of recriminations in the CPM. For a discussion, see Asha Krishnakumar, *Frontline*, August 15, 2003.

49. Peter Evans, "Looking for Agents of Urban Livability in a Globalized Political Economy," in *Livable Cities? The Politics of Urban Livelihood and Sustainability,* ed. Peter Evans (Berkeley: University of California Press, 2002).

50. M. P. Parameswaran, a prominent KSSP leader, notes that as early as 1972 the KSSP was promoting the concept of sustainable development well before it became fashionable in development circles (personal communication, May 23, 2000, Thiruvananthapuram).

51. For an account of the role of the KSSP, see M. P. Parameswaran, "Role of the Kerala Sastra Sahitya Parishad in the Movement for Democratic Decentralisation," paper presented at the International Conference on Democratic Decentralisation, Thiruvananthapuram, May 23–27, 2000. See also Thomas Isaac and Franke, *Local Democracy and Development*, chapter 4, and Véron, "The 'New' Kerala Model."

52. T. M. Thomas Isaac, Richard Franke, and M. P. Parameswaran, "From Anti-Feudalism to Sustainable Development: the Kerala People's Science Movement," *Bulletin of Concerned Asian Scholars* 29, no. 3 (1997): 36.

53. N. Jagajeevan and N. Ramakanthan, "Grama Sabhas: A Democratic Structure for Development Planning," paper presented at the International Conference on Democratic Decentralisation, Thiruvananthapuram, May 23-27, 2000, 3.

54. Thomas Isaac and Franke, *Local Democracy and Development*, 90-91.
55. The seminar schedule for early 2000, for example, included "the total sanitation village," "micro hydel projects," "social auditing," "rain water harvesting," "labour contract societies," and last but not least, "rabbitry."
56. The data is for 990 *panchayats*. For a full account and analysis, see Chaudhuri and Heller, "The Plasticity of Participation."
57. M. P. Parameswaran, "From Voters to Actors: People's Planning Campaign and Participatory Democracy in Kerala," Kerala Sastra Sahitya Parishad, Trichur, 2001.
58. In one *panchayat* alone, B. Manjula ("Voices from the Spiral of Silence: A Case Study of Samatha Self Help Groups of Ulloor," paper presented at the International Conference on Democratic Decentralisation, Thiruvananthapuram, May 23–27, 2000) documents the formation of two hundred women's micro-credit schemes. See also T. N. Seema and Vanitha Mukherjee, "Gender Governance and Citizenship in Decentralised Planning," paper presented at the International Conference on Democratic Decentralisation, Thiruvananthapuram, May 23–27, 2000, and Vanita Mukherjee, "Democratic Decentralisation and Associative Patterns," unpublished paper, Trivandrum, 2002.

4

Feminism, Poverty, and the Emergent Social Order

Mary E. John

I

It is a sign of our times that when it comes to giving a face to poverty in contemporary India, that face will, more likely than not, be female. Whether it be the endangered girl child or the destitute widow, the images are compelling. Concepts such as the feminization of poverty emanate from everywhere—whether from the state, NGOs, or women's groups, not to speak of international organizations. Much of this visibility is arguably a mark of success, the result of sustained feminist initiatives. The women's movement in India can count itself among the lucky ones—an "old" social movement that has played a substantial role in contemporary struggles, ebbing, flowing, and reinventing itself in myriad ways. Indeed, when compared to other social movements, the impact of "women" on contemporary institutions, ideologies and practices may well be unique. And yet, for reasons that I hope will become clearer in the course of this essay, thinking about issues of women and poverty today seems to throw up more questions than answers, and the future has never been more uncertain. In other words, we are not in the fortunate position of being able to build on cumulated wisdoms, and even less in a situation of consensus over the issues at stake. There is perceptible fatigue in some quarters as the movement ages, with old problems persisting even as the world is being so rapidly transformed. Not everyone believes that the multiple strands and differences that have come to characterize the Indian women's movement should be counted among its strengths.

Precisely because of the experience of being overtaken by enormous changes, by events few would have predicted at the time but which are bound to cast a long shadow into the years ahead, it may be useful to step back from the immediacy of the present to gain a perspective on the historicity of a movement such as the women's movement. More specifically, how and in what ways has poverty figured in this history?

While it is common to go back as far as the mid-nineteenth century to plot the beginnings of public debates over women's rights in the context of social reform movements, especially in the regions of Bengal and Maharashtra, it is only from the turn of the twentieth century that women's organizations were formed in order to stake their own claims, and that women's voices gained a hearing in more numerous locations within the sub-continent. Especially from the 1920s onwards, a multi-stranded movement was clearly in evidence. We are beginning to rediscover and appreciate women's involvements in a range of social movements during the turbulent decades of the early twentieth century, and not only as the force behind more mainstream organizations such as the WIA (Women's Indian Association) or the AIWC (the All India Women's Conference). Women were active in the anti-caste movements in southern and western India, in tribal and peasant struggles, in the overseas anti-indenture campaigns, in nationalist, Gandhian, and communist-led movements. Unfortunately, the historical record remains quite sparse where many of these agitations are concerned, so that the nationalist and Gandhian streams continue to leave the strongest legacy.[1]

Interestingly enough, even though the poverty of India was a major plank in the nationalist attack against colonial rule, this is not central in the more culturally oriented "status of women" debates of the time. Upper class and caste biases are clearly in evidence in many of the well-known women's struggles of the early twentieth century—such as over the franchise and reservations of seats in political bodies, the publication of Katherine Mayo's book *Mother India,* the introduction of birth control, and the campaign for passing the Sarda Act to raise the age of marriage.[2] According to Geraldine Forbes, if the first generation of women involved in the major women's organizations justified their demands in terms of "the ideology of social feminism, . . . ty[ing] their arguments about women's rights to women's obligation to perform traditional roles and serve the needs of the family,"[3] certainly by the 1940s this ideology was also found wanting. More radical ideas, often drawn from socialism and communism, became influential.

A distinct shift in outlook is visible, for instance, in the deliberations of Nehru's sub-committee on Women's Role in a Planned Economy, initially set up in 1938, which resulted in the first policy document on women as workers and citizens of the new nation-in-the-making. This radical modernist text conceived of women as "individuals," with economic rights occupying pride of place (in employment, as property inheritors, in marriage and divorce), while questions of "culture" and "tradition," clearly still on the horizon, were accommodated somewhat uneasily. An extraordinary document in many ways, one which sought to "plan" a new future for all working women (in plantations, factories, and a wide range of mainly urban occupations, but without forgetting housewives, domestic servants, even prostitutes), it is significant that in spite of its central emphasis on women's lack of economic rights, this did *not* require addressing poverty as such. When at all, poverty came up rather tangentially and fleetingly. One such instance was the brief discussion of birth control: "Where population is increasing by leaps and bounds, and where poverty increases in the same proportion, control of population is absolutely necessary";[4] another was the practice of prostitution.[5]

No active attempts were made to implement the recommendations of the subcommittee on women in the years following independence. This in itself is not particularly surprising. But what has yet to be adequately explained is the complete absence of any references to the document itself once the new state and development planning were institutionalized.[6] Be that as it may, it is with the era of development that our story really begins. Development has been the epochal ideology that enabled a Third World nation such as India after independence to make a break with the colonial past and will itself a fully modern future.[7] Sustaining the nation in its initial decades before entering a crisis during the 1970s and 1980s, it is this ideology, moreover, that has been in a state of decline since the 1990s, so much so that we are today at a new conjuncture represented by the rise to dominance of transnationally powerful regimes of economic liberalization and globalization, however confused our understanding of these successor ideologies might be.

The era of development is critical for understanding the post-independence rebirth of the women's movement, and for a number of reasons. First of all, it is not accidental that the heyday of the development decades—the 1950s and 1960s—have, until very recently, been referred to as the "silent period" of the women's movement in India. Though assessments may differ, feminist scholars have investigated the "accommodation and acquiescence" if not "euphoria" of a pre-independence generation of women leaders who placed their hope and trust in the new nation-state and its constitutional claims of gender equality, and so withdrew as a pressure group.[8] The repressive capabilities of this state in crushing struggles such as the Telengana people's struggle (1946–1952)[9] and the insurrections in Tebhaga did little to mar the hegemonic articulation of state, nation, and the economy through a secular-universalistic language of inclusiveness, through proclamations of "unity in diversity" in the forward march to achieve growth through development.

It was only in the late 1960s and '70s that signs of crisis in the Nehruvian model of state-led development planning became palpable, leading to the first loss of legitimacy for the Congress government and the rise of a range of new social movements, all of which culminated in the imposition of a state of Emergency in 1975. And yet, as I have argued elsewhere, it was precisely at this time of crisis that "the coding of the Indian nation as socialist, guided by aims of national self-determination still shaped political discourse to such a degree that these were also formative for a number of oppositional struggles."[10] The emergence of a new phase of the women's movement from the 1970s onwards therefore took shape in a context where the primary institution to address was the Indian state. This could and did emanate from very different positions—by extreme left groups such as the Progressive Organisation of Women (POW) who wished to expose the state's vested interests, by left-liberal women who sought to rewrite state policy to include women, and by "autonomous" groups who campaigned against the custodial rapes of Mathura and Rameezabee, and who made legal reform a major plank of their activism.[11] For those women who had taken the claims of Nehruvianism and the constitutional guarantees of equality seriously, the biggest shock of the 1970s was the realisation of the invisibility of women in the overall developmental process. This was manifested in the form of startling evidence pointing to processes of impoverishment and deteriorating circumstances for the majority, especially rural women, during the very decades devoted to the welfare and progress of all its citizens.[12]

Middle-class in its leadership, a freshly charged women's movement therefore drew on all the cultural and social capital available to it, raiding the social sciences in order to better grapple with as yet poorly understood relations between women and poverty. The key discipline here was economics, and the biggest advances of the 1970s and early '80s were made in the spheres of women's work, its measurement, problems of undervaluation, declining work participation rates, grass-roots organizing, and so on. Other areas grew in tandem with these developments such as an awareness of the significance of women's health, and the first discoveries by demographers such as Pravin Visaria and Asok Mitra of a secular declining trend in the female-male sex ratio since the turn of the twentieth century (which until then had simply been put down to the under-counting of women in the Indian census).[13]

Within the limited space of this essay it is not possible to provide a fuller account of the multiple beginnings of the women's movement during the 1970s, nor of its further evolution in the 1980s (including the establishment of women's studies as an inter- and anti-disciplinary field), as fresh challenges were encountered, and new areas of concern opened up. But some clarifications may be necessary before moving on, in order to guard against possible misreadings of this period. First of all, I do not wish to imply that questions of women and development—synonymous with the problems of poor women—were the most significant or novel issues to have been addressed at this time. Indeed, in the minds of many, it was the agitations against violence—against rape and dowry-deaths—that led to the first major nationwide campaigns for legal reform and resulted in widespread media publicity, thus fueling the belief that a new phase of the women's movement was genuinely in evidence. Nor do I wish to suggest that there were few differences during these years. The battles over "autonomy" by newly formed women's groups in relation to political parties and their women's wings, especially those from the left, were but one of many sources of division. The main point really is this: A unique synergy was achieved in relation to critiques of development that was larger than the disparate actors who contributed to it. Local struggles over work, land, and livelihoods, militant feminists with a far-left orientation, "nationalist" women close to the state apparatus, academics in research centers and universities, and international agencies, often quite critical of each other, created a new cause—poor women at the "grassroots," whose disenfranchisement none could dispute.

If pressed further, one might say that in the formative period of the post independence phase of the women's movement in India—namely the 1970s and early '80s—the first efforts to conceptualize and campaign around women's issues coexisted at different and complex levels, making it impossible to typify them in textbook fashion into, say, "liberal," "socialist," and "radical" versions of feminist politics. Some organizations undoubtedly espoused the universalist language of "women's oppression," and drew on individual legal casework to create awareness among a larger public about the widespread structures of violence against women. Others prioritized mass-based mobilization, especially among peasants, agricultural laborers, or in relation to trade union demands. However, even in the case of an avowedly Marxist-feminist group such as the Progressive Organisation of Women in Hyderabad—and with all their emphases on the "toiling masses"—it is worth noticing that their very first activity in 1974 was a campaign against "the dowry system which is prevalent mostly in the middle and upper classes," which was followed by a similar campaign against "eve-teasing" (as the harassment and humiliation of women on city streets and buses has been called).[14] In her study of women's organizations in the cities of Bombay and Calcutta, Raka Ray has argued that it is within regionally shaped "political fields" that women's movements evolved their agendas and self-understanding, so much so that a simple distinction between "autonomous" and left-identified groups cannot do justice to the actual ideologies, programs, and constraints of a particular women's organization.[15]

The task of analyzing the political frameworks of different strands within the women's movement becomes even more complex after the 1980s, when issues of communalism, a growing anti-Muslim upsurge, and a reconfigured nationalism speaking the language of Hindutva also became issues that feminists had to confront. Struggles of a more directly economic nature undoubtedly benefited from existing critiques of development. Early trenchant critiques (such as those that were later published in the collection edited by Devaki Jain and Nirmala Banerjee in 1985)[16] were deepened by analyses such as Bina Agarwal's review essay of the relationships among women, poverty, and agricultural growth in India. Agarwal's discussion drew on a wide variety of studies to highlight the negative effects of the new agricultural technologies on women's labor, the special vulnerabilities and increasing numbers of "female headed households," and growing evidence of a systematic bias against girls and women in the intra-household distribution of food and health care. It is telling that her essay ends with the following claim: "Existing state policies and programmes (even those aimed at alleviating poverty) offer little scope for optimism. . . . The point of hope, however, lies in the growth of consciousness among rural women in recent years of the need to organise and unite for fighting against oppression, both outside the home and within it."[17] These and other criticisms of the state notwithstanding, no one was prepared for just how the state itself responded in the decade that followed.

II

With the 1990s, the quieter liberalization measures begun in the mid 1980s led to India's first serious balance of payments crisis of 1991. This in turn resulted in the announcement of a New Economic Policy involving a comprehensive program of economic reform aiming towards structural adjustment in all sectors, thus fundamentally revising, if not undoing, more than four decades of development planning. First publicly initiated when the Congress returned to power in 1991, these policies were subsequently taken forward under the coalition government headed by the Bharatiya Janata Party (BJP) which took control in 1996. "Economic facts" should not, however, blind us to the transformed larger ideological climate by virtue of which a country like India, as a relative latecomer to the processes of stabilization, structural adjustment, and liberalization, has entered the contested terrain of globalization.

As successor ideologies, liberalization and globalization appear as deeply contradictory, indeed, even as negative paradigms. Their economic rhetoric consists of a retreat from the productive and welfarist dimensions of the state in favor of market- and export-led growth, and the creation of a culture built around consumption. The fact that other Third World nations have referred to their time of economic restructuring during the 1980s as "the lost decade," and that our new models—the Asian tigers—witnessed major crises during the very years when India began to globalize, has accentuated two things— the extraordinarily intense modes of ideological reconstruction of the new Indian global citizen being deployed today (acutely visible in the heightened place occupied by the media in everyday life), and the severe erosion and loss of authority of alternate paradigms, especially with the collapse of the socialist bloc. Promoters of liberalization persist in referring to the opening of the economy as an "irreversible" process, as not happening quickly enough.

What does all this mean for a social movement such as the women's movement and for contemporary approaches to issues of poverty? In the face of the deeply negative climate of the 1990s (in contrast to the more buoyant and idealistic years of the women's movement's rebirth in the 1970s), and precisely because of the apparent absence of options, one must approach such a question from a range of vantage points. Such an approach is all the more necessary today because the impact of the women's movement is both widespread and uneven. At this stage in its development, the movement has increasingly become more institutionalized, and the future of earlier modes of mobilization is particularly uncertain. Feminists who played an initiating role in the 1970s and 1980s are today "spokespersons" on a number of issues. As I mentioned at the beginning of this essay, the multiple forms of visibility of women's issues (including their co-optation and annexation in unintended ways) could well be a unique feature of contemporary Indian social and political life. Whether it be the legacy of local struggles, the shifting concerns of the state, or the very relationship between globalization and poverty, "women" constitute a significant presence. The rest of this essay will therefore make different inroads into the broad and heterogeneous thematic of women and poverty in the contemporary context, sometimes with the help of detailed examples, sometimes more briefly. In the process, I also hope to illustrate the difficulties involved in gaining an adequate perspective on what "globalization" represents, quite apart from possessing the right language to challenge it.

My first approach for thinking about the changes wrought under the sign of liberalization and globalization will be through a discussion of the trajectories of two recent local movements spawned in the name of "women." The key to the life of the women's movement in India so far is that it is not simply composed of more or less high profile leaders—whether activists, writers, or from political parties, the administration, and the academy. Most accounts of major campaigns of the women's movement, as well as of specific struggles and organizations, have dwelt on their formative period, and there is little on the changes wrought since the 1990s.[18] During the 1990s, two women's struggles in particular achieved considerable attention, and in ways that spilled beyond their regional confines. Quite different in their origins and organizational structures, each of them tells a distinct story about the kinds of problems women's movements are facing, especially in relation to the Indian state. My examples are the Women's Development Programme (WDP) in Rajasthan and the anti-arrack (distilled country liquor) agitation in Andhra Pradesh.

The WDP was launched in 1984 (with initial funding provided by UNICEF) as a unique program of empowerment of rural grassroots women in several districts of Rajasthan in northwest India, a region castigated for its "feudal"— i.e., socioeconomic and cultural—backwardness. What set the WDP apart from other state-led schemes was its emphasis on communication of information, education, and awareness raising (rather than employment generation), based on an interactive network linking government officials and NGO staff. The most important figures within this organizational structure have been the village-level workers or *sathins* (literally female companions), who were entrusted with the task of building women's groups within their villages. These groups were able to generate sensitivity towards each other's problems, build an environment in which women could begin a process of collective questioning, and so support women in their struggle to resolve issues together.[19] Toward this end a great deal of emphasis was placed on the training of the *sathins* in the WDP, a process that was intensive, innovative, and deeply committed. Commentators who toured districts where the WDP was active noticed marked differences among the women they met. In the space of a few years it was clear that the WDP had made a significant impact, with women's groups monitoring drought relief works, participating in health education programs, taking up small savings schemes, contributing to the monthly newsletter, and organizing against specific practices such as mass child marriages to older men.[20]

Of course, this is not to say that the WDP did not encounter plenty of challenges, difficulties, and criticisms from different quarters. *Sathins* did not find it easy to build groups and hold meetings, whether due to domestic duties, opposition from men, or heavy work schedules especially during the harvest season and religious festivals. Lower caste *sathins* encountered further obstacles to their leadership. More importantly, from the perspective of the organizational structure of the WDP, after the initial years of flexibility and innovation, the district administration and *panchayats* wished to take advantage of the *sathins'* village level rapport and activism to draw them into government schemes such as family planning, child immunization drives, and poverty alleviation programs. The family planning programs in particular became the focus of agitation by the *sathins* after they obtained evidence of several forced sterilizations and of the linking of famine relief with family planning targets. *Sathins* were soon criticized for becoming too independent and for participating in alternative women's organizations. Five *sathins* were fired when they attended the National Conference of the Women's Movement held in Calicut (Kerala) in 1990. (These national meetings, first begun in 1980 in the city of Bombay, have been held every two to three years in different cities, and bring together thousands of participants from all over India. Since then there have been gatherings in Tirupati in 1993 and Ranchi in 1996.)

In the early 1990s, the *sathins* decided to form their own union (the Sathin Karamchari Sangh) to press for their demands, which included an increase in their honorarium (set at Rs. 200 per month to cover incidental expenses) and proper recognition of their status as government rather than "voluntary" workers. It probably goes without saying that such a demand flew in the face of the liberalization policies set in motion during these very years, when the last thing the government was prepared to contemplate was the induction of poor, predominantly illiterate rural women into the state apparatus. Instead, efforts to dismantle the program have been initiated on a number of fronts—by leaving vacant posts unfilled, by attempting to "integrate" *sathins* into service delivery schemes such as the World Bank–funded ICDS program (Integrated Child Development Scheme), and by announcing that the *sathin* model for women's empowerment would be replaced by a new model—the *sangam* or *samooh* (group) model—that no longer required the special skills of leaders such as the *sathins*.

The *sathins* have continued with their struggle, sometimes appearing to gain marginally from outside support such as was provided by the National Commission of Women[21] or by political changes in the Rajasthan government from the BJP to the Congress in 1999.[22] In February 2001, the five *sathins* who were fired in 1990 won a decade-long legal battle for their reinstatement. In March 2002, the contradictions besetting this state-sponsored women's program reached a flash point, when the government of Rajasthan issued a notification ordering the closure of the entire program on grounds of its financial unviability. However, the state appears to have been ill-prepared for the mobilization that followed—a broad platform of women's groups was set up in Rajasthan to oppose the government directive, and *sathin* union activists lobbied intensively in the capital of Delhi. All the protests did appear to bear fruit—the order for closure was revoked and the status quo maintained. Indeed, the state government has even made appointments of new *sathins* in districts where there were none before. It remains profoundly unclear, however, whether this can be termed a victory. In the intervening years the program has been effectively hollowed out and turned into something else: *Sathins* are no longer provided with any kind of training or collective network, and the single important activity appears to be creating self-help groups (SHGs) among village women.

The second example I wish to discuss here is the anti-arrack agitation that arose in parts of Andhra Pradesh in 1992, especially in the eastern district of Nellore. Perhaps the only common thread with the WDP is that the primary initiators of the anti-arrack movement were also poor rural women with no prior experience in politics as it is conventionally understood. Sporadic struggles against government-backed sales of arrack had been taking place in many districts of the state since the 1980s, and gathered unprecedented momentum in 1992 in Nellore when peasant women, working only in their villages, enforced the closure of local arrack shops and targeted the excise department officials and excise police. In so doing, they were able to effectively confront the state and destabilize its economy, one that had become quite dependent on the massive excise revenues from increasingly aggressive arrack sales.[23]

Arrack became a focal point in the women's struggle, enabling them to comprehend many of their daily problems related to work, the family economy, health, education, and their personal lives. For instance, women felt the acute injustice of a situation where water had to be brought from long distances in villages without schools or hospitals, but which were being regularly supplied with arrack. Some women had no difficulties in tackling their husbands directly over the issue. Others found it easier confront men by taking them on collectively in a public space like the arrack shop, thus bringing about major changes in gender relations at the village level. The movement had many origins, the most catalytic of which was the government-initiated program to eradicate illiteracy, taken up in each district by voluntary organizations. Women and girls formed the backbone of the literacy drives, and some of the stories written in the neo-literacy primers about problems related to arrack inspired those attending the classes. Women stopped the arrack carts from entering their villages, forcibly closed arrack shops, resisted pressure tactics and attacks by contractors and excise personnel. It was only much later that an anti-arrack coordinating committee was formed, and that women's organizations and political parties began to realize the full extent of what was going on.

As the result of the dispersed and localized nature of the anti-arrack agitation—led by dalit, backward caste and Muslim women—the state was unable to isolate its leaders and simply repress the movement. Women did not take on the state directly but managed to destabilize its power by severing the nexus of the government and the liquor contractors at those points where it functioned most effectively—the arrack shops, stock points, and auctions. What is remarkable is both how the movement spread to neighboring villages and the extent to which a variety of interest groups, including ultimately the state government itself, felt compelled to support it. The state government first announced a ban on arrack in the district of Nellore in April 1993, followed by a similar ban throughout the state six months later. Everyone sought to appropriate the anti-arrack women, and political parties—both those in power and those in opposition—imaged the women as social reformers and modern *durgas* (avenging goddesses) who were cleansing the nation of the evil of arrack. They thus "predicated onto the woman in the anti-arrack agitation an assortment of complex narratives of which she was the sole heroine."[24] In January 1995, soon after the Telugu Desam Party defeated the Congress and returned to power, the Chief Minister N.T. Rama Rao introduced total prohibition as a populist ploy, and the focus shifted from *arrack* to liquor in general, from the struggle of poor rural women to one of the urban middle-classes.[25] But by March 1997, the dry laws were lifted since they were seen to have opened the door to bootlegging, apart from being blamed for severely jeopardizing business interests in the globalizing city of Hyderabad.

The state, in the meanwhile, inaugurated thrift and savings schemes in the very villages where the women had been so active. Awards were instituted to those women who were the most successful micro-entrepreneurs. The government gave such a strong push to these credit schemes that even the Ninth Five Year Plan (1997–2002) document of the Planning Commission introduced a special box item on "Podupulakshmi—Pride of Nellore Women— a success story" in their chapter on poverty alleviation schemes.[26] Co-opted in this way, it is perhaps needless to add that the struggle in and around Nellore, which not so long ago had been able to achieve a measure of empowerment among women by calling to account the most oppressive structures controlling their lives, was betrayed. Women's efforts were largely directed towards micro-economic activity. Quite apart from the disputed positive potential of such schemes, they are hardly a substitute for the basic demands raised in the wake of these women's effective exposure of the state's regressive and exploitative policies towards its rural working populations.

Each of these struggles—around the Women's Development Programme in Rajasthan and the anti-arrack agitation in Andhra—has clearly been shaped by their respective regional contexts. In a drought-prone backward region with strong norms of female seclusion, the *sathins* emerged as local leaders and mobilizers, thanks to the initiative provided by the state and NGOs (including international funding). Their main demand has been for stronger institutional support, to the point of inclusion within the local state apparatus but without compromising on their unique non-service oriented modes of functioning. Nellore, on the other hand, is part of Andhra's relatively prosperous coastal rice-growing belt. Here, rural women were agitating against the deprivation and violence they were experiencing due to the drain of men's earnings into *arrack*. Both these local movements only subsequently gained the attention and support of women's organizations. And in both cases, it is the state that has been in a position to deflect these rural women's protests in similar ways, by refusing to be accountable and by inserting models of "self-help" and economic entrepreneurship among poor rural women instead.

Indeed, the most disorienting aspect of the emerging social order has to do with the changeling and dissimulative discourse and practice of the state. The "social mobilization" of women (and other so-called weaker sections) is a catch-phrase frequently deployed by government agencies and spokespersons and can be found in numerous documents. From "welfare to development to empowerment" is yet another contemporary slogan meant to demonstrate the state's steady advancement in addressing women's issues over the last half century. It certainly cannot be said that poverty has disappeared from the state's agenda. (This is what many had initially feared would be the direct effect of the new rhetoric advocating the retreat of the state from economic development, especially with the entry of the BJP-led coalition government in 1996.) One has to look beyond official texts to gain a sense of how the dominant order is attempting to shift its priorities and strategies. This brings me to my second point of entry into the current conjuncture. The greatest challenge facing a movement such as the women's movement in these rapidly changing times could well be the new consensus that has emerged around the question of population control.

A closer look will reveal just why the population question has turned out to be such a major stumbling block. To begin with, ever since its post-independence rebirth in the 1970s and '80s, the women's movement has been fundamentally opposed to agendas of population control, a position that has been shared by "autonomous groups" as much as by left-identified organizations.[27] Moreover, such opposition appeared to have been only too well-founded in the wake of the Emergency years of 1975–1977. In the sterilization camps organized by the then Youth Congress leader Sanjay Gandhi, young single men were among those forcibly sterilized, official deaths alone numbered over two thousand, and these widely condemned crimes were among the most shocking violations of the period. The ineffectiveness of the Family Planning Programme, as it was then called, stood starkly exposed. Others believed that these excesses did not represent the dominant agenda of the state, and took comfort from the international propagation of the slogan "development is the best contraceptive" by Indira Gandhi's cabinet minister Karan Singh at the World Conference on Population in Bucharest in 1974. Feminist critiques of India's initial health policy during the first post-independence decades have been more concerned to highlight its strong urban bias and the fundamental inability of the system of Primacy Health Centres to serve vast rural populations. Moreover, the state paid no attention to maternal health in this period (the 1950–1970s), concentrating solely on trying to improve child survival in the hope that such a strategy would bring down fertility rates.[28]

The latter years of the '70s and especially the '80s brought about dramatic changes, and in ways no one could have anticipated. After the Emergency, the Family Planning Programme—still under a cloud—was rebaptized as Family Welfare and integrated within the existing system of general health services. However, far from inaugurating a more genuinely comprehensive approach to the health care needs of poor families, family welfare has been progressively usurping outlays meant for overall public health, especially for the control of communicable diseases: Claiming 15 percent of the total health budget in the 6th Plan (1982–87), family planning jumped to consuming as much as 35 percent of the 8th Plan budget a decade later, and this rising trend continues.

Even more disorienting for the women's movement has been the scrambling of the discourses and practices of population control with those of women's empowerment: Every potentially emancipatory aspect of a poor woman's life—her education, her employment, her decision to marry, her control over resources, indeed, her very autonomy, is today open to annexation—or so many in the women's movement in India believe—by forces whose primary concern is to reduce population growth. Hesitant attempts by the state to increase female sterilization and contraception which began in the late '60s, received a major boost post-Emergency, when the program was restructured, leading to the official abandonment of target-based approaches, and a decisive shift from focusing on men to concentrating on women. But in 1994, women's organizations—again across a wide spectrum— were shocked and even betrayed by the proposals of the Expert Group on the Population Policy set up by the Indian state: For the first time in post-independence history, a government document—the Draft National

Population Policy—announced that population growth was playing a causative role, not only in spreading poverty, but also in exacerbating environmental degradation.[29] It even went so far as to suggest a range of legislative steps against those with more than two children. It is therefore particularly telling just what aspects of the critiques of India's population policies—leveled by women's organizations and health groups since the 1980s—were subsequently redeployed by the Indian government to produce an updated, target free, voluntary, pro-woman national population policy for the new millennium.[30]

Today there exists a population policy couched in the language of empowering women for improved health and nutrition, through the ostensible convergence of health issues, free and compulsory education up to the age of fourteen, raising the age of marriage, focusing especially on "underserved" populations. However, feminists and health activists have shown that, as it turns out, current policy is largely concerned with inducting long-acting, provider-controlled, and women-centered hormonal contraceptives in the name of women's "unmet needs," leaving precisely all the major issues of macro-economic policy unaddressed. Indeed, India seems to be aiming for the historically unprecedented goal of achieving demographic transition and population stabilization without parallel changes in the economy. There is a further twist here: One of the facets of the post-liberalization period has been the growing political autonomy of the different states within the Indian federal system, in spite of being in greater financial crisis. While the overt language of policy at the national level may well be voluntaristic and democratic in tone, this is not the case at the state levels. There are now regional population policies in states such as Madhya Pradesh, Maharashtra, Rajasthan, and Andhra, where strong incentives and disincentives have been promoted; where fresh targets have been set; and where a two-child norm is being used to penalize women—preventing anyone with more than two children from standing for election in the *panchayats* and municipalities,[31] or from receiving government aid, including food rations in the public distribution system. Local women's groups and others in these states are therefore doing what they can to campaign against their respective state governments, while those at the "center" in Delhi are discovering the limits of lobbying for change in the national capital.[32]

In my view, there is a further aspect to the current scenario that is special cause for concern. Unlike even a few decades ago, population control has fully entered middle-class "common-sense," for whom it is the single most critical problem facing the country. One could cite numerous instances to substantiate this, but I will mention just two: Even as eminent a personage as Justice Ventakatachaliah, who gave up his chairmanship of the Human Rights Commission to convene the controversial review committee of the Constitution of India, has gone on public record to state that it is precisely in the face of the most burning problems of the country such as the population problem, that a constitutional review is required. School textbooks have also not been spared: Since 2001 the proposed revision of school syllabi by the National Council of Educational Research and Training (NCERT) has been much in the news because of the surreptitious alterations made in the history syllabus to advance right-wing agendas. Less commented upon in all the debate and opposition are other changes and additions: For instance, in the proposed English syllabus for class V primary school children, population growth and gender equality are to be taught together as part of "population education."[33]

The women's movement thus finds itself in a climate where population reduction is no longer a relatively marginal matter of covert and coercive "excesses" but enjoys widespread and far-reaching consent.[34] The situation has been further complicated by new divisions and differences within the movement: Those who draw upon the perspectives of public health initiatives and the need for improvements in the economy in order to address women's health needs are deeply suspicious of the contemporary language of women's reproductive rights. They see this as yet another ploy by both international agencies and the state to advance an older agenda of population control. Imrana Qadeer has critiqued feminist approaches that "place reproductive health centre stage" with its narrow biological and medicalist focus on a woman's lifecycle.[35] Others, however, do not see how the annexation of the rhetoric of reproductive health per se diminishes the legitimacy of addressing this sphere of women's lives. Instead, they have argued for broadening the scope of population policies by creating the necessary "enabling conditions" and "social rights" within which women could make more genuine reproductive choices.[36] Suffice it to say, therefore, that the entire problematic being covered in the name of population control—with women's reproductive and sexual "choices" now at its heart—has become one of the hardest areas for the women's movement to confront, where older strategies forged during the development era serve feminists poorly under the present dispensation.[37]

Let me now shift to the third entry-point for approaching questions of poverty, namely its place in relation to the big questions of globalization and liberalization. In a recent article reviewing India's "micro-movements" from the 1970s to the present, D. L. Sheth has argued that the very onset of globalization has revitalized the entire spectrum of social movements (many of which had become moribund or routinized after the initial elan of the 1970s), and is even producing a "high degree of convergence on a wide range of issues concerning globalisation."[38] There are many fascinating and informative aspects to Sheth's account. However, having rightly seen how the entry of globalization has become the new frame of reference and target for numerous social movements (including the women's movement), this slides into the problematic claim that a "counter-discourse" of converging positions is consequently in the making. The multiple strands of the women's movement illustrate the extent to which divergent and contrary positions have actually been hardening in recent years. Even when allowance is made for the fact that these positions often focus on different dimensions of liberalization and globalization, their range is truly remarkable, while they are all feminist and committed to social justice. Compared to the extensive debates within the movement on issues such as the question of a uniform civil code, or over reservations for women in local self-government and in Parliament, similar public debates have not taken place over the immensely critical nature of the new conjuncture of "globalization." Whether positions are being adopted unequivocally or with considerable uncertainty, it is time that they are reflected on at greater length. No discussion of poverty takes place today without reference to globalization, its discourses, policies, and institutional restructuring.

The most frequently heard and strongest voices within the women's movement have condemned and attacked the New Economic Policies right from their inception a decade ago. Their basis is that globalization can only inaugurate a widening of disparities across and within nations and regions, leading to a deepening of processes of impoverishment for the majority. The special sufferers here will be poor women, for such women will have to increasingly bear the disproportionate burdens arising from the unequal allocation of resources and poorer self-care, even as they work harder to make up for falling real incomes, reductions in social welfare, and the privatization of services. As women take on multiple jobs, their daughters will either follow them, or take charge of the household, thus being debarred from an education. Greater levels of stress will also lead to a worsening of men's ability to cope, which then takes such forms as growing violence or increased desertions. Following this line of argumentation, large sections of the women's movement, not only those coming from the left, have been mobilizing repeatedly against economic reform, whether it be over disinvestment of the public sector, conditions of work in export processing zones, or food security subsidies.

In order to show how seriously they viewed the announcement of the New Economic Policies in 1991, the Indian Association of Women's Studies devoted its sixth national conference in 1993 (a three-day event held every two years with plenaries and simultaneous sessions) entirely to the theme of the "New Economic Policy and its Implications for Women." While numerous consultations have followed, actual in-depth studies of the consequences of the new policies in the lives of women are just beginning to appear. One of the earliest efforts was by activists and scholars in Bombay, who questioned claims in favor of the feminization of the labor force during structural adjustment, by showing that major manufacturing industries in the city of Bombay have in fact been retrenching women at unprecedented rates since the 1980s.[39] A parallel critique of the feminization thesis has been leveled by Nirmala Banerjee.[40]

Less visible in the concerted attacks against liberalization have been the frameworks and perspectives being deployed by those who oppose the current regime. In my view, the absence of self-reflexivity about their ideological frames of reference constitutes a major impediment that is blocking the advancement of such oppositional agendas. As I mentioned earlier on, it is never enough, especially not today, to think that facts somehow speak for themselves. What, then, are the ideological subtexts fueling current opposition, and whom do they address? The major problem here is that these oppositional voices invariably speak from positions that have precisely lost their authority in the present climate. They either stem from the era of developmentalism and economic nationalism that has lost out in the current conjuncture, or hark back to an even earlier time, to a cultural past free from all forms of capitalist and imperialist domination. This has also led to the situation where Marxists, whose frameworks continue to be pinned to state-centered welfare and socialist planning, share a common platform with eco-feminists such as Vandana Shiva, whose opposition to multinational capital arises from a fundamentally different world-view, one based on the desire to preserve the indigenous local knowledges and pre-modern relationship to nature that she imputes to Third World women farmers.[41] As the result of the coming together of such incommensurable frameworks, there is a definite air of eclecticism in some the current oppositional rhetorics being deployed. This adds to the problem of coming across as speaking not from the present but from the past.

In comparison, the voices of those who have offered some kind of qualified acceptance to globalization, though often couched in a more tentative or speculative language, nonetheless appear to gain simply by virtue of being more rooted in the present. Here again, positions are quite diverse. A figure like Madhu Kishwar, for example, seems to be basing her assent to the current economic regime less out of any careful assessment of its claims than from her opposition to any state-centric—or what she identifies as western-inspired—world-view, whether of development or women's empowerment.[42] From a very different perspective, the Marxist-feminist Rohini Hensman views the greater integration of the world economy as a necessary stage in the evolution of global capitalism. She goes further to assert that this demands a correspondingly international level of intervention and struggle, whether through the promotion of coordinated class actions by globally disenfranchised workers or by taking advantage of international standards such as the highly controversial World Trade Organization (WTO) directive to link trade with labor standards in developing nations like India. The anti-globalization agenda doesn't make sense for groups like women workers in Third World contexts, she goes on to argue, who have potentially more to gain through "concerted action to shape the global order in accordance with a women's agenda for justice and equity as well as caring and nurturing. . . . Can a socialist feminist vision of an ideal world include national boundaries maintained by nationalism, with its potential for developing into fascism, imperialism and war?"[43] The weakness in her otherwise cogent account has to do with her audience—neither the international working class nor transnational feminist groups are particularly visible today. (It is the anti-globalizers who seem to be steadily gaining in global visibility—most recently at the third social summit organized in Mumbai, India, in January 2004, which included several feminist organizations. And yet, there have been some telling reformulations in the rhetoric deployed at these meetings—calls for a movement of "counter-globalization" and opposition to "imperial globalization" rather than direct opposition to globalization per se may well be indicative of a nascent political formation critical of both nationalisms and certain versions of globalization.)

The third example of qualified support to globalization comes from the work of Gail Omvedt, and is surely the most provocative. Omvedt has argued that globalization and the new economic order may actually help those very groups whom the development era effectively marginalized. Her analysis is based on the expectation that globalized markets will, on the one hand, rein in the Indian bourgeoisie, its unviable monopolies, and the inefficient upper caste state bureaucracy, and, on the other hand, give the small farmer a better global price for produce which was previously underpriced due to state intervention. As she has put it polemically, "if the choice is between a high caste capitalist Indian economy with a highly privileged all-male workforce . . . producing steel or automobiles, and a relatively labor-intensive multi-national linked company in a rural area employing women [or lower castes, in leather trades, fruit and vegetable production and so on] then we will prefer the multinational."[44] This argument (which shares common ground with some feminization arguments elsewhere) begs as many questions as it raises, the most important of which would be the following: Are these hitherto marginalized groups—peasants, dalits, backward castes, and women—socially positioned to take advantage of globalization, and on what basis can we expect the hitherto dominant urban classes and castes to lose out in the current realignments taking place?

My final example of a different voice is that of SEWA, the Self-Employed Women's Association, as mediated by its leaders Ela Bhatt and Renana Jhabvala. The history of SEWA goes back to the early 1970s, and grew out of its founder Ela Bhatt's formative experience as a Gandhian with the Textile Labour Association in Ahmedabad. SEWA describes itself as a trade union of poor, self-employed workers, and has a membership of over 200,000 women. Its main centers are in Gujarat, though there are newer ones in a few other states as well. Their approach to women's issues is one of economic empowerment—the "second freedom" Bhatt believes is India's struggle after political freedom was won in 1947[45]—by providing the necessary economic and financial security to women workers in the informal or unorganized sector, through a system of cooperative banking, maternal and child care, and most recently through an insurance program set up in collaboration with insurance companies. I would call their response to liberalization one of pragmatism. Recognizing that the living standards of the poor may well have declined after structural adjustment was initiated and that the hitherto secure entitlements of the organized sector may also get eroded, they wish to take the "positive" approach of creating the necessary social security systems that could potentially address the needs of the vast majority of the country's workers. In contrast to the public sector and the private sector (the backbone of India's experiment with a mixed economy during the development era, and towards whom all national policies have been aimed), they have mooted the concept of "the people's sector"—unorganized labor and self-employed producers in rural and urban India, subjects of neglect yet on whom the economy effectively depends.[46] With their emphasis on women's economic agency, processes of decentralization, increased levels of financial and managerial participation by the "beneficiary" population, and the reduced role of the state, it is perhaps not surprising that SEWA has been picked up as a model by international agencies such as the World Bank—and not just for Third World countries, but even for First World nations who are themselves seeking to dismantle their welfare systems in favor of neoliberal policy orientations. SEWA is therefore at the hub of a number of highly contentious issues. What are the elisions underwriting the liberal concept of women's "economic agency" and greater efficiency in managing poverty, and what dangers does this portend for the future?[47]

III

This chapter has attempted to identify some of the major challenges posed by the contemporary conjuncture to feminist politics in ongoing battles against poverty. I have in particular concentrated on the effects of a shift in paradigm from the once dominant era of state-led development planning (within which a new phase of the women's movement emerged) to the current rise to dominance of ideologies of liberalization and globalization. Contrasting perspectives—the new hegemonic location of population control for reducing poverty; problems of sustaining local struggles; and the diverse positions in the women's movement towards globalization—have been presented. Of course, there is a great deal more that needs to be examined on all of these, and I have done no more than skim the surface.

If one can venture to say anything with some degree of confidence, it is that the state has been steadily abdicating from its own role, in the past decade not even setting much store by its own agendas for the eradication of poverty. This may be why the erstwhile "think tank" for the government, the Planning Commission, has provided such optimistic estimates of current trends. If the projections of the recently concluded Ninth Plan are to be believed, poverty in India should have declined from an estimated poverty ratio figure of 29.2 in 1996–1997 to 18 in 2001–2002 (to drop further to 9.5 in 2006–2007 and 4.3 in 2011–2012).[48] It is not so much that others have disputed these estimates as being quite off the mark, but that we have entered an era where extensive and serious debates on poverty are increasingly confined to journals such as the *Economic and Political Weekly*. The government, on its part, has been far more concerned to interface with the middle classes, business interests, and the media through the tax proposals of its annual budgets. Why else has the Tenth Plan (2002–2007), due to begin in April 2002, received practically no public attention?

But instead of lamenting the failures of planning, the purpose of this concluding section is to take note of other emergent processes whose significance in the years to come is likely to grow. Ironic as it might seem, and in considerable contrast to the divergent—indeed, somewhat chaotic—responses to "globalization," the one subject of growing consensus today is the resignificance of the "local." Obviously, different conceptions of the local abound. But the version that everyone subscribes to is the need for greater political decentralization and local autonomy, a cause espoused by those who might otherwise be pro- or anti-state, liberalizers, or leftists. The revival of local self-government in the late 1980s, after widespread institutional neglect following independence, coupled with a reservations policy granting one-third seats for women in village *panchayats* and urban municipalities (passed without any debate, let alone opposition, by Parliament during 1993 and '94), clearly constitutes an unprecedented opportunity: more than a million women representatives across the country are now in a position to tackle local problems, not by waiting to be served from distant centers of power, but right at the grassroots.

There is little question of the radical potential of this revival. The journey, however, has barely begun. The only state where a major devolution of power in financial and developmental terms has taken place is Kerala. It is a telling comment on the extent of the masculinization of politics and political parties in that state, however, that women representatives have yet to make a real difference, all the positive social and educational indicators among Kerala women notwithstanding.[49] In most other states, the burden has been to demonstrate that women elected to local bodies are not mere "rubber stamps" for more powerful male relatives, and that they can function in spite of patriarchal constraints. The danger today is that unless genuine powers are vested at these local levels, the new energies will become moribund and get dissipated.[50] Furthermore, the somewhat narrow focus by feminists and others on the alleged advantages or disadvantages of women representatives (Are they less corrupt? Are they more vulnerable? and so on)[51] has been at the cost of shying away from the institutional consequences that accompany the participation of women in "governance." On the one hand, the "autonomy"

of major sections of the women's movement from political parties has been
something of a founding principle. On the other hand, the rise to dominance
of right wing parties such as the BJP, boasting prominent support from
women, has been a major source of crisis. Active, vigorous, and accountable
"good governance" cannot be separated from direct involvement in the institutions that promote the political process. What, then, might be the relations
between party politics, women in power, and the politics of feminism?

If the participation of women in the electoral process brings new opportunities and dangers, the rise of a politics based on caste and minority status
also poses radical questions to the women's movement. We have come a
considerable way from the reductive and technicist battles over the determination of poverty during the 1970s that focused on the appropriate measurements of calorie intake for determining BPL (below poverty line) populations. And yet, the power of economic ideologies is such that material
concepts of disadvantage, lack of entitlements, and unmet basic needs continue to dominate contemporary debates. Furthermore, there has been a
tendency during the last decade to uphold struggles over poverty in opposition to those being raised in the name of so-called "identity politics," especially in the wake of the re-emergence on the national stage of the politics of
caste and community. Such misgivings have been voiced in the women's
movement as well. To my mind, this polarization blocks the chance of actually transforming our understanding of poverty itself. It could be argued, and
I am going to do so here, that one of the failures of the developmental era
was its inability to account for inequalities and hierarchies such as those
based on caste and community, other than as residues of the past. It therefore required major national crisis points—the anti-Mandal agitation of 1990
against the implementation of reservations for the Other Backward Castes in
administration and higher education, the demolition of the Babri Masjid in
1992 and the anti-Muslim riots that followed, and the rise of new regionalisms, among others—for hitherto largely invisible structures of disparity
based on caste, community, and region to gain some measure of recognition
in their own right. One of the potential gains of the last decade, therefore,
would be to acknowledge that the *multiple inequalities of the present* must
be taken into account (rather than transcended or sought to be bypassed) in
ongoing struggles against poverty.[52] For the women's movement—already
accused of having "divided" prior struggles by introducing questions of
gender—the way forward may not be easy. But it is not for nothing that contemporary studies of poverty have begun to notice that dalits, major sections
of the backward castes, tribals, Muslim minorities, and female-headed
households practically exhaust the categories of the poor. Feminists will
have to play their part to turn such lists into live zones of coalition building.[53]

The diversity in the experiences and forms of poverty in India today may
thus require unlearning inherited ways of conceptualizing our underdevelopment, which the women's movement can ignore only at its peril. Perhaps

this is still less controversial than the final issue I would like to raise, one that is bound to be more debatable since it involves going beyond the "poor." To put it most provocatively: Has the heavy emphasis on representations of poverty—at the cost of a parallel understanding of class dynamics—also become one of the weaknesses of the women's movement? Poverty and class continue to be conflated with one another (not unlike the conflation of women and gender), and to the detriment of *both*. Class analysis—that is to say, analysis that focuses on the non-poor as well as the poor—has seen no significant advancements in the last few decades. The mode of deployment of class in campaigns and struggles within a movement such as the women's movement has suffered considerably, and operates to a remarkable degree within a social and epistemological vacuum. At least two dimensions of class analysis need much more attention. The first is the strategic location of the Indian middle classes and their key role in articulating the hegemony of the ruling bloc. They have arguably been at the heart of the major "critical events" of the decade of the 1990s—liberalization, "Mandal," and "Ayodhya."[54] And yet we do not even have a minimal sense of the social composition of this class, its degree of heterogeneity, and its ideological functions.[55] Moreover, leadership of the women's movement has invariably arisen from this class, whose mandate has therefore been one of *representation,* understood in all its various aspects.

The second aspect of class analysis that is urgently in need of redressal centers on the intermediate classes and castes, which, for lack of a better description, I will call the non-poor. An indispensable dimension of such analysis would include patterns of mobility across class fractions, processes that enable some groups to move out of poverty and possibly gain some measure of prosperity while others strategize to prevent themselves from "falling." Isn't it curious how little we wish to know of such trends? Now it could of course be argued that since a movement must have its priorities, the problems of the non-poor cannot be expected to figure very highly. However, such a short-sighted approach has come home to roost today. As far back as the first shocked discovery of the prevalence of dowry murders among urban lower middle class families almost three decades ago, there has been evidence of *greater* gender biases in families beyond the pale of dire need. In more recent years, considerable anxiety has emerged over the worsening of female-male sex ratios, which are sharpening outside the classes of poor, leading to speculations of the "paradox" of the "prosperity effect,"[56] the negative effects on women of fertility decline,[57] and the mismatch between measures of "backward" districts according to economic and gender indicators.[58] The results of the 2001 Census in particular, where child female/male ratios in the 0–6–year age group have dropped precipitously in many districts of the most economically advanced states of the country, especially in urban areas, have led to dystopic speculations of various kinds. (The worst state averages for 2001 are Punjab (793), Haryana (820), Gujarat (879), and

Himachal Pradesh (897), and the all-India figure is 927 girls per 1,000 boys.) There is every reason to believe that these are not isolated patterns but a potential sign of things to come, as men and women make "choices" under conditions of limited gains and potential losses in an expanding, increasingly competitive economy. And yet, analysis is still largely impressionistic, mobilization quite weak and often not sufficiently sensitive to the genuine problems involved.[59] The women's movement often appears caught in a kind of cleft stick—denouncing poverty and the "evils" of the new consumerist culture in one and the same breath. Sometimes the question is posed: If poverty is bad for women, could prosperity be worse?

Perhaps, then, the way forward may have little to do with actually getting the right perspective on "globalization." Nor can we rest content with celebrating "local" initiatives. A marginal presence barely two decades ago, feminists surely have good reason to feel vindicated as more and more institutions address the constituency of "women." Today, however, this very gain in legitimacy could result in the stagnation of the movement. And yet, it need not. For feminism to retain its constitutive force and to believe that it can be a part of social transformations, the task is nothing less than to go beyond certain inherited constructs of "poor women" in order to contest existing accounts of social change as such. Feminism must, on the one hand, realize that its future is tied up with the multiple languages of poverty and disparity that are straining to be heard. On the other hand, even at the cost of overload, there are no stopping places where gender loses its urgency—"success" stories in class terms are not being mirrored in the egalitarian life-chances of sons and daughters.

Above all else, the future of the women's movement will depend on its ability to rejuvenate itself. It cannot simply rely on older strategies devised during the development era. This is by no means an argument in favor of the "retreat of the state," but simply to note that the state itself should be one of many sites of contestation. The strength of the women's movement in India—as this chapter should have made amply clear—has derived from its capacity to take on new challenges, to break out of narrow definitions of patriarchy and gender oppression. Today these qualities will be needed more than ever before. If it is the exclusiveness of the emergent social order that is blocking democracy in our times, broadening the terrain on which battles of gender and poverty must be fought may well be a risk worth taking.

NOTES

Different parts of this paper have been presented in Berkeley, Delhi, and Bangalore. An earlier version has been published in *Feminisms in Asia,* Special Issue of *Inter-Asia Cultural Studies* 3, no. 2 (2002): 351–67. I am particularly grateful to Mary

Katzenstein and Raka Ray for their thoughtful and detailed comments on earlier drafts, which helped considerably in revising my arguments. Of course, I remain solely responsible for the views expressed here.

1. It might be of interest to readers to know that the social reform movements of the nineteenth century have attracted more in-depth historical analysis to date, at least among feminist scholars located in India, than the early twentieth century period when women's organizations first became established. Significant texts on women in the colonial period include Geraldine Forbes, *Women in Modern India* (Cambridge: Cambridge University Press, 1996); Radha Kumar, *A History of Doing: An Illustrated Account of the Movements for Women's Rights and Feminism in India, 1800–1990* (New Delhi: Kali for Women, 1993); J. Krishnamurthy, ed., *Women in Colonial India: Essays on Survival, Work and the State* (Delhi: Oxford University Press, 1989); B. R. Nanda, ed., *Indian Women from Purdah to Modernity* (New Delhi: Vikas, 1976); Bharati Ray, ed., *From the Seams of History: Essays on Indian Women* (Delhi: Oxford University Press, 1995); Kumkum Sangari and Sudesh Vaid, eds., *Recasting Women: Essays on Colonial India* (New Delhi: Kali for Women, 1989); and Susie Tharu and K. Lalita, eds., *Women Writing in India: From 600 B. C. to the Present*, 2 vols. (New York: The Feminist Press and Delhi: Oxford University Press, 1991 and 1993).

2. In the words of the feminist historian Mrinalini Sinha, during the 1920s and '30s "liberal Indian feminism played a pivotal role in fashioning a bourgeois liberal Indian modernity." See Sinha, "Refashioning Mother India: Feminism and Nationalism in Late-Colonial India," *Feminist Studies* 26, no. 3 (Fall 2000): 626.

3. Forbes, *Women in Modern India*, 7.

4. *Women's Role in a Planned Economy*, Report of the Sub-committee (Bombay: Vora and Co., 1947), 175.

5. As the authors of the report put it, "the foundation of prostitution is hunger." While professing to hold no moral or sexual attitudes against this occupation, they believed that its eradication would be feasible only in "a planned society where economic conditions will change, education will predominate and the dual standard of morality be replaced by a common but higher and healthier standard of life between man and woman" (*Women's Role in a Planned Economy*, 186, 192).

6. Instead, the 1950s and '60s saw the re-emergence of "women" in the community development programs (financed by the Ford Foundation) whose projects were geared to enable village women to become, in the words of the director of the Women's Programme in 1959, "a good wife, a wise mother, a competent housewife, and a responsible member of the village community" (cited in Rekha Mehra, "Rural Development Programmes: Neglect of Women," in *Women and Rural Transformation—Two Studies*, ed. Rekha Mehra and K. Saradamoni [New Delhi: Concept, 1983], xx). Women's work and labor are not alluded to anywhere.

7. For a fuller discussion, see Satish Deshpande, "From Development to Adjustment: Economic Ideologies, the Middle Class and Fifty Years of Independence," *Review of Development and Change* II, no. 2 (July–December 1997): 294–318.

8. See Neera Desai, "From Articulation to Accommodation: Women's Movement in India," in *Visibility and Power: Essays on Women in Society and Development*, ed. Leela Dube, Eleanor Leacock, and Shirley Ardener (Delhi: Oxford University Press, 1986), 287–299, and Nirmala Banerjee, "Whatever Happened to the Dreams of

Modernity?' The Nehruvian Era and Women's Position," *Economic and Political Weekly* 28, no. 17 (May 1, 1998): WS-2-7.

9. Stree Shakti Sanghatana, *"We were making history"* . . . *Life Histories of Women in the Telangana People's Struggle* (New Delhi: Kali for Women, 1989).

10. Mary E. John, "Gender and Development in India, 1970s–1990s: Some Reflections on the Constitutive Role of Contexts," *Economic and Political Weekly*, November 23, 1996, 3072.

11. General overviews of the women's movement are to be found in Indu Agnihotri and Vina Mazumdar, "Changing Terms of Political Discourse: Women's Movement in India," *Economic and Political Weekly* 30, no. 29 (1995): 1869–1878; Nandita Gandhi and Nandita Shah, *The Issues at Stake: Theory and Practice in the Contemporary Women's Movement in India* (New Delhi: Kali for Women, 1992); Madhu Kishwar and Ruth Vanita, eds., *In Search of Answers: Voices from Manushi* (London: Zed Press, 1987); Kumar, *A History of Doing*; Nivedita Menon, ed., *Gender and Politics in India* (Delhi: Oxford University Press, 1999); and Gail Omvedt, *We Will Smash This Prison! Indian Women in Struggle* (London: Zed Books, 1980), among others.

12. The "founding text" here is the *Towards Equality Report,* produced by the Government of India's Department of Social Welfare through setting up the Committee on the Status of Women in India. Unbeknownst to its team of authors, this report was meant to be the country study for India at the first International Year for Women in 1975 organized by the UN.

13. The first discussion of the declining sex ratio was introduced by Pravin Visaria, "The Sex Ratio of the Population of India," *Census of India 1961*, vol. 1, Monograph no. 10 (1969). The equally significant essay by Asok Mitra, "Implications of Declining Sex Ratio in India," first published in 1979, has recently been reprinted with a number of new articles in *Enduring Conundrum: India's Sex Ratio; Essays in Honour of Asok Mitra,* ed. Vina Mazumdar and N. Krishnaji (New Delhi: Rainbow, 2001), 143–98.

14. K. Lalita, "Women in Revolt: A Historical Analysis of the Progressive Organisation of Women in Andhra Prodesh," *Women's Struggles and Strategies*, ed. Saskia Wieringa (Aldershot: Gower, 1988), 60–61.

15. Raka Ray, *Fields of Protest: Women's Movements in India* (Minneapolis: University of Minnesota Press and New Delhi: Kali for Women, 1999).

16. Devaki Jain and Nirmala Banerjee, eds. *Tyranny of the Household: Investigative Essays into Women's Work* (New Delhi: Shakti Books, 1985).

17. Bina Agarwal, "Women, Poverty and Agricultural Growth in India," *Journal of Peasant Studies* 13, no. 4 (1986): 213.

18. See Amrita Basu, *Two Faces of Protest: Contrasting Modes of Women's Activism in India* (Berkeley: University of California Press and Delhi: Oxford University Press, 1993); Ilina Sen, ed., *A Space within the Struggle: Women's Participation in People's Movements* (New Delhi: Kali for Women, 1990); Kumud Sharma, "Shared Aspirations, Fragmented Realities: Contemporary Women's Movement in India, Its Dialectics and Dilemmas," New Delhi: Centre for Women's Development Studies, Occasional Paper no. 12; Raka Ray; *Fields of Protest.*

19. Kavita Srivastava and Jaya Sharma, "Training Rural Women for Literacy" (Jaipur: Institute of Development Studies, 1991).

20. Maitreyi Das, *The Women's Development Programme in Rajasthan: A Case Study in Group Formation for Women's Development* (Washington, D.C.: The World Bank, 1991).

21. National Commission of Women, *The Sathin as an Agent of Women's Development* (New Delhi: Government of India, 1996).

22. Sathin Karamchari Sangh, "The Sathin Issue: A Collective Strategy, the Need of the Hour," unpublished pamphlet.

23. For details of the anti-arrack agitation, see Anveshi, "Reworking Gender Relations, Redefining Politics: Nellore Village Women Against Arrack," *Economic and Political Weekly,* January 16–23, 1993, 87–90.

24. Susie Tharu and Tejaswini Niranjana, "Problems for a Contemporary Theory of Gender," in *Subaltern Studies IX: Writings on South Asian History and Society,* ed. Shahid Amin and Dipesh Chakrabarty (Delhi: Oxford University Press, 1996), 254.

25. Uma Maheswari, "Anti-arrack Movement, Prohibition and After: *Eenadu's* Strategic Support and Silence," *Journal of Arts and Ideas, Special Issue on Gender, Media and the Rhetorics of Liberalisation,* nos. 22–23 (1999): 73–86.

26. The box item explains that "podupu" means saving, Lakshmi being the Goddess of Wealth. The *podupulakshmi* "movement" ("the sequel to the total literacy campaign and the anti-arrack movement"), it is said, is going beyond conventional thrift schemes and carrying out a wide variety of women-centered activities, with the aid of local government functionaries such as the public health worker (ANM), school teacher, fair price shop dealer, and *anganwadi* (child care) worker. (Planning Commission, Government of India, *Ninth Five Year Plan 1997–2002, volume II, Thematic Issues and Sectoral Programmes* [New Delhi, 1999], 17.)

27. This unequivocal stance against population control is itself a mark of the distinctiveness of the women's movement in the post-independence era. In the pre-independence period of the 1920s and '30s, when the question of birth control was first publicly debated and was a highly controversial subject indeed, it was not uncommon to find advocates of birth control among women's organizations who also viewed it as a means to contain poverty, as we saw in the deliberations of Nehru's Sub-Committee on Women.

28. See Monica Das Gupta, Lincoln Chen, and J. N. Krishnan, *Women's Health in India: Risks and Vulnerabilities* (Delhi: Oxford University Press, 1995); and Imrana Qadeer, "Maternal Health in India," in *Gender, Population and Development in India,* ed. Maitreyi Krishnaraj, Ratna Sudarshan, and Abusaleh Shariff (Delhi: Oxford University Press, 1998), 270–90.

29. Government of India, *Draft National Population Policy* (New Delhi: Ministry of Health and Family Welfare, 1994).

30. Government of India, *National Population Policy* (New Delhi: Ministry of Health and Family Welfare, 2000).

31. In a recent study of women councillors in the municipalities of the metropolitan city of Delhi and the small town of Karnal in rural Haryana, one of the questions put to the councillors was their response to the recent order in both the states debarring those with more than two children from standing for election. Much to the surprise of the interviewers, they found the councillors in both contexts unanimous in their support of the policy. The interviewers' final comment was that with such widespread consent, it was feminist opposition to such policies that was clearly misplaced! (Marg, *Daughters of the 74th Amendment: A Study of Delhi and Karnal* [New Delhi: Marg, 2001]).

32. *Healthwatch Update,* Issue 11 (September–December 2000) and Mohan Rao, "Population Policies: States Approve Coercive Measures," *Economic and Political Weekly,* July 21, 2001, 2739–41.

33. This is mentioned in the National Council of Educational Research and Training, *Guidelines and Syllabi for Primary Stage* (New Delhi, 2001), 30.

34. Middle class consensus over population control has also been bolstered by stoking fears regarding the unbounded multiplication of Muslims. This became manifest when 1991 Census data on the break-up of the population by religion—which showed that Muslims had grown slightly faster than Hindus in the 1981–91 decade—was used as "proof" in numerous newspaper articles and public exhortations soon after it was published in 1995 that Muslims practice polygamy, resist contraception, and are swamping the Indian nation with Islam. Interestingly, high levels of poverty among Muslims (especially in urban areas) were not part of these discussions.

35. Imrana Qadeer, "Reproductive Health: A Public Health Perspective," *Economic and Political Weekly* 33, no. 41 (1998): 2676–78.

36. T. K. Sundari Ravindran, "Women and the Politics of Population and Development in India," *Reproductive Health Matters*, no. 1 (1993): 26–38, and Gita Sen, Adriane Germaine, and Lincoln Chen, eds., *Population Policies Reconsidered: Health, Empowerment and Rights* (Cambridge, Mass.: Harvard University Press, 1994).

37. For further discussions of these dilemmas, see Tharu and Niranjana, "Problems for a Contemporary Theory of Gender"; Mary E. John, "Globalisation, Sexuality and the Visual Field: Issues and Non-Issues for Cultural Critique," in *A Question of Silence? The Sexual Economies of Modern India*, ed. Mary E. John and Janaki Nair (New Delhi: Kali for Women, 1998), 368–96; and Vanita Nayak Mukherjee, "Gender Matters," in *Beyond Numbers: A Symposium on Population Planning and Advocacy, Seminar*, no. 511 (2002): 67–75 .

38. D. L. Sheth, "Globalisation and New Politics of Micro–movements," *Economic and Political Weekly,* January 3–9, 2004, 47.

39. Nandita Shah, Sujata Gothoskar, et al., "Feminisation of Labour Force and Organisational strategies," *Economic and Political Weekly*, April 30, 1994, WS 39–48.

40. Banerjee has also opposed a tendency to generalize about the relationship between new work opportunities for women and their empowerment or subordination, advocating a more contextual approach instead. See Nirmala Banerjee, "How Real Is the Bogey of Feminisation?" *The Indian Journal of Labour Economics* 40, no. 3 (1997): 427–38.

41. Vandana Shiva's analyses can be gleaned from lectures such as "Trading Our Lives Away: Free Trade, Women and Ecology," Durgabhai Memorial Lecture, 1996 at the Council for Social Development, New Delhi, and in essays such as Vandana Shiva, *Globalisation of Agriculture, Food Security and Sustainability* (New Delhi: Research Foundation for Science, Technology and Ecology, 1998). A series of phases of globalization—colonization by Europe; the universalization of production and consumption in the name of "development"; and, finally, the current trade treaties focused on biodiversity and genetic resources—are opposed to the potential of "decentralized agricultural communities," which, like pre-modern paradigms of the "home" are somehow without hierarchies—whether of ecology and economics, domestic or commodity production, natural or human economies, or relations of gender.

42. In a set of proposals canvassed in *Manushi*, Madhu Kishwar wishes to set in motion a "freeing up of the entrepreneurial skills of the people," especially women, who have been made dependent and prevented from taking their place in the pub-

lic sphere of the economy due to an over-bloated, over-centralized bureaucracy, and a larger culture of criminalization and violence (Madhu Kishwar, "Laws, Liberty and Livelihood: Towards a Bottom-Up, Woman Friendly Agenda of Economic Reforms," *Manushi*, no. 122, [January–February 2001]: 8–12).

43. Rohini Hensman, "Globalisation, Women and Work," *Economic and Political Weekly*, March 6, 2004, 1034. See also Rohini Hensman, "World Trade and Workers' Rights," *Economic and Political Weekly*, April 8–14, 2000, 1247–54.

44. Gail Omvedt and Chetna Gala, "The New Economic Policy and Women: A Rural Perspective," *Economic Review* (October 1993): 15.

45. Ela Bhatt, "Doosri Azadi: SEWA's Perspectives on the Early Years of Independence," *Economic and Political Weekly*, April 15–May 1, 1998, WS 25–27.

46. Renana Jhabvala and R. K. A. Subrahmanya, eds. *The Unorganised Sector: Work Security and Social Protection* (New Delhi: Sage, 2000).

47. For further discussions and criticisms see World Bank, *Gender and Poverty in India* (Washington D.C.: The World Bank, 1991); John, "Gender and Development in India"; Marilyn Carr, Martha Chen, and Renana Jhabvala, eds., *Speaking Out: Women's Economic Empowerment in South Asia* (New Delhi: Vistaar, 1997); and A. R. Vasavi and Catherine P. Kingfisher, "Poor Women as Economic Agents: The Neoliberal State and Gender in India and the U.S.," *Indian Journal of Gender Studies* 10, no. 1 (January–April 2003): 1–24.

48. Planning Commission, Government of India, *Ninth Five Year Plan 1997–2002, volume I: Development Goals, Strategies and Policies* (New Delhi, 1999), 33.

49. Indeed, one of the major architects of Kerala's decentralization process has candidly admitted the following in a discussion of women political representatives: "Most of them were young, educated only up to matriculation or below, from poor or lower middle class backgrounds and without prior experience in elected office. Forty percent of them did not have any previous exposure to public activity. They had to work in an unfriendly social environment and often faced slander and gossip. This triple burden of work, family duties and responsibility as an elected representative gave rise to family tensions, although they were within manageable limits" (T. M. Thomas Isaac and Richard Franke, *Local Democracy and Development: People's Campaign for Decentralised Planning in Kerala* [New Delhi: LeftWord, 2000: 227]). Unfortunately, the largely uncritical if not celebratory approach that has been adopted towards the "empowered" women of Kerala, at least till recently, has been at the severe cost of any nuanced understanding of contemporary practices and gender relations in that complex state.

50. A genuine contradiction is evident in the means whereby decentralization is to be implemented, since it depends on the "giving up" of power by the higher tiers of the state apparatus. The contradiction involved is even sharper than it would have been during the development era, because, if anything, political power and regional autonomy among individual states in relation to the center has increased in the last decade.

51. There is a growing literature on the subject, mostly in the form of case studies and training manuals by NGOs. Some examples would be Bisakha Datta, ed., *And Who Will Make the Chapatis? A Study of All Women Panchayats in Maharashtra* (Calcutta: Stree, 1998); Nirmala Buch, "Women's Experience in New Panchayats: The Emerging Leadership of Rural Women," Centre for Women's Development Studies

(Occasional Paper no. 35, 2000); Institute of Social Sciences; *Women and Political Empowerment: Proceedings* (New Delhi: The Institute, 1995); Susheela Kaushik, *Women and Panchayati Raj* (New Delhi: Har-Anand, 1993).

52. For an early effort in this direction, see Mary E. John (with K. Lalita), *Background Report on Gender Issues in India* (Sussex: Bridge, IDS and ODA, UK, 1995).

53. It would, however, be exceedingly naïve to suppose that the deprivation and marginalization experienced by these groups would somehow act as a natural magnet drawing them together as a majority, whether socially or politically. It is not for nothing that recognition of the "cultural" dimensions of poverty is emerging at a time when the nation has witnessed the revival of a very different majoritarian project, that of Hindutva. Recent developments in states as different as Uttar Pradesh and Gujarat are but an indication of how the most vicious conflicts can take place between groups adjacent to one another in strictly economic terms. Moreover, there is a longer history of anti-reservation *resentement* whereby the small but never invisible members of lower castes within the middle classes have not been allowed to forget who they are, a strategy that has been reproduced to deadly effect in the successful destruction of lives and livelihoods of all classes of Muslims in Gujarat. The current agenda of the Hindu Right to produce a Hindu Rashtra by incorporating sections of the most backward castes, dalits, and tribals within its fold cannot be countered by purely economistic conceptions of deprivation. And yet, as the extraordinary results of the just-concluded Lok Sabha elections of 2004 would indicate, the aggressively marketed "India Shining" campaign of the BJP, which—more than anything else—sought to make the poor invisible if not irrelevant, has backfired in a way no one predicted beforehand.

54. Deshpande, "From Development to Adjustment."

55. D. L. Sheth, "Secularization of Caste and Making of New Middle Class," *Economic and Political Weekly* 34, nos. 34–35 (1999): 2502–10.

56. Barbara Harriss-White, "Gender-Cleansing: The Paradox of Development and Deteriorating Female Life Chances in Tamil Nadu," in *Signposts: Gender Issues in Post-Independence India*, ed. Rajeswari Sunder Rajan (New Delhi: Kali for Women, 1999), 124–53.

57. Monica Das Gupta and P. N. Mari Bhatt, "Intensified Gender Bias in India: A Consequence of Fertility Decline," in *Gender, Population and Development*, eds. Maithreyi Krishnaraj, Ratna Sudarshan, and Abusaleh Shariff (Delhi: Oxford University Press, 1998), 73–93.

58. Preet Rustagi, "Identifying Gender Backward Districts Using Selected Indicators," *Economic and Political Weekly*, November 25, 2000, 4276–86.

59. To date, the main reason advanced for the falling numbers has been the burgeoning practice of prenatal sex determination tests followed by the selective abortion of female fetuses, frequently called "female foeticide." Although such sex determination tests have been banned by law as far back as 1986 (as the result of feminist campaigns), unscrupulous doctors and radiologists are said to be making enormous profits with their ultrasound machines in cities, towns, and relatively more prosperous rural areas. Thus far not a single doctor has been apprehended, and the practice continues more or less secretly. However, much more information and understanding are required at the level of family practices across different classes and social groups before any further explanations, let alone interventions, can be offered.

5

Who Are the Country's Poor? Social Movement Politics and Dalit Poverty

Gopal Guru and Anuradha Chakravarty

Appointed in 1953, the first Backward Classes Commission observed that a low position in the caste hierarchy was the key determinant of social and economic backwardness. No less in contemporary times, caste continues to be deeply imbricated in the perseverance of poverty. The proportion of scheduled castes classified as marginal landholders (owning about a third of a hectare) has risen from 68.9 percent in 1980–1981 to 72.2 percent in 1990–1991, and the proportion of scheduled caste landless agricultural laborers is growing.[1] In 1993–1994, the proportion of rural scheduled castes and scheduled tribes falling below the poverty line was 49.0 and 49.5 percent respectively, as compared to 32.8 percent of rural, non-scheduled households generally.[2] According to a report from Human Rights Watch, "An estimated forty million people in India, among them fifteen million children, are bonded laborers, working in slave-like conditions in order to pay off a debt. A majority of them are dalits."[3]

This strong colinearity of low caste status and poverty has long been recognized. But debates have raged over the reasons for and the fitting response to this social and economic reality. For Gandhi, the problem was not caste (*varna*) but untouchability. For Nehru, the problem was first and foremost poverty: Supplant poverty with equitable growth and the excrescences of caste would fade. For B. R. Ambedkar, the Untouchable leader and statesman, as long as caste as a social system persisted, so would grievous deprivation.

In this chapter, even as we are most persuaded by Ambedkar's understanding, we address the political complexity of dismantling caste concurrent with the intent to redress poverty. In India's democratic polity, we argue, organizing against caste has required organizing on the basis of caste. In the process of addressing this "democratic paradox," we trace how the common thread running through the varied approaches of India's political formations has been the shortchanging of strategies that address the wrenching problems of material poverty. We organize the discussion that follows first by exploring the caste basis of Indian poverty; we then turn to the development of state policies and to the ways these policies shaped the approaches of social movements as they sought to combat poverty. We subsequently consider three particular responses: the radical challenge and failed adaptation of the Dalit Panthers, the capture of state power by the Bahujan Samaj Party (BSP) with its attendant compromises and contradictions, and finally, the soft resistance to the State's neoliberal agenda by dalit NGOs.

DALITIZATION OF INDIAN POVERTY

Following from the dominant logic of class analysis of Indian poverty, both mainstream neo-classical economists and radical Marxist analyses have generally neglected the study of the economic consequences of the caste system. In the few instances that neo-classical approaches have been applied to examine the independent effects of caste on the economic structure, the animating questions have pertained to the origins and persistence of caste as an economically inefficient institution or of the impact of caste on unemployment patterns. The literature is largely silent on the issue of income distribution.[4] In its turn, the Marxist literature's tendency to treat the social structure of caste as the residue of feudal or semifeudal modes of production constrains our ability to understand the economic impact of caste under conditions of capitalism and the globalized market. Also, the Marxist understanding of social relations as superstructure determined by the economic base limits an appreciation of the independent impact of social structure on the control of the means of production, specific patterns of appropriation of surplus value, etc.[5]

Obviously, these approaches for understanding the nature of poverty in India miss an important point, i.e., the mutually reinforcing effects of caste and class hierarchies condemning those at the bottom to a doubly-reinforced structural trap. Various independent surveys at the national level and across different states have concurred that the dalits are backward on more criteria than any other caste grouping.[6] Suffering from cumulative disabilities, the dalits are backward on all counts such as mental and physical health, dwelling status, sources of livelihood, land ownership, debt levels, etc.[7] Contemporary indices reveal some characteristic features of the economic status of dalits. They have a high dependence on wage labor—particularly unskilled manual labor. They comprise a negligible proportion of the self-employed. Unemployment levels are twice that of the other caste groups, and the daily wage earning is the lowest among all castes. All of these factors collude to result in low consumption expenditures limited to the barest subsistence, little to no savings, and very high poverty levels.[8] Although about 16 percent of the total population of India,[9] the dalits comprise fully three-quarters of the ranks of the poorest of the poor. An indication of the very long-term historical impact of this structural trap is manifested in the slow and barely perceptible process of inter-generational mobility out of this position at the bottom of the economic and social hierarchies.

The two available exits from this severely disempowering location are the State and the market. Unfortunately, the market has proven ruthless and the State unreliable. The State in its commitment to social justice and fundamental rights of citizens has over the years enacted a series of legislations designed to abolish the practice of untouchability, to carry out land reform, to declare as illegal the institution of bonded labor, etc.[10] Through a policy of reservations in government employment, on elected assemblies and in public educational institutions, the State has also sought to create opportunities for dalits to exercise political power, to attain economic security and the capacity for upward mobility. Unfortunately, the State stands implicated for its failure to enforce the above laws, for its active collusion with the propertied classes and upper castes preventing the full implementation of land reform and for the failure of its "development" agenda to impart either the necessary education for gainful employment or to create sufficient jobs for educated dalit youth.

The case of land reform is a telling example of the extent to which the State has abdicated its commitment to justice, leaving the dalits to face the ruthless logic of market forces. Eighty-one percent of India's dalit population lives in villages. More than three-quarters of this population are landless agricultural laborers, sharecroppers, and rural non-farm workers. The program of land redistribution did not rely much on confiscation and redistribution. Instead, some redistributed land was sliced away from the local commons; other portions were made available to dalit families as upper-caste landowners sold off tiny slivers of land in a gesture toward meeting the new laws.[11] This inconclusive and half-hearted program resulted in ownership by dalit families of generally uncultivable land ranging from a tiny percentage of an acre to a couple of acres at the maximum. Less than 1 percent of dalit farmers have access to irrigation facilities. Upper caste farmers usurp available water resources and also use rights to transport and other infrastructure connecting the village to the market.[12] This produces and sustains economic relations of severe dependence of dalits on the landed classes. These upper and middle caste families have retained ownership of hundreds of acres of land—some of it in blatant violation of land ceiling laws, some of it exempted by the State from the land ceiling laws, and most of it as disguised holdings. The income of dalit families from agricultural labor or cultivation of their miniscule land holdings is barely enough to ensure two full meals a day. It means the utter inability to generate savings or to make small productive capital investments, to provide for adequate clothing or much-needed medicine.[13] In fact, 48 percent of the dalit population in rural India lives below the poverty line.[14]

This desperate poverty also means that despite high enrollments in government schools (87 percent according to government figures), families cannot afford to lose a pair of working hands during the long gestation period that goes with the completion of school education. This factor, along with faint employment prospects in the future, leads to a high dropout rate among dalit students (66.7 percent) as families begin to use schools largely as crèches, keeping young children there only until the point that they become more useful in helping to provide subsistence for the family.[15] As market prices of food grains and other essential commodities soar, the iron grip of poverty tightens, setting in motion the migration of dalit peoples to urban and semi-urban areas. Here, the dalits constitute a new urban proletariat, working in stone quarries and brick kilns from dawn to dusk in deplorable conditions for wages below the market rate.[16] Tribals join the ranks of the dalits in these occupations—having been dislocated from their forested lands by crushing poverty—to be bought and sold between middlemen and then delivered to proprietors for what is for all practical purposes a new system of bonded labor.[17] The informal sector with its low incomes, irregular work, and lack of organizational structures for workers is another arena that absorbs the dalit masses. Ragpicking, construction work, scavenging for coal or scraps of metal in the drains, rickshaw pulling, etc., are a few of the primary activities in this sector—requiring only unskilled labor. Their huts and shanties in the slums are not safe from the government's eviction and demolition squads trying to "clean up" the city.[18] In order to earn a livelihood from ragpicking and scavenging, they root about in mounds of garbage with stray dogs and pigs for company—thereby conflating the ritual pollution line with the poverty line. A competitive enterprise, this work also requires that scavenging zones be guarded against violation at all times of the day or night. As they work around the clock, the doubly reinforced social and economic structural trap remains firmly shut.

What then are the options for survival open to dalits? It is an established fact that government jobs (e.g., bureaucracies, public enterprises, railways, army) are the main source of employment in the formal sector. The economic security along with the social prestige associated with it has enabled the emergence of a class of dalits that is vastly better off, socially conscious, and more politically aware than its brethren in the urban slums or villages. The State program of investing in the education of dalits through provision of free schools, hostel facilities, scholarships, and training centers has met with relative success, as evinced by a slow but definite growth in literacy levels. In the year 1961, the literacy level among dalits was 10.27 percent. This rose to 21.38 percent in 1981 and stands at 37.4 percent in recent years.[19] Now a certain number of dalits can also compete with upper-caste candidates for middle-level positions.[20] However, given the shrinkage of the welfare state (not offset by the growing availability of jobs in the private sector which does not observe affirmative action policies), dalits face the risk of further marginalization. Without some fundamental social and economic change, dalits will continue to be at a far remove from top-level educational qualifications and access to white-collar jobs.[21] Where self-employment opportunities are concerned, these are more difficult to come by for the dalits than for other social groups. The hotel and hospitality industry, for example, is closed (except for the most menial of tasks like sweeping) because of the ritual pollution aspect. Without access to credit facilities or lobbies in the corridors of power, capital-intensive industries such as that of oil and petrol are also off limits to dalit peoples.[22]

As life becomes a series of movements from margin to margin, dalits cannot but question the fruits of economic development. Symptomatic of the growing alienation from the State are the metaphors they use to think about their lives and livelihood. The revolutionary poet Narayan Survey has suggested that for the dalits, the *roti* (*bhakri*) is not only round as the moon but also just as distant.[23] "Poison bread"[24] is another symbol of the diminution of human dignity each time dalits eat leftover food from the homes of the upper castes as a matter of routine survival, or are forced to consume wild leaves or the flesh of dead animals during bad times such as droughts.

THE EVOLUTION OF POLICY AND MOVEMENT RESPONSE

Efforts to oppose the scourge of untouchability and the idea of caste ascription have a long history. Indeed, as Myron Weiner has argued, "More than one hundred years of social reform movements, public pronouncements by political leaders, constitutional declarations, and legislation" have undermined the "orthodoxy"—the belief in—if not the "orthopraxy"—the practice of—caste hierarchy.[25]

The paradox of "*naming*" and thereby *inscribing* caste in order to *disinter* its strictures from its deeply embedded place in Hindu society also reaches back into pre-democratic colonial times, even as post-Independent democratic practices reinforce these processes. The 1953 Backward Classes Commission report referred to at the opening of this chapter was not the first official acknowledgment of the role of caste as an independent factor in determining the class structure. The Untouchables and the lower castes[26] had been categorized under the rubric "*backward classes*" in the 1870s by the colonial administration in Madras. By 1925, particularly in the Bombay and Madras presidencies, seats were reserved in local assemblies and educational institutions for the *backward classes*—an overarching category constructed to include the "*depressed classes*" (Untouchables and Tribals) and low castes other than the *depressed classes*. The colonial state then created through the Government of India Act 1935 a new nomenclature "*scheduled castes*" for the Untouchables who became entitled to the benefits of an affirmative action policy in the spheres of education and representation in the state apparatus.

The efforts to dismantle the detriments of untouchability through the targeted practice of preferential identification continued with the Constitution of independent India. Article 17 abolishes untouchability, while Article 46 simultaneously requires the state to promote with special care the educational and economic interests of the weaker sections, particularly the so-named Scheduled Castes and Tribes. Similarly, Article 335 provides for preferential treatment of Scheduled Castes and Tribes in appointments to government services and posts; and Articles 330 and 332 provide for seat reservations in parliament and the state legislative assemblies, while still other constitutional provisions do the same for the local councils (*panchayats*). Interestingly, the post-colonial state has continued to institutionalize this particular identity for Untouchables and beginning in the early 1990s further codified the term "*other backward classes*" (OBCs) by authorizing job preferences designating eligibility by the social and economic status of the lower castes.

In the Constitutional Assembly debates, however, a strong preference emerged to overlook the structuring effects of caste on the grossly iniquitous economic system. Nehru's socialist leanings implied that economic change and modernization would become the preferred instruments to do away with caste, other abhorrent social legacies, and, of course, poverty. The imperative of national unity also contributed to this tendency to underplay the consequences of the divisive caste structure. Another powerful force operating in this context was "colonial shame," or the need to deny British characterizations of India as backward and caste-ridden.[27] Thus a whole nexus of causes conspired to neglect the fundamentally social basis of poverty in India. Defeating Ambedkar's argument in Parliament that the backward classes were "but a collection of certain castes,"[28] Nehru's Congress government successfully engineered the dominant consensus that held that the most appropriate strategy to combat poverty and implement social justice was one centered around economic class identification rather than that of caste. In fact, by 1961, this government had decided that although the scheduled castes and scheduled tribes would continue to enjoy the benefits sanctioned by the Constitution, it would not be useful to compile a caste-based list of OBCs, nor would it be desirable to have a reservation policy for OBCs at the Center.[29]

From this time until the mid-1970s, the political opportunity structure continued to be fairly stable and generally inopportune for explicit caste-based political mobilization as well as other identity movements more generally. This is not to deny that the broad structure of constraints and opportunities was undergoing a slow and perceptible change. A split in the hegemonic Congress party followed Nehru's death in 1964. The economy also landed in serious trouble leading to falling support for the party. With these changes, some political space began to open up for mobilization by competing parties and identity-based social movements. As the mid-1970s approached, "dalit" identity emerged as a powerful frame used by the scheduled castes to galvanize a political movement around their pressing concerns. It resonated with Ambedkar's famous argument (*contra* Gandhi) that the scheduled castes had political interests separate from the rest of the Hindu masses and should therefore mobilize on that distinct social basis.[30]

However, even as the Constitution and its pursuant legislation permitted—indeed, seemed to require—claims-making based on caste, the degree to which class and poverty matters were to be incorporated in movement agendas was a more indeterminate question. In the 1970s, the mobilization frames that were constructed proved to be predominantly class-based. For example, the Dalit Panthers emerged as a radical movement of urban slum-dwelling scheduled caste youth in Maharashtra. A substantial section of the Dalit Panthers embraced a discourse animated by the ideas of revolutionary Marxism, and although the movement did not involve armed struggle, it was a call to the dalit peoples to demand an improvement in their rapidly deteriorating conditions of life. In socialist magazines and through brief flirtations with Marxist groups, the Panthers expressed their total rejection of the ideology of the caste system and determined to break the reinforcing effects of the economic and social hierarchies, of which the dalits were at the very bottom. In other parts of the country, the increasingly assertive dalits threw in their lot with the Naxalites, a radical Marxist-Leninist group which organized armed struggles of the rural poor against the exploitation of the upper-caste landed classes and colluding state governments.[31]

Indeed, economic class continued to be the mainframe of Indian politics as Indira Gandhi and the Congress party surged into power in the 1972 general elections on the wave of the hugely successful manifesto "*Garibi Hatao!*"[32] which resounded deeply with the impoverished masses. Class-based populist strategies of mobilization around the program of nationalizing industries and imposing land reforms during the imposition of Emergency between 1975–77 are also indicative of the incentives for class mobilization inherent in the political opportunity structure. Emergent dalit movements adapted to this opportunity structure that opened up space for contentious political mobilization and simultaneously ensured its articulation through a class-based lens.

It was not until the late 1980s, when the Mandal Commission recommendations were resuscitated by V. P. Singh's government, however, that caste became an overtly political issue at the national level with significant electoral incentives for political parties mobilizing on that basis. Caste questions began to occupy center stage in national debates about modernity and citizenship in India. In the following years, the politics of identity continued to become increasingly important as the Babri Masjid was demolished and in its wake bloody communal riots (re)established religion as another live political issue. A notable feature of this new political opportunity structure is that it has generated not only identity-based social movements but has also prompted the direct quest for political power through electoral competition. In the state of Uttar Pradesh, for example, two main contenders for political power are the *Bahujan Samaj Party* (BSP, a dalit-based political party) and the *Bharatiya Janata Party* (BJP, a Hindu-right political party). On the one hand, the BSP seeks to defend its dalit constituency from co-optation by the BJP's upper-caste–dominated, all-encompassing Hindu fold; on the other hand, the BSP seeks to thwart the BJP's Hindu revivalist politics by projecting a secular front comprising the dalits, scheduled tribes, some lower castes and other members of religious minority groups, particularly Muslims. In the intertwining of the politics of caste and religion, dalit politics has been recast and redefined along these dimensions, but somewhere along this road, the focus on class and poverty as the important political issues of the day has been lost.

IDENTITY FORMATION AS STRATEGY TO DEAL WITH POVERTY

Given both the material reality of the intersections of untouchability and poverty, and the caste frame embodied in state policy, it should have been no surprise that movement politics looked to caste as a basis of mobilization. But what was less "predetermined" was how caste politics would confront class commonalities and differences. Would those organizing around dalit identities seek out or eschew alliances with other groups and, if the former, what would be the basis of such coalitions?

Right from the earliest days of post-Independence, it was clear that, instead of being passively defined by their poverty, dalits would be active agents in developing strategies to struggle for human dignity and equal opportunity. In consonance with Ambedkar's belief that the assertion of the scheduled castes must be undertaken by the scheduled castes themselves, the *All India Scheduled Castes Federation* was formed as a political party representing the interests of the scheduled castes specifically. Its poor showing in the first general election prompted Ambedkar to rethink the best strategy for mobilization. He began to seriously contemplate the possibility of an alliance bringing the low-castes (OBCs), tribals, and scheduled castes together. After all, he argued, "it is obvious that these three classes are naturally allies."[33] Not only were these groups either outcaste or on the fringes of an oppressive Hindu society, but they were also the most pauperized sections of the country's population.

This strategy of alliance building has gone through several kinds of articulation. After Ambedkar's death, the *Republican Party of India* (RPI) was formed as a broad-based political party to mobilize the scheduled castes as well as the scheduled tribes and OBCs. It committed itself to "organize the peasantry, the landless laborers, workers in factories and other wage earners" and under its banner agitations were organized to demand the effective implementation of the Minimum Wages Act 1948, improvement of urban slums, redistribution of idle and waste land to landless laborers, etc.[34] However, the RPI could not really win the allegiance of the non-scheduled caste poor. It faced the hegemonic and broad-based aggregative Congress party, which by the mid-60s had successfully built a strong base in rural India, particularly in the northern heartland. The Congress's mainly upper caste–upper class leadership had made enough concessions to woo the tribals, scheduled castes, and other weaker sections that comprised the rural poor.[35] Perhaps more significant was the fact that the RPI encountered impediments in the differences and divisions among the scheduled castes, the scheduled tribes and OBCs as distinct groups. Despite Ambedkar's observations about the economic and social interests they had in common, it turned out to be very difficult to construct a broad cross-caste, class-based coalition. Indeed, this, particular difficulty was to plague the dalit movement repeatedly in the future.

These early years proved to be a lesson in why alliances were not easily forged: The census in colonial India played a historic role in the social construction and categorization of particular groups on the basis of caste identity. Caste classifications implied the creation of separate identities and interests and spurred the formation of caste-based pressure groups and associations.[36] Ironically, this process was reinforced by the post-colonial state, which in its effort to do away with the historical burden of caste-based economic and social inequality has had to create separate caste-based categories of social-political identifications (e.g., scheduled castes and tribes versus OBCs) and separate structures of economic-political incentives. The Hindu social order based on graded inequality has also been vital to the feeling of separateness and competition among caste groups. Ambedkar had noted that "the Shudra, while he is anxious to pull down the Brahmin, is not prepared to see the Untouchables raised to his level. . . . The result is that there is nobody to join the Untouchable in his struggle. He is completely isolated. Not only is he isolated, he is opposed by the very classes who ought to be his natural allies."[37] Making political capital of these divisions have been India's political parties. In the late 1960s and through most of the 1970s, the scheduled castes remained a constituency of the Congress party, while the OBCs were divided in their support for socialist parties and right-wing political formations. This political divide has led to violence between dalits and OBCs on numerous occasions.[38] More recently, for example, there have been incidents of violence between supporters of the *Bahujan Samaj Party* (generally perceived as a party representing the interests of the dalits) and the *Samajwadi Party* (with its Yadav-dominated OBC constituency) in Uttar Pradesh.

A final factor of considerable importance relates to the disparate economic positions of dalits and OBCs, particularly in the rural economy. While dalits comprise disproportionate numbers of landless laborers, a growing number of small and middle cultivators are emerging from the ranks of the OBCs.[39] The challenge of the OBCs to the landed upper castes is only one of the sources of growing violence in states like Bihar. Causing great bitterness and animosity are the emerging disparities between dalits and OBCs.[40] It is worth noting here that the OBCs are a group composed of a great number and variety of low castes. Some of these castes (like the Yadav) have become much better off than the others—so much so that there is a distinction to be made between the *most backward classes* (MBCs) and the other backward classes.[41] This complex syndrome of causes has undermined prospects for cross-caste solidarity between the poor and the desperately impoverished and should caution against simplistic proposals for unity.

The identity "dalit" came into widespread currency in the mid-1970s through the Dalit Panther movement and the explosion onto center stage of a radical dalit literature. Though this identity was chosen deliberately by the Panthers and used proudly,[42] the strategic dilemmas of the earlier periods continued with reference to the question of the substance of "dalit" identity and its implications for social and political mobilization. Was it meant to symbolize the assertion of only the scheduled castes, or could it potentially weld together a coalition of all the socially marginalized and economically impoverished masses, all those who have been "broken, ground down by those above them in a deliberate and active way"?[43] The promise of the "dalit" identity lay in its epistemological and political capacity to forge a unity drawing on the material social experience of the subjects it sought to simultaneously represent and constitute.[44] It was asserted that "dalit is not a caste. He is a man exploited by the social and economic traditions of this century. He does not believe in God, Rebirth, Holy Books teaching separatism, Fate and Heaven because they have made him a slave. He does believe in humanism. Dalit is a symbol of change and revolution."[45]

These views did not find universal acceptance, nor did the articulation of such ideas result in the unified radical struggle of all the impoverished. Instead, the organization of the Dalit Panthers disintegrated under the stresses produced by divergent ideas among its leadership about the substance and direction of the dalit struggle. Namdeo Dhasal led the Marxist faction within the organization that favored a broad-based class struggle of various caste groups and a closer relationship with the revolutionary Naxalites. The Ambedkarite faction headed by Raja Dhale argued, to the contrary, that this class-based strategy would dilute the urgency of the concerns of the scheduled castes.[46] This meant an interpretation of dalit identity as representative of only the scheduled castes. In fact, it is this understanding of "dalit" that has stuck in most academic literature and social-political activism.

Still another strategy emerged in the middle of the next decade of the 1990s. Without explicitly referring to a class-based strategy for the mobilization of the impoverished, and rejecting the default position that the struggles of the dalits must be waged by dalits alone, this movement speaks in the majoritarian language of liberal democratic politics. It identifies a *bahujan samaj* (majority community) that does not deny the divisions and differences between its constitutive parts, yet hopes to contain the contradictions in the name of the numerical majority of the oppressed. It is aided significantly by the incentive of a direct route to capture of state power that its majority strength implies. This purposive political framing by the political party BSP draws inspiration from the ideas of Jotirao Phule in mid-nineteenth century Maharashtra, and Swami Achhutanand in early twentieth century Punjab and the United Provinces. These reformers had articulated the expression "*bahujan samaj*" to indicate that should the Untouchables and *shudras* (low castes) unite politically, they could comprise the majority of the population and be in a position to govern themselves.[47] The BSP is not only following through on the promise of the *bahujan*, but also responding to the logic of the changed political opportunity structure that is enabling of identity-based political mobilizations around caste and religion. Thus, it has sought a broad strategy of inclusiveness without denying the diversity and specificity of identities within its political constituency comprised of dalits, scheduled tribes, some OBC castes and religious minorities such as Muslims. The BSP's projection of itself as a dalit-based secular party is an attempt to challenge and subvert the logic of the upper-caste dominated Hindu revivalist BJP. Important questions remain, however. Is the *bahujan* identity merely one of political convenience, or is the practice of a *bahujan* politics shaping and constituting a cross-caste community of solidarity that the "dalit" frame has not been able to create? And what of poverty? Unfortunately, in doing away with the weaknesses of the "dalit" frame, the BSP has compromised the dalit movement's main virtue, i.e., its central focus on the urgent question of impoverishment. Given the threatening nature of globalization in terms of the shrinkage of state employment opportunities, reduction of social spending, and the rise in food prices, this neglect could be an egregious betrayal of the pauperized *bahujan*.

Finally, there have been efforts to unite the scheduled castes, low castes and tribal peoples under the broad banner of race. The *Dravida* movement began in the late nineteenth century as an appropriation of colonial discourse on the Brahmin-dominated Aryan invasion into the Indian subcontinent. This was a strategy to reject the Sanskritizing influence of the twice-born castes and to build in its place an egalitarian, ethnicized identity as the original inhabitants of the land. The *Self-Respect movement* was later founded by Periyar who had left the Congress arguing for a new society based on equality (*samadharma*) and a rejection of the caste system. The dravidian identity in particular, and the politics of race in general, have continued to inspire the formation of political parties and other social movements led by non-Brahmins in the southern states. The Dalit Panthers were deeply interested in the struggles of African Americans in the United States and named themselves after the Black Panther movement that emerged in 1966. Elsewhere, dalits see themselves as the black Untouchables of India.[48] Indeed, the politics of race remains significant as a category for the mobilization of dalits and other oppressed peoples, though it has never become a primary site of dalit struggle.

The following sections of this chapter will explore the accomplishments and limitations of three different kinds of dalit struggle for empowerment. Each has, in its time frame, become the rallying point for the mobilization of thousands of dalit peoples.

THE DALIT PANTHERS—FAILED ADAPTATION OF AN EMERGING RADICALISM

In 1972, hundreds of dalit youth raised their pens in a powerful protest against their dehumanizing poverty and the "Hindu feudal order."[49] Most of the Panther youths were children of poor peasants, landless laborers, or urban workers. As first-generation educated, yet continuing to experience hunger, unemployment, and social discrimination on account of their "untouchability," they mobilized in revolt against these oppressive economic and social conditions. Their voices rose from the slums and factories, teahouses and public libraries, exposing the inadequacies of Independence, developmentalism, and social justice. They demanded land redistribution through the just implementation of the land ceiling acts, control of food grain prices, daily minimum wages for laborers, benefits for unemployed dalits, confiscation of foreign capital, control of the means of production, the removal of casteist and communal prejudices in employment and educational institutions, and an equal treatment for all in the name of human dignity. The Panthers' Manifesto concluded that "true independence is one that is snatched forcibly out of the hands of the enemy. One that is like bits thrown to a helpless beggar is no independence."[50]

There was discernibly a vital disconnect between their revolutionary aspirations and the strategies they adopted for radical struggle. Instead of a revolutionary armed struggle, as one would perhaps expect from a reading of the Manifesto, theirs was a movement focused on developing a revolutionary consciousness by countering the ideological hegemony of the upper castes which, based on the ancient scriptures and religious-moral philosophy, legitimated the oppression of dalits. The young poets and writers of the Dalit Panthers publicized their trenchant critiques in socialist magazines and at dalit literary conferences. In their contestation of the ideological, moral, and cultural superstructure of the political-economic system, the Dalit Panthers adhered to a Gramscian brand of Marxism rather than a Marxist-Leninist approach to system change. They missed, however, a key insight of Gramscian Marxism: Although challenging discourses are necessary instruments of system change, this is inherently a long-term process and does not constitute a direct or immediate route to the achievement of desired outcomes. What becomes indispensable to bringing about actual change is the degree of political organization, the strength of political alliances, and the relations of force within a particular historical bloc of contention.[51] In these vital respects, the Dalit Panthers found themselves unprepared. They could not adjust to the political flux produced in the wake of the de-institutionalization of the Congress party, nor could they engage other important political actors who had become active as political space opened up at both the national and regional levels. They seemed hesitant to take any initiative beyond cultural activism.[52] Ultimately, organizational weaknesses and fundamental differences between its leadership on the direction that Panther activism should take split the organization from within. The inability also to develop a coherent agenda of class-caste struggle, the failure to build political alliances around such an agenda and to position itself in the rapidly changing scenario hastened the decline of the Dalit Panther movement.

The confusions of the Dalit Panthers during the pre-Emergency days extended well into the Emergency period and speak volumes about the paralysis that engulfed the organization. Instead of building relationships with political forces on the left or developing a viable economic program as an alternative to that of the Congress whose economic vision had over twenty-five years of independence yielded little to the dalits, the Panthers found themselves in support of Indira Gandhi's call to banish poverty, nationalize industries, etc. There was also a strong reluctance on the part of the faction led by Raja Dhale to participate in the rural struggles led by the radical Naxalites in Bihar and Andhra Pradesh who were at that time facing the inevitable problems in bringing the lower castes and dalits together in an armed struggle on the lines of a class war.[53] The conspicuous lack of effort by the Panthers themselves to organize the rural dalits has been a valid criticism of their political strategy. Certainly no dalit movement can be effective without mobilizing the vast masses of rural India.[54]

In the tradition of Ambedkar, the Dalit Panthers also harbored a deep suspicion of the mostly Brahminical leadership of the socialist parties. Jayprakash Narayan's socialist movement building on a rural-urban coalition failed to attract the Dalit Panthers. In organizational terms, too, the Dalit Panthers floundered. Though membership grew to around 25,000 by the mid-seventies, there were no cadre-training programs, no full-time workers for the organization, and no established method of generating resources for their work. Branches of the Dalit Panthers emerged spontaneously with an uncertain relationship to the main leadership or central commitments of the movement. The Dalit Panthers began to resemble a large, indisciplined crowd rather than a focused political organization. Finally, as the differences between Namdeo Dhasal and Raja Dhale became more irreconcilable, the Panthers underwent the first split in 1974, followed in quick succession by three more splits in 1975, 1976, and 1977.[55] During this period, its activism was broadly centered on organizing meetings, processions, and propaganda to protest atrocities against dalits. Over the next two decades, the Dalit Panthers were immersed in the struggle to defend the state assembly decision to rename the Marathwada University with the name of Dr. Ambedkar. This decision by the state assembly had sparked pogroms against dalits as villages were attacked, thousands of poor people fled their homes, and women were raped. Over time, some organizational splinters of the Panthers were absorbed into the Congress and mainstream politics.[56] There remained, however, several organizations by the name of Panther,[57] drawing inspiration from the effervescence of the 1970s and determined to continue the struggle of dalit assertion in the villages and slums of India. This strong "expressive link"[58] can be counted as one of the Panthers' main successes.

The other major success of the Panthers has been the vital legacy of dalit cultural assertion. Baburao Bagul, the prominent dalit poet, declared "dalit sahitya is not a literature of vengeance . . . dalit sahitya first promotes man's greatness and man's freedom and for that reason it is an historic necessity."[59] Beginning in the '70s in a major way, dalits have emerged as creators of culture in their own right. There is today a great profusion of novels, short stories and poems, debates on cultural memory and social change,[60] and considerable effort underway in various parts of the country to recover, record, and preserve dalit folk traditions.[61] Literary contributions by dalits have also included innovations of style and content. Using a starkly minimalist approach in the use of language, the poets and writers of the Dalit Panthers exploded their subaltern world into a complacent middle class, upper-caste consciousness. Namdeo Dhasal's collection of poems *Golpitha*, based on life in Bombay's red-light district, aroused considerable indignation among middle-class intelligentsia. The deliberate use of crude and direct language to represent the violence and stark poverty of their lives has often disturbed middle-class sensibilities. It is worth quoting from Vijay Tendulkar's[62] introduction to Dhasal's *Golpitha* poems:[63]

> In the calculations of the white collar workers, "no man's land" begins at the border of their world, and it is here that the world of Namdeo Dhasal's poetry of Bombay's Golpitha begins. This is the world of days of nights; of empty or half-full stomachs; of the pain of death; of tomorrow's worries; of men's bodies in which shame and sensitivity have been burned out; of overflowing gutters; of a sick young body, knees curled to belly against the cold of death, next to the gutter; of the jobless; of beggars; of pick-pockets; of Bairaga swamis; of Dada

bosses and pimps; of Muslim tombs and Christian crosses; of film star Rajesh Khanna and the gods on the peeling wall above the creaking bed.

Because refined cultural tastes and literary sophistication is generally defined by an upper class position, high culture is often used as an instrument to mark class boundaries and exclude lower classes from access to social and cultural commodities.[64] Thus, the confident and bold use of language, metaphor, and images unpalatable to the upper castes and upper classes testifies to the spirit of resistance among dalit writers. And in the creation of an original and authentic dalit literary work there is enacted the more radical practice of cultural assertion and social empowerment.

BAHUJAN SAMAJ PARTY—REDEFINITION AND THE POLITICS OF COMPROMISE

The BSP is the vehicle through which a certain class of dalits has aimed, through electoral victory, to capture State power and control public policy. It represents the efforts of a generation of dalits who have benefited from the State's development programs and affirmative action policies in education, employment, and politics. Despite the general failure of the postcolonial State in eradicating poverty or improving the quality of life for the vast majority of dalits, it is surely a portent of future possibilities that this small success (i.e., the emergence of a class of upwardly mobile and politically conscious dalits) has in its turn become an investment into a future of empowerment for the dalit masses. With an authoritative say in the allocation of resources and the direction of public policy, it may be possible to bring about the kind of fundamental changes that previous governments have generally been constrained to do. This trajectory of change, though bound to be gradual, could also be considerably deep, because inherent in the use of State power by dalits are multiple possibilities for crafting a future such as were unavailable before.

The launch pads for the BSP were two earlier organizations built by Kanshi Ram. The *All-India Backward and Minority Employees Federation* (BAMCEF), founded in 1973, was a forum to establish networks and spread an Ambedkarite social consciousness among educated dalit government employees in the west and north Indian states. This was followed in 1982 by the *Dalit Shoshit Samaj Sangharsh Samiti* (DS-4), which functioned as a "quasi-political party"[65] and mobilization organ of the dalit masses particularly in rural areas. It organized rallies and peoples' parliaments,[66] launched fundraising drives,[67] contested elections, and published its own newspaper, *The Bahujan Times*. This publication could not sustain itself and died out, followed by the weekly *Bahujan Sangathak*[68] which continues to be regularly published today in various languages under the auspices of the BSP. Formed in 1984, the BSP carefully propagates the political relevance of a *bahujan* (majority) community that includes, besides the dalits, various other poor and oppressed sections of the population such as the scheduled tribes, some OBC castes—particularly the MBCs, and Muslims. It is to enact and symbolize this community that BSP leaders refer to their work in terms of a movement, not that of a political party. For all practical purposes, however, the BSP is a dalit-based political party committed to the pursuit of power.

The *bahujan* identity has achieved some success in forging a unity between these different social groups on the strength of which the BSP has, in the '90s, emerged as an important national-level party, also winning a place in governing coalitions in Uttar Pradesh (UP) several times. Significantly, each time that the BSP has participated in a coalition government, there have been indications as to how tense and tenuous the *bahujan* identity can be. For instance, despite being coalition partners with the BSP in the 1993 UP government, Mulayam Singh Yadav's OBC-based *Samajwadi Party* (SP) worked to undermine the cohesiveness of the *bahujan* community by trying to wean away Muslim and MBC votes toward itself. Deeper problems surfaced as well, such as the resistance of the SP toward the appointment of dalits (instead of dominant OBCs, such as the *Yadavs*) in the bureaucracy; the growing resentment of the OBCs toward dalits in the rural economy leading to violent clashes between them, etc.[69] It came as no surprise when this coalition government was torn apart from within and collapsed. Two years later, in 1995, the BSP entered into a political alliance with the BJP to form the state government in UP. As an upper-caste–dominated Hindu revivalist party, the BJP happens to be the antithesis of everything the BSP purportedly stands for. It was inevitable that this partnership should be a "fragile and contradictory"[70] one; if the contradictions of the 1993 alliance were not readily apparent at the start, this time around the tensions stood out in bold relief. The BSP had to be alert to the BJP's potential to subvert the *bahujan* community by absorbing dalits and lower castes into its Hindu fold on the basis of an anti-Muslim agenda; it also had to defend its program for the empowerment of dalits from the stiff resistance put up by the BJP. This government collapsed by the end of that year, only to be resuscitated after the assembly polls of 1997. The endless recriminations continued between these two parties, particularly when the BJP attempted to reverse programs put in place by Chief Minister Mayawati, such as the recruitment of dalits to key positions in the bureaucracy, implementation of reservation quotas for MBCs, increased expenditures on health and family planning schemes for the dalits, etc. This government, too, did not manage to last its tenure.

There is one important difference between situations like those outlined above and that of the present government in UP. The 2002 post-election alliance (once again) between the BSP and the BJP is marked by a balance of power preponderantly in favor of the BSP and Chief Minister Mayawati. The BJP, having lost considerable political ground at the national level in the aftermath of the Gujarat riots and the assembly polls in several states, has high stakes in the survival of this particular government. For the time being at least, the BSP has been able to proceed with programs aimed at its *bahujan* constituency without strenuous opposition from its partner-in-government. However, a new strategy used by the BSP to counter the influence of the BJP has made vulnerable the authenticity of this very constituency. This is the practice of issuing party tickets to upper-caste candidates. Though it is not clear if this will be enough to wean away upper-caste Hindu votes from the BJP, it does open to question the integrity of the *bahujan* community. Will this dilute the BSP's commitment to the dalits and other backward groups? What about its commitment to secular politics? Will the carefully constructed unity of the *bahujan* and the agenda lying at its heart be compromised in the heat of electoral competition and identity politics? It is very likely that capitulation by the BSP on issues perceived by the dalits to be of great importance could cost the party their support. Clearer answers than this will emerge only with the passage of time.

There is one particular critique, however, that can be made with reasonable accuracy. This pertains to the BSP's abdication of the poverty question. Urgent issues at the heart of dalit welfare, such as land redistribution and minimum wages, have been generally ignored, and the single-minded quest for political power has not been accompanied by a comprehensive economic or social vision for the dalits and other constituent members of the *bahujan* community. When in power, the party has, on the one hand, focused on building a cultural consciousness by renaming roads and building statues to honor dalit leaders. This is important in itself, but given the neglect of fundamental structural questions, substantial improvements in the life conditions of dalit masses appear to be far from likely. On the other hand, the BSP has been busily engaged in a "transfer of power,"[71] as reservation quotas are filled and dalits appointed in large numbers to high administrative posts. Though this is a long-term system change underway, the direct benefits of this empowerment are more likely to go to the upwardly mobile, educated dalit class than to the vast numbers of impoverished and illiterate masses. Failure to attend to the critical question of poverty indicates the exercise of power without purpose—an egregious error for a dalit-based political party that has come so far.

NGOS AND SOFT RESISTANCE TO
THE STATE'S NEOLIBERAL AGENDA

In the 1990s, there has been a striking proliferation of non-governmental organizations (NGOs) as principled issue actors in contestation against the State. In the struggles of NGOs against this powerful actor, the repertoire of contention has generally included highly visible advocacy campaigns, information dissemination strategies, network building with other NGOs within the State and beyond its borders, and pressure tactics at domestic and international fora to embarrass and expose the State in the hope of compelling it to reconsider faulty policies, implement programs consistent with highly valued norms and to secure justice for its citizens.[72] While globalization processes have continued to intensify with the largely unaccountable decisions of State elites and representatives of transnational capital, there has been a growing disjuncture between its promised benefits and the very basic needs of poor peoples worldwide. This means that instead of an emancipatory force, globalization has become irrelevant, if not a direct threat to the security, welfare, and livelihood of millions of vulnerable people.

NGOs have been in the forefront of struggles to reform or reverse this alienating process. A reformist strand of NGO activism believes in the potential of capitalism to achieve greater social good, but acknowledges that unrestrained global capitalism generates inequities, subverts democracy, and creates conditions for instability and violence. In keeping with this philosophy, they press States for guarantees of basic incomes, protectionist measures for vulnerable social groups, and greater opportunities for such groups to participate in and benefit from globalization. In contrast, radical NGO activism sees globalization as inherently damaging to social democracy, economic justice, and cultural pluralism. Though deglobalization seems to be the only appropriate solution to these problems, radical opposition campaigns at the global level, such as the NGO-dominated battle of Seattle, have yet to gain a momentum critical enough to bring about a substantive reversal of the globalization project.[73]

A survey of NGO activism on the Indian stage similarly reveals the absence of radical politics, particularly on the question of dalit poverty. Among dalit-led NGOs, there seem to be two main foci of activism. On the one hand, there are organizations engaged in information dissemination, skill generation, and capacity building among dalits. These projects, like the ones conducted by the *Women's Voice* in Bangalore, enable impoverished dalit families to create avenues for self-employment and learn other technical skills. On the other hand, there are dalit-led NGOs such as *Drushti* in the Bidar district of Karnataka,[74] that are mobilizing the dalits for political agitation on questions such as minimum wages essential to their survival. This kind of activism has yielded some successes in parts of Andhra Pradesh, specifically in the coastal Andhra and Telengana regions.

Focused specifically on human rights issues such as the daily occurrence of atrocities against dalits (and therefore related only indirectly to the poverty question) are NGOs like the *Peoples Union for Civil Liberties* (PUCL) under a primarily non-dalit leadership.[75] Other NGOs such as the *Mazdoor Kisan Sangharsh Samiti* (MKSS)[76] seek to weld together a broad class-based coalition of workers, peasants and other toiling masses. But it has not demanded fundamental changes in the social and economic structures that produce poverty; nor is the MKSS agitation (focused on issues such as corruption, the need for transparency and the right to information) explicitly linked to the question of impoverishment. It is also unfortunate that there has been a general failure on the part of NGOs concerned about dalit peoples to galvanize an all-India social movement. The reasons for this are many; for example, the inability of activists to generate consensus on the question of according primacy to reservation policy and denunciation of caste atrocities *or* to issues relating to poverty.[77]

There is, however, one strategy that is being increasingly adopted by NGOs building transnational alliances with non-governmental organizations in other countries. Identified as a "boomerang"[78] pattern of activism, domestic NGOs working on the concerns of dalits are able to bring pressure to bear on the State by activating their transnational networks. Thus, member NGOs in other countries begin to pressure their respective states or, if necessary, an intergovernmental forum, so that these actors are in turn persuaded to urge, pressure, and compel the original State to implement the required policy changes. In this manner, domestic NGOs are able, by activating external sources of influence, to bring about the desired change when a solely domestic advocacy campaign would not have been sufficient. The growing preference for this kind of activism is evidenced by the proliferation of transnational linkages such as the *International Dalit Solidarity Network*, the World Council of Churches' *Dalit Solidarity Program,* and the growing participation of dalit activists in UN activities such as the *Seminar of Experts on Racism, Refugees and Multiethnic States* (Geneva, 1999), the *First Session of the Preparatory Committee for the World Conference against Racism* (Geneva, 2000), and the organization of international conferences such as the *Global Conference against Racism and Caste-based Discrimination* attended by social activists from South Africa, Japan, Germany, Denmark, Netherlands, United States, United Kingdom, Sri Lanka, Pakistan, Nepal, Bangladesh and of course India (New Delhi, March 2001). The agenda of dalit activists at this particular conference was the inclusion of the question of dalit rights onto the agenda at the *World Conference against Racism* to be held at Durban. It is worth noting that they were able to succeed in this endeavor.[79]

CONCLUSION

The gradual "transfer of power" to dalits, and the relentless diminution of their human dignity are simultaneous realities in post-colonial India. Dalit assertion and dalit acquiescence are the twin facets of dalit experience. The revolution underway is indeed "silent,"[80] "democratic,"[81] and "unfinished"[82]; it has also become increasingly bloody, especially in the countryside, as landed upper castes resort to violence to quell the rising tide of dalit empowerment. The dalit acquiescence, in its turn, is evident in the sometimes painfully modest expectations of the people from the government. The case of the ragpickers of Pune is an eloquent example of this extreme self-effacing behavior. Their only demand from the Pimpri-Chinchvad municipal corporation was that they be issued identity cards to ward off harassment at the hands of the police and middle-class urbanites. Not for them the temerity or the initiative to demand better housing in the slums or some alternative employment opportunities.[83]

This chapter has not explored the radical activism of dalit groups localized in a few regions of India. In rural Bihar and Andhra Pradesh, the agrarian struggles of the dalits continue under the Naxal banner; other local struggles are waged by dalits on land-related questions, such as the struggle for the *Panchama* land in Tamil Nadu[84] or the struggle for the *Gairan* land in Maharashtra.[85] In states with long-standing Communist Party–dominated governments such as West Bengal and Kerala, the condition of dalits in the rural economy is better on most counts. Still, much remains to be done even in these oases of relative security. For instance, left parties have been unable to take up the concerns of the urban unorganized sector in any consistent fashion. The party executive committees are also skewed in favor of the upper castes.[86]

This chapter has focused rather, on three examples of the more "mainstream" forms of activism in which dalits have been engaged: the erstwhile Dalit Panther movement, the BSP party organization, and NGO politics targeting conditions among low caste groups. The picture these three cases paint is mixed: On the one hand, the Dalit Panthers as a political movement rapidly lost steam, but on the other hand they spawned a cultural effervescence that continues with great vitality and promise. Similarly with the BSP: On the one hand, the party demonstrated that dalit political leadership can mobilize large vote banks that can have significant electoral clout at the state level; on the other, the electoral logic of democratic politics can lead to alliances that undermine the representation of dalit interests and voice. This dual tale applies as well to the recent history of NGOs which have, on the one hand, served a vital role in bringing human rights abuses into the open, and on the other hand been frustrated by the limitations of the patchwork service functions of nonprofit philanthropic work even as vast structural inequalities remain in place.

Perhaps most worrisome is the possibility that the historic moment amenable to a consideration of mass poverty and social justice may have lapsed. The failures, the compromises, and soft resistance of social movements, political parties, and NGOs indicate that for one reason or another, the fundamental economic and social questions relevant to the security and welfare of dalits are being sidetracked. Our own review, regrettably, has not revealed otherwise.

NOTES

1. National Commission to Review the Working of the Constitution; A Consultation Paper on the Pace of Socio-Economic Change under the Constitution, Chair: Justice

Dr. K. Ramaswamy, May 11, 2001, chapter 9, 5 (http://lawmin.nic.in/ncrwc/final report/v2b1-4.htm).

2. Ira N. Gang, Kunal Sen, and Myeong-Su Yun, "Caste, Ethnicity, and Poverty in Rural India," Department of Economics, Rutgers University, School of Development Studies, University of East Anglia and the Department of Economics, Tulane, February 2004 (http://oll.temple.edu/economics/Seminars/GangSenYun-IndiaPoverty Caste.pdf).

3. Human Rights Watch, "Broken People; Caste Violence against India's Untouchables," New York, March 1999. Summarizing this nexus between caste and poverty in India's "heartland" of Uttar Pradesh, Valerie Kozel and Barbara Parker write that the vast majority of respondents, rich and poor alike, saw social identity (low caste) as a strong predictor of "who is and is not poor, who is illiterate, who is employed in low-paid low-status agricultural labour, and who lives in poorly constructed housing with limited access to basic services." Kozel and Parker, "A Profile and Diagnostic of Poverty in Uttar Pradesh," *Economic and Political Weekly*, January 25, 2003. None of this is to suggest that there has not been change. In a recent survey of Rajasthan in which he discusses the emergence of a new strata of "political entrepreneurs," Anirudh Krishna writes: "Caste continues to be a primary source of social identity in these villages, people live in caste-specific neighborhoods, and the clothes that they wear reveal their caste identity. Yet insofar as political organization is concerned, caste no longer has primary importance." Krishna, "What Is Happening to Caste? A View from Some North Indian Villages," *Journal of Asian Studies* 62, no. 4 (November 2003): 1171–93.

4. See S. K. Thorat and R. S. Deshpande, "Caste System and Economic Inequality: Economic Theory and Evidence," in *Dalit Identity and Politics*, ed. Ghanshyam Shah (New Delhi: Sage Publications India Pvt. Ltd., 2001), for an excellent overview of the economic literature dealing with the economic consequences of caste. For an application of the neo-classical approach to the caste system, see George Akerlof, "The Theory of Social Customs of which Unemployment May Be One Consequence," *Quarterly Journal of Economics* 94, no. 4 (June 1980); George Akerlof, "The Economics of Caste and of Rat Race and Other Woeful Tales," *Quarterly Journal of Economics* 90, no. 4 (November 1976); and Deepak Lal, ed., *"Hindu Equilibrium," Cultural Stability and Economic Stagnation*, vol. 1 (Oxford: Clarendon Press, 1988).

5. See, for example, E. M. S. Namboodiripad, "Caste, Classes and Parties in Modern Political Development," *Social Scientist*, November 1977, and B. T. Ranadive, "Caste, Class and Property Relations," *Economic and Political Weekly*, February 1997.

6. To mention only a few sources, see Census of India 1991; National Sample Surveys over the years—particularly the rural labor inquiry reports, the landholding surveys and the employment/unemployment surveys; Second Backward Classes Commission (Venkatswamy report) 1986: 2 volumes, Government of Karnataka.

7. This is the finding of forty IAS officers in several villages across the country in 1995. See Sanjay Sinha, "Profile of the Poorest among Poor," *The Administrator* XLII (January–March 1997): 173–83.

8. See Thorat and Deshpande, 57–71.

9. Scheduled castes in India (data sheet): Planning Commission (Backward classes and Tribes Division), Government of India, November 2000.

10. Minimum Wages Act 1948; Zamindari Abolition Act 1952; Untouchability Offences Act, 1955 and the Protection of Civil Rights Act, 1976; Bonded Labor System

(Abolition) Act 1976; SC and ST (Prevention of Atrocities) Act, 1989. These are the more prominent among the myriad legislations designed to empower the dalits and other impoverished sections of the population which are mostly the low castes comprising the OBCs. There are also the justiciable fundamental rights guaranteed in the Constitution and the nonjusticiable Directive Principles that are supposed to guide State policy in its program of social justice.

11. See Oliver Mendelsohn and Marika Vicziany, *The Untouchables: Subordination, Poverty and the State in Modern India* (Cambridge: Cambridge University Press, 1998), 30–36.

12. P. Sainath, *Everybody Loves a Good Drought* (New Delhi: Penguin Publications, 1996), 123; Tangraj, *Dalit in India* (Mumbai: Vikas Adhyayan Kendra), 23.

13. For an account of the land reform project in Uttar Pradesh and the survival strategies of several generations of an impoverished and powerless dalit family, see Siddharth Dube, *In the Land of Poverty: Memoirs of an Indian Family 1947–97* (New York: Zed Books Ltd., 1998), chapter 12.

14. Scheduled castes in India (data sheet): Planning Commission (Backward Classes and Tribes Division) Government of India, November 2000.

15. See Gopal Guru, "Education as Baby-sitting," *The Hindu*, May 27, 2000.

16. See Mendelsohn and Vicziany, *The Untouchables*, chapter 6, for an account of the mobilization of workers in the stone quarries of Faridabad. About eight of every ten laborers in these quarries is a dalit—the others are tribal peoples. This struggle faltered in the face of the failure of the Central Government to enforce the laws that already existed; the blatant contempt by Haryana's state government of Supreme Court directives in favor of the laborers; and the corrupt nexus between the ruling party in Haryana and the contractors.

17. Mahasweta Devi, "Contract Labor or Bonded labor?" *Economic and Political Weekly* 16, no. 23, June 6, 1981. For an insight into the extreme exploitation of people at the intersection of low caste, low class, and gender, see also a collection of narratives on the exploitation of impoverished dalit and tribal women. Mahasweta Devi, *Outcaste: Four Stories*, trans. Sarmistha Datta Gupta (Calcutta: Seagull Books Pvt. Ltd., 2002).

18. See, for example, the editorial "Bombay: Whose Grandfather's Property?" in *Dalit Voice* (April 1–15, 1983), a fortnightly newspaper published in Bangalore, Karnataka. Reprinted in Barbara Joshi ed., *Untouchable! Voices of the Dalit Liberation Movement* (London: Zed Books, 1986), 69–71. In 1999, one such eviction effort in Bombay made headlines as a dalit woman whose little hut was demolished hit Commissioner Khairnar in anger and desperation.

19. Vijendra Kumar, *Rise of Dalit Power in India* (Jaipur: ABD Publishers, 2001), 7. Also see Tangraj, *Dalit in India*, 23.

20. Mendelsohn and Vicziany, *The Untouchables*, 266–68.

21. Jan Breman (*Wage Hunters and Gatherers: Search for Work in the Urban and Rural Economy of South Gujarat* [Delhi: Oxford University Press, 1994], 8) has pointed out that "it seems reasonable to assume that workers in the formal sector are mostly recruited from the higher social strata whose education level is much higher; conversely, low social position and informal sector activities are likely to go together."

22. Advocacy for non–farm-related, self-employment opportunities for dalits is gaining momentum in India, but there is need to pay greater attention to the problems peculiar to the dalit situation. See, for example, Martin Ravallion, "What Is

Needed for a More Pro-Poor Growth Process in India," *Economic and Political Weekly*, March 25, 2000. It should be mentioned here that dalits are taking the initiative in establishing their own sources of credit and finance, e.g., Siddharth Bank (Pune), Ambedkar Bank (Jalgaon), and the Dalit Chambers of Commerce (Ahmedabad). Because they are very recent phenomena, there are no concrete evaluations available of these institutions.

23. See Narayan Survey, *Sanad* (Mumbai: Granthali, 1987), 34. Dalit writers such as Surajmal Chaun also echo this sentiment. See his autobiography, *Gehu Ki Roti* (Hindi).

24. See Arjun Dangle, ed., *Poison Bread* (New Delhi: Orient Longman, 1983).

25. Myron Weiner, "The Struggle for Equality: Caste in Indian Politics," in *The Success of India's Democracy*, ed. Atul Kohli (Cambridge: Cambridge University Press, 2001).

26. "Low castes" refers to the vast number of castes subsumed under the nomenclature *Shudras* (those other than the twice-born Hindu castes), but even so, the low castes are positioned as a group a rung above the Untouchables in the caste hierarchy.

27. On this point, see Nicholas B. Dirks, *Castes of Mind: Colonialism and the Making of Modern India* (Princeton, N.J.: Princeton University Press, 2001), 281.

28. Parliamentary Debates, vol. XII–13 (part II), col. 9006.

29. See Christophe Jaffrelot, *India's Silent Revolution: The Rise of the Lower Castes in North India* (New York: Columbia University Press, 2003), 228. Various states, however, went ahead with reservation for OBCs. In this regard, the southern states were much more progressive than other parts of the country.

30. With this in mind, Ambedkar had argued in favor of separate electorates for the scheduled castes. He was opposed to Gandhi, who advocated that the scheduled castes be called "harijans" (literally "God's people") to be incorporated into a reformed Hindu fold. This position denied that the scheduled castes represented a distinct political constituency. Ultimately, the Poona Pact (1932) was signed with Ambedkar conceding the demand for separate electorates, achieving in its place the right of reserved seats on elected assemblies.

31. Mendelsohn and Vicziany, *The Untouchables*, 204.

32. Literally meaning "Remove Poverty!"

33. B. R. Ambedkar, "Untouchables or the Children of India's Ghetto," in *Writings and Speeches,* vol. 5, compiled by Vasant Moon (Bombay: Government of Maharashtra 1989), 115–16. Cited in Gail Omvedt, *Reinventing Revolution: New Social Movements and the Socialist Tradition in India* (New York: M. E. Sharpe, Inc., 1993), 51.

34. See Sudha Pai, *Dalit Assertion and the Unfinished Democratic Revolution: The Bahujan Samaj Party in Uttar Pradesh* (New Delhi: Sage Publications India Pvt. Ltd., 2002), 75–78, for a description of the manifesto of the RPI and an analysis of the reasons behind the decline of the party and, ultimately, its absorption into the Congress.

35. See Omvedt, *Reinventing Revolution*, 52.

36. For a detailed history of colonial ethnography and the role of the census in objectifying the caste system, see Bernard Cohn, *Colonialism and Its Forms of Knowledge: The British in India* (Princeton, N. J.: Princeton University Press, 1996), and Dirks, *Castes of Mind*. On the inclusion of caste in the Government of India 2001 Census, there has been a renewed debate over these questions—see Nandini Sundar, "Caste as Census Category: Implications for Sociology," *Current Sociology* 48, no. 3 (July 2000).

37. Cited in Dube, *In the Land of Poverty*, 210.

38. For example, in the 1974 Worli riots, which occurred on the occasion of Parliamentary by-elections in central Bombay, dalits supporting the Panthers clashed with the OBCs who supported the Shiv Sena. See Omvedt, *Reinventing Revolution*, 50–51.

39. This is not to say that all dalits are landless laborers in the rural economy, or that all landless laborers are composed of the dalits. See Mendelsohn and Vicziany, *The Untouchables*, 56.

40. The formation of caste-based militias is an indicator of the hostility and violence that engulfs the rural economy in Bihar. The Yadavs (OBC) have their Lorik Sena, the Kurmis (OBC) their Bhumi Sena, the Bhumihars (upper-caste dominant land-owning class) have their Brahmarshi Sena. The dalits have generally thrown in their lot with the Lal Sena (Red Army) of the Naxalites, who are the revolutionary Marxist-Leninist groups.

41. In 1971, the first Bihar Backward Classes Commission identified 93 castes as MBCs. In Uttar Pradesh, the Most Backward Classes Commission was appointed in 1975, which submitted its report in 1977 identifying 36 castes as MBC, while 18 castes were noted as being OBC. The criteria for the UP Commission were the significance/insignificance of landed property, representation in the state administration, etc. It was revealed that MBCs were even less represented in the lower rungs of the bureaucracy than the dalits. See Jaffrelot, *India's Silent Revolution*, 250–51. For an account of the progress made in the southern states in terms of reservation policies for OBCs and the identification of MBCs, see pp. 237–49.

42. See Eleanor Zelliot, *From Untouchable to Dalit: Essays on the Ambedkar Movement* (New Delhi: Manohar Publications, 1992), 267.

43. This is the literal meaning of the term "dalit." See Eleanor Zelliot's argument that there is inherent in the word a rejection of pollution, karma, and justified caste hierarchy. Zelliot, *From Untouchable to Dalit*, 267.

44. Gopal Guru, "The Language of Dalit-Bahujan Political Discourse," in *Dalit Identity and Politics*, ed. Ghanshyam Shah (New Delhi: Sage Publications India Pvt. Ltd., 2001), 102.

45. Gangadhar Pantawane, founder-editor of *Asmitadarsh* (mirror of identity), the chief organ of dalit literature. Cited in Zelliot, *From Untouchable to Dalit*, 268.

46. The debate within the Dalit Panthers organization was framed around a choice between a Marxist or an Ambedkarite position. As Omvedt has pointed out, this obviously overlooked Ambedkar's own ideas about creating an allied struggle of various oppressed caste groups. See Omvedt, *Reinventing Revolution*, 54.

47. See Jaffrelot, *India's Silent Revolution*, chapters 5 and 6.

48. See V. T. Rajshekhar, *Dalit: The Black Untouchables of India*, 3rd edition (Atlanta: Clarity Press, 1995).

49. The Dalit Panthers' Manifesto (Bombay 1973) declared that Hindu feudal rule has been much more ruthless in suppressing the dalits than either the Muslim rulers or British imperialists. It further argued that all the arteries of production, the bureaucracy, judiciary, army, and police forces are in the hands of Hindu feudal landlords, capitalists, and religious leaders, enabling them to serve their vested interests.

50. See the Panthers' Manifesto in Joshi, ed., *Untouchable!*, 141–147.

51. For Antonio Gramsci's selected writings on hegemony, relations of force, and the idea of the historic bloc, see David Forgacs, ed., *An Antonio Gramsci*

Reader: Selected Writings, 1916–1935 (New York: Schocken Books Inc., 1988), 189–221.

52. On the important issue of preparedness for radical struggle, Omvedt writes that "Much of the Panther elan had been built up in dialog and clash with the brahmanic elite, its figureheads, and its symbols; now they seemed unable to move beyond this. They found themselves the center of radical attention in a way for which they were unprepared." Omvedt, *Reinventing Revolution*, 53.

53. See Sumanta Banerjee, *In the Wake of Naxalbari: A History of the Naxalite Movement in India* (Calcutta: Subarnarekha Publications, 1980).

54. See Lata Murugkar, *Dalit Panther Movement in Maharashtra: A Sociological Appraisal* (Bombay: Popular Prakashan, 1991), 100.

55. For a detailed account of the organizational dilemmas that plagued the Dalit Panthers, see Murugkar, *Dalit Panther Movement in Maharashtra*, chapter 4.

56. Guru, "Language of Dalit-Bahujan Political Discourse."

57. For instance, an organization by the name of Dalit Panther was born in Uttar Pradesh in the 1980. They were a militant group using fiery rhetoric and violent demonstrations to press their claims. By 1986, however, the UP Panthers had waned and its leadership arrested on charges of threat to national security. See Vivek Kumar and Uday Sinha, *Dalit Assertion and the Bahujan Samaj Party: A Perspective from Below* (Lucknow: Bahujan Sahitya Sansthan, 2001), 53.

58. Omvedt, *Reinventing Revolution,* 57.

59. Quoted in Zelliot, *From Untouchable to Dalit,* 278.

60. See, for example, D. R. Nagaraj, *The Flaming Feet: A Study of the Dalit Movement in India* (Bangalore: South Forum Press and ICRA, 1993) for an insight into the social and political debates embedded in the emerging dalit literary oeuvre in Karnataka.

61. For an account of the profusion of works of dalit folk traditions, see Zelliot, *From Untouchable to Dalit,* 317–33.

62. A major playwright and dramatist in Marathi theatre.

63. Quoted in Zelliot, *From Untouchable to Dalit,* 277.

64. For a defining work on the social critique of the judgment of taste, see Pierre Bourdieu, *Distinction: A Social Critique of the Judgement of Taste,* trans. Richard Nice (London: Routledge, 1986).

65. Pai, *Dalit Assertion and the Unfinished Democratic Revolution,* 91.

66. Kanshi Ram argued that the peoples' Parliament would provide dalits with "the opportunity for debate and discussion on their burning problems which are side-tracked in the national Parliament. . . . Such a debate by peoples' Parliament without any power will be a constant reminder for the oppressed and exploited masses to make the national Parliament a truly representative one as early as possible." Cited in Kumar and Sinha, *Dalit Assertion and the Bahujan Samaj Party,* 62.

67. For a fascinating account of Kanshi Ram's fund-raising strategies, pursued independently of big business support by going directly to the impoverished masses for a single rupee per head in donation, see Kumar and Sinha, *Dalit Assertion and the Bahujan Samaj Party,* 65–69.

68. *The Bahujan Times* had a precursor in *The Oppressed Indian,* a monthly magazine published in English by the BAMCEF. This too faded away eventually.

69. See Pai, *Dalit Assertion and the Unfinished Democratic Revolution,* chapter 4.

70. Pai, *Dalit Assertion and the Unfinished Democratic Revolution,* 178.

71. Jaffrelot, *India's Silent Revolution*, v.

72. See Margaret Keck and Kathryn Sikkink, *Activists Beyond Borders: Advocacy Networks in International Politics* (Ithaca, N.Y.: Cornell University Press, 1998).

73. For a comprehensive discussion of the multiple dimensions of globalization, see Jan Aart Scholte, *Globalization: A Critical Introduction* (New York: Palgrave, 2000). For the distinctions between reformist and radical responses to globalization, see pp. 33–39.

74. *Drushti* is led by Rev. Karkaer Namdeo. There are also several dalit-based NGOs in Andhra Pradesh such as those under the leadership of Chinnaih in Hyderabad.

75. Other prominent human rights NGOs are, for example, the *Society of Depressed People for Social Justice* and the *All India Human Rights Group*.

76. Active in the state of Rajasthan in western India. See Aruna Roy, "Democracy, Ethics and the Right to Information," Dept. of Education, Delhi University, December 19, 2000.

77. See V. Suresh, "Dalit Movement in India," in *Region, Religion, Caste, Gender and Culture in Contemporary India,* vol. 3, ed. T. V. Satyamurthy (New Delhi: Oxford University Press, 1996), 379.

78. See Keck and Sikkink, *Activists without Borders*, 13.

79. At Durban, however, the *National Campaign on Dalit Human Rights* was not able to make much headway with their demand for an international recognition of dalit rights. For an analysis of the unpreparedness of dalit activists to deal with hard-nosed intergovernmental diplomacy at Durban, see *Human Rights Features,* "Caste Away—or How the Dalit Cause Was Lost in Durban," www.hrdc.net/sahrdc/hrfeatures/HRF44.htm (accessed July 25, 2003).

80. Jaffrelot, *India's Silent Revolution*.

81. Gail Omvedt, *Dalits and the Democratic Revolution: Dr. Ambedkar and the Dalit Movement in Colonial India* (New Delhi: Sage Publications India Pvt. Ltd., 1994).

82. Pai, *Dalit Assertion and the Unfinished Democratic Revolution*.

83. Gopal Guru's interview with the ragpickers of Pimpri-Chinchvad, February 21, 2001.

84. S. Anandhi, *Land to the Dalits: Panchama Land Struggle in Tamil Nadu* (Bangalore: Indian Social Institute, 2000).

85. Guru, "Language of Dalit-Bahujan Political Discourse."

86. Ross Mallick, *Development Policy of a Communist Government: West Bengal since 1977* (Cambridge: Cambridge University Press, 1993).

6

Red in Tooth and Claw?

Looking for Class in Struggles over Nature

Amita Baviskar

Authoritative commentaries on "environmental movements" in India generally agree that these movements represent an "environmentalism of the poor." It is believed that, unlike the post-materialist concerns driving First World environmentalism, Southern mobilization around the use and abuse of nature is intrinsically linked to issues of material distributive justice. Struggles over natural resources are therefore perceived as combining shades of both "green" ecological concerns and "red" class politics. This paper draws on a comparative analysis of contemporary social movements in India to point out that there are diverse struggles over "green" issues or sustainable natural resource use, of which only some are identified as "environmental movements." However, the practice of representing a social movement as "environmental" is not arbitrary; it is closely related to the nature of capital that a movement confronts, and to the intervention of metropolitan[1] audiences. The representation of a social movement as "environmental" shapes the process of making claims in both enabling and disabling ways. In order to explore the political implications of adopting the environmentalist mantle, we need to locate environmental movements within a discursive framework constituted by unequal structures of global political economy, while also examining the negotiation of meanings between the different groups that constitute social movements. Through this account, I attempt to show that the complex, often contradictory, relationships between the "red" and "green" aspects of environmental movements defy categorization. To provoke further reflection on what has now become conventional wisdom on this subject, this paper ends by arguing that the defining feature of "environmental movements" in India is not that they represent an "environmentalism of the poor," but that they emerge through collaborations with middle-class actors and audiences.

ENVIRONMENTALISM OF THE POOR

Ramachandra Guha, one of the foremost scholars of environmentalism in India and abroad, notes that the "Indian environmental movement" is an umbrella term that covers a multitude of local conflicts, initiatives, and struggles where the poor confront the rich in order to protect the scarce, diminishing natural resources that are needed for survival.[2] Beginning with the Chipko movement in the Garhwal Himalaya in the 1970s and reaching global prominence with the movement against the Narmada dams in the next two decades, India has witnessed a series of popular movements in defense of community rights to natural resources. According to Guha, "most of these conflicts have pitted rich against poor: logging companies against hill villagers, dam builders against forest tribal communities, multinationals deploying trawlers against traditional fisherfolk in small boats. Here one party (e.g., loggers and trawlers) seeks to step up the pace of resource exploitation to service an expanding commercial-industrial economy, a process which often involves the partial or total dispossession of those communities who earlier had control over the resource in question, and whose own patterns of utilization were (and are) less destructive of the environment."[3] Since the agents of more intensive resource exploitation are supported by the state, local communities have no recourse except direct action in protest against injustice. Guha argues that these movements address a new form of class conflict, one rooted in a "lopsided, iniquitous and environmentally destructive process of development in independent India."[4]

According to Madhau Gadgil and Guha, this pattern of development can be attributed to the dominance in Indian society of an "iron triangle" of politicians and bureaucrats who use public resources to extend patronage to, and receive support from, industry, large landowners, and urban middle class populations. These resource "omnivores" live on islands of prosperity at the cost of India's vast numbers of "ecosystem people" who are submerged in a sea of poverty. Faced with a diminishing resource base, their subsistence rendered more and more precarious, ecosystem people—the rural landless and marginal farmers, artisans, pastoralists, tribal groups, and fisherfolk—end up becoming "ecological refugees," joining the ranks of impoverished migrant laborers in urban slums. Whereas their economic and political power enables the omnivores to insulate themselves from the effects of ecological crisis, the poor ecosystem people experience it directly in their everyday lives. This deepening of social disparities is a direct consequence of the subversion of democratic processes by omnivores. By centralizing state power in the hands of technical and scientific experts, justified in the name of "national interest," India's rich traditions of decentralized governance, especially in the sphere of natural resource management, have been dismantled.[5] When threatened ecosystem people unite and mobilize to assert their rights to resources, they question not only the distribution of resources, but the very premises of power and knowledge on which state policies are based. These structures of decision-making and the forms of knowledge that they privilege, are challenged by the "environmentalism of the poor."[6]

Guha contrasts Indian "environmentalism of the poor" with First World environmentalism, especially in the United States. In the United States, environmental movements have predominantly emerged in a postmaterialist or postindustrial society where questions about the "quality of life" are not rooted in the politics of production but in forms of consumption. Thus nature is not primarily valued as the source of material subsistence but in terms of its aesthetic, spiritual, and moral qualities, which have been promoted through the wilderness movement. The variety of environmentalism shaping the wilderness movement does not question the social and ecological basis of American affluence, its dependence on a global network of social exploitation and resource extraction. In contrast, Indian environmentalism links issues of ecology with questions of human rights, ethnicity, and distributive justice. This rootedness in issues of subsistence and survival has "also prompted a thoroughgoing critique of consumerism and of uncontrolled economic development." Guha acknowledges that his broad-brush comparison needs to be qualified by taking into account the environmental justice movement in the U.S. and versions of the wilderness movement among wildlife conservationists in India. But "these caveats notwithstanding, there remains, on the whole, a clear distinction in terms of origins and forms of articulation, between how environmental action characteristically expresses itself, in the North and in the South."[7]

The work of Guha and Gadgil translates into scholarly terms the ideological position espoused by several leading environmentalists in India. The key statement that "environmental degradation and social injustice are two sides of the same coin"[8] is endorsed by Anil Agarwal of the non-governmental organization (NGO) Centre for Science and Environment, as well as by Medha Patkar, leader of the *Narmada Bachao Andolan* [Movement to Save the Narmada] and Father Tom Kocherry of the Kerala Fishworkers' Forum. The need to assert a "red" agenda for Indian environmentalism, and the anxiety to maintain a distance from First World environmentalism, stems also from the desire to establish a link with Indian socialism. Indian environmentalism has always been suspect in the eyes of the organized Indian Left which, by and large, still subscribes to the notion that the development of capital-intensive technologies is a progressive trend. The two Communist Parties of India, in particular, support a model of industrial development led by a centralized state and either ignore concerns about ecological degradation or see them as inevitable costs attached to the quest for development. Indian environmentalists' disenchantment with the industrial-urban complex is perceived by many leftist groups as either atavist (regressing to a rural past) or elitist (affluent groups out of touch with the problems of the Indian working class). The fact that a major section of Indian environmentalism lays claim to the Gandhian values of ecological prudence and frugality, and to the Gandhian model of decentralized democracy at the level of the village,[9] is another ground for conflict, given the Indian Left parties' historic hostility to Gandhi. The claim that the sustainability of natural resource use (the ecological question) is intrinsically dependent on the social relations of ownership, control and management (the equity question) is thus a bid to recover a submerged stream of socialist thought[10] so as to repudiate environmentalism's associations with affluent consumers.

The claims about an "environmentalism of the poor" are made with reference to certain social movements, most notably the Chipko and Narmada struggles, but also to movements such as the *Chilika Bachao Andolan* [Movement to Save Chilika Lake] against intensive aquaculture, the Kerala Fishworkers' Forum's campaign against mechanized trawlers, the mobilization against eucalyptus plantations on common lands in Karnataka, and several smaller campaigns against dams, power projects, and military installations. While there has so far been a consensus among environmentalists that these movements combine "red" and "green" aspects, this consensus has not been an easy one to forge. Not only has their ideological formulation been ignored or dismissed by mainstream "red" political activists, with only a few Marxist-Leninist or Maoist factions willing to enter into a discussion with environmentalists, but even scholars of these movements have struggled to come to terms with the complexity of ideologies that the movements represent. Gail Omvedt argues that the shift away from the earlier class-based movements towards those of dalits, farmers, women, and *adivasis* should be understood as an attempt to redefine the sphere of economic production within which exploitation occurs.[11] She notes that rural movements in India are wary of being labeled "environmentalist," yet she goes on assert that "the survival movements of the rural poor" in India constitute "new green movements."[12] Guha resolves the difference between how villagers in the Garhwal Himalaya perceive their struggle, and how it is understood by others, by noting that the Chipko movement has two different faces—one "public" and the other "private." According to Guha, although Chipko is not an environmental movement and is best described as peasant resistance, it has gained popular legitimacy by its use of the formal ideology of environmentalism and Gandhian *satyagraha* (non-violent resistance). In the successful fusion of its "private" and "public" aspects lies the strength of Chipko.[13]

The politics of naming movements as "environmental" or otherwise is not settled quite so easily. I have argued elsewhere[14] that the representation of social movements as "environmentalist" emerges from a discursive encounter between different groups within the movement and their supporters. The multiple contending meanings that different groups bring to the terrain of struggle are negotiated and new understandings created in an ongoing process of dialogue between unequally situated actors. In the case of the anti-dam struggle in the Narmada valley, I have pointed out that "there is a difference between people's perception of what they are fighting for—basic subsistence denied by the state, and the claims made by intellectuals who postulate that 'indigenous' resistance is a comprehensive critique of development based on the 'traditional' adivasi [tribal] way of life, distinguished by its reverence for nature and simplicity—values that challenge the dominant worldview's desire for mastery over nature and material wealth. Although the ideology that perceives environmental conflict in terms of sustainability is external to *adivasi* consciousness, it is employed strategically to gain the sympathy of urban supporters."[15] As I shall discuss later, the "strategic essentialism"[16] of metropolitan activists who represent poor *adivasi* practices as innately environmentalist has political implications that need to be considered more carefully. The case for the "environmentalism of the poor" becomes quite confused when we examine the diversity of grounded struggles over nature in India today. The next section analyzes the current state of some significant social movements in order to illustrate the inherent problems in assuming an identity between "red" and "green" issues in the Indian context.

REVISITING CHIPKO, NARMADA, AND OTHER ENVIRONMENTALIST ICONS

The Chipko movement, India's first celebrated environmental struggle, started in the early 1970s and pitted hill villagers against state forestry policies that gave priority to commercial exploitation over subsistence use.[17] The Forest Department's replacement of the mixed deciduous forests with pine plantations in the Garhwal region undermined an economy where forests provided fuel, fodder, timber, and many other basic requirements. Protest in the hills was marked by the large-scale involvement of women, leading some scholars to claim that Chipko was an "ecofeminist" movement.[18] The campaign to manage forests for guaranteeing subsistence usufruct acquired an explicitly ecological dimension after the devastating floods of 1970, which brought into public consciousness the links between deforestation, soil erosion, floods, and landslides. A key element in Chipko ideology since then was opposition to commercial tree felling on both ecological and social grounds. Of the diverse ideological streams comprising the Chipko movement,[19] the most well-known is associated with Sunderlal Bahuguna, the charismatic saintly figure who has spread the Chipko message in India and abroad through his tireless *padayatras* (journeys on foot) across the Himalaya, fasts, lectures, and writing. Bahuguna's indefinite fast in 1981, demanding a total ban on commercial felling above an altitude of 1,000 meters, was a major success for the movement. It was in response to this event that the government imposed a fifteen-year moratorium on commercial forestry in the region.[20]

In the 1980s, the Chipko movement subsided, with only a small section associated with Bahuguna continuing to protest against the construction of the Tehri dam. However, part of the Chipko critique, that government policy in the Uttar Pradesh hills was insensitive to the region's ecological and social specificity and was driven by the concern to maximize revenues which were appropriated by a bureaucracy based in the plains, formed the core of a movement for regional autonomy.[21] This movement for a separate state raged throughout the 1980s and 1990s and was marked by a series of public protest rallies and demonstrations, some of which were violently suppressed by the state (most notably the brutal assault on women protestors at Muzaffarnagar in 1994). The state of Uttaranchal was finally carved out of the hill districts of Uttar Pradesh in 2000. Can the transition from a movement that sought to safeguard a hill ecology for meeting subsistence needs to a movement for ensuring better political representation and self-government for hill populations be interpreted as an instance of successful "environmentalism of the poor," with struggle centered around control over productive resources? The present situation in Uttaranchal belies this hope. While claiming that the new state will redress the historic inequalities between the plains and the hills perpetuated by the Uttar Pradesh government, the movement makes no mention of social disparities *among* hill people.[22] Nor has it made any effort to incorporate an environmentalist agenda into its program. Since its formation, the Uttaranchal government has been financially bankrupt. Its plans to get over this crisis entail the same development schemes that the Chipko movement had opposed: forest exploitation and dam construction. As these plans indicate, decentralizing political control in the region may even accelerate ecological degradation. Meanwhile Sunderlal Bahuguna, the veteran Chipko leader, continues to oppose the Tehri dam and other construction in the hills, but has now joined hands with a right-wing religious group, the *Vishwa Hindu Parishad* (VHP) [World Hindu Committee]. In the summer of 2000, Bahuguna participated in a VHP-organized campaign protesting against any activity that would block or sully the sacred river Ganges (the Tehri dam is being built on the Bhagirathi River, one of the main tributaries of the Ganges).[23] Bahuguna is also reported to have been one of the VHP delegates who met the prime minister in 2001, pressing for the early construction of a temple at the site of the Babri Mosque that was demolished by Hindu fundamentalists in 1994.[24]

Whether Bahuguna's association with Hindu fundamentalists is an instrumentalist alliance or one based on shared meanings and concerns about Hindu sacred geography, one is struck by how this turn of events has taken scholars and environmentalists by surprise. The voluminous literature on the subject of the Chipko movement does not provide us with the analytical tools to understand these developments. Even Haripriya Rangan's recent account,[25] which has the temporal advantage of being able to address both Chipko and the Uttarakhand movements, constructs an explanation in terms of regionalism and ignores the "saffron" tinge in hill politics. The dominant perspective on Chipko as a subaltern environmental movement, as represented by Bahuguna and publicized across the world by Guha, Vandana Shiva, and Anil Agarwal, now seems to warrant closer examination. Were there particular cultural understandings that villagers brought to the struggle that were ignored or glossed over in the accounts of the movement that circulated globally? Was the "environmentalism of the poor" only a momentary conjuncture to have metamorphosed within a decade into a movement for regional autonomy with no environmentalist orientation? Or was Chipko's environmentalism a metropolitan construction, fueled no doubt by Bahuguna's representations of the struggle, that glossed over or selectively interpreted aspects of a movement for decentralized control over resources?

Questions about the multiple representations of class, region, and ecology that inform the ideology of environmental movements also arise in the case of the Narmada Bachao Andolan. This movement against the construction of several dams across the river Narmada in central India has mobilized and united strikingly different social groups in its campaigns. In the case of the Sardar Sarovar dam, the movement brings poor hill *adivasis* together with prosperous caste Hindu farmers of the plains.[26] In the case of the Maheshwar dam, it unites poor low-caste boatmen with well-to-do caste Hindu farmers. In both these instances, the common bond that brings these groups together is the threat of displacement, the loss of land, and livelihood. The anti-dam movement has made conspicuous the figure of the *adivasi* ("indigenous" person, member of India's Scheduled Tribes), whose distinctive life in the forested hills of the river valley and dependence on forests and a close-knit village community, makes restitution or compensation impossible. While displacement with very little possibility of adequate rehabilitation is undoubtedly a grievous social injustice, the question of tribal displacement is perceived by metropolitan supporters of the Narmada struggle as an issue that combines equity with ecology—"red" with "green." Interestingly, there is less discussion about the ecological impacts of the dam due to the impounding of water in its reservoir or on downstream ecosystems and in the command area and more on how the dam will submerge a unique tribal lifestyle that is ecologically sustainable. The identification of *adivasi* natural resource use with ecological wisdom ignores a complex history of subjugation that has left *adivasis* impoverished, forced to expand cultivation by clearing forest slopes.[27] *Adivasis* can, at best, be described as "environmentalists by default;"[28] while their resource use is less destructive compared to the intensive extraction promoted by the state, it fails to provide them with secure or sustainable livelihoods. The significant presence of prosperous farmers, beneficiaries of capital-intensive farming technologies subsidized by the state, who make up the majority of those fighting against displacement in both Sardar Sarovar and Maheshwar submergence zones, also dilutes the argument that the Narmada movement constitutes an "environmentalism of the poor." Yet, the movement conducted a successful campaign with the help of environmental NGOs such as the International Rivers Network, Environmental Defense Fund, Friends of the Earth, Sierra Club, and European Green groups to stop World Bank funding for the Sardar Sarovar dam. In the late 1990s, the movement succeeded in forcing the withdrawal of the foreign partners in the consortium led by an Indian firm to build the Maheshwar dam.

When, despite the World Bank's withdrawal from the Sardar Sarovar project, the dam continued to be built, the Narmada movement petitioned the Supreme Court to stop the project. The court ordered a temporary halt on construction in 1995, but allowed the dam height to be raised slightly in 1999. It was then that the celebrated author Arundhati Roy wrote an eloquent essay on the Narmada issue, passionately espousing the movement's cause.[29] The essay was widely circulated in the press and over the Internet, renewing metropolitan interest in the movement. The Narmada struggle came back into the limelight, thanks to the lecture-cum-film screenings organized by Roy and film-maker Jharna Jhaveri who toured Europe and North America as well as the Indian metros. Buoyed by the enthusiastic response to her call to support the movement, Roy also organized a highly publicized "Rally for the Valley" in September 1999. The rally consisted of a few hundred supporters, mainly from the ranks of the "metropolitan causeratti,"[30] who traveled through the submergence zone accompanied by a large contingent of journalists. Their coverage of the event tended to focus on Roy, whose power as a star attraction and spokesperson for the cause outshone even that of Medha Patkar, the charismatic leader who had started the movement and steered it towards its current prominence.[31] For the media, Roy, rather than Patkar or the affected *adivasis*, was more newsworthy. Even in the aftermath of the Supreme Court verdict allowing the dam to be built, a decision that consigned most of the affected people in the Narmada valley to a grim future, media coverage focused more on Roy's reaction and on her skirmishes with the Supreme Court over whether her writings constitute "contempt of court" than on the people threatened with imminent displacement. The priorities of the media in determining newsworthiness privilege images and accounts of a "celebrity" over those of the people in the Narmada valley. Yet the skewedness in coverage is something that the movement's leadership has accepted, and even tacitly promoted, as a means of attracting metropolitan supporters to their cause.

In the same district of Madhya Pradesh where the Narmada movement has been campaigning against the Maheshwar dam, the *Adivasi Mukti Sangathan* [Tribal Liberation Organization], which had mobilized adivasis to stake a claim over state-controlled forest lands, was brutally suppressed by the administration.[32] The Sangathan's rapid expansion among *adivasis* in the area threatened the power base of the deputy chief minister of the state who was supported by local traders, money-lenders, and their *adivasi* allies. After a series of confrontations, some of them violent, with state officials and state-sponsored gangs, the organization was branded in the media as "Naxalite" (violent, extreme Left), and accused of destroying forests and sabotaging community forestry initiatives such as Joint Forest Management. Notwithstanding its attempts to secure *adivasi* control over natural resources such as land, forests, and water, the Adivasi Mukti Sangathan was portrayed by the state and perceived by metropolitan opinion as "anti-environmentalist."

In the eastern part of Madhya Pradesh (now the state of Chhattisgarh), the *Chhattisgarh Mines Shramik Sangh* [Workers' Union] has been organizing for the rights of workers employed in public sector mines and private ancillary industries over the last three decades. The Union has fought for secure and remunerative employment, as well as for environmental safeguards for workers' health and safety.[33] The organization's leader Shankar Guha Niyogi (who was murdered in 1991 by assassins hired by a group of industrialists) also founded the *Chhattisgarh Mukti Morcha* (CMM) [Liberation Front] which mobilized small and marginal farmers (who also work as part-time laborers) against the ecological degradation of agricultural land and the pollution of water by mining-related activities. The Front has had enough local support to get its candidate elected to the state legislative assembly for the last fifteen years. Despite its sustained engagement with ecological issues in agriculture and industry as they affect the working poor, a commitment reflected in the red and green CMM flag, the Front has not been perceived as an environmental movement.

Finally, I round off this red and green miscellany by citing recent events in Delhi where an "activist" judiciary has been acclaimed by the intelligentsia for its environmentalism. In response to a petition by M. C. Mehta, an environmentalist lawyer, a Supreme Court bench headed by Justice Kuldip Singh, the "green judge" as he was dubbed by the media, ordered the closure of all industries in Delhi that failed to meet pollution control norms and that violated the zoning provisions of Delhi's Master Plan. The Court also responded to other "public interest" petitions by consumer rights and middle-class residents' associations and directed the Delhi government to remove all squatter settlements on public lands. Delhi's political establishment, politicians as well as administrators who had for decades enabled violations of the Master Plan and the proliferation of slums for gaining illicit incomes and electoral support, pleaded before the court that its orders were impossible to implement but found their arguments dismissed. Representatives of trade unions and small-scale manufacturers who protested against the loss of jobs and the economic loss to the city were similarly ignored. Upper-class opinion has been overwhelmingly on the side of the Supreme Court and Shri Jagmohan, the Minister of Urban Development in the central government who has supported the Court's actions. From early 2000, Jagmohan spearheaded the campaign for a "clean and green" Delhi, even as tens of thousands of working class families lost both their homes and their means of livelihood.[34]

What do these contemporary examples tell us about the connections between ecology and equity? At first glance, there seems to be something arbitrary in the way in which some social movements come to be perceived as "environmental" movements. In the Chipko case, there is no clear connection between regional autonomy and ecologically sustainable development. Nor does the combined struggle of marginalized hill *adivasis* and capital-intensive farmers against displacement by the Narmada dams warrant the environmental label. On the other hand, social movements such as the Adivasi Mukti Sangathan and the Chhattisgarh Mukti Morcha that mobilize poor people for rights to natural resources, or for safe and non-polluting industrial processes, are not perceived as "environmentalist" in their orientation. "Environmental" movements display a similar diversity with respect to the concern for equity. In Delhi, environmentalism directly undermines working class livelihoods. In the Narmada valley, the disparate constituencies of poor and prosperous landowners unite against a common threat. In the Chipko case, equity is understood in *regional* terms as an opposition between a hill society and a state and economy dominated by the plains, rather than in terms of class or caste. These examples indicate that so-called environmental movements bring together social groups with diverse class backgrounds and even contradictory structural locations, whose practices sometimes do not even exemplify ecological sustainability. At the same time, social movements that do, in fact, attend to ecological concerns and issues of equity may not be perceived as "environmental."

The apparent arbitrariness of this labeling gives way, upon closer examination, to some distinct patterns. Social movements that are represented as an "environmentalism of the poor" are often organized against particular forms of capital and in collaboration with metropolitan interlocutors and audiences. As I shall argue, these two elements are not unconnected. "Environmental" movements are more effective when confronting large capitalist firms (especially transnational ones) and international financial institutions such as the World Bank. Thus the Narmada movement was able to influence the World Bank, the Japanese and German governments, as well as German firms, to withdraw funding from dams. The Chilika Bachao Andolan was successful in campaigning against the state government's lease of large parts of Lake Chilika to the Tatas, one of India's biggest industrial conglomerates. Groups have organized successfully in Orissa against transnational mining interests just as they have mobilized in Kerala against international fisheries firms that own mechanized trawlers. The "environmentalist" representation has been less successful against smaller, more dispersed capital with its very different structures of accountability. While large, transnational capitalist firms and institutions have to respond to the pressure of metropolitan environmentalist organizations which have emerged as an influential element in shaping global political economy, smaller firms that do not have to care about their corporate images escape such monitoring. In the absence of an effective regulatory framework for environmental protection in India, petty capitalist firms can get away with environmental murder.[35] Thus, despite staving off the Tatas, the Chilika Bachao Andolan has not been able to break the nexus between local traders and financiers who are linked to local farmers and fishermen and who are impervious to environmentalist arguments. This is not to suggest that large capitalist firms are necessarily more ecologically benign or easier to regulate than smaller firms, but to point out that the former have had to become more responsive to metropolitan environmental organizations that have emerged as an important force in mobilizing particular understandings of "environmental" issues. Related to the goal of campaigning against transnational capital in particular forms is the nature of alliance-building which "environmental movements" in India have chosen to prioritize. A limited grassroots base has often been buttressed by the mobilization of dispersed metropolitan support in India and abroad among environmental and human rights organizations.

"Environmentalist" arguments have had very mixed fortunes when used against the Indian state. While the Narmada Bachao Andolan could compel the World Bank to impose stringent conditionalities on the Indian government, the failure to meet which resulted in the suspension of Bank funding for the Sardar Sarovar dam, the movement failed to convince the judges of the Supreme Court who asserted that dams were necessary in the national interest for food security and economic growth. The Indian state has often mobilized the claim of "national interest" to justify policies and projects that adversely affect the poor, just as it has deployed to great effect the claim of "national sovereignty" to insulate itself from pressure by transnational supporters of Indian environmental movements.[36] State institutions have generally been suspicious of, if not hostile to, social movements that bring to the fore issues of control and access to natural resources. By and large, when state intervention by the Supreme Court judiciary and by the central government has been on the side of environmental conservation, it has privileged the preservation of wilderness areas such as forests, often at the cost of curtailing resource use by local people. Only when local people are presented not as "poor villagers who destroy the environment to make both ends meet" but as ecologically wise *adivasis* or "hill people" is there likely to be some sympathetic consideration of their rights.

The connections between "environmentalist" representations of social movements, the nature of capital that they oppose, and their collaborations with metropolitan audiences and interlocutors, shape the political trajectory of these struggles. I draw attention to these features not in order to construct a typology of social movements—indeed, such a typology with its suggestion of the unvarying determinacy of certain structural conditions (e.g., if a transnational corporation, then an environmental movement), would afford little analytical purchase. I would stress here the element of political choice available to actors within social movements. To paraphrase Karl Marx, social movements create collective identities and make claims, both material and symbolic, within unequal structures of power and under circumstances not of their choosing.[37] These constrained choices are simultaneously enabling and disabling. Particular circumstances may shape the choice of adopting the discursive framework of "environmentalism," even as this framework imposes its own disciplinary logic on the movement. The environmentalist discourse has an affinity for certain forms of claims over others. It favors particular representations of people and places over others. Village community, hill women, tribal/indigenous, religious/traditional are valorized[38] whereas other representations—wage-worker, dalit, slum dweller—are not so privileged. Similarly, the relationships that environmental movements forge with metropolitan supporters in turn shape their practices and conditions of possibility.

Like the globalizing discourse of development,[39] the discourse of "environmentalism" divides the world in ways that direct attention and justify intervention. Just as the "Third World" is created as an object for intervention by the development industry, metropolitan environmentalist imaginings valorize parts of the world as marked by "unique" ecological value (e.g., the rainforest), disaster (e.g., sub-Saharan Africa), or emancipatory politics (e.g., the Narmada valley or the Himalaya).[40] Metropolitan sensibilities are often shrewdly played upon by grassroots social movements to strengthen their claims to natural resources. Environmentalism is particularly prone to positing organicist links of the "blood and soil" variety that fuse nature and culture. Thus, notions of *adivasis* as ecologically noble savages, ancient stewards of the land, were deployed by the Narmada Bachao Andolan to oppose displacement. The Chipko movement was able to use the image of hill villages as timeless, unitary communities to secure metropolitan support for their cause. While appreciating the political mileage that such representations bring to further a social movement, it is important to note the issues that are excluded as well. For instance, social differentiation within the village community or region or between *adivasis* is obscured,[41] sometimes in ways that further disenfranchise the most powerless members among these groups. In the Narmada valley, mobilization has focused on those groups who stand to lose their "ancestral" lands, lands that are suffused with enduring cultural meanings. Left out of this strategy of claims-making are the Dhankava Naiks, a dalit group who are the poorest of the poor, who have no land but only legends about how, many generations ago, the *adivasis* conquered them and captured their forests. Like the Dhankava Naiks, environmentalist valorization of the "indigenous" leaves out the vast majority of the world's poor, who live on the margins of subsistence and in the most degraded ecological conditions but who cannot claim to be "indigenous people" in the limited definition accorded that term.[42] The empowering politics of being indigenous has its inverse in the profound disempowerment experienced by migrants. For instance, recent migrants to urban areas can establish no authentic genealogies; their claims are the most tenuous even though they may be the most ecologically deprived and socially vulnerable group. Environmentalist movements have so far proved to be inadequate for addressing issues of urban poverty or rural landlessness.

Environmentalist discourses also hold the poor to impossibly high ecological standards, standards that metropolitan supporters themselves certainly do not live by. It is expected that the poor are ecologically frugal and, if given control over natural resources, would manage them sustainably. The experience that most social groups, on achieving upward mobility, immediately embark upon resource-intensive production and consumption patterns is somehow ignored. The assumption in the "environmentalism of the poor" argument that the poor are innately endowed with ecological virtues can lead to environmentally disastrous consequences. The Sixth Schedule areas of northeastern India where tribal autonomous councils have full control over natural resources have seen deforestation at an unprecedented rate over the last few decades. The probability of a similar debacle in the newly formed state of Uttaranchal highlights the shortcomings of such analyses. At another level, the glorification by metropolitan audiences of certain Indian movements as environmentalist and their extending support to them deflects attention away from mobilizing on environmental politics closer to home. College students in Delhi and Mumbai are more likely to participate in a Narmada rally than to reflect critically on changing their own resource use patterns or joining the battle in their immediate urban environment between the homeless and those who wish them elsewhere. When they do not examine the role of metropolitan classes, environmentalist alliances may end up reproducing rather than changing structural inequalities that create ecological degradation in the first place.

The reliance on dispersed metropolitan support necessitates using the media to connect the grassroots with audiences abroad. Since media attention requires constant renewal and refreshment, and environmental movements have to continuously stage new spectacles to stay in the public eye. I have described elsewhere[43] how *adivasis* and middle-class activists successfully collaborate in the production of such protest events. However, the failure to "perform" in ways that grab attention relegate movements to the sidelines. A preoccupation with mobilizing people to turn out in large numbers for events overtakes the movement's other responsibilities of widening and deepening its political base. In the case of both the Chipko and the Narmada movements, grassroots support has dwindled even as these movements have gathered strength among metropolitan audiences. Media attention is organized not only around "events" rather than "issues," but it is also attracted to glamour more than to substance. As in the case of the Narmada movement, while Roy's celebrity endorsement brought fresh publicity to the anti-dam movement, the coverage was generally focused on Roy's persona as a crusader rather than on the cause that she was supporting. The media thrives on controversy so that extremist positions receive more attention than moderate ones; violent confrontations gain more air-time and column space than measured debate, negotiation, and compromise. Conducting a social movement through the media brings with it attendant hazards that shape the movement's trajectory.

Rather than contrasting the "environmentalism of the poor" and the "environmentalism of the rich," as Guha does, I would argue that the two are in fact interconnected. Environmental movements that rely on metropolitan support build alliances with the rich who have an interest in imagining heroic people and pristine places *elsewhere,* so that their own patterns of resource use are unaffected. The ideology that drives poor people's struggle for subsistence may actually intersect with the rich person's notion of tribal homelands where *adivasis* protect the environment. Finally, while we address the contradictions of class that exist within environmental movements, we must keep in mind that the "environmentalist" representation of particular social movements is only one among several contending and converging subjective meanings that people attach to these struggles. A social movement is powerful precisely because its meanings are ambiguous and shifting: for some hill *adivasis,* the Narmada movement is a fight to hold on to their precious land; for the engineering student, it may encapsulate the hope of a technologically-appropriate utopia; for the leftist radical from Kerala, the dam represents the evils of global capital; for the veteran Gandhian, the movement promises to breathe life into a vision of village-centered development. Rather than a reductive search for what an "environmental movement" is "really" about—whether class, race or gender—we need to appreciate its ideological hybridity and the ways in which the tensions and contradictions between different, unequal groups are negotiated.

NOTES

This paper has benefited greatly from responses received at seminars at Berkeley, Cornell, Delhi, and Iowa. In particular, I would like to thank Ram Guha, Mary Katzenstein, Raj Patel, and Raka Ray for their incisive comments.

1. By "metropolitan" I mean upper-class educated Indians, Ashok Rudra's "intelligentsia," as well as their counterparts in other countries. See Rudra, "The Emergence of the Intelligentsia as a Ruling Class in India," *Economic and Political Weekly* 24, no. 3 (1989): 142–50.

2. Ramachandra Guha and Juan Martinez-Alier, *Varieties of Environmentalism: Essays North and South* (Delhi: Oxford University Press, 1998), 4.

3. Guha and Martinez-Alier, *Varieties of Environmentalism*, 5. Also see Ramachandra Guha, *Environmentalism: A Global History* (Delhi: Oxford University Press, 2000), 99–124.

4. Guha and Martinez-Alier, *Varieties of Environmentalism*, 17.

5. Madhav Gadgil and Ramachandra Guha, *Ecology and Equity: The Use and Abuse of Nature in Contemporary India* (New Delhi: Penguin, 1995), 34–45.

6. This point seems to contradict Guha's contention that "it is impossible to say, with regard to India, what Jürgen Habermas has claimed of the European green movement: namely, that it is sparked not 'by problems of distribution, but by concern for the grammar of forms of life'" (Guha and Martinez-Alier, *Varieties of Environmentalism*, 21). Collective action over natural resources not only raises questions about ownership and control, but often also claims to represent a different way of relating to nature, one that repudiates the cultural values enshrined in the ideology of capitalist development. To quote E. P. Thompson, "every contradiction is a conflict of values as well as a conflict of interest." On the continuities and discontinuities between New Social Movements in India and Europe, also see Amita Baviskar, *In the Belly of the River: Tribal Conflicts over Development in the Narmada Valley* (Delhi: Oxford University Press, 1995), 39–43.

7. Guha and Martinez-Alier, *Varieties of Environmentalism*, 17–19. It is puzzling that Guha does not consider the struggles of Native Americans to reclaim alienated land, or against the siting of hazardous products, or the burgeoning organic farming movement, to be significant strands in the U.S. environmental movement. Perhaps the problem stems from his conflation of the terms North and South with nation-states. If one were to imagine North and South not as polar categories separating nations across the globe but as metaphors for the inequalities created by the convergence of class, nation, race, and gender, then the environmental justice movement in the United States would appear not as an anomaly in the North, but as sharing political space with other Southern struggles, separated though they may be by national borders.

8. CSE (Centre for Science and Environment), *The State of India's Environment: A Citizens' Report* (New Delhi: CSE, 1982).

9. M. K. Gandhi, *Hind Swaraj, or Indian Home Rule* (Ahmedabad: Navjivan Publishing House, 1938).

10. This socialist stream can be traced to Gandhi's views about Indian villages and their patterns of resource use, views that were (somewhat ironically) influenced by colonial constructions of Indian rurality (cf. Maine's village republics), and also to early twentieth-century German and Russian Marxist debates about the peasantry that influenced socialists such as Ram Manohar Lohia and those associated with the Sarvodaya movement led by Jai Prakash Narayan in the 1970s.

11. Gail Omvedt, *Reinventing Revolution: New Social Movements and the Socialist Tradition in India* (New York: M. E. Sharpe, 1993).

12. Gail Omvedt, "India's Green Movements," *Race and Class* 28, no. 4 (1987): 36.

13. Ramachandra Guha, *The Unquiet Woods: Ecological Change and Peasant Resistance in the Himalaya* (Delhi: Oxford University Press, 1989), 173–77, 196. It must be noted that Guha and Omvedt's analyses acknowledge and attempt to grapple with the complexity of social movement strategy and practices. In contrast, Tom Brass renders a reductive reading of Indian "New Social Movements" as essentially neopopulist and interested in safeguarding the status quo. (See Brass, "Moral Economists, Subalterns, New Social Movements, and the (Re-)Emergence of a (Post-)Modernised (Middle) Peasant," *Journal of Peasant Studies* 18, no. 2 (1991): 173–205.

14. Baviskar, *In the Belly*, 237–242.

15. Baviskar, *In the Belly*, 237.

16. Peter Brosius, "Analyses and Interventions: Anthropological Engagements with Environmentalism," *Current Anthropology* 40, no. 3 (1999): 280.

17. Guha, *Unquiet Woods*.

18. Vandana Shiva, *Staying Alive: Women, Ecology and Survival in India* (New Delhi: Kali for Women, 1988). This characterization is repudiated by Guha, who cautions against interpreting women's participation in Chipko in terms of a modern conception of feminist self-assertion (Guha, *Unquiet Woods*, 175; also Ramachandra Guha, "The Malign Encounter: The Chipko Movement and Competing Visions of Nature," in *Who Will Save the Forests?: Knowledge, Power and Environmental Destruction*, ed. Tariq Banuri and Fredrique Apffel Marglin [London: Zed Books, 1993], 101). Guha also states that Chipko's base has not been restricted to any one section of Uttarakhand society. Bina Agarwal points out that Shiva's analysis fails to locate the link between women and the environment as embedded in the structures of class (/caste/race) organization in terms of production, reproduction, and distribution (Agarwal, "The Gender and Environment Debate: Lessons from India," *Feminist Studies* 18, no.1 [1992]: 127). Both Guha's and Shiva's conception of hill village society has been criticized as simplistic and romantic by Subir Sinha, Shubhra Gururani, and Brian Greenberg, "The 'New Traditionalist' Discourse of Indian Environmentalism," *The Journal of Peasant Studies* 24, no. 3 (1997): 65–99. For a review of these debates, see Indrani Chaudhuri, *Women and Environment in the Development Process: A Case Study of the Chipko Movement in Uttarakhand,* M.Phil. Sociology dissertation, University of Delhi, 1996.

19. Guha, *Unquiet Woods*, 179–84.

20. It is important to note that there were many other leaders and activists associated with Chipko, most notably Chandi Prasad Bhatt. Bhatt's activism has been more low-key and democratic; whereas Bahuguna projects his individual self, Bhatt works closely with a group of village men and women. Bhatt's ideology has also been less environmentally radical than Bahuguna's. Instead of advocating a complete cessation of developmental activity in the region (e.g., road-building), he stresses the need to generate employment through ecological sound technologies (Guha, *Unquiet Woods*, 182–83). While Bhatt is widely respected in the region, he is little known outside it. Metropolitan environmentalists in India are more familiar with the ascetic figure of Bahuguna. Bahuguna's success in wresting a ban on felling from the central government owes a good deal to the personal intervention of Prime Minister Indira Gandhi to whom he secured direct access. How Indira Gandhi's "love for nature," the aesthetic sensibilities of a key politician, shaped conservation policies in India while en-

abling her to win the support and admiration of scientists, naturalists, and activists tells us a great deal about the political processes of Indian environmentalism (see Mahesh Rangarajan, "The Politics of Ecology: The Debate on Wildlife and People in India, 1970–95," *Economic and Political Weekly* 31, nos. 35–37 [1996]: 2392–93).

21. Haripriya Rangan, *Of Myths and Movements: Rewriting Chipko into Himalayan History* (Delhi: Oxford University Press, 2000), 167–70, 180–84.

22. In fact, in opposing the imposition of caste-based quotas in government jobs and educational institutions, it may even seem that the movement *denies* the existence of caste inequalities. Even scholarly writings on hill societies aver that villages are "relatively egalitarian," glossing over the differences between caste Hindus and Scheduled Castes with respect to the ownership of land, education, and relationship with the plains economy. While the difference between men and women in terms of a division of labor are acknowledged, they are not addressed through any gendered strategy for social change.

23. Mukul Sharma's current research explores the connection between parts of the environmental movement and the Hindu Right. According to Sharma, "it is delightfully naïve to assume that the entire content of emerging environmental issues and movements is necessarily progressive. The panoply of environmental politics in India today reveals some political allegiances and affinities with Hindu conservative forces. Rather than uncritically endorsing all environmental movements, or all visions of the environment, we should analyze their limitations, intractabilities and contradictions in relationship to communalism" (Sharma, "Saffronising Green," *Seminar* 516 [2002]: 31). See also Amita Baviskar, "Vanishing Forests, Sacred Trees: A Hindu Perspective on Eco-consciousness," *Asian Geographer* 18, nos. 1–2 (1999): 21–31.

24. Personal communication from Mahesh Rangarajan.

25. Rangan, *Of Myths and Movements*, 193.

26. Baviskar, *In the Belly*.

27. See Amita Baviskar, "The Fate of the Forest: Conservation and Tribal Rights," *Economic and Political Weekly* 29, no. 38 (1994): 2493–2501.

28. Baviskar, *In the Belly*, 239.

29. Arundhati Roy, *The Greater Common Good* (Bombay: IndiaBook Distributors, 1999).

30. Harsh Sethi, "Movements and Mediators," *Economic and Political Weekly* 36, no. 4 (2001): 269.

31. This is not to suggest that Roy's initiative was seen by the movement's activists as upstaging Patkar or otherwise problematic. The main Andolan activists have welcomed Roy's involvement and have even defended her against criticism by Ramachandra Guha (see Chittaroopa Palit, "The Historian as Gatekeeper," *Frontline,* January 5, 2001). However, other activists associated with the movement have voiced their disquiet at the way in which a relative newcomer was immediately elevated to the top ranks of the movement and lionized, while long-time supporters who had suffered police brutality and imprisonment for the sake of the movement remained uncelebrated (see Yogesh Divan's letter in *Jansatta*, Delhi edition, August 1999). Harsh Sethi also points out that the involvement of media-savvy mediators changes dynamics within movements (Sethi, "Movements and Mediators," 270).

32. Amita Baviskar, "Written on the Body, Written on the Land: Violence and Environmental Struggles in Central India," in *Violent Environments*, ed. Nancy Peluso and Michael Watts (Ithaca, N.Y.: Cornell University Press, 2001).

33. Anil Sadgopal and Shyam Bahadur Namra, eds., *Sangharsh aur Nirmaan: Shankar Guha Niyogi aur unka Naye Bharat ka Sapna* [Struggle and Construction: Shankar Guha Niyogi and His Dream of a New India] (New Delhi: Rajkamal Prakashan, 1993).

34. Amita Baviskar, "The Politics of the City," *Seminar* 516 (2002): 40–42; Amita Baviskar, "Between Violence and Desire: Space, Power and Identity in the Making of Metropolitan Delhi," *International Social Science Journal* 175 (2003): 89–98.

35. The ecological havoc wrought by small-scale firms in Indian towns is documented in CSE, *State of India's Environment: The Citizens' Fifth Report* (New Delhi: CSE, 1999). Many of these industries argue that, if they were to conform to environmental norms, they would become uneconomical. They assert that there is a trade-off between generating employment (and profits) and protecting the environment which a poor country like India can ill afford.

36. On the issue of the accountability of the Indian state, see Satish Deshpande, "From Development to Adjustment: Economic Ideologies, the Middle Class and 50 Years of Independence," *Review of Development and Change* 2, no. 2 (1997): 294–318.

37. Karl Marx, *The Eighteenth Brumaire of Louis Bonaparte* (Moscow: Progress Publishers, 1852).

38. These concepts have been analyzed critically by scholars of environmentalism: on community, see Arun Agrawal, *Community in Conservation: Beyond Enchantment and Disenchantment,* CDF Discussion Paper (Florida: Conservation and Development Forum, 1997), and Tania M. Li, "Images of Community: Discourse and Strategy in Property Relations," *Development and Change* 27, no. 3 (1996): 501–27. On indigeneity, see T. M. Li, "Articulating Indigenous Identity in Indonesia: Resource Politics and the Tribal Slot," *Comparative Studies in Society and History* 42, no. 1 (2000): 149–79; and Anna L. Tsing, "Becoming a Tribal Elder, and Other Green Development Fantasies," in *Transforming the Indonesian Uplands: Marginality, Power and Production*, ed. Tania M. Li (Amsterdam: Harwood, 1999).

39. Arturo Escobar, *Encountering Development: The Making and Unmaking of the Third World* (Princeton, N.J.: Princeton University Press, 1995).

40. On globalization and the construction of place, see Arjun Appadurai, *Modernity at Large: Cultural Dimensions of Globalization* (Minneapolis: University of Minnesota Press, 1996), and Satish Deshpande, "Hegemonic Spatial Strategies: The Nation-Space and Hindu Communalism in Twentieth-Century India," *Public Culture* 10, no. 2 (1998): 249–83.

41. Amita Baviskar, "Tribal Politics and Discourses of Environmentalism," *Contributions to Indian Sociology* 31, no. 2 (1997): 195–223.

42. Akhil Gupta, *Postcolonial Developments: Agriculture in the Making of Modern India* (Durham, N.C.: Duke University Press, 1998), 289.

43. Baviskar, *In the Belly*; Amita Baviskar, "Who Speaks for the Victims?" *Seminar* 451 (1997): 59–61.

7

Farmers' Movements and the Debate on Poverty and Economic Reforms in India

Gail Omvedt

"EVERYBODY TALKS ABOUT RURAL POVERTY, BUT . . ."

Everyone talks about it, everyone has ideas of what to do about it, yet rural poverty persists.

From the time of the British, from the time of independence, the misery of India's rural poor has been a subject for debate and for legitimation of public policy. The British justified their rule by what they could do for the peasantry and the poor. The independent Indian government combined Nehru and Gandhi to proclaim a "socialism" that could provide both welfare and growth. Neither has had much success. British imperialism produced poverty, or at least held India back while Europe went ahead, partly: while in 1800 the living standards of various parts of the world, from China to England, were more or less the same, by 1950 these world level inequalities had vastly increased. Similarly, the Nehru era of "brahmanic socialism" saw the "Hindu rate of growth" (3.5 percent) and a high and almost stable level of poverty for three decades. It is not that India has made no progress in reducing poverty in the years since independence, but that this progress has been so meager in comparison with what has been possible and what other Asian countries have achieved.

What of the era of liberalization? Varying voices rise from civil society and the social movements. A free society and open economy is the road to prosperity, or liberalization, globalization and privatization ("LPG" in the current left jargon) are the worst thing that can happen to India, "worse than a hundred Kargills" in one overdone speech.

The issue should at least be taken as a matter for investigation rather than beginning with assumptions. There is in fact a large amount of socio-economic data on such issues. Opponents of economic reforms claim that in the "neo-liberal" era all public responsibilities are being forsaken and the old social ideals and values are being lost. Indeed, at one level the society does seem to be plunging into an era of hedonism and consumerism, of unabashed striving for individual success as a new generation reacts to the Gandhian-socialist disdain for accumulation in the earlier period (the "yuppies"). Paradoxically, however, the presence and pressure of a strong critical force has meant as much if not more monitoring of poverty than earlier. Along with the heated debates of the 1990s have come some impressive economist evaluations.

SOCIAL MOVEMENTS AND POVERTY

Though it may seem to jar with the theme of this book, I argue that there is no inherent connection between social movements and poverty. No social movement takes "ending poverty" as such as its goal; rather they fight for various special interests that are usually distributional. (This chapter assumes that distributional movements may alleviate poverty on a short-term basis, but long term eradication requires economic growth to generate resources.) Where the connection between social movements and poverty is made, it is through the ideology of the leadership of these movements, rather than through the inherent interests of the section being organized.[1] Thus, nearly all movements do ideologically link their goals with general welfare of a people (usually a nation, sometimes humanity as a whole), but these ideologies make this link in very different ways and with very different terminologies. Since similar social movements can have very different types of leadership, this connection is indirect and variable.

To take just one example, working class movements have taken place under socialist leadership (communist or social-democratic), under liberal leadership (of a social liberal variety), or under conservative, even reactionary leadership. Probably the historically dominant form even in the labor movement has been not socialist but liberal; the "rights" discourse itself is a liberal one.[2] Currently in India, it is the Bharatiya Mazdur Sangh that has the biggest union membership today, while the World Trade Organization (WTO) has been headed by a former labor leader, Michael Moore. Under all types they have won significant gains without any necessary step towards the achievement of the goal of the broader ideology of the specific movement. The perspective on poverty and the role of the working class movement in ending it vary according to leadership.

In other words, social movements which organize specific sections of people on specific issues may do so with a variety of ideologies. These can mostly still be classified in terms of the great ideologies of the post-

Enlightenment period—socialism, liberalism, conservativism. In the Indian context this classification would be as follows:

1. Gandhism—and especially the neo-Gandhism that is the ideology of most environmental movements in India—is a version of romantic conservativism. It is a village-oriented ideology, but of a type that romanticizes the life of the traditional village (including the traditional caste system, with children following the professions of their fathers) and the "limitation of needs"; it expresses a thoroughgoing distrust of industrialism and development itself.

2. Liberalism has not been strong until recently, though during the pre-independence period it found exponents among early social reformers and especially among leaders of the anti-caste movement. (For instance, in Ralph Dahrendorf's classification of different types of liberal ideologies, Phule, Ambedkar, and Periyar can be called social liberals).[3]

3. The main guiding ideologies of India in the post-independence period have been varieties of socialism. These include the various forms of democratic socialism (e.g. Lohiate socialism) as well as Communism. However, the dominant trend has been what is generally called today "Nehruvian secularism" or "Nehruvian socialism." Its dominance is what leads to the question of the relationship, in India, between social movements and poverty.

Finally, while "Hindutva" or "Hindu nationalism" is often considered an ideology, I would argue that it is not; it contains many trends which borrow rather indiscriminately from all of the classic ideologies; thus it could not be classified as an ideology in this sense but rather as a discourse or frame.[4]

With this in mind, it is necessary to examine social movements in India, particularly the farmers' movement, in terms of the background of political-economic developments after independence.

NEHRUVIAN STATE, GANDHIAN VILLAGE:
POST INDEPENDENCE POLICIES ON POVERTY AND GROWTH

The Congress party which had led the fight for independence claimed goals of both economic growth and poverty removal. As the All India Congress Committee stated in 1948.

A quick and progressive rise in the standard of living of the people should be the primary consideration governing all economic activities and relevant administrative measures. . . . The achievement of a national minimum standard in respect of all the essentials of physical and social well-being within a reasonable period must be pursued as the practical goal of all schemes for economic development.[5]

This emphasis on poverty removal was particularly connected with Gandhism, however, and here the dilemma lay: how to reconcile Gandhian romantic conservativism with Nehruvian socialism in a combined development policy.

Basically, this was done by allocating the achievement of growth to Nehruvian methods, and the achievement of poverty reduction and removal to Gandhism coupled with special programs for the poor. The combination assumed a dichotomy between growth as such, and poverty alleviation as such.

The version of socialism that we call Nehruvian socialism (or "brahmanic socialism")[6] focused on industrial growth, based on the development of heavy industries and the state, which was to own the main industries, the "commanding heights of the economy," and regulate thoroughly the remaining "private" sector as a "license-permit raj." Nehru was not a socialist in envisioning a major role in governance by the working class; he was a socialist in the sense of public management by an elite. The Nehru-Mahalanobis policies for growth themselves assumed a marginalization of agriculture and the villages, since capital investment was to be focused on industry, which would be capital intensive and thus a relatively small employer of labor. (This also assumed that most Indians would continue in their traditional village occupations and life.) As an early planner put it, while there was no articulated idea of extracting surplus from agriculture, what "Indian planners effectively did was to treat agriculture as a 'bargain sector'"—that is, one that would provide cheap raw materials, cheap labor, and cheap food for industry, thereby lowering the cost of production for capitalists—a form of extracting resources from agriculture that he called "incremental primitive socialist accumulation."[7] It was here that Gandhian economic themes, with their romanticization of village life, came in: peasants with their traditional ploughs, artisans with their traditional instruments, and weavers with their traditional (perhaps slightly upgraded) *charkhas* would supply the "basic needs" of food, shelter, and housing. The theme was that crucial to poverty alleviation was a large amount of employment which it was assumed would come only through industries that were not capital intensive.[8] In textiles, efforts to discriminate against mill cloth to favor handlooms resulted in the burgeoning of powerlooms and an undercapitalization of the whole industry, which now stands far behind that of most other Asian countries.[9]

Beyond this, poverty removal was seen as coming through distributional methods and special state-administered programs. The first phase of these efforts was exemplified in the land reform efforts (in almost all left, including left-Congress, rhetoric, land reform was the symbol for the removal of the poverty of the rural poor).[10] The second phase came with Indira Gandhi's slogan of *garibi hatao* and the creation of a variety of central government schemes, Integrated Rural Development Programme

(IRDP), Training of Youth for Self Employment (TRYSEM), Jawahar Rozgar Yojana (JRY), Development of Women and Children in Rural Areas (DWRCA) and so on.

The decade of liberalization has brought a new phase of emphasis on economic growth, but even here, arguments that growth by itself is a major factor (if not the only one) in removing poverty have been made by only a few economically-oriented politicians; most have concentrated on stressing distributive measures that would ease the pain of transition. Slogans have been used of "structural reform with a human face," the "middle way," and so on, but the thinking has still been that the "human face" would necessarily involve a slowing down of the growth process.[11]

The dominant mental framework in India—affecting politicians and bureaucrats alike, as well as most of the intellectuals—was thus a dual one. It was one that envisaged steel mills, computers, and universities for the elite, and *charkhas* and ploughs (and usually missing schools) for the villages—Vedas for the twice-born, Puranas for the *shudras*. Even the issue of "reservation"—compensatory discrimination for the Dalits and *Adivasis*—was looked at in a similar dual fashion: the assumption was that "merit" had to be sacrificed to achieve "social justice," much as growth had to be sacrificed (or at least compensated for) to remove poverty. In other words, arguments that the representation of all sections of the population in governance and economic power (diversity) would promote efficiency, or that growth itself would help in reducing poverty, were rarely taken up.[12]

THE NEW SOCIAL MOVEMENTS, NEW FARMERS' MOVEMENTS

The term "new social movements" for India refers to those movements arising in the 1970s which were "new" in the sense of organizing new sections of the population (dalits, other backward castes [OBCs]/*Bahujans,* women), around new issues (environment, caste, gender, production for the market/oppression by the state) and using new concepts and analyses as frameworks for their struggle. Their methods of struggle—including closing off villages to officials, rail and *rasta rokos* (blockages), massing in large numbers for rallies—were also sometimes new and dependent in part on the methods of communication and transportation available in India by that time, though for the most part these could find a precedence in earlier movements. They generally distinguished themselves from "old" movements, most notably those of the left and national movements, by an explicit rejection of "class" as the main basis for struggle and by asserting their autonomy from political parties. In *Reinventing Revolution,* my earlier study of these, I distinguished four major movements (each comprising different organizations and local forms and with different trends within them)[13]—the anti-caste movement, the women's movement, the

environmental movement, and the farmers' movement. This broad classification blurred over some specificities—for instance, regional "nationality"
movements like that for Jharkhand were taken up in the chapter on environment, while *Adivasi* movements (which hit a peak somewhat later) were
not discussed in detail. It also did not satisfactorily answer the question—indeed few studies of "social movements" have done so—whether Hindutva
or "Hindu nationalism" could be considered a social movement: if so, it
would negate the general impression of "social movements" or "new social
movements" as a basically progressive force.

In any case, as we noted, most social movements as such do not normally
have a focus on poverty removal as their goal, and this can be said to have been
true of the new social movements also. Even the Dalit movements, which arguably have mobilized the poorest sections of the population, have not analyzed poverty as such: they have been most concerned with atrocities, the
achievement of the recognition of their humanity, and representation in the
highest levels of employment and power. The fight for political power and symbolic issues which represent the fight for identity and recognition as human be-
ings (like the naming of Marathwada University after Dr. Ambedkar) have become major issues of struggle. The demand for land has been important, but
the analysis of this has by and large been taken from theoreticians of the Left.

As for the women's movement: where activists have talked of the economic
aspect of gender issues, they have generally followed the main theoretical
framework of the organizations of the husbands/families of the women activists. Only a few of the well-known feminists have struck out on their own
on such issues. Environmental movements also have not really dealt with the
issue of poverty. In fact, the dominating environmental ideological trend, a
neo-Gandhian romantic anti-industrialism, has tended to argue that the interpretation of traditional subsistence villages as "poor" is mistaken, that true
wealth lies in other factors. While there are indeed many kinds of human
wealth, this definition if pushed to its logical conclusion would render mean-
ingless all efforts at development and alleviation of poverty.

Among the new social movements, the farmers' movements have been perhaps the only ones to take the ending of rural poverty as an explicit goal and
to articulate an ideology that sought to explain rural poverty. This ideological
frame has differed in crucial ways from the economic perspective of the various socialist trends in India, but like them it has been a discourse focusing
heavily on economic factors (in Sharad Joshi's terms, it has been "economistic" but has rejected the "class" concept as used by conventional Marxists).

In a broad sense, "farmers' movements" can be defined as those which organize rural producers of all "classes" and sections. They differ from traditional "peasant" movements in that they are involved in production for the
market to some degree or other and/or are affected by the various developmental projects of the capitalist era.[14] They include:

1. The autonomous, "non-party" farmers' organizations which sprang up in the 1970s and came to be a prominent influence in the 1980s.
2. Rural environmental movements, including movements of dam evictees, of farmers of drought-prone areas; though some of these (like the Narmada Bachao Andolan [NBA]) have been depicted as primarily organizing "tribals," in fact the large majority of people they have organized have been farmers or peasants. They also organize producers from all sections, rural poor and laborers as well as better-off farmers. The NBA for instance has had one of its strongest bases among the rich farmers of the Nimad area of Madhya Pradesh. One of the up-coming movements of this type, the Krishna Valley water movement (Pani Sangarsh Calval) in southern Maharashtra, includes in its strategy bringing together drought-affected farmers with dam evictees. This movement does not oppose "big dams" but rather seeks equal water distribution and just rehabilitation for evictees in the command area of the dams.
3. The official farmers' organizations of the political parties (most important of these have been the Kisan Sabhas of the CPI and CPM, and the Bharatiya Kisan Sangh (BKS) of the BJP. Today the left parties generally have separate agricultural laborer organizations, though their "Kisan" groups include all "classes" of farmers. It might be noted that the BKS has been emerging as the most effective and largest of these party-linked organizations (just as the BMS is now the largest trade union in the country); it can also be noted that unlike the Communist parties, the BJP does not try to organize agricultural laborers separately.
4. Unorganized struggles which have sprung up here and there, on all kinds of issues, including protest against displacement for developmental projects or urban expansion. Most notably in recent years the issue of access to water has been a focus of struggles.

This chapter, then, focuses on the autonomous farmers' movements.

AUTONOMOUS FARMERS' MOVEMENTS: A HISTORICAL SKETCH

The movements arose in the 1970s in a first wave of struggle, with early organizations in the Punjab (the Zamindara Union, later to call itself the Bharatiya Kisan Union or BKU) and Tamilnadu (the Vyavasayigal Sangham) with a powerful movement led by Narayanaswamy Naidu. The second wave arose at the beginning of the 1980s and saw the formation of new state-level organizations: the Shetkari Sanghathana in Maharashtra led by Sharad Joshi; the Karnataka Rajya Rayatu Sangha (KRRS) in which Prof. Nanjundaswamy eventually emerged as dominant leader; the BKU of Uttar Pradesh (UP) led by Mahendra Tikait and the Khedut Samaj of Gujarat.

The organizations were regionally based, using themes and rhetorical imagery drawn from regional cultures, primarily at home in the vernaculars, yet always seeking the elusive national alliance. Efforts at unity began in 1980 with Narayanswamy Naidu taking the lead; this resulted in most organizations coming together as the All-India Bharatiya Kisan Union, and then splitting in 1982. Sharad Joshi then took up the effort, forming a more "federal" coordinating committee in October 1982, which became the Kisan Coordinating Committee (KCC). He also took up unity efforts on a campaign basis, leading farmers from Maharashtra in 1984 to participate in a major struggle of wheat farmers of the Punjab. This climaxed in an agitation with nearly forty thousand farmers besieging the state capital in Chandigarh in May and announcing a forthcoming blockade of all foodgrains from the state. The threat this could have had for India's national foodgrain economy—with the public distribution system (PDS) depending heavily on supplies of wheat and even rice from the northwest and especially the Punjab—clearly frightened the government. Whatever power the farmers' movement might have had, though, was diverted as the fight against "extremists" in the Punjab was carried by the Indian state into a raid on the Golden Temple in Amritsar in June. This event, which led in November 1984 to the death of Indira Gandhi, in many ways marked the climax of the power of the farmers' movement and the beginning of the communalization of Indian politics.

Nevertheless, a new upsurge was seen, though now of different character. In 1986, the holding of a massive conference of women farmers at Chandwad (first conference of the Shetkari Mahila Aghadi) signaled a broadening from what Joshi had described as a "one-point" program. At the same time, increasing discontent with Congress rule saw a coming together of opposition forces under V. P. Singh, a former finance minister who had resigned from the party. Singh now led an alliance of the newly formed Janata Dal (a socialist formation) and left parties, backed by nearly all the "new social movements" of the period—Dalits, farmers, women, an independent working class movement led by Datta Samant of Bombay. This oppositional "third force" came to form a National Front government (with the backing of the still-weak BJP) in 1989.

From then on, however, things began to fall apart, both for the farmers' movement and for the political third force. Farmers' organizations campaigning for the left–Janata Dal alliance attempted to come together on their own with a planned mass rally—over five lakhs expected—announced for Delhi on October 2, 1989. This crashed with a personality/leadership conflict between Sharad Joshi and Tikait. (At this point underlying political-philosophical differences which existed were not determinant). The farmers' movement split in two at a national level, with Nanjundaswamy and most socialist-led smaller organizations lining up with Tikait, while the Gujarat Khedut Samaj and Punjab BKU (but emerging splits in the Punjab BKU resulted in one of the factions joining the Tikait-Nanjundaswamy alliance) allied with Sharad Joshi and the Shetkari Sanghatana.

Overall, the split meant a weakening of the movement. Sharad Joshi went on to head up a task force on agriculture, for the formation of a National Agricultural Policy under the V. P. Singh government, but by the time its report was submitted in 1990 the government itself had fallen from power in the storm that burst out over the implementation of the Mandal Commission report. From then on and for a long time, economic issues, including those of farmers, were sidelined by what was referred to as "Mandal-Mandir" politics: the demands of OBCs and backward castes on one hand, and the rise of Hindu communalism on the other as the BJP slowly rose to contend with the Congress as the strongest national party in India.

In 1991, in the wake of a shock of another assassination, a new Congress government headed by Narsimha Rao came to power and immediately announced a "new economic policy" (NEP). It was the beginning of the era of liberalization, itself a shock for India's left forces and a puzzle for the social movements. The left immediately took up the task of denouncing all change as the result of imperialist conspiracy. The slogans varied, with the "Dunkel Draft" and NEP as enemies eventually replaced by "LPG" (liberalization, privatization and globalization"), but the rhetorical opposition to all change remained even as Communist-led governments in Kerala and West Bengal began to implement reforms. This opposition to liberalization carried with it most of the well-known leaders of social movements—with the exception of the farmers' movement. Sharad Joshi emerged in the 1990s as the most powerful mass leader to support liberalization and globalization boldly and aggressively. "I'll pin a medal on Arthur Dunkel myself if he comes here," he began by saying. The result was that the existing split within the farmers' movement took on ideological dimensions, with Nanjundaswamy now becoming the main voice for opposition. Given the degree to which the media, at least for most of the decade, was dominated by anti-liberalization forces, this meant that Nanjundaswamy came to be projected on a world scale as the main farmers' leader in India. In 1993 the two opposing factions held rallies in Delhi of about equal size (roughly fifty thousand), one arguing against the WTO, the other proclaiming itself as "Farmers for Freedom."

As a whole the farmers' movement, like most social movements, has found itself in a period of decline in the 1990s and the early years of the new century. Leaders have grown old. Splits and ideological uncertainties have affected all organizations. The Punjab BKU now has three units, one linked to the Sharad Joshi–led national federation, another to the Nanjundaswamy-Tikait alliance, the third with Marxist-Leninist leadership. Nanjundaswamy's organization, the KRRS, itself suffered a major split after their European "caravan" of farmers, with the opposition, led by a former Member of the Legislative Assembly (MLA), Puttannaiah, charging foreign funding and favoritism in their use.[15] The majority of the KRRS apparently followed him. Shetkari Sanghatana has suffered an erosion of leadership, with the majority of "past presidents" (men and women) joining various political parties, ranging from the Nationalist Congress Party of Sharad Pawar to the BJP. Tikait's BKU has found itself outdone in many agitations by the BJP-led Bharatiya Kisan Union. Efforts of the Shetkari Sanghatana, the KRRS, and other organizations to form independent political parties on their own have been a dismal failure.

Yet force still remains. The new century has seen a weakening of all mass movements, though the farmers' movement still can mobilize impressive numbers in agitations. Farmers are still facing tremendous obstacles and sporadic local struggles constantly take place over water issues, over prices, over bureaucratic harassment. The old issues remain, while problems of water, drought, and technology (symbolized by the "GM seeds" issue) seem to be emerging as connected and important issues.

PERSPECTIVES ON POVERTY 1: THE 1980S

In the 1980s, the farmers' movement spoke with one voice, though many accents, on the issue of rural poverty and exploitation; in the 1990s, with the split over liberalization, two major voices emerged.

In the 1980s, the perspective of the movement was fairly simple: exploitation by the Indian elite (identified variously as the state, urban India, etc.) was responsible for the poverty of the entire rural population. This was put most forcefully by Sharad Joshi in his "India versus Bharat" imagery which spread throughout India—"India" standing for the modern, westernized, urban elite, "Bharat" for the rural poor. It was not simply an urban-rural distinction, as Joshi spoke of "refugees from Bharat in India" (i.e., the urban poor) being on the side of farmers, and of the rural elite being representatives of "India." In Marathi, the identification of the enemy was very often as "village thugs and urban goondas," and all Sanghatana activists and ordinary members I have spoken to have been clear about this identification of allies in the cities. (In fact, most of them have had relatives in the urban working class, and generally urban manual workers have supported the movement even while middle-class intellectuals, including the left, have condemned it as "rich farmer"–led). In Joshi's words,

> Before independence it was the British government which took their raw materials for a song, processed the raw materials in London and Manchester and then sold the finished product at enormous profit. Today, Pune, Calcutta and Bombay are the London and Manchester. And our current rulers have replaced the British in grabbing the wealth of the country. I do not believe in sophisticated terms like "class struggle." You may call this whatever you like. But I call

this the struggle between Bharat and India, the fight for liberation by Bharat from India.[16]

Clearly some rhetoric at least was being borrowed from the nationalist and left movements. Farmers were speaking of exploitation, and as the main slogan of the Maharashtra movement went, *bhik nako, have gamace dham*— "we don't want alms but the reward of our sweat!" [return of our labor]. Farmers were demanding as a right, charging that it was they who produced the wealth on which the elites were living.

This placing of the major line of contradiction between the exploiting urban/state-based elite and the rural community as a whole was common to all the regional movements, though they spoke of it in different ways. In Karnataka, Nanjundaswamy and other leaders with a Lohia socialist background spoke of "internal colonialism" and a bondage maintained by upper-caste capitalists (especially Brahmans) over the peasants as producers and industrial workers and urban employees as consumers. Tikait in UP talked of urban exploiters. There was an anti-Brahmanism in much farmers' movement discourse, explicit in the case of Tikait and to some degree Karnataka, while in Maharashtra, the Marathi imagery of Sharad Joshi often drew heavily from the language of Phule and the non-Brahman movement.[17]

The notion of the exploitation of agriculture as a basis for development could itself be given a Marxist twist or a liberal (conventional economic) one. Joshi, sometimes describing himself as the "only true Marxist in India," the only farmers' organization with a "red badge," pointed to Rosa Luxembourg and Marxist theories of the accumulation from agriculture—either that of countries dependent on imperialism, or domestic agriculture in the case of those countries which did not have external colonies. From the perspective of most Indian leftists, however, it has been associated with liberalism and even "neoliberalism."[18]

A second major theme was the unity of all rural sections in the face of this exploitation. To the left this was a denial of "classes" and the main source of their charges that the movement actually was in the interest of richer farmers. Differences of caste and gender as well as economic status (the "rich farmer/poor farmer" and agricultural labor/farmer groups) were recognized but treated as strata or "diversity" and not as "classes" in the Marxist sense. The common interests of rural people in opposition to their exploitation by overriding urban or state forces were seen as overriding these. This unity was aggressively asserted by Joshi with a denial of the relevance of "class" distinctions among the farmers, by the Nanjundaswamy by speaking of his movement as a "village movement."

A third major theme, connected to the notion that the state was responsible for exploitation, linked a new vision of development to the initiative of the farmers once freed from state control. As Sunil Sahrasabudhe put it,

An important feature of the peasant movement is that none of its demands are for development in the rural areas. They have neither asked for easier terms of credit or for the opening of hospitals and schools. . . . When the peasant gets the extra money, which is his due, he will invest it in the manner he deems fit. It will be up to him to decide whether to build roads and canals, establish schools and hospitals, develop research laboratories, carry out research on the farm or do whatever else he may think necessary and useful. Let not anyone else try to determine what he should do with his money. His money has always been spent by someone else and the result is there for everyone to see. Eradication of the poverty of the rural people, not through development, but by giving them fair returns for their produce is the strongest and most radical argument for decentralization. . . . This may give some idea of what one means when one says that the peasant movement today exhibits signs of transcending modernity in continuing with Gandhian ideology.[19]

Assadi also argued that this reliance on Gandhian alternatives such as decentralization of power, support for cottage industries, eliminating market dependency through biofertilizers and locally produced goods, was a common feature of most farmers' organizations.[20] This was an anti-Nehruvian (anti-statist) form of Gandhism that appeared to be a unifying theme, with almost all sections of the farmers' movement in this period identifying strongly with Gandhi. In the end this unity proved to be superficial: the Shetkari Sanghatana emphasized the anti-statism to the point of open liberalism while at the same time expressing the modernity of the farmer and his need for development and technology (in this sense Joshi was closer to Marx and Ambedkar), while the KRRS's Nanjundaswamy and the Lohiate socialists following him carried the Gandhism to the point of anti-developmentalism and united it with a dependency version of socialism to stress opposition to "multinationals" and all forms of "neo-colonial" control.

A refusal to make demands from the state ("we are not asking anything from the state, but to stop exploiting us") was emphasized by Sharad Joshi. It tended to become a differentiating point, just as the "one point program" was seen as a differentiating point from the charter of demands often put up by other organizations. Tikait's BKU, as well as the KRRS, tended to make populist demands from the state, e.g., education facilities, roads, and employment, and reservations of jobs for farmers and used the concept of a state-enforced "parity" of prices between urban and rural production.[21] However, hostility to the state was seen everywhere, and expressed in the common form of defiant struggle in which farmers sought to close off their villages and ban entry of politicians and policy-makers, linking the notion of village autonomy once again to Gandhism and decentralization.

In the 1980s, differences existed among and within the different organizations, but they were muted: at a level of struggle the movement fought the state and its agencies; at the ideological level it seemed to express a combination of Gandhism and anti-statism; at the level of alliances it worked with the left parties, Dalit organizations, women and important sections of the industrial working class. Up to the end of the 1980s, it appeared that differences in the movement were largely those of personality and regional styles.

PERSPECTIVES ON POVERTY 2: THE 1990S POLITICAL AND ECONOMIC DEBATES

Events up to 1989–1990 gave the general impression not only of a unifying trend within the farmers' movement, but of the various new social movements coming together. In spite of differences erupting, such as among farmers in the October rally in Delhi, V. P. Singh was elected prime minister at the end of 1989 with the support not only of the left but of the farmers' movement, Dalit and OBC groups and environmentalists. This did not last. Differences over what stand to take on liberalization and globalization now became salient, as the unity that appeared to exist in the 1980s in which the "single issue" moving each major social movement could bring all together proved to be spurious.

It is clear now that major differences exist among every social group over opposition to or support of the "new economic policy" and all it implied. In spite of talk of the dominance of "neoliberalism," in India active vocal support for policies of economic reform has been limited, with the result that political reforms have been carried forward almost surreptitiously and apologetically. A large section of political leaders and intellectuals (including most of the major daily newspapers) have been anti-reform or hesitant. The "Left" opposition has appeared strong (especially in the beginning several years) and along with the growing voice of Hindu-nationalist *swadeshi* advocates was influential among social movements.[22]

Splits also took place within social movements. In the women's movement and Dalit movement these were not so obvious; little organizing anyway had taken place on economic issues. Most leading activists tended to follow the left in their critiques of liberalization; those who did not for the most part quietly continued their activities—and indeed most organizing was on issues irrelevant to the overall policy debate. Among Dalits, though there has always been an underlying sentiment in favor of globalization, if not liberalization, it has been muted until recently. Only in the last year or so have new voices been heard from the Dalit movement, seen most visibly in the Bhopal Document, which takes inspiration from U.S. "affirmative action" programs in a section called "Let's Go Globe-Trotting," and which envisages land reforms as part of an overall project aimed at "democratizing capital" to help create Dalit independent smallholders, entrepreneurs, businessme, and millionaires.[23]

Among women, Madhu Kishwar, editor of *Manushi,* was the most high-profile activist to boldly take a stand in favor of liberalization; but by this time she was refusing the designation of "feminist." Other women activists supporting liberalization tended to find themselves isolated. In the environmental movement, the most famous sections, spearheaded by the Narmada Bachao Andolan, quickly took a position opposing reforms, opposing "globalization" on a general anti-development platform in which "subsistence production" and a romanticized view of traditional peasant (especially *adivasi*) life was central. While there were many activists organizing on issues of dam eviction or similar themes (for instance, the movement in the Krishna basin region of Maharashtra) who had very different perspectives on irrigation and development, these did not publicly contest the NBA at this time and had no clear differences on globalization and liberalization.

In the farmers' movement, however, the split was stark from 1991 onward. Sharad Joshi became the most prominent mass leader in India to support liberalization, while Nanjundaswamy of Karnataka quickly became a major Indian spokesman against globalization. Indeed, through much of the 1990s Nanjundaswamy gained a new media image through semiviolent campaigns attacking Cargill (a symbol of multinationals seeking to enslave farmers through seeds), McDonald's, and finally Monsanto, which with its Indian subsidiary Mahyco was developing a new cotton seed with an inserted gene to protect it from the bollworm, and carrying on experiments in selected farms. With Sharad Joshi were the Gujarat organization, a developing farmers' movement in Haryana, and one section of the Punjab BKU, while Nanjundaswamy allied with Tikait and another section of Punjab farmers.

FARMERS AND THE DEBATE ON LIBERALIZATION AND TECHNOLOGY

The split within the farmers' movement has not been simply over abstract support of or opposition to liberalization. It has centered around very concrete issues, linking technology, seeds, irrigation, and development to the question of liberalization. These have posed farmers' movements not only against the state, but against each other and against other social movement organizations.

The first such issue to develop in confrontational form was that of irrigation. The NBA's stand against "big dams" as such had alienated nearly all of the Gujarat population, and the increasing desperation of farmers in many parts of Gujarat resulted in the end of 1999 in an effort to organize a mass movement in support of the Sardar Sarovar Project (SSP, the major Narmada dam). It was led by Joshi and named "Narmada Jan Andolan." This was suppressed by the Gujarat government almost as much as they had tried to suppress opposition to the dam, but for a time media had a field day posing the battle in personalistic terms as one of Sharad Joshi versus Medha Patkar.[24]

An even more widely publicized issue has revolved around seeds, in particular the new biotechnology which has created new varieties of seeds through genetic modification (GM) technologies. These were being opposed in general by the environmental middle class left, but the opposition has been most strongly expressed in relation to farmers and by the section of the farmers' movement headed by Nanjundaswamy and the Karnataka Rajya Rayata Sangh, and it has been directly linked to the issues of globalization, multinational dominance, and indigenous culture.

The heart of this opposition was expressed in the terms of the very identity of farmers. The opponents of liberalization, patent rights, and multinational corporation (MNC) domination have pictured the ideal farmer as a subsistence oriented producer, living in harmony with nature—a basically Gandhian image of a harmonious village life. In this, control of one's own seeds is seen as almost a defining factor of the traditional farmer, while in contrast, multinationals developing new seeds are depicted as enslaving the farmers, forcing them into dependence on market production and on a monopoly supply of seeds. Although this opposition has most recently expressed itself against GM seeds and biotechnology, the rhetorical opposition to "Green Revolution" technology is just about as strong. "Hybrid" seeds are denounced and connected with a "hybrid" culture that presumably takes the indigenous farmers away from their own culture; see, for instance, the attitude reflected in Vasavi's study, based in Bijapur district, which does not even consider the possibility of provision of water from the Almatti dam.[25] Assadi has stressed the cultural opposition of the KRRS opposition to the Dunkel Draft, and quotes Nanjundaswamy as arguing that "Major decisions that affect our farmers are no longer being made by farmers and their organizations or state legislatures or even by Parliament . . . [but] in Washington and Geneva and IMF/World Bank headquarters and at the GATT [General Agreement on Tariffs and Trade] secretariat." Like the left as a whole, this section of the farmers' movement saw a "new colonialism" and the transformation of farmers from autonomous producers with control over land and seeds to "low wage laborers for agrobusiness." This displacement of the farmer was the destruction of Indian culture.[26]

This links the neo-Marxist category of "neocolonialism" control by MNCs, the world finance institutions and the transformation of farmers into wage laborers to a general cultural assertion. Thus the opponents of the new GM seeds could assert that the wave of suicides by farmers was also related to seed-providing MNCs, and continually referred to the pauperization in Third World countries resulting from globalization as well as the increase in "consumerism at the expense of the common man."

How did the KRRS and its supporters plan to deal with this global threat? At this point, earlier critiques of the state began to shift to policies that implicitly

asked for what Assadi calls a "strong but autonomous state." The state should
be of the peasantry, with democratic and decentralized decision making
(every treaty should be referred to Parliament and to states for ratification, the
KRRS claimed, seeking to challenge India's signing of the WTO agreement in
the Supreme Court), but it would have to be strong enough to impose a
"Khadi Curtain" that would keep out western hegemony and multinationals.[27]

In contrast to this view, Joshi and other supporters of liberalization have
depicted a modern, rationally minded farmer producing for the market, already accustomed to buying new hybrid seeds (and picking and choosing
among them). Farmers have been seen almost as the ideal entrepreneurs, attempting to carry out a toilsome but honorable occupation under the very
difficult conditions imposed by the Nehruvian state and its "license-permit
raj." The market is defended on moral grounds just as the KRRS attacks it on
moral grounds, as promoting self-reliance and freedom to the benefit of hon-
est producers such as farmers, and as leading to rapid development and the
removal of poverty. If the anti-liberalizers spoke the language of nationalist
swadeshi and the fight against colonialism, Joshi evoked the heritage of the
anti-caste movement in Maharashtra which had severely critiqued the indigenous elite. The 1993 conference of the Shetkari Sanghatana at Au-
rangabad was preceded by vigorous campaigning for open trade, and in the
conference Joshi won wide applause when he said, "They talk about a new
East India Company—we would welcome it in comparison to these black
Englishmen who rule over us now!" or, "If we have to be ruled we would
prefer it be done by someone competent."[28]

In its discussion of exploitation and surplus, the Sanghatana had always at
least a Marxian tone and attitude, and this has also been seen in its perspective
on technology: the development of technology is viewed as a part of human
advance. Thus, the Green Revolution was seen as necessary for advances in
production at the time and for freeing India from dependence on imported
foodgrains, though now the overuse and disadvantages of chemical fertilizers
and pesticides are becoming evident. As a solution to this, rather than simply
rejecting chemicals for traditional forms, Sanghatana activists and farmers now
look to the promise of biotechnology, both for increasing production and for
reducing the dependence on pesticides. Similarly, the solution to the developing power of western patented improved seeds is seen not as in the total rejection of patenting, but to develop Indian research and reward Indian innovation, which patenting would make possible.[29] All innovators, including
farmers, would benefit from this. Finally, Sharad Joshi's Marathi speeches included a critique of traditional Brahmanic tendencies to treat knowledge as a
secret possession. With patents, at least knowledge was made public, though
at a cost; but the refusal to allow even experiments by Monsanto and its Indian
partner Mahyco (Maharashtra Hybrid Seeds Company) on cotton plants was
compared to Brahmans denying *Shudras* the right to read the Vedas.

The access to technology thus is seen not only as a crucial right of farmers as producers, but one that has added urgency with the argument that in today's world Indian farmers can be competitive only through upgrading productivity. This was an important modification officially admitted by the Sanghatana in its liberal faith that opening up markets would be sufficient: now it was admitted that farmers were technologically backward, that the centuries of caste oppression had indeed taken their toll, and that liberalization required a simultaneous access to and use of the most modern technologies.

From this perspective the multinationals or large seed companies would not pose a threat as long as the farmer has sufficient choice among them—indeed they would be an ally in developing the technologies of modernization. Activists have pointed out the complex of interests involved in opposing GM seeds—charging, for instance, that pesticide companies (whose interests are threatened by new seeds which do not need chemical pesticides to resist pests) have financed the opposition campaign. Knowing that Indian per-acre productivities being the lowest in the world for the major crops, they have also argued urgently for upgrading of technologies in order to compete in the world market, even to produce for India itself.

In the attitude toward technology, the "Marxist" themes in Shetkari Sanghatana discourse are clearly taking precedence over their "Gandhism." Advances in technology, in the forces of production, have been looked upon as human advances; in contrast to the eco-romanticist depiction of the farmer as rooted in the soil and a natural life, the Sanghatana discourse sees him/her as an oppressed human being, searching for a better life, aspiring to move ahead. Tom Brass has characterized the ideology of peasant or farmers' movements as sharing romanticist-holistic themes with environmentalism;[30] this is true for the section of the movement led by Nanjundaswamy. The Shetkari Sanghatana approach has in contrast been rationalistic and materialistic, upholding Gandhi for his village focus and as an alternative to Nehruvian statism, seeing him not as opposed to economic development but rather visualizing development coming as a natural process based on keeping the surplus in the villages.[31]

The different leaders of the farmers' movement thus now appear to be in an almost total ideological confrontation; the position regarding liberalization is now linked to that of technology and development: pro-liberalizers are pro-technology; anti-liberalizers are now opposing both contemporary biotechnologies and Green Revolution technology. These positions are connected with strong assertions about their implication for poverty. For the anti-technologists, it has been on the one hand "Green Revolution" and now agricultural biotechnologies that threaten the livelihoods of the poor; dams that displace and oppress them; world trade that would enslave them. For the pro-technological liberalizers, it is "subsistence farmers" who are the poorest; it is drought that is the greatest agent of displacement; and—with all their faults and ambiguities—it is the rise in productivity in agriculture (a result first of Green Revolution technology and now of biotechnology) that can provide both the income and employment opportunities that will alone help the rural poor to move ahead (for an eloquent statement of this position, see Michael Lipton's Consultative Group on International Agriculture Research (CGIAR) paper and International Fund for Agricultural Development (IFAD) seminar presentation). The divide on technology is similar to the divide on trade: Will Indian farmers—including the rural poor—prosper by becoming part of world trading networks, or by trying to hide behind a "khadi curtain"?

It was clear that by the beginning of the new millennium, there are deep rifts in Indian society, among social movements and within the farmers' movement itself over basic perspectives on poverty and development. However, while debates among the leadership and among intellectuals continue, it appears that farmers themselves are voting for technology and openness. Nanjundaswamy's ability to claim leadership of the farmers' movement in Karnataka itself is now under question, and his main opponent, Puttanaiah, appears to be gradually evolving an independent approach.[32] As a recent paper by Stig Toft Madsen and Staffan Lindberg puts it, while the Indian government hesitates in approving Bt cotton, farmers are going ahead and planting it. The KRRS campaign was failing to unite farmers against genetically engineered crops, and "while the head says 'no,' the feet say 'yes' to the seeds as well as to the way they were obtained."[33]

Thus, while the division among leaders remains, the majority opinion among the farmers, in regard to both dams and the latest seed technologies, seems to be on the side of the pro-technologists and pro-liberalizers.

HAS THERE BEEN POVERTY REDUCTION?

Interestingly, more research and publication seemed to focus on the issue of poverty in the 1990s as compared to the two earlier decades. This is certainly true of India's most important general intellectual publication, the *Economic and Political Weekly*. Clearly, both the opponents and defenders of reforms were concerned to monitor the effects on poverty.

The initial phase came with a series of articles in 1995 which showed an increase in poverty based on the most prestigious of India's sample organizations, the NSS (National Sample Survey).[34] These data became used quite widely as proof of the morass of poverty which awaited the rural poor. However, the main problem with the studies was that their latest period was the 1991–1992 NSS survey; this was less than a year after the true beginning of reforms and the growth in poverty mainly reflected the decline in the general economic growth rate that came in 1991–1992 before the 1990s shift to higher growth rates. The 1993–1994 NSS survey showed, in contrast, an almost stagnant situation in poverty between the 1987–1988 survey and 1993–1994.

Evidence remained inconclusive and much debated since there were only smaller samples ("thin" samples) of the NSS until its full round was taken in 1999–2000. By the time this took place, there had been many intervening studies and debates about the accuracy of the NSS data, their divergence from the statistics collected officially (in the NAS). Among other issues of concern were differences in data regarding answers to questions about consumption in the last week, versus the last month (a thirty-day period). The NSS in 1999–2000 used both, and then showed rather surprisingly a high decline in rural poverty. This was questioned by skeptics of reform such as Arjun Sen, while supporters cited comparisons with other studies. K. Sundaram then wrote a series of articles using as base not the poverty statistics as such, but data on employment, arguing that there had been a rise in the real income of the lowest sections of unorganized workers; this, he noted, fit the claims for a decline in poverty. The debate ranges from name Bhalla's argument that poverty has declined[35] to as much as 15 percent to the much more cautious assessment of World Bank economists that it has declined minimally—and much less than what has been possible—from about 39 to 34 percent.

Another interesting event of the debate about reforms and GATT (now WTO) process was that, according to the official measurements used to calculate the "aggregate measure of support" given to agriculture, studies for nearly all crops in India showed that this was negative.[36] This was used by experts to argue for the greater competitive quality of India's agricultural products, and by Sharad Joshi and other farmers' movement spokesmen to support their claim of exploitation of rural production: the "negative subsidy" of India (otherwise called a "tax" in many studies of the "political economy of agriculture" produced by World Bank economists) now became a byword to argue against the government. A major culprit here has been the continuing subsidization by developed countries of their agriculture.

The evidence appears to support a decline in poverty, but not a very large one for rural areas. The assessment of Datt, Kozel, and Ravallion that the decline has been only modest and has been slightly slower than the decline from 1987–1988 to 1993–1994; this they argue has been the failure of pro-poor growth. Agricultural growth has lagged behind, and this has been crucial for the poor. Similarly, the problems of joblessness and lack of growth in educational opportunities remain. There has also been little visible fundamental change in the funding of education and health, especially with a minister at the center who interprets "human resources development" in terms of promoting Vedic mathematics and astrology—i.e., Brahmanic values. Subsidies for higher education are promoted (for instance with the Indian Institutes of Management) while primary education has continued to be neglected. There is also evidence for a growing rural-urban gap, and severe caste differential in poverty rates.[37]

Thus we can argue that not only was the earlier "Nehru model" of development rather anti-agriculture, the implementation of reforms in the 1990s focused on industry rather than on agriculture. At the international

level, the process of subsidizing agriculture in developed countries continued; while in India itself not only was agriculture kept under fairly tight
restrictions (for instance, there was only very slow approval of new GM
technologies, while monopoly purchasing schemes such as those in cotton continued for much of the period), but above all, public sector investment in agriculture showed a declining trend. Through much of the
1990s rains were good; but then in the early years of the twenty-first century severe drought hit several parts of the country (notably in Maharashtra, Andhra, Karnataka and Tamilnadu), continuing for several years.
While poverty has declined in the 1990s, it is still seriously high—India
has perhaps the most poor people of any country in the world. Poverty is
worse in rural areas; there is indeed some evidence that the rural-urban
gap has been increasing. In other words, while the rural poor/farmers
have benefited to some degree from the general economic growth of the
1990s, it has not been by very much.

The conditions of exploitation which gave rise to the farmers' movement
remain. The issue of rural poverty remains equally alive in India. The result
has recently been given a political expression. In a surprising result, the
people of India in May 2004 general parliamentary elections gave a decisive
rejection to the BJP, which had been full of confidence after overwhelming
victories in several state assembly elections in December, and chose a
Congress-led alliance. The BJP had been projecting a grandiose image of a
powerful "India shining"; this was fairly decisively rejected. The role of the
left and the promise of "reforms with a human face" now brought a new focus on dealing with poverty and unemployment. However, with foreign-
born Sonia Gandhi refusing to be prime minister, the position devolved
upon Manmohan Singh—considered the original architect of India's economic reforms. Thus the road ahead is now open.

Two factors stand out from this survey of the farmers' movement and perspectives on poverty. First, it is clear that throughout varying political and
economic regimes—first the state-oriented "Nehru model" and more recently
the market-oriented decade of reforms—agriculture has continued to be discriminated against, and this has had the consequence of maintaining often
severe rural poverty even in the face of economic development. Powerful
and massive mobilization of farmers against this has had little political effect;
in spite of fears of the influence of the "farmers' lobby," India's urban bias
has remained in place. And second, the widely varying perspectives seen in
the farmers' movement (and indeed in all social movements) have reflected
the different intellectual orientation of the leadership of local and regional
movements, rather than the mass base character of farmers themselves. Neither the analysis of poverty nor its alleviation has proved a simple matter in
independent India.

NOTES

1. See my paper for the Farmers' Movement Organisation project, which argues that precisely in the case of the farmers' movement, you can find movement organizations with almost identical mass base and contrasting ideologies. See Gail Omvedt, "Ideology and Organization in the Farmers' Movement: Shetkari Sanghatana from 'Remunerative Prices' to 'Farmers for Freedom,'" Paper for Farmers' Movement Organization project, Copenhagen, Denmark: Nordic Institute for Asian Studies, June 2000.

2. Samuel Bowles and Herbert Gintis, *Democracy and Capitalism: Property, Community and the Contradictions of Modern Social Thought* (London: Routledge and Kegan Paul, 1986).

3. Ralf Dahrendorf, "Liberalism," in *The New Palgrave: The Invisible Hand*, ed. John Eatwell, Murray Milgate, and Peter Newman (New York: W. W. Norton, 1987).

4. The terminology of "ideology" has specific implications with which I do not always agree, but I am using it anyway to indicate the major, broad worldviews that have arisen with industrial-capitalist society. Broader concepts used in sociological literature are "frame" or "discourse," and in this sense each of the specific social movement organizations should be described as having a discourse or using a framework.

5. Cited in V. S. Vyas and Pradeep Bhargava, "Public Intervention for Poverty Alleviation: An Overview," *Economic and Political Weekly*, October 14–21, 1995.

6. See the chapter on "Brahman Socialism and the Hindu Rate of Growth" in Gail Omvedt, *Dalit Visions: The Anti-Caste Movement and the Construction of an Indian Identity* (New Delhi: Orient Longman, 1995).

7. Sukhumoy Chakravarty, *Development Planning: The Indian Experience* (New Delhi: Oxford University Press, 1987), 19, 21.

8. One consequence of this was that trade unions also consistently opposed automation, out of fear that this would reduce the availability of employment; the idea that growth could continually create new areas of employment was hardly recognized in popular discourse.

9. Nilanjan Banik and Saurabh Bandopahyay, *Cotton Textile Industry in India in the Wake of MFA Phase-Out*, New Delhi: Rajiv Gandhi Institute for Contemporary Studies, Working Paper No. 9, 2000.

10. See, for instance, Narasimha Rao's "novel," *The Insider* (New Delhi: Viking [Penguin Books India]), 1998, which makes land reform the center for the heroic efforts of his hero.

11. Remarkably, Nobel Prize–winner Amartya Sen's arguments that globalization would be helpful for the poor if education, health, and land reform measures are taken and that in turn these would help in producing growth, have been ignored by his otherwise enthusiastic left supporters in India.

12. The first enthusiastic presentation of this I have heard was from a Chinese woman, daughter of Communist Party members, trained as a finance economist in the United States, and returning to China to work as a venture capitalist: Mannie Liu, "Venture Capital, Growth and Poverty," presentation at the Seminar on Profiles of Poverty and Networks of Power, Madurai, February 14–16, 2001.

13. For this reason I refer to them in the plural in this paper: Dalit or farmers' "movements" and not "movement."

14. The term "farmer" is sometimes used to suggest those rural producers involved in commodity production as contrasted with the more subsistence-producing "peasant." It is significant, however, that the distinction makes no sense in Indian languages where one word serves for both—*kisan, shetkari, rayat,* etc. This fits a situation where almost all producers do sell in the market as well as consume a portion of their produce.

15. Stig Toft Madsen, "The View from Vevey," *Economic and Political Weekly,* September 29, 2001; S. K. Ramoo, "Karnataka Farmers' Organisation Splits," *The Hindu,* November 16, 2000.

16. Quoted in *Sunday,* December 1980.

17. Muzaffar Assadi, "'Khadi Curtain,' 'Weak Capitalism' and 'Operation Ryot': Some Ambiguities in Farmers' Discourse, Karnataka and Maharashtra 1980–95," in *New Farmers' Movements in India,* ed. Tom Brass (London: Frank Cass, 1995), 220–21.

18 . Among conventional economists, the point was expressed in the idea of "taxation" of agriculture put forward in the 1980s by several World Bank volumes on "The Political Economy of Agriculture." Anne O. Krueger, Maurice Schiff, and Alberto Valdes, *The Political Economy of Agricultural Pricing Policy, Volume 2: Asia, A World Bank Comparative Study* (Baltimore and London: Johns Hopkins University Press, 1991); D. Gale Johnson, "Agriculture in the Liberalization Process," in *Liberalization in the Process of Economic Development,* ed. Lawrence B. Kruse and Kim Kihwan (Berkeley: University of California Press, 1991), 283–391. The famous phrase "getting prices right" was originally used in connection with agriculture (see C. Peter Timmer, *Getting Prices Right: The Scope and Limits of Agricultural Price Policy* [Ithaca and London: Cornell University Press, 1986], and Theodore W. Schultz, "Economic Growth from Traditional Agriculture," in *Chicago Essays in Economic Development,* ed. David Bell [Chicago and London: University of Chicago Press, 1972], 3–22). Theodore Schultz, it may be noted, is not only considered a founding figure who "did so much to establish development studies in Chicago" (introduction to Bell, *Chicago Essays in Economic Development,* ix); his major research connection was with India. More social-liberal agriculturally oriented economic institutions such as the International Food Policy Research Institute (IFPRI) stressed similar themes, e.g., Romeo M. Bautista and Alberto Valdes, *The Bias Against Agriculture: Trade and Macroeconomic Policies in Developing Countries* (San Francisco: International Center for Economic Growth and International Food Policy Research Institute, 1993). The report of South Commission, set up as a body of developing nations only and headed by Julius Nyerere, warned against trying to finance development through policies of exploitation of agriculture through discriminatory pricing, expressing also questions about PDS–type policies of procuring cheap food for state-financed distribution; see South Commission, *The Challenge to the South: Report of the South Commission* (Delhi: Oxford University Press, 1992), 83–91.

19. See Sunil Sahrasabudhe, "Peasant Movement and the Quest for Development," in *Peasant and Peasant Protest in India,* ed. M. N. Karna (New Delhi: Intellectual Publishing House, 1989).

20. See Assadi, "'Khadi Curtain,'" 214.

21. See Zoya Hasan, *Dominance and Mobilisation: Rural Politics in Western Uttar Pradesh, 1930–1980* (New Delhi: Sage, 1989), 176.

22. In the end, however, the strongest base for opposition to reforms seems to simply come from entrenched bureaucratic interests, who have benefited from the rhetoric of both right and left in their resistance to any erosion of power.

23. See Bhopal Document, Government of Madhya Pradesh, 2001; Bhopal Declaration (from Dalit Conference, January 12–13, 2001).

24. See Gail Omvedt, "Struggle against Dams or Struggle for Water? Environmental Movements and the State," in *Indian Democracy, Meanings and Practices,* ed. Rajendra Vora and Suhas Palshikar (New Delhi: Sage, 2003).

25. A. R. Vasavi, *Harbingers of Rain: Land and Life in South India* (Delhi: Oxford University Press, 1999).

26. Assadi, "'Khadi Curtain,'" 220.

27. Assadi, "'Khadi Curtain,'" 220–21. It was Nanjundaswamy who first used the phrase in an interview in 1988.

28. Such extreme rhetoric has Dalit correlates: "The problem with the British is that they came too late and left too soon!" from a prominent Dalit intellectual at a 1999 conference in Chandigarh.

29. A major spokesman for "intellectual property rights for farmers" in India has been Anil Gupta of the Indian Institute of Management, who has long been attempting to record and publish farmers' innovations in his *Honeybee* (in English, Gujarati, and Hindi) and has urged protection for farmers' rights. But there has been no connection with Shetkari Sanghatana activity.

30. Tom Brass, introduction to *New Farmers' Movements in India,* ed. Tom Brass (London: Frank Cass, 1995), 14.

31. Sharad Joshi, *Swatantra ka Nasle?* [What Went Wrong with Independence?] (Parbhani: Renuka Prakashan, 1998), 59–60.

32. See Stig Toft Madsen, "The View from Vevey"; *The Hindu,* January 25, 2002, Karnataka edition.

33. Staffan Lindberg and Stig Toft Madsen, "Farmers' Movements in South Asia: Contemporary Trends in a Historical Context," *Cambridge Review of International Affairs* (forthcoming).

34. S. P. Gupta, "Economic Reform and Its Impact on the Poor," *Economic and Political Weekly,* June 3, 1995; Suresh D. Tendulkar, "Economic Reforms and Poverty," *Economic and Political Weekly,* July 10, 1995; Suresh D. Tendulkar and L. R. Jain, "Economic Reforms and Poverty," *Economic and Political Weekly,* June 10, 1995.

35. Abhijit Sen, "Estimates of Consumer Expenditure and Its Distribution: Statistical Priorities after NSS 55th Round," *Economic and Political Weekly* (December 16, 2000); Deepak Lal, Rakesh Mohan, and I. Natarajan, "Economic Reforms and Poverty Alleviation: A Tale of Two Surveys," *Economic and Political Weekly* (March 24, 2001) provided early examples of the disagreement. K. Sundaram then wrote a series of articles using as base not the poverty statistics as such, but data on employment, arguing that there had been a rise in the real income of the lowest sections of unorganized workers; this, he noted, fit the claims for a decline in poverty (Sundaram, "Employment-Unemployment Situation in the Nineties: Some Results from NSS 55th Round Survey," *Economic and Political Weekly,* March 17, 2001; "Employment and Poverty in 1990s: Further Results from NSS 55th Round Employment-Unemployment Survey, 1999–2000," *Economic and Political Weekly,* August 11, 2001; "Employment and Poverty in 1990s: A Postscript," *Economic and Political Weekly,* August 25, 2001).

See also K. Sundaram and Suresh D. Tendulkar, "Poverty in India in the 1990s: Revised Results for All-India and 15 Major States for 1993–94," *Economic and Political Weekly*, November 15, 2003; Surjit Bhalla, "Recounting the Poor: Poverty in India, 1983–99," *Economic and Political Weekly*, January 25, 2003; and Gaurav Datt, Valerie Kozel, and Martin Ravallion, "A Model-Based Assessment of India's Progress in Reducing Poverty in the 1990s," *Economic and Political Weekly*, January 25, 2003.

36. See Ashok Gulati and Seema Bathla, "Capital Formation in Indian Agriculture: Re-Visiting the Debate," *Economic and Political Weekly* (May 19, 2001); Ashok Gulati, Rajesh Mehta, and Sudha Narayanan, "From Marrakesh to Seattle: Indian Agriculture in a Globalising World," *Economic and Political Weekly*, October 9, 1999: 2931–42; Ashok Gulati and C. N. Hanumantha Rao, "Indian Agriculture; Emerging Perspectives and Policy Issues," *Economic and Political Weekly*, December 31, 1994); Ashok Gulati and Anil Sharma, "Agriculture Under GATT: What It Holds for India," *Economic and Political Weekly*, July 16, 1994; Ashok Gulati and A. N. Sharma, "Subsidising Agriculture: A Cross-Country View," *Economic and Political Weekly*, September 26, 1992.

37. For data on caste, see Sundaram and Tendulkar, "Poverty in India in the 1990s."

8

Miracle Seeds, Suicide Seeds, and the Poor

GMOs, NGOs, Farmers, and the State

Ronald J. Herring

GOLDEN RICE, FLOUNDER GENES, AND INSULIN: TRANSGENIC POLITICS

Both sides in the globally contentious politics surrounding genetically modified organisms—or "GMOs"[1]—have a poverty story to tell. Instrumental discourses counterpoise disaster scenarios against promises of improving the human condition through technological innovation.[2] The public debate is dominated by the antinomies of the dangerously unnatural—"Frankenfoods," and "suicide seeds"—against a solution to a gathering Malthusian crisis of world hunger. These disputes do not follow familiar North-South tectonics. Broadly, one can distinguish an American view that has been more supportive of GMOs and a European view that has been skeptical or oppositional. India has been poised between these alternatives, as have activists in social movements claiming to represent farmers, the poor, and the environment. On March 26, 2002, India became the sixteenth nation in the world to certify a genetically altered crop for commercialization, albeit provisionally and in the face of continuing opposition. Since then, there has been a veritable explosion of entrants into the transgenic seed arena in India, some sanctioned by the state and some generated by an opportunistic rural anarcho-capitalism enabled by biotechnology.

Conflicts surrounding GMOs represent a special category of politics; interests are mediated by incomplete science and discontinuities in ethical, even cosmological, systems. Opponents deploy arguments entailing ecological disaster, unnatural acts, and the hubris of "playing god." Though it is the most novel and intractable politically, the dimension of novel and unnatural processes and products constitutes only one of the breaking points in this debate. Much of the overt contest in India has been about property as a sub-set of the globalization dispute. Property disputes are demonstrably subject to conciliation, bargaining and compromise—familiar terrain for the political economy of interests. Moreover, property is at the core of any serious con-sideration of the poor, current fads notwithstanding.[3] Disputes about the na-ture of the natural, and consequent risks of the unnatural, take on a different politics, dependent on an expertise that is asymmetrically distributed both locally—on the ground within movements—and globally. These latter ques-tions create a new politics less susceptible to ordinary bargaining solutions, but it is an inescapable politics generated by the genomics revolution.

As the major players in the genomics revolution are multinational firms, and opposition speaks explicitly of the vulnerability of poor people and poor nations facing globalization and radical technical change, some in-credulity meets the notion that biotechnology could be pro-poor. Yet India's Prime Minister Atal Bihari Vajpayee stated on September 7, 2001, that na-tional policy was based on a vision of "shaping biotechnology into a premier precision tool of the future for creation of wealth and ensuring social justice—especially for the welfare of the poor."[4] Biotechnology is to be de-veloped to fight obdurate diseases, increase agricultural production, combat nutritional deficiencies, and protect the environment. Any and all of these outcomes could be pro-poor if realized.

Those who claim to speak for farmers have taken different positions on this promise. The first overt politics around GMOs were oppositional—a loosely-jointed movement against the government's decision to allow field-testing of transgenic crops throughout India. Protests were held, trial crops were burned in the fields, courts were moved. The oppositional discourse was constructed in terms of threats: threats to national independence, in the form of dominance of agriculture by multinational corporations; threats to farmers, in the form of bondage to monopoly seed corporations; threats to na-ture, in the form of "biological pollution" (horizontal gene flow); threats to human health, in the form of undiscovered allergens. The recuperative op-posites were posed in terms of universal valents: biodiversity over biological reductionism; self-reliance in place of subordination to foreign market power; safety over uncertainty and risk; the natural over the unnatural.

Opposition in India, as in Europe, specifically centered on seeds—and not on pharmaceuticals. There is some biological justification for this dis-tinction: transgenic seeds are released into the environment; pharmaceuti-cals can in theory be sequestered—though the increasingly common pro-duction of pharmaceutical components by plants in the field through "pharming" blurs the distinction. "Golden rice" and tomatoes with flounder genes—the first real, the second a hoax—come up regularly, but not in-sulin. Human insulin is produced by a genetically modified organism; the alternatives involve the pancreas of dead pigs or cows, carrying hardly salubrious connotations in several world cultures. Bovine insulin in India is cheaper than human insulin, yet the latter is increasing in usage.[5] Nevertheless, social movements do not target transgenic insulin. Seeds evoke multiple and overlapping cultural meanings, enabling a politics not available to those worried about transgenics in pharmaceuticals. Vandana Shiva, the dominant voice in opposition, explicitly compared the seed to the spinning wheel of the Independence movement: "The seed has become for us the site and symbol of freedom in the age of manipulation and monopoly. . . . In the seed, cultural diversity converges with biological diversity. Ecological issues combine with social justice, peace and democracy."[6] Seeds are constructed as carriers of the many virtues of a peasant society under threat of extinction. Seeds so understood are embedded in more encompassing cultural tropes of cyclicality and renewal.[7] But the most important conclusion may be that it is politically impracticable to attack life-saving drugs, as European non governmental organization (NGOs) explicitly recognize; foreign seeds present a different opportunity structure altogether.

"CREMATE MONSANTO": SUICIDE SEEDS AND THE TERMINATOR

Direct action against transgenic seeds began in 1998, targeting the transnational giant Monsanto. The firm was accused of planning to unleash a biocultural abomination on India. What is technically gene use restriction technology (GURT) was dubbed the "terminator," evoking a fairly dramatic image for those familiar with the internationally popular film of the same name. The term itself, and the alarm to India, originated with the Rural Advancement Foundation International (RAFI) of Canada. RAFI linked terminator technology to "suicide seeds." The terminator would in theory permit engineering of plants that could not produce viable seeds, forcing farmers to return each season to buy new seeds—generating a biological dependence of farmers on firms unmatched by customary arrangements. More important symbolically, the venerable cycle of "self-organizing" agriculture would be replaced by dependency and cash nexus.

   This construction—linking multinational capital, globalization, and a cultural abomination of suicide seeds—created a capacious symbolic opening. Monsanto was powerful and American, and it carried baggage of history. Clubbed together with Dow Chemicals, which together "brought us Bhopal and Vietnam," Monsanto was accused of planning to "unleash genetic catastrophes."[8] Real attributes of the firm's record were combined with a false attribution to Monsanto of property rights for engineering sterile seeds—the terminator.

   A social tragedy deepened this symbolic opening. A rash of suicides by debt-ridden farmers—most notably in Warangal district, Andhra Pradesh, but widely spread—was linked explicitly by activists to globalization of agriculture and new technologies.[9] Vandana Shiva, with colleagues, produced in 2000 a volume *Seeds of Suicide*, "dedicated to the farmers of India who committed suicide." Deepening dependence on hybrid seeds of multinationals—variously called "seeds of death" or "suicide seeds"—did not distinguish transgenic seeds from other hybrids; nevertheless, field trials of transgenic cotton in 1998 were tainted as an opening wedge of terminator technology in India.[10] Terminator seeds were specifically banned by the government of India in response to this movement, as announced in assurances in the *Lok Sabha* and *Rajya Sabha*, and via Office Memorandum No. 82–1/98 PQD, dated May 25, 1998. None of these assurances stopped the campaign.[11]

Monsanto's marketing director for India responded that the farmers' suicides had nothing to do with Monsanto at all, but ironically might have been prevented by its technology. With transgenic cotton, Monsanto argued, farmers would have had less debt from pesticide purchase and less loss of yield—less poverty, fewer suicides. Glenn Stone noted that "India is a key battle line in the global war over GM crops, and both sides interpret the Warangal suicides as supporting their position."[12]

It was the extranational vector of introducing transgenics into India that provided a handle for mobilization of farmer opposition. Indeed, it is a fascinating counter-factual to imagine the politics had the GMOs come through the Indian public sector—as is now unfolding with both Chinese and Indian versions. But in the event, biotechnology and globalization were welded at the hip in social-movement constructions. Vandana Shiva's *Biopiracy: The Plunder of Nature and Knowledge* was published in 1997; its themes provided the main frames for the connection between globalization and transgenics in India. Chapter 1 sets the stage: "Piracy through Patents." Chapter 2 throws down the rhetorical gauntlet: "Can Life Be Made? Can Life Be Owned?" Dr. Shiva's overriding concern with biotechnology is that techniques are being made available for "the control of agriculture by multinational corporations."[13] In the resulting movement, concern with intellectual property rights and corporate power was married to cultural and nationalist themes of self-reliance, nonviolence, local knowledge, and biodiversity.

Protests on the ground began with the *Karnataka Rajya Raitha Sangha* (KRRS; Karnataka State Farmers' Organization). Founded in 1980, the organization's original objectives were issues around which farmers have historically mobilized—debts, taxes, prices. Like most farmer organizations in India, it was led by richer farmers. Opposition to multinationals predated the transgenic seeds initiative. In 1992, KRRS activists occupied and ransacked the offices of the seed giant Cargill in Bangalore and Bellary. In 1995, activists raided a Kentucky Fried Chicken restaurant in Bangalore.[14] Critiques of multinational penetration of India connected a state-level farmers' organization to national and international public intellectuals contesting globalization. KRRS became a member organization of the international umbrella *Via Campesina*. The leader of the KRRS, Professor M. D. Nanjundaswamy, summarized their position at the demonstration against the World Economic Summit in Cologne in 1999: "We do not want Western money, technologies, or 'experts' to impose their development model on us." Their alternative was "a world where local people are in control of their local economy, where centralized political and economic power disappear. . . ."[15] In both theory and method, the movement resonated strongly with Gandhian precedents.

Monsanto provided a charged political target and a redirection of the KRRS campaign. In 1995, the Indian firm MAHYCO (Maharashtra Hybrid Seeds Company) obtained permission to import and test transgenic cotton seeds obtained from Monsanto. It was widely reported in India, and asserted by NGOs mobilizing opposition, that Monsanto had taken over MAHYCO, India's largest seed company; the actual ownership share was 26 percent. MAHYCO's interest was in Monsanto's Bollgard cotton, which was genetically engineered to produce pesticide in the plant's tissues. Bt is the generic designation for seeds to which a gene from a soil bacterium—*Bacillus thuringiensis*, hence the name Bt—has been added. This gene enables the plant to produce a protein that is toxic to some types of insects (*lepidoptera*) that consume its tissues, most importantly for India the especially destructive American bollworm (*Helicoverpa armigera*). For unclear ecological reasons, India suffers from particularly intensive bollworm infestations in comparative terms. Cotton is a crop especially vulnerable to pests. In India, more than half of all pesticides consumed are used on cotton; the cost of pesticides used against the bollworm alone is about 11 billion rupees [US $235 million] annually. Unserviceable cash debts to pesticide firms figured prominently in the suicides of ruined farmers in 1998. As farmers in India have encountered the pesticide treadmill—more poisons are required over time for less effect—the Bt plant was potentially attractive. But there is also an enormous social externality of pesticide use: contamination of farm workers, soil, and water, as well as damage to nontarget insects, birds, and aquatic life. Moreover, cotton in India is often in crisis, as dramatized by the farmer suicides. India has more acreage in cotton than any other country, almost nine million hectares, but yields are among the lowest in the world—about 320 kg of cotton lint per hectare.[16]

MAHYCO produced an Indian Bt cotton from Monsanto germplasm by making back-crosses with local varieties after obtaining approval from the Department of Biotechnology. The firm then applied for permission to conduct large-scale field trials. These trials were necessary to obtain approval for commercial release from the Genetic Engineering Approval Committee of the Ministry of Environment and Forests (GEAC). Though similar tests were taking place throughout the country, on five agricultural crops, it was Bt cotton that sparked protests. The transnational connection through Monsanto was central to protest politics.

In the beginning of Operation Cremate Monsanto, Bt cotton crops were burned on two test plots in Raichur and Bellary districts of Karnataka in 1998. The KRRS explained its action as explicit resistance to foreign domination of the seeds of Indian farmers, and thus of India. The alternative name for the campaign was "Monsanto, Quit India," reflecting again the Gandhian evocation. For the burning of a crop in Savalanga, activists from the youth wing of the KRRS—*Hasiru Sene* (Green Army)—surprised their leaders and police and burned a field of a farmer—Ganagdharaiah—who claimed he did not know there was Bt cotton on his land. President of the north Indian farmers' organization *Bharatiya Kisan Sangh,* Choudhary Mahendra Singh Tikait, was present at the protest. The claim of the *Hasiru Sene* was that Bt cotton was a threat to both the environment and traditional agriculture. Characterization of the transgenics as a problem of globalization solidified international protest linkages. The first field burning was accomplished when the leader of the KRRS, Professor Nanjundaswamy, came to the fields with activists from Spain and Germany.[17]

Though the terminator debate was prominent internationally and in India, this technology was neither developed nor owned by Monsanto.[18] Monsanto's representative in India rebutted charges of suicide seeds: "Since the so-called terminator gene does not exist today in any plant in any country in the world, the question of its involvement in the field trials currently on in India does not arise." MAHYCO-Monsanto Seeds chairman B. R. Barwale emphasized that the seeds being tested had been approved by the Department of Biotechnology for trials and have "nothing to do with the so-called terminator genes."[19] Nevertheless, suicide seeds were presented in movement iconography as an assault on India as nation; Vandana Shiva wrote:

> Freedom from the first cotton colonisation was based on liberation through the spinning wheel. . . . Freedom from the second cotton colonisation needs to be based on liberation through the seed. . . . The freedom of the seeds and freedom of organic farming are simultaneously a resistance against monopolies . . . like Monsanto and a regeneration of agriculture. . . . The seeds of suicide need to be replaced by the seeds of prosperity.[20]

As in many social movements in India, the KRRS explicitly linked mobilization to Gandhian ideals, primarily organized around the concept of *swadeshi* (self-reliance). Multinationals were cast in imperial terms, seeking dominance of Indian farmers and India. This critique of neocolonial dependencies is organically linked to a widespread and vigorous re-thinking of internal democracy that increasingly occupies social movements outside political parties and government institutions. Concern with the processes and institutions of democratic development valorizing "the people" generically largely displace class or sectoral interests in movement strategy. The movement *Lok Swaraj* (People's Self-rule), for example, seeks "to assert people's sovereignty over decisions and resources that affect their lives and livelihood . . . to save the country being hijacked by a new form of colonialism." A subtheme, *Bija Swaraj* (Seed Self-rule), then locates seed struggles both within a broader ideology asserting the people's sovereignty in the face of threats from globalization within a national context of incomplete democracy. *Lok Swaraj* implies a form of participatory and transparent democracy inconsistent with rule by distant experts, whether biological scientists or economists. The government's cotton tests were criticized as top-down, even illegal—an imposition by technocratic elites with foreign allies on unsuspecting people in rural India.[21]

The KRRS was the epicenter of on-the-ground protests against GMO seeds, along with Andhra Pradesh, but there were other venues and tactics. In Delhi in September 2000, a *Bija Panchayat* (seed tribunal) met to hear testimony on the crisis of farmers and urge a moratorium on transgenic seeds. Public intellectuals seem to have dominated. Justice V. R. Krishna Iyer spoke to a group including foreign NGOs and Indian farmers on the plight of farmers caught up in dependency relations. The *panchayat* also heard testimonies of farmers from Punjab, Andhra Pradesh, and Karnataka. Testimony as recorded by the press asserted that many farmers "were forced to commit suicides and sell their kidneys to repay loans and protect their family honor."[22]

The composition of the *Bija Panchayat* was typical of the anti-GMO coalition: public intellectuals from India, international NGOs and their Indian partners and sporadic involvement of some farmers. Sociologically similar coalitions represent one of the last vestiges of an active pro-poor agenda in India today: they are often exactly the same people.

Politics surrounding "farmers' movements" inevitably raise the question of who speaks for the farmer. In the initial protests by KRRS, a third trial plot, in Adur village, Haveri *taluq*, was not burned. The reasons proved to be diagnostic of the weakness of the movement. The farmer who owned the plot, Shri Shankarikoppa Mahalingappa, reportedly was willing to cooperate until the state-level unit of the *Bharatiya Kisan Sangh* (Indian Peasant Union) asked him not to. In my own conversation with Mahalingappa, he stressed that he could not count on the KRRS explanation of the new technology, but had to see for himself. He then asked for and received police protection for his crops. Mahalingappa found that the "suicide seeds" actually sprouted— at a 95 percent germination rate—and called arguments of Professor Nanjundaswamy about the danger of the transgenic seeds "a cheap publicity stunt." Neighboring farmers watched his experience closely and were eager to obtain the new seeds.[23] He noted that the foliage did not harm insects other than the bollworm, nor mammals; as far as he could tell as a farmer, there was no danger from the new seeds. Once a member of the KRRS, Shankarikoppa Mahalingappa turned against the movement on the issue of destroying test crops in the field. His desertion proved to be politically prescient. His dissent illustrated one historic problem of mobilization: cultural and practical distance of elites from nominal members. Leaders of the movement were decrying terminator technology even as Shankarikoppa Mahalingappa was testing out the germination rate—and finding it high. The KRRS was especially suspect on this dimension of cultural distance and dubious representation.[24] Professor Nanjundaswamy claimed a membership of ten million farmers for KRRS; yet, the KRRS failed to secure any seats when it transformed itself into a political party.[25]

Less noted than the political importance of Shankarikoppa Mahalingappa's dissent and withdrawal from the KRRS was his testing of germination rates and safety of Bt seeds growing on his land. The rhetoric of suicide seeds was turned on its head: the Monsanto seeds did well in the soil. Mahalingappa told me that the "terminator" talk was "just propaganda."

THE SUICIDE SEEDS SPROUT: COTTON FARMERS VS. DELHI'S *RAJ*

Opposition to the field trials of Bt cotton was in part opposition to Delhi's rule. Protesters held that democratic norms were violated in a top-down imposition of technology driven by global pressures. Opponents claimed specifically that states were bypassed in an opaque process. Approval for contained field trials for collection of data was granted by the Department of Biotechnology through the Review Committee on Genetic Manipulation; permission for large-scale field trials was granted by the Genetic Engineering Approval Committee (GEAC) of the Ministry of Forests and Environment in 1998 under provisions of the Environment (Protection) Act, 1986, and Rules (1989). The tests were to determine potential problems with gene flow, gene stability, animal nutrition, insect resistance, and other ecological effects of Bt seeds. State Biotechnology Coordination Committees headed by the chief secretary of each state are mirrored in theory by district level committees. This complex regulatory structure is meant to prevent unsafe or unwise commercialization of new organisms. Field tests of new seeds were to reassure mass publics that the state's final decisions were authorized by science.[26] The theory is decentralized, with many access points for transparent consideration. The reality was experienced by opponents as opaque and closed. The institutional matrix for approving transgenics is elaborate, in conformity with international biosafety norms, but regulation is a different matter altogether.

By mid-October 2001, there were reports of actually existing fields, in the thousands of hectares, of illicit Bt cotton growing in the state of Gujarat; unknown quantities were reported in other states as well.[27] The Genetic Engineering Approval Committee in Delhi on October 18 ordered the Gujarat State Biotechnology Coordination Committee to uproot and burn the Bt crop. In this ironic replay of the "cremate Monsanto" campaign, the roles of activists and state were reversed; farmers mobilized to prevent the burning of their fields. Federalism immediately became a political issue; Gujarat expected Delhi to compensate its farmers, but in the first instance questioned the need for a scorched earth policy.[28] By October 31, the GEAC had modified its order to bend to reality. Because the variety—*Navbharat* 151—flowers early, most had already gone to market: there was no cotton to burn, its lint could in no way be distinguished in the market, and the seeds had been kept or dispersed to other farmers. The GEAC then ordered recovery of cotton from the market to the extent possible, procurement of unpicked cotton at the support price, destruction of seeds and storage of lint, and uprooting and complete destruction of crop residue. Licenses of seed dealers who had spread the illegal variety were canceled. The government lodged a complaint against Navbharat in Metropolitan Magistrate Court in Ahmedabad on December 11 for penal action for violation of the Environment (Protection) Act.

Why were farmers paying premium prices for a technology that prominent public intellectuals and a significant farmers' movement had said would bankrupt and endanger them? The clearest answer is that there were significant profits, despite very high costs of black-market seeds.[29] Indeed, after the discovery of illegal Bt cotton in Gujarat, farmers throughout cotton areas began clamoring for Bt seeds; charlatan suppliers cropped up to take advantage of the frenzy.

Though material benefits of growing transgenic cotton now seem clear—at least to this observer—there is considerable dispute on the magnitude of income effects, the varieties that work best, and the time required to give a reasonable assessment. Comprehensive data over any significant length of time are not available. Union agriculture minister Ajit Singh estimated from official field trials that the productivity increases are on the order of 30–35 percent.[30] Data from field trials of the Department of Biotechnology obtained by the author in June of 2002 indicate a similar picture, but quite differentiated by variety and region. Looking across twenty-three of the twenty-five locations for the 1998–1999 trials, these data indicate a financial benefit of about Rs 4,500 per acre in Maharashtra and Madhya Pradesh and Rs 7,800 per acre in Gujarat, Andhra, and Karnataka. The major source of increased revenue is yield increase—on the order of 30 percent—and savings on pesticide—ranging from Rs 1,500 to 3,000 per hectare. The data for the 2001–2002 trials are more dramatic, because of the bollworm infestation: for

MECH184Bt, a yield increase over non-Bt cotton of 96 percent in the field sites; for MECH12Bt, 69 percent, and for MECH162Bt, 80 percent. Even if these data are cooked, as charged by NGOs, the results are consistent with the Indian Council of Agricultural Research (ICAR) data and—more telling—the rush to obtain Bt seeds in cotton areas, a phenomenon that was acknowledged in my conversations with NGO activists opposed to the seeds. It must be emphasized that the size of the financial benefit to farmers is dependent on the level of pest infestation. In years of heavy bollworm presence, the savings on pesticide will increase as well as the yield advantage.[31] In years of light infestation—for example in times of drought—the extra cost of Bt seeds is essentially the price of insurance; the more risk-averse the farmer, the more the value of this expenditure.

Delhi's order to uproot and burn crops ignited farmer protests, on both economic and political grounds. Sharad Joshi, president of the farmers' organization *Shetkari Sanghathana,* said at a rally October 30, 2001: "They will have to walk over our corpses to destroy this crop. This is our *satyagraha.* This is a question of the farmer's freedom to select his seed and access technology." A group of farmers estimated to number in the thousands pledged that they would not allow the government to touch their crop. This pledge was taken at the Nilkantheshwar temple on the banks of the hallowed Narmada river.[32] In a rally about two weeks later, a crowd estimated at between twelve and thirteen thousand cotton farmers protested in Wardha near Nagpur. This large protest was not in Gujarat, but in neighboring Maharashtra; either the seeds had surreptitiously spread to Maharashtra or the farmers there anticipated growing them. This protest too was under the leadership of the *Shetkari Sanghatana.* A *rail roko* (train stopping) agitation at Wardha and Sewagram stations was meant to interrupt traffic on the Central Railway's Mumbai-Howrah route. This protest took place even though the government was by that time promising that the crop would be burned only after purchase: there was to be no financial loss to agriculturalists. But more than money was at stake; Sharad Joshi posed the question as one of farmers' freedom and, implicitly, urban bias: "Development should not be locked up in the cities. The marvel of technology should reach the villages."[33]

Despite the elaborate regulatory apparatus of the state, and the belligerent vigilance of the NGOs opposed to transgenics, the discovery of Bt cotton resulted from neither; business rivalry uncovered the underground seeds. The variety growing in Gujarat was supplied by Navbharat Seed Limited, which had registered the seed as a hybrid and subsequently claimed no knowledge of its transgenic nature. MAHYCO, which had spent about US$8 million preparing the Bt cotton seeds for commercialization in India and originally received permission from Delhi for field trials, reported Navbharat to the GEAC for selling illegal seeds. MAHYCO might not have discovered this fact had the bollworm infestation that hit Gujarat in 2001 not been so devastating that the few healthy fields attracted notice. Farmer leader Sharad Joshi wrote:

Through a lucky stroke a nondescript seed company managed to play Robin Hood and smuggle into Gujarat one line of anti-bollworm gene. For three years nobody noticed the difference and then came the massive bollworm rampage of 2001. Gujarat saw all its traditional hybrid cotton crop standing devastated, side-by-side the Bt-gene crops standing resplendent in their glorious bounty. The Government was upset and ordered destruction and burning of the bountiful crop.[34]

The origin of the Navbharat seeds is unclear. The irony is that despite the mobilization around "terminator technology" and "suicide seeds," Navbharat was probably using offspring of Monsanto's patented seeds—acquired either in the United States or in India—to breed a new line in quantity. If Shankarikoppa Mahalingappa's case is typical, farmers may well have been sequestering transgenic seeds from the field trials, illegally, and replanting them—though everyone involved with the field trials that I have spoken with thinks this unlikely to have been a major source of transgenic cotton. One outcome, too dynamic to treat here, is well summarized by Dr. Suman Sahai, of Gene Campaign: "The market is awash with the illegal, unregulated cotton varieties." The net result is what has been called "transgenic chaos"—as farmers experiment with new crosses, hucksters appear with cheaper seeds of dubious lineage and miracle claims, and the characterization of the original subterranean appropriation of Bt cotton genetic material as a "Robin Hood" act catches on in the media.[35]

BOUNDED FRAMING: MOVEMENTS AND INTERESTS

The farmers in whose name protagonists in the seed war speak are divided. Though often clubbed together in naïve political analysis, there is no reason to assume unity of farmer interests—objective or subjective. Farmers' movements are deeply divided by ideology, faction, personality.[36] Moreover, there is on the ground continuous differentiation of economic interests. Contrary to organicist conceptualizations of rural society, there is no coherent interest of "rural India" or of "farmers." Rice farmers may have no interest at all in Bt cotton, or in any cotton.[37] Additionally, in the arena of transgenic crops, a multifaceted ideational divide looms as well—variations in trust in government and science, assessment of risk, the nature of the unnatural.

Intellectuals have framed the issues for farmer movements: Gene Campaign, the Research Foundation for Science, Technology, and Ecology (RFSTE), Greenpeace-India, KRRS. But for this political intermediation to be successful, both framing and objectives must resonate with enough of the world as experienced by farmers to generate support. The micro-economic and biological success of Bt cotton outweighed the more indirect, distal, and hypothetical arguments about foreign control and dangerous genes. Gujarat

Khedut Samaj president Vipinbhai Desai said at the *Shetkari Sanghatana* rally on the Narmada: "We have tested the seeds. This is the third yield using Bt cotton seed. The government says it is hazardous. If that is so, why are they not proving it scientifically."[38]

Farmers with whom I have discussed these issues are not terribly concerned about the theoretical risks asserted by environmentalists. The attitude could be summarized as one of wait-and-see pragmatism. Nevertheless, the early framing of this debate has remained significant, however bogus are some of the claims. In July 2003, at a meeting in Palakkad district, agrarian leaders continued to tell me and each other of threats from "the terminator." The most recent farmer organization in a district already very heavily organized is the *Deshiya Karshaka Samrakshana Samithi* (National Farmers Protection Society); protection was explicitly from globalization, personified by Monsanto.

In this microcosm of seeds and seed choices we then have another light on the puzzle Ashutosh Varshney[39] poses for Indologists: if material interests drive mobilization, why has rural India not formed itself as political actor? Surely the GMO controversy created ideal conditions for a social movement of indigenous *Bharat* against a globalizing India. This was precisely the construction of the KRRS; the metropole represented by Delhi was caving in to globalization pressure that would subordinate and bankrupt the Indian farmer. Varshney's own answer is essentially primordialist: there are cross-cutting social cleavages of caste and community that undermine horizontal solidarity in rural India. But objective interests themselves are deeply divided in rural India. The surplus farmer who gains from higher food prices gains at the expense of the deficit farmer and the landless. These divides alone are sufficient to explain the absence of a rural political bloc.[40] But in addition to divisions among farmers and other rural classes introduced by objective class structure, seed politics introduces a knowledge gradient that divides social movements. Ideational divides over transgenics are deeply etched not only because of knowledge asymmetries—is there or is there not a terminator threatening farmers' livelihoods?—but also because of deep normative ambiguities concerning the nature of the unnatural and the legitimacy of collective risk. These interests—both material and ideational—provide ample reason for rural divides without reliance on primordial loyalties.

The pro-Bt stance of cotton farmers was certain to win at the national level; the Kisan Coordinating Committee composed of the Shetkari Sanghatana, Bharatiya Kisan Union (Punjab), Indian Farmers Federation (Andhra Pradesh), Khedut Samaj (Gujarat) among others threatened civil disobedience and the planting of Bt cotton seeds if the Centre did not approve the new seeds.[41] Three Bt cotton varieties were approved provisionally for commercialization on March 26, 2002, and more are under consideration. This outcome is not surprising. Farmers possess a diffuse residual power across regimes in India, particularly when unstable coalitional governments rule in Delhi. Moreover, the biotechnology project has been a state project from the mid l990s. The Confederation of Indian Industries likewise takes a strong stance in favor of biotechnology. As political power becomes more regionalized, and coalitions rule in Delhi only on the basis of aggregating regional parties, the assumption of a strong central state moving against locally entrenched farmers becomes less and less credible. Moreover, even in national politics, no populist stands against farmers, and no political coalition wins without populism. One strand of this populism stands on antiquated but culturally powerful tropes of sturdy peasants in agrarian villages; if India does not stand for the *kisan,* for what can it stand?

Despite the triumphalism of the pro-biotech treatment of the Bt outcome, there is a societal risk: for all the romanticization of local knowledge, it is not clear that the sons of the soil always know best. Farmers adopted insecticides, not from concern for social externalities, but rather because they had to protect their crops. A small farmer in South Africa, T. J. Buthelezi, who had experienced both Monsanto and Bt cotton, captures the logic: "But even if they [Monsanto] weren't good to us [and they were], Bt cotton has proved to be the best thing to put money in our pockets. I wouldn't care if it were from the devil himself." The GMO debate turns from benefits to risk; what is the threshold of social risk?[42] What institutions could provide answers that would be accepted?

Despite its limited scope and scale, the mobilization against transgenic seeds illustrates some genuinely new strands in farmer mobilization, as well as continuities with historical movements. The new features can be understood as elements of an emergent politics of expertise, driven by the effects of uneven globalization of knowledge. In the politics of expertise, interest is mediated by forms of knowledge not easily accessible to participants in the movement. The risks are unknown, as the science is necessarily incomplete. This is genuinely new terrain for the species. One then expects both innovation and continuities in political strategy.

The failure of the movement against Bt cotton is in some ways surprising. The leadership had an easy target that was symbolically charged, considerable international support, great facility with language and politics, outstanding access to courts and media, the convening power of prominent public intellectuals and activists. The strategy seemed exactly right, from our understanding of peasant protest historically. Ranajit Guha, in his classic *Elementary Aspects of Peasant Insurgency,* emphasized the political utility in agrarian movements of strategic metonymy—making a singular part stand for the complex whole. For example, in successful agrarian movements, the most decadent local landlord was presented as encapsulating in his person the evils of landlordism as a social system, and was strategically attacked as such.[43] Monsanto symbolized globalization, and thus dominance of weak farmers by powerful multinational firms, as well as environmental reckless-ness. The images of power and control conferred by market size were dra-maturgically rich. Vandana Shiva spoke of "technological totalitarianism." The new seeds were dubbed one of "capitalist patriarchy's life threatening projects," part of "Monsanto's totalitarian empire."[44] Raising the ante so high lays the groundwork for continuity with peasant struggles' enduring depen-dence on evocation of moral outrage. Transgenic seeds became a site for contesting foreign threats to seeds embodying indigenous knowledge and culture. Theft in the form of "biopiracy" was seen as the objective of global life-science firms working in India. Suicides of farmers were linked to out-rages of globalization, encapsulated in the metaphor of "suicide seeds." Moral outrage at market power and technological juggernauts merged with defensive nationalism. Gandhian notions of *swadeshi* were opposed to neo-classical arguments for openness of economy.

In the moral economy of anti-GMO mobilization, as in much peasant protest, markets appear as a form of dominance, in contrast to the realm of freedom portrayed by neoliberal apologists—this is the ideological divide between the *Karnataka Rajya Raitha Sangha* and the *Shetkari Sang-hatana.* Farmers were represented in the oppositional movement as in dan-ger of being forced to grow new seeds, of becoming bonded to seed firms. *The Indian Farmers Petition,* a resolution of the Forum of Farmers Organi-zations on Globalization and Agriculture, opposed "the spread of capital in-tensive agriculture in which innocent Indian farmers are being trapped in the lust for high profits and being driven to indebtedness."[45] Farmers are presented here with the innocence of colonial representations of peasants; they lack the autonomy to resist "lust for profits." In the *Charter of Farm-ers' Rights to Safe Seeds* issued by a coalition of farmers' organizations con-vened by *Navdanya,* a right is asserted to "safe seeds and freedom from risks."[46] The normative conceptual framework of capitalism—reward for risk—is contravened by appeal to an alternative moral economy of safety first. The marketplace is treated as a sphere of dominance, in competition with an arena of freedom. Choice is eclipsed by structure. Uttar Pradesh farmer leader, Mahendra Singh Tikait, observed from his experience with the Inter-Continental Caravan: "When we told European farmers that they should not export their products to India, they simply laughed at us. They told us that we should not buy their products if we did not want them. We are nothing compared to them."[47]

Despite continuities with historic struggles, the transgenic protests broke new ground for farmers' movements. Most important were global reach and contestation of science. But transnational alliances have risks as well as benefits. Indian farmers in the Inter-Continental Caravan to Europe had their authenticity as farmers called into question; many were quite removed from actual agricultural operations and were not poor enough for the Europeans' imagination of Asian peasants—though it is hard to know what European NGOs expected given that everyone arrived by international commercial flights. There are persistent rumors I've heard in various parts of India that the Caravan and the Bt protest at home were funded by pesticide firms fearful of losing their profitable stranglehold on farmers. The experience of the KRRS specifically on the global stage had an impact on the movement in India, contributing to its fragmentation and ineffectiveness. Because of the asymmetric distribution of knowledge globally, the public face of resistance to GMOs frequently came from Indians connected to international NGOs—Greenpeace, for example. Reciprocally, the web pages of international opponents of transgenics depend heavily on the output of Vandana Shiva, who came to represent Indian farmers, sometimes India itself. Her global reach indicts "imperialist science." Supporters of transgenics attack Shiva and other activists for deployment of "junk science." The politics of expertise is then enmeshed in an international contest over the meaning of "science."

Because the science is contested, and inevitably incomplete, multiple claims to representation have some staying power; it is unclear how the public—in India or elsewhere—understands genetic engineering and its products. *The Washington Post* (October 16, 1999) reported a poll by Environics, a Toronto-based public environmental polling firm, of one thousand citizens each in twenty-five countries in which India ranked high in acceptance of biotechnology for both pest resistant plants and development of new medicines (76 and 81 percent respectively); comparable percentages for the techno-optimist United States were 78 and 87. Despite clear evidence of farmers' demand for transgenic cotton seeds, as evidenced by their willingness to pay premium prices for unofficial Bt seeds, the RFSTE and Navdanya published a pamphlet entitled "The Hazards of Bt Cotton" in which it is claimed that "the major farmers' unions of India have rejected Bt. cotton."[48] If so, there are serious problems of representation.

Both global stage and knowledge asymmetries reinforce the historic problem of representation in farmers' movements. Farmers are more than ever represented by those with specialized knowledge and elite connections. In constructing these contests dramaturgically, conjured threat and anxiety loom large. These are the conditions under which the late Murray Edelman[49] posited the greatest power for symbolic politics. The Bt cotton controversy illustrates how the strategic deployment of resonant symbols evoking fear and doubt may succeed, but simultaneously how such constructions may be "hoist on their own petards" when symbolic freedom of maneuver meets the limits of ground realities. Framing is plastic, but bounded.

A BIOTECHNOLOGY FOR THE POOR?

Visions of food security and nutritional improvement via genetic engineering resonate with earlier debates in Indian agriculture. The "green revolution" as political symbol crystallized cleavages on two dimensions: Malthusian assumptions and technological fixes. Critics pointed to class-skewed rates of adoption and inequality of outcomes; scholars such as Michael Lipton (1989) argued from aggregate effects that poverty would have worsened in the absence of massive production increases. Political parties addressing poverty adopted either a land-redistributive stance (on the left) or moved to subsidize agriculture with nominal targeting for the poor (the dominant response). Neither worked very well on a national scale for the simple reason that a coalition for the poor is hard to mobilize; nominally pro-poor public programs confront local power that can either veto or capture. A comparable precipitation of politics around the poor and genetic engineering has not yet emerged, but these fault lines are unlikely to disappear.

The moral high ground of aiding the poor through biotechnology—claimed primarily by multinationals selling seeds—typically depends on an underlying Malthusian logic: increased population pressure on food stocks necessitates more productive and adaptable technologies if the poor are to be fed. In this view, the "green revolution" has reached a point of diminishing returns, and thus needs an infusion of potential from the "gene revolution." The Malthusian argument in contemporary India is undermined by the tens of millions of tons of grain surpluses—something in the range of 63 million tons in 2002. Adequate storage is not available for these grain "surpluses," resulting in much spoilage. It is not clear how more surplus production would alleviate hunger. It should not be necessary to stress again that these questions lie more in the realm of rights and entitlements than in genetic potential of seeds.

Despite transparent weaknesses in the Malthusian argument, biotechnology as part of a pro-poor development strategy is not implausible. This is a sector in which low-income countries could have a developmental comparative advantage based on biodiversity and knowledge. Development of the sector potentially valorizes, perhaps remunerates, local knowledge, which is everywhere in danger of extinction.[50] Developing this new sector is enthusiastically embraced by both Indian firms and state governments and by the state via the Ministry of Science and Technology.[51] The distinguished scientist M. S. Swaminathan posits "the power of genetic modification to do immense good to agriculture and food security." He discusses, for example, transgenes' conferring drought and salinity resistance as a potential means of coping with global climate change in poor nations. But Swaminathan argues: "Unless research and development efforts on GM foods are based on principles of bio-ethics, bio-safety, bio-diversity conservation and bio-partnerships, there will be serious public concern about the ultimate nutritional, social, ecological and economic consequences of replacing numerous local varieties with a few GMOs."[52]

The potential importance of pro-poor biotechnologies is buttressed by the biological externalities of current practices of intensification. This path is not only producing lower rates of yield increases at the margin, but threatens ecological heath and future production. The poor are the first victims of environmental degradation; they lack the means of mobility, flexibility, and adaptation possessed by the wealthy. Additionally, the poor face nutritional deficiencies that result directly from restricted dietary choice imposed by poverty. Re-engineering plants through traditional breeding techniques is both slow and inefficient, as many traits are transferred in each cycle, generating more genetic roulette than necessary. President of the Rockefeller Foundation Gordon Conway argues that the future depends on a "doubly green revolution" that utilizes biotechnology along with traditional techniques rooted in a sustainable agroecological view of farming (green manuring, biological pest control, etc.).[53] Half of Conway's solution—implying agro-ecological approaches to sustainable farming—is acceptable to opponents of transgenic plants in India, but the other half is not. Arguments similar to those of Gordon Conway—essentially walking on both legs—have produced something of a consensus in the foundation and development community internationally around the potential of genetic engineering. The United Nations Development Program (UNDP), in its recent *Human Development Report*—"Making Technologies Work for Human Development"—cautiously endorsed transgenics, including potential benefits specifically for the poor.[54] Supporters of sustainable agriculture and ecological regeneration in India objected strenuously to what was felt to be betrayal by a perceived ally.[55] The potential coalition for the poor, already quite weak, faces fracture on the knife edge of technology. Pro-poor potentialities of genetic engineering are widely believed by opponents to be no more than ideological constructions of firms seeking profits and governments that back them: neither market nor state confers legitimacy.

International optimism about biotechnology and the poor, which is approaching a consensus narrative in powerful institutions, resonates with the Nehruvian faith in science and technology.[56] In an organicist fashion, modernization overwhelms poverty, which is a residue of backwardness. Opponents of GMOs find faith in either the state or science hard to maintain in contemporary India. Science is rhetorically tainted with instrumental use, thus with interests. The state's certification of safety is suspect because of its declared interest in promoting biotechnology. Science as method—as a means of testing and adjudicating truth claims—is reconstructed rhetorically as legitimation in strategic deployment of findings by corporations, government agencies and NGOs. No one I talked to in the opposition camp, for example, believed that the Department of Biotechnology field data on Bt cotton trials would settle anything, even if published; their very secrecy was a sign of inauthenticity.

The assumption of a large part of the potentially pro-poor coalition that transgenics are inherently inimical to the interests of the poor lacks nuance. For example, pest-resistant crops such as Bt cotton reduce applications of pesticides in controlled experimental data available and in accounts of individual farmers.[57] Cash requirements and potentially the debt burdens of poorer farmers are reduced—assuming timely credit on reasonable terms can be obtained—but so is demand for labor in application of pesticides, perhaps at the expense of wage laborers. On the other hand, where laborers are paid by the quantity harvested, increases in yield increase income; reciprocally, there is no work in cotton fields when bollworms devastate the crop. Moreover, those laborers may gain some health advantage from fewer poisons in the fields, and certainly gain from increased production in those areas in which payment is by harvested weight.[58] Whoever drinks surface water or shallow well water—often the poor—benefits from less poisoning, as do gleaners of fishes, but there may be less wage labor in agriculture. Though the discourse of GMOs from both movements has centered on small farmers, the landless are the truly awkward class. Poverty is highly correlated with landlessness, and the poverty of the landless is the most obdurate developmental dilemma.

Returns to farmers will depend on seed prices.[59] The seed technology is at least as divisible as the pesticide technology; small farmers should in principle be able to improve their net returns. There is some evidence of this outcome in South Africa and other countries.[60] Management to prevent or slow development of resistance to Bt toxin by bollworms via planting of *refugia* is on the basis of current anecdotal evidence unlikely, yet it is also unclear whether or not alternative hosts in India make this consideration less threatening than first thought. MNCs assume in their propaganda lower food prices from greater production, a benefit to the urban and many rural poor, yet the yield advantages of most transgenic crops are not to date dramatic, nor in foods for the poor. Finally, genetic engineering could in principle address the specific needs of the poor. A plant engineered for drought resistance and tolerance of poor soil, for example, could assist those pushed to the margins of land and water systems by agrarian power dynamics in a way no other feasible policy could. Likewise, nutritionally enhanced grains may prove important, as the poor are disproportionately dependent on grain calories and micro-nutrient deficiencies are serious.

Pro-poor outcomes are then certainly conceivable, and there is some evidence for realization among small farmers.[61] Much depends on property regimes nationally and internationally; on government policy toward seeds; on the priorities of scientific research. Opponents highlight the foreign threat, yet predatory firms are not the only actors. Immediately following the agronomic success of illegal Bt cotton came announcement of an agreement between Nath Seeds and the Biocentury Transgene (China) Company, to introduce transgenic cotton technology in India. Biocentury's patents are for Bt and Bt+ genes developed by the Biotechnology Research Institute (BRI) of the Chinese Academy of Agricultural Sciences and applicable across a range of crops besides cotton. Subsequently there has been significant development of transgenic research in the public sector in India, in small seed firms and in consortia of seed firms.[62] The easy assumption that globalization is conceptually coherent and monolithic is dubious.

Poverty is mostly an outcome of property institutions; there is no mystery how to make purposive alterations should regimes wish to do so.[63] It has been politically difficult to separate analytically the question of genetically engineered crops from property entanglements. These questions are complicated by international pressures for the final dismantling of the nationalist economic project of Nehru and global convergence of neoliberal property regimes. Appropriate property institutions—most importantly a strengthening of both national and international biological commons—would answer many of the critics of genetic engineering, but not all. Owning nature is a venerable question,[64] to which genomics adds untested complexity. New technologies enable property claims unimaginable a generation ago, raising profound questions of valuation in both the economic and ethical sense.

Deep concerns about intellectual property among opponents of transgenics in India specifically protested convergence of global property law, driven by Trade-related Aspects of Intellectional Property Rights (TRIPS) and the World Intellectual Property Organization (WIPO), that supports a patent regime favored by multinational capital.[65] Patents are anathema to the antiglobalization coalition. As suggested above and below, the property regime proposed by global capital seems not so threatening as this construction has it, but neither is it so normatively unproblematic as neoliberal ideology would have it. Patents are seen by industry and many economists as necessary to spur investment, but the historical record is not so clear as is often assumed.[66] The property system enabled by genetic engineering is indeed one currently dominated by Western capital,[67] but not from any inherent necessity. The first wave of Bt cotton came via Monsanto; the next may well come from China, derived from public sector research there, or from the advanced public-sector research in India. The number of unofficial or illicit Bt cotton varieties in India continues to multiply, even as new firms acquire Monsanto's license to produce new official varieties. There could not be a less apt description of the current transgenic arena in India than "monopoly." And whatever the mix of licensed and stealth seeds available in the fields, in practice, farmers seem quite willing to ignore everyone's property claims in seeds.

Winning political strategies in India do well to claim the poor, or at least the farmer; there is both real and constructed overlap between the categories.

Who speaks for the poor is always unclear. The poor know very well what different distributions of land, credit, and wages mean for their well-being, having sustained long-standing struggles on these issues. But biotechnology produces a murky politics of expertise: much that needs to be known is simply not known. By focusing on Monsanto and the dependency construction of technical change, foes of GMOs arguably made a strategic error. Leaders spoke of a novel and dangerous "terminator technology" enslaving farmers; on the ground transgenic seeds were being widely and vigorously propagated, sold, and exchanged because they gave better results. Somewhat more freedom from pesticide firms and debts incurred from increasingly ineffective chemicals meant more on the ground than a hypothetical threat of dominance by a distant Monsanto. It was not clear in the fields how Monsanto or Delhi could force any Indian farmer to plant or not plant anything. Farmers vote with their plows, as the stealth movement for Bt cotton demonstrated.

But Bt cotton will not solve the problems of the rural poor. Development of a bioengineering sector that could benefit the poor assumes three preconditions. First, serious concerns of safety and risk must be settled, implying the creation of national capacity, disaggregated to the local level, to implement the Biosafety Protocol of the Convention on Biological Diversity. For this safety regime to be effective, there will have to be a double revolution in the legitimacy of science and government in public perception. Second, getting the property system wrong will lower the probability of biotechnology's being justifiable in developmental terms—i.e., improving the life chances of the poor. And finally, social direction of research in the public interest will have to recover ground lost to privatization, where the incentive structure is not pro-poor. The strong assumption is that social direction itself can be made pro-poor.

CONCLUSION: BIOPOLITICS, STATES, AND MARKETS

There are two political conclusions from the Bt episode. First, a potential coalition for the rural poor is divided by the ideational constructions of biotechnology; the outcome is to lessen the chances for pro-poor outcomes. Science itself is constructed in ways that divide the left. All my activist friends in India think the story outlined in this chapter is contrary to their values and my own. It does not help that the Bush administration rails against both European caution on GMOs and the resistance of African countries to transgenic food aid. Yet the evidence from the Bt cotton episode seems fairly clear: there are no suicide seeds. There are, however, both persistent risks and social institutions producing desperation among Indian farmers: structural vulnerabilities induced by class, droughts, and floods, international market-rigging in agriculture, official skewing of attention and favors toward the better-connected. Poor farmers face great and debilitating insecurity; insecurity is in a way the core of poverty. Markets in agriculture are risky places, especially for the poor, and no currently wealthy nation exposes its farming sector to market risks in the way India does. Nor are international development agencies with clout friendly to pro-poor market-rigging. Given these dynamics, seeds cannot carry the weight assigned them by either side of the GMO mobilization: other variables drive poverty, not least of which are distributions of landed property and political coalitions.[68] Yet well-known structural adversities, international and domestic, do not mean that farmers are so incapable of knowing and pursuing their interests and assessing their risks as the movement opposing GMO seeds has constructed them. Whether their pursuits are congruent with larger societal interests in environmental safety is another question altogether; farmers took to the pesticides that now ruin them and their environment, regardless of externalities, driven by a perceived necessity born of real vulnerability.

The second conclusion concerns politics of framing. There is no doubt that framing has enormous power in a field of high anxiety and low information.[69] Activists in Palakkad district in 2003 recounted to me as fact the suicide-terminator-Monsanto construction against any evidence I could produce. If farmers actually bought transgenic seeds, I was corrected, they did so because they were duped. If they planted such seeds, they were ruined by Monsanto's monopoly. Any other construction was ideological— pro-market, pro-globalization, pro-multinational. The fear of globalization strikes deep. Frames filter information. Oppositional NGOs and the Indian press continue to promulgate stories to the effect that "Bt Cotton Has Failed." Reality seems a bit more nuanced: the Bt transgene in quite a few varieties of cotton seems to find favor with farmers; some varieties do better than others; farmers experiment with different Bt varieties and make choices among them, based on large price differences and performance differentials under variable agronomic conditions. Some varieties increase profits considerably. "Bt cotton" is itself an ideological construction devoid of agro-economic meaning—there are numerous cultivars, some with and some without ability to produce the Cry1Ac protein lethal to bollworms.

Any movement claiming to represent farmers should intuit these outcomes. The Bt cotton enterprise, official and underground, is expanding; unless we assume farmers to be incapable of calculating their interests, the suicide-seed construction is bound to fail as a mobilizing trope for agrarian movements. Despite its powerful cultural resonance, that narrative runs counter to the experiential base of farmers, who know what grows in their fields and what does not; the experience of Shankarikoppa Mahalingappa turned out to be normative. Not surprisingly, the political strategy of opponents now seems to emphasize more the ecological threat than the agrarian—to claim, for example, that successful transgenic cultivars such as *Navbharat* 151 are products of "biological pollution," rather than inspired—and undoubtedly crafty—plant breeding. Since there is no way of disproving a negative—that something will not happen—and since the science on horizontal gene flow is indeed incomplete, this strategy for stopping transgenics via raising the anxiety threshold may stand a better chance. More likely, whatever the findings on risk and uncertainty, whatever the debunking of miracle and suicide seeds, farmers will prove difficult to control by either patent claims of high-tech firms or a panoptic state.

The final comment is then on states and markets, the theme of this volume. The Indian state has never been particularly pro-poor on the ground where it counts, though individual state governments certainly have been, and effectively so.[70] Delhi now promotes biotechnology, with a passing nod to its pro-poor possibilities.[71] Indian national policy calls for a form of regulation that structures markets in a way that multinationals prefer. Monsanto would prefer to be the only approved purveyor of transgenic seeds—it could then have a better claim on the monopoly Vandana Shiva grants it. Yet in the Bt episode, neither state nor Monsanto could enforce their preferences on farmers in a dynamic anarcho-capitalism built on stealth and opportunism.[72] How typical this outcome may be, and what it predicts about the pro-poor possibilities of biotechnology, remain to be seen. But to dismiss the potentialities of technical change in improving the life chances of the poor—as many nominally pro-poor forces have—is increasingly recognized internationally as groundless and aloof. These characterizations do not augur well for effective political representation of the poor.

NOTES

1. I have been helped by comments and suggestions from Sivramiah Shantharam, Lloyd and Susanne Rudolph, Urbashi Poddar, Sanjeev Chopra, Phil Oldenburg, C. S. Prakash, Ann Grodzins Gold, Suman Sahai, Anatole Krattiger, and especially Kameswara Rao and Stig Toft Madsen. Dia Mohan provided important research assistance.

Though prejudicial as a description of transgenics, "GMO" is employed here because of its universal currency. All existing crops are genetically modified—that is the purpose of plant breeding—often by unnatural means of inducing mutations. See, e.g., Mark L. Winston, *Travels in the Genetically Modified Zone* (Cambridge: Harvard University Press, 2002). *Transgenic* is more precise as a name for plants that result from recombinant DNA technology—moving a gene from one species to another. Though often reduced by opponents to genetic engineering, agricultural biotechnology frequently utilizes tissue culture and marker-aided selection. The text adopts the language of the political movements, eliding these distinctions.

2. For representative examples, see Kristin Dawkins, *Gene Wars: The Politics Of Biotechnology* (New York: Seven Stories Press [Open Media Pamphlet Series], 1997); Per Pinstrup-Anderson and Ebbe Schiøler, *Seeds of Contention: World Hunger and*

the *Global Controversy over GM Crops* (Baltimore: Johns Hopkins University Press, 2000); Vandana Shiva, *Stolen Harvest: The Hijacking of the Global Food Supply* (Cambridge, Mass.: South End Press, 2000); Robert L. Paarlberg, *The Politics of Precaution: Genetically Modified Crops in Developing Countries* (Baltimore: Johns Hopkins University Press, 2001); Alan McHughen, *Pandora's Picnic Basket: The Potential and Hazards of Genetically Modified Foods* (Oxford: Oxford University Press, 2000); M. S. Swaminathan, "GM to Do Good to Agri and Food Security," *The Economic Times*, November 13, 2001; Dan Charles, *Lords of the Harvest: Biotech, Big Money, and the Future of Food* (Cambridge, Mass.: Perseus Publishing, 2001); Vandana Shiva, Afsar H. Jafri, Ashok Emani, and Manish Pande, *Seeds of Suicide: The Ecological and Human Costs of Globalization of Agriculture* (Delhi: Research Foundation for Science, Technology and Ecology, 2000); and Winston, *Travels in the Genetically Modified Zone.*

3. Ronald J. Herring, "The Political Impossibility Theorem of Agrarian Reform: Path Dependence and Terms of Inclusion," in *Changing Paths: The New Politics of Inclusion*, ed. Mick Moore and Peter Houtzager (Ann Arbor: University of Michigan Press, 2003).

4. Department of Biotechnology, Ministry of Science and Technology, Government of India, *Biotech News* 2, Issue 2 (November 2001).

5. In 2001, when the issue of comparative cost was raised in Parliament, animal-based insulins cost Rs 65 per vial and human insulin Rs 200 per vial in India. Plans for import substitution through the Department of Biotechnology were aimed at reducing the cost by eliminating dependence on American producers.

6. Vandana Shiva, "Ecological Balance in an Era of Globalization," in *Global Ethics and Environment,* ed. Nicholas Low (London: Routledge, 1999), 47–69.

7. Ann Grodzins Gold, "Vanishing: Seeds' Cyclicality," *Journal of Material Culture* 8, no. 3 (2003): 255–72.

8. Press Release, Asian Social Forum [Hyderabad] Seminar, "Beyond Bhopal and Bt.: Taking on the Biotech Giants," Delhi, Research Foundation for Science, Technology and Ecology, January 4, 2003.

9. For a technical explanation of the terminator, G. V. Ramanjaneyula and A. Ravindra, *Terminator Logic: Monsanto, Genetic Engineering and the Future of Agriculture,* Science for People/Research Foundation for Science, Technology and Ecology, New Delhi, January 1999. On the debt nexus as a cause of suicides, see Centre for Environmental Studies Warangal, *Citizens' Report: Gathering Agrarian Crisis—Farmers' Suicides in Warangal District (A.P.) India,* Kishanpura, 1998; Department of Agriculture and Cooperation, Ministry of Agriculture, Government of India; *Report of the Study Group on Distress Caused by Indebtedness of Farmers in Andhra Pradesh,* New Delhi, September 1998; Glenn Davis Stone, "Biotechnology and Suicide in India," *Anthropology News* (May 2002); Shiva et al., *Seeds of Suicide,* 64–110; Srinand Jha, "Seeds of Death, GMO Cotton, India," www.tompaine.com, May 30 2001; interview with Devinder Sharma, "The Introduction of Transgenic Cotton in India," *Biotechnology and Development Monitor,* no. 44 (March 2001): 10–13.

10. Paarlberg, *Politics of Precaution,* 99-100; Geeta Bharathan, "Bt-Cotton in India: Anatomy of a Controversy," *Current Science* 79, no. 8 (October 25, 2000): 1067–75.

11. In a communiqué of February–March 2000 and a news release of February 20, 2000, RAFI produced a refutation to the notion that the terminator had been stopped.

"Terminator 2 Years Later: Suicide Seeds on the Fast Track," RAFI International Office, Winnipeg, Manitoba, Canada. RAFI noted that the international campaign to renounce the technology had been endorsed by many governments and by the Director General of the United Nations Food and Agriculture Organization (FAO), Jacques Diouf. Nevertheless, RAFI notes that research on the terminator continues. See also, "Terminator Technology Not Terminated," Agra/Industrial Biotechnology Legal Letter 1, no. 1 (January 2000), 4.

12. Stone, "Biotechnology and Suicide," 1.

13. Vandana Shiva, *Biopiracy: The Plunder of Nature and Knowledge* (Cambridge South End Press, 1997), 91.

14. Darryl D'Monte, "Gandhi's Disputed Heritage," *UNESCO Courier*, 2000, 1–4; Stig Toft Madsen, "The View from Vevey," *Economic and Political Weekly*, September 29, 2001, 3733–42; Ranjit Dev Raj, "Indian Farmers Take the War to Europe," Inter Press Service, May 24, 1999; Shiv Visvanathan and Chandrika Parmer, "A Biotechnology Story: Notes from India," *Economic and Political Weekly*, July 6, 2002, 2714–24; various issues of *Deccan Herald*, "Operation Cremate Monsanto: Raitha Sangha to Burn Bollgard Cotton in Bellary," in December 2,1998, Bangalore; and *The Hindu* (Shimoga), January 3, 1997; see also Omvedt, this volume.

15. Professor Nanjundaswamy, "Statement of Professor Nanjundaswamy at the Demonstration Against the World Economic Summit, Cologne, June 19th, 1999," GreenFiles, WWF-I, New Delhi.

16. On the biology and economics of cotton production, see Clive James, *Global Review of Transgenic Crops: 2001 Feature: Bt Cotton,* ISAAA Briefs No. 26, Ithaca, N.Y.: ISAAA, 2002; D. Sharma, "The Introduction of Transgenic Cotton in India," 10–13. On desperation of farmers, consider the example of Popatbhai Ramjibhai Patel, a farmer in Gujarat: he explained that his costs of cultivation had doubled in the previous five years and many farmers were thinking of abandoning cotton. "This new seed may be a good alternative for us. We have run out of options." Dionne Bunsha, "A Can of Bollworms," *Frontline* 18, Issue 24, November 24–December 7, 2001.

17. D'Monte, "Gandhi's Disputed Heritage," 1-4; *The Hindu* (Shimoga Edition), 3 January 1999; *Deccan Herald*, "Operation Cremate Monsanto: Raitha Sangha to Burn Bollgard Cotton in Bellary," December 2, 1998, Bangalore.

18. The patent is held by Delta and Pine Land Company, in collaboration with the United States Department of Agriculture's Agricultural Research Service—U.S. Patent 5,723,765 entitled "Control of Plant Gene Expression," granted March 3, 1998, on a concept referred to as the Technology Protection System (TPS). Monsanto's attempt to purchase Delta and Pine Land failed, though this fact did not change the protest focus on "Monsanto's terminator." Despite its prominence in discourse, terminator technology was not commercialized, due in large part to vigorous international protests and intervention of the President of the Rockefeller Foundation, Gordon Conway [personal communication]. See also, Scott Kilman, "Monsanto Won't Commercialize Terminator Gene," *Wall Street Journal*, October 5, 1999. There have been, to my knowledge, no applications for field testing of this technology. Syngenta seems to be the current leader in GURT technologies but has not deployed it in any crop.

19. Quoted in Dow Jones Agnet, November 20, 1998; Sharad Mistry, "Terminator Gene a Figment of Imagination: Monsanto Chief," *Indian Express,* December 4,1998.

20. Shiva, *Stolen Harvest.* For a more nuanced view of the complex relationship between seeds, agricultural practices, political economy, and suicide, see A. R. Vasavi, "Agrarian Distress in Bidar: Market, State and Suicides," *Economic and Political Weekly,* August 7, 1999, 2263–68.

21. *Lok Swaraj* has subdivisions of *anna swaraj* (for food), *bhu swaraj* (land), *jal swaraj* (water), *van swaraj* (literally forest, but connoting commons in general). *Navdanya* ("Nine Seeds") is the major organizer, linked to the Research Foundation for Science, Technology and Ecology in Delhi.

22. *Times of India,* "Farmer Suicides Lead to GM Moratorium Call," September 26, 2000. Discussion of farmer suicides mentioned high costs of production and bogus pesticides that bankrupt farmers; for an empirical analysis, Centre for Environmental Studies Warangal, *Citizens Report.* Ironically, these are problems Bt cotton was meant to alleviate. The press report mentions "more than 100" participants; twenty-five farmers' organizations reportedly participated in organizing.

23. Interview, June 7, 2004; Madsen, "The View from Vevey," 3733–42; see also N. R. Birasal, "Haveri Farmers Will Resist KRRS Destruction Trial," *Times of India,* December 5, 1998. Visvanathan and Parmer, "A Biotechnology Story," 2714–24.

24. One participant in Nanjundaswamy's Inter-Continental Caravan complained of the *neta-chamcha* (leader-sycophant) character of relations in the movement. *Chamcha,* literally "spoon," carries an even more derogatory connotation than "sycophant." Use of English language by leaders was also criticized by rank-and-file farmers. Vandana Shiva's critiques of KRRS's style of leadership received international circulation: www.natural-law.ca/genetic/NewsJan-Feb99/GEN1-9IndiaUpdates Brad.hhml. "Coercion" and "undemocratic methods" are singled out as reasons for "failure to bring the farmers along." See also Madsen, "The View from Vevey," 3733–42; Reungchai Tansakul and Peter Burt, "People Power vs. the Gene Giants," *Bangkok Post,* August 1, 1999.

25. Stig Toft Madsen, "Post Festum: The Lotus and the Mud in an Indo-Global Context," Conference on Globalization and Democratic Developments in Asia," Lund University, May 18–20, 2000, cited with permission of author.

26. Interviews in Delhi, July 2001, June 2002 supplement cited sources for this and later discussions of regulatory structure and practice, surveillance, and discovery of illicit Bt plants. See also Department of Biotechnology, Ministry of Science and Technology, Government of India, *Revised Guidelines for Research in Transgenic Plants and Guidelines for Toxicity and Allergenicity Evaluation of Transgenic Seeds, Plants and Plant Parts,* New Delhi, August 1996. Government of India, Ministry of Environment and Forests, *Rajya Sabha,* Unstarred Questions, various volumes.

27. Personal communications with agricultural scientists in India and press reports indicate plantings in Maharashtra, Andhra Pradesh, Rajasthan, Karnataka, Punjab and Haryana as well. The only means of distinguishing Bt cotton is by testing genetically for the Cry1Ac gene. Seeds locally known as 151 *Navbharat biyaran* in Gujarat, were sold under names such as *Jay, Vijay,* and *Digvijay* in Andhra Pradesh, evidently without widespread knowledge of their transgenic character.

28. See *Rajya Sabha: Unstarred Question No. 205*, 01.03.2002, Minister Shri T. R. Balu, "Cultivation of Bt Cotton Using Navbharat Seeds"; Parvathi Menon, "Waking Up to GM Cotton," *Frontline* 18, Issue 23, November 10–23, 2001; Vinod Mathew, "India's GM Cotton Story Gets Bigger—'Uproot & Destroy' Begins on Gujarat Farms," *The Hindu* Business Line, October 20, 2001; Darshan Desai and Sonu Jain, "Government Gets Cotton Farmers to Pay for Its Incompetence," *Indian Express*, October 21, 2001; Bunsha, "Can of Bollworms"; R. Ramachandran, "Green Signal for Bt Cotton," *Frontline* 19, Issue 8, April 13–26, 2002.

29. C. S. Prakash, "The Biotech Miracle," *Indian Express*, Letters to the Editor, November 5, 2001, reports a cost ratio of roughly 7 to 1, Bt seeds to traditional seeds. Purvi Mehta reports a somewhat higher differential, but still high profits among the Gujarati farmers with whom she works (personal communication, December 15, 2001). Karamsibhai Ladabhai Patel reported a ratio of Navbharat seeds to his usual hybrid seed of Rs 550/bag to Rs 300/bag (Bunsha, "A Can of Bollworms"), with very large savings on pesticides. Shankarikoppa Mahalingappa, the KRRS dissident, reported a 25 percent increase in yields along with large savings on pesticides: flatly, "it was profitable." It is clear that bollworm infestation on Bt fields is reduced, increasing yields and reducing pesticide cost. Ramachandran (Ramachandran, "Green Signal for Bt Cotton") reports Indian Council of Agricultural Research trial data for Bt cotton showing an economic advantage to farmers of Rs 8,000–10, 000 per hectare—the same range as the MAHYCO trials. Matin Qaim and David Zilberman ("Yield Effects of Genetically Modified Crops in Developing Countries," *Science* 299 [2003] 900–902) created a small firestorm by projecting the very large gains in Indian field data to farmers in other regions of the world ("Bt Cotton: Confusion Prevails," EPW Commentary, *Economic and Political Weekly*, May 25, 2002). Suman Sahai has much more pessimistic figures based on farmer interviews.

30. Singh's comments reported in *Financial Express* (Delhi), October 5, 2001; Sonu Jain, "Bt in Bt Cotton Means Blocking the Seed, Trashing the Fact," *Indian Express*, October 27, 2001, reports yield increases in the field trials of 297 kilograms per hectare, based on Department of Biotechnology data. Savings to the farmer from reduction of pesticide purchase alone in those data were Rs 1,856 per hectare. With a market price of Rs 22/kg, the average farmer gained Rs. 6,534 per hectare from using Bt cotton.

31. The *Science* article of Matin Qaim and David Zilberman, "Yield Effects of Genetically Modified Crops in Developing Countries," *Science* 299 (2003), 900–902, extrapolating from Indian data to global farmer benefits was widely criticized on this point. See, e.g., Ian Scoones, "Regulatory Manoeuvres: The Bt Cotton Controversy in India," IDS Working Paper No. 197, Brighton, U.K., August 2003.

32. The temple is named for the "blue necked" Shiva, alluding to Shiva's voluntarily taking the poison of demons into his bowl and consuming it, turning his neck blue before it was metabolized into a safe substance. Shiva took poison in the public interest; Bt cotton, according to its proponents, will alleviate the threat of poisons to the body public, as did Shiva's taking the poison into his body. Whether this association was planned by organizers or not is unknown to me, but seems possible.

33. Joshi quoted in Sajid Shaik, "Farmers Decide to Defend Their Bt Gene Cotton Crops," *The Times of India*, October 31, 2001; description of rallies in *Indian Express*, November 13, 2001. On the pro-technology stance of the *Sanghatana*, see Omvedt, this volume.

34. Sharad Joshi, "Unquiet on the Western Front," *The Hindu*, Business Line, December 19, 2001. Joshi's account of discovery conforms to accounts given me by two people who toured fields in Gujarat at the time as part of their jobs: Purvi Mehta–Bhatt and Deviprasad Mishra, personal communications. See also *Rajya Sabha* (op. cit.).

35. Suman Sahai, "Bt Cotton: Confusion Prevails." See, e.g., Scoones, "Regulatory Manoeuvres."

36. Dipankar Gupta, *Rivalry and Brotherhood: Politics in the Life of Farmers in Northern India* (Delhi: Oxford University Press, 1997); Omvedt, this volume.

37. However, I found in Palakkad district in 2003 that much of the discourse surrounding the risks of Bt cotton had been transferred to Bt rice, as there is little cotton grown in the district.

38. Desai quoted in Shaikh, "Farmers Decide to Defend."

39. Ashutosh Varshney, *Democracy, Development and the Countryside: Urban Rural Struggles in India* (Cambridge: Cambridge University Press, l995).

40. Ronald J. Herring, review of Varshney, *American Political Science Review* (Fall 2000).

41. These threats were widely reported in the press; see, for example, Asia Intelligence Wire, March 26, 2002.

42. Buthelezi in Virginia Baldwin Gilbert and Thomas Lee, "Genetically Altered Cotton Transforms Farming in South Africa," *St. Louis Post-Dispatch*, November 26, 2001. The primary risks are rapid development of Bt-resistant varieties of insects, rendering less effective an organic pesticide naturally available; so far unknown effects on microflora in the soil, gene flow to other species or to traditional crop varieties. Though "tests" have been run to guard against ill effects, these are fairly minimal. See, for example, *Rajya Sabha*, Unstarred Question No. 2782, 14.12.2001; not much time has passed, and any assumption of a strong bio safety regime in rural India is wishful thinking.

43. Ranajit Guha, *Elementary Aspects of Peasant Insurgency* (Delhi: Oxford University Press, l983).

44. Vandana Shiva, "Monocultures, Monopolies, Myths and Masculinization of Agriculture," paper prepared for the International Conference on Women and Agriculture, 1998. Her panel, which she did not attend, was entitled "Women's Knowledge, Biotechnology and International Trade—Fostering a New Dialogue into the Next Millennium." Obviously the fostering failed.

45. The forum, held May 30, 1998, in New Delhi, included farmers' organizations across the political spectrum, from the communist All-India *Kisan Sabha* to BJP associations. Organizational impetus came from *Navdanya*, a seed-preserving pro-biodiversity NGO linked to the Research Foundation for Science, Technology and Ecology in New Delhi. *Navdanya* [literally "nine seeds"], partly because of the international lecture tour of Francis Moore Lappe, has become, like Grameen Bank, something of a pilgrimage site.

46. Press release, Research Foundation for Science, Technology and Ecology, New Delhi, November 1, 2001. The classic work on "safety first" as the core of peasant moral economy is James C. Scott, *The Moral Economy of the Peasant* (New Haven, Conn.: Yale University Press, 1976).

47. Personal communication from Tikait to Stig Toft Madsen, quoted with permission.

48. Research Foundation for Science, Techology and Ecology/Navdanya, New Delhi. No date, but after May 2002.

49. Murray Edelman, *Politics As Symbolic Action* (Champaign/Urbana: University of Illinois Press, 1962).

50. Anil Gupta, "Rewarding Local Communities for Conserving Biodiversity: The Case of the Honey Bee," in *Protection of Global Biodiversity: Converging Strategies*, ed. Lakshman D. Guruswamy and Jeffrey A. McNeely (Durham, N.C.: Duke University Press, 1998), 180–89; Charles Weiss and Thomas Eisner, "Partnerships for Value-Added through Bioprospecting," *Technology in Society* 20 (1998), 481–98.

51. Confederation of Indian Industry, *Biotechnology on the Fast Track*. Unpublished conference proceedings, New Delhi: Department of Biotechnology, Ministry of Science and Technology, Government of India, 2001; *Biotechnology: A Vision*, New Delhi.

52. M. S. Swaminathan, "GM to Do Good."

53. Gordon Conway, *The Doubly Green Revolution: Food for All in the 21st Century* (New York: Penguin Books, 1997). For a treatment sensitive to the obstacles and realistic about the excessive promises of miracle seeds, but decidedly Malthusian, see Pinstrup-Anderson and Schiøler, *Seeds of Contention*. For a tenor of the pro-GMO position, see Dennis T. Avery, "Biotech Foods . . . Safe, Tested and Ready for the World," *Global Food Quarterly*, Churchville, Va.: Hudson Institute, Center for Global Food Issues, 1999. The article's lead-in states: "The real risk is starvation in poor countries, not genetically engineered food."

54. United Nations Development Programme, *Human Development Report: Making Technologies Work for Human Development* (New York: Oxford University Press, 2001).

55. Smitu Kothari and Michelle Chawla, eds., *UN DeePer in the Techno-Corporate Mire* (New Delhi: Kalpavriksh, Lokayan, et al., 2002).

56. Ashis Nandy, *Science, Hegemony, and Violence* (New Delhi: Oxford University Press, 1990).

57. Early attacks by sucking insects—aphids, jassids, thrips—are not affected by the Bt toxin, nor are all bollworm varieties equally affected in all regions, but bollworm spraying is typically reduced significantly.

58. This is the finding of a very large survey of Bt farmers commissioned by MAHYCO/Monsanto. See A. C. Nielsen, "Nationwide Survey by A. C. Nielsen ORG-MARG Underscores Benefits of Bollgard™ Cotton. Press Release," *The Economist*, June 21–27, 2003. A. C. Nielsen ORG-MARG, Mumbai, 2004. Devparna Roy, based on work in Gujarat cotton fields, reports that one reason farmers in her sample like Bt cottons of various varieties is efficient harvesting (personal communication 2004).

59. See Sahai, "Bt Cotton: Confusion Prevails," for a pessimistic projection for Bt cotton, contrary to the analysis of Matin Qaim and David Zilberman, "Yield Effects." MAHYCO believes that at a price ratio of 4 to 1 over traditional varieties, farmers will increase margins, and the firm will profit; the rule of thumb is that the farmer should get two-thirds of the benefit, the company one-third. Personal communication, Raju Barwale, Managing Director, MAHYCO, May 31, 2004. The seeds are selling.

60. Yousouf Ismael, Richard Bennett, and Steven Morse, "Biotechnology In Africa: The Adoption and Economic Impacts of Bt Cotton in the Makhathini Flats, Republic of South Africa," paper presented for AfricaBio Biotechnology Conference for Sub-Saharan Africa, Johannesburg, South Africa, September 26–27, 2001; James, *Global Review of Transgenic Crops*; Qaim and Zilberman, "Yield Effects," 900–902.

61. The literature is too large to consider here. See G. J. Persley and M. M. Lantin, eds., *Agricultural Biotechnology and the Poor*, Washington, D.C., Consultative Group on International Agricultural Research, 2000, for a grounded range of possibilities. The most recent comparative summary is UNFAO, "The State of Food and Agriculture 2004: Agricultural Biotechnology—Meeting the Needs of the Poor?" Rome, 2004.

62. E.g., K. S. Jayaraman, "India Produces Homegrown GM Cotton," *Nature Biotechnology* 22, no. 3 (March 2004): 255–56; *The Economic Times,* December 26, 2001; *The Hindu,* February 16, 2004; Asha Krishnakumar, "Biotechnology: Bt cotton, again," *Frontline* 21, Issue 10 (May 8–21, 2004).

63. Ronald J. Herring, "The Political Impossibility Theorem of Agrarian Reform: Path Dependence and Terms of Inclusion," in *Changing Paths: The New Politics of Inclusion,* ed. Mick Moore and Peter Houtzager (Ann Arbor: University of Michigan Press, 2003), on the fads in pro-poor rhetoric and the reasons for retaining a property focus.

64. Ronald J. Herring, "State Property in Nature," in *Land, Property and the Environment,* ed. John F. Richards (Oakland, Calif.: Institute for Contemporary Studies, 2002).

65. Sahai, "Bt Cotton: Confusion Prevails"; Vandana Shiva, *Patents: Myths and Reality* (Delhi: Penguin, 2001).

66. Ha–Joon Chang, *Kicking Away the Ladder: Development Strategy in Historical Perspective* (London: Anthem Press, 2002).

67. In Indian Farmers Petition, a resolution of the Forum of Farmers Organizations on Globalization and Agriculture, May 30, 1998, New Delhi :"The liberalization and globalization regime have been destroying India's resilient crop diversity and culture of sustainable agriculture through multifold attacks. . . . The loot and patenting of our bio-resources have increased under the WTO and trade liberalization regimes."

68. The political optimism about coalitions expressed in Herring, *Political Impossibility Theorem,* is undermined by the current divisions over biotechnology in pro-poor organizations in India. For a comparative treatment, see John Harriss, "Do Political Regimes Matter: Poverty Reduction and Regime Differences Across India," in *Changing Paths,* ed. Peter Houtzager and Mick Moore (Ann Arbor: University of Michigan Press, 2003).

69. See John Dryzek, *The Politics of the Earth* (New York: Oxford University Press, 1997. On anxiety and symbolic politics, Edelman, *Politics As Symbolic Action.*

70. Harriss, "Do Political Regimes Matter"; Ronald J. Herring, "Political Conditions for Agrarian Reform and Poverty Alleviation," Institute for Development Studies Discussion Paper 375, University of Sussex, Brighton, U.K., June 2000.

71. When I asked in the Department of Biotechnology for examples of pro-poor biotechnology, vermiculture was the dominant response. This is not a fair sampling

of policy, nor of potentialities; official publications recite many other possibilities, including bioprospecting. Nevertheless, the biotech impulse in India is more that of taking advantage of the "information revolution," generating investment and growth, capitalizing on India's scientific knowledge capital, and preventing descent in the global hierarchy—China's public sector makes very good Bt cotton, and most Chinese farmers grow Bt cotton.

72. The final irony is that the inability of Monsanto to enforce its property claims in India—and Brazil, more dramatically—will add to the pressure to prioritize research on gene use restriction technology (GURT)—a.k.a. The Terminator.

9

Strong States, Strong NGOs

Neema Kudva

I would like to liken nation-building to a chariot driven by five horses. These are: the Central government; the State governments; Panchayati Raj Institutions; the private sector; and last, but not the least, voluntary organizations and community-based groups. The chariot will run fast and in the right direction only when all the five horses run in tandem.

—Atal Bihari Vajpayee[1]

A key question which we have asked ourselves all those 22 years is: who are "we" vis-à-vis Government? Then and now Government exists as the largest development agency. We are often wrongly presented as "extension wing of Government or as implementing agency for achieving targets set by others or as contractors, or merely as Non-Government." The term Non-Government Organization is a negative one, and does not reflect the true nature of volunteerism, civil society and a positive role in processes of genuine empowerment and change.

—Nafisa Barot[2]

In April 2002, then Prime Minister Atal Bihari Vajpayee, and a nongovernmental organization (NGO) activist, Nafisa Barot from Gujarat, made these statements in New Delhi at a planning commission–sponsored All-India Conference on the Role of the Voluntary Sector in National Development. Likening nation-building to a charging chariot, a disturbing metaphor emblematic of the prime minister's political party, the Bharatiya Janata Party (BJP), Vajpayee voiced a vision of NGO–state relations where each brought particular strengths to the task of nation-building. He added, "no-doubt greater involvement of voluntary organizations will help the government in providing more efficient delivery of services at substantially lower costs.[3] In contrast, Barot sought to distance voluntary organizations from the state.

The two comments provide a glimpse into the complicated nature of NGO–state relations at one point in time. These relations are key to understanding the possibilities that exist for Indian NGOs to play a meaningful role in poverty alleviation. This chapter will argue that NGO impacts on poverty are best understood in the context of parameters set by the state. To do so, it will start by presenting the growth and development of the large and increasingly diverse NGO sector, focusing on changing NGO–state relations in post-independence India, as it transformed from a Nehruvian democratic socialist state to one where market triumphalism and religious nationalism have become dominant forces. NGO–state relations are shaped by changes in state-society relations and by the position of the state as regulator, funder, and political force at several levels, providing in turn multiple points of contact and possibilities for conflict and collaboration with NGOs. Following the historical narrative through three stages outlined by the editors of this volume, it will draw on case literature from the States of Karnataka, West Bengal, and Tamil Nadu, to demonstrate that the efficacy of NGO-driven, or state-driven but NGO-assisted policies for poverty alleviation turn on the question of the ability of a strong state to create openings that NGOs can then use to push for change.

In the story of changing state-society relations in post-independence India, NGOs rise to prominence in the third phase (from 1989 to the present) with "the NGO-ification of civil society," as the editors note, "arguably crowding out some of the more protest-oriented forms of organizing within the social movement sector." NGOs are characterized as forming part of the network of "global soup kitchens" (Fowler 1995, 1), working as service providers and sub-contractors to the state, providing cost-efficient, innovative, and targeted services that withdrawing states cannot, or refuse to, provide.

Proponents of NGOs like Barot argue in contrast that the location of these social actors in civil society provides them with an opportunity and opening for a renewed engagement in redistributive politics. NGOs can work across existing divisions; their "location at the margins are crucial standpoints for struggles, and thus for altering the terms of public debate and the concrete management of economic and social life."[4] In this perspective, NGOs work to empower communities and build social capital in civil society.

The debate on the role and effectiveness of NGOs continues, even as several commentators have pointed out that the sector, though large, is still small compared to the Indian state in terms of the amount of funding and support it brings to addressing problems of poverty and social change.[5] Equally important is the fact that the majority of Indian NGOs tend to be small, with annual budgets that are below Rs. 500,000 per year.[6] For many observers, the quality of NGO impacts in the face of pervasive poverty are captured in Sheldon Annis's frequently quoted comments on how size and small scale can be synonymous with insignificance, low cost can simply mean underfunded and of low quality, and political independence can signify powerlessness.[7] Despite these reservations, what we do know is that the growing NGO sector, small though it may be in comparison to the state, does have some impact and is becoming increasingly diverse. This diversity reflects not just regional differences and variation in state governments but also the influence of donors and the need for NGOs to demonstrate success. The same factors also lead to the uneven distribution of NGOs within programmatic sectors and across India.

One caveat needs to be emphasized: the relationship between social movement and NGO sectors is not systematically examined here, reflecting, in part, a serious gap in the NGO literature. The assertion that NGOs crowd out and dilute social movement claims has been made by many theorists and some activists, though others reflecting the perspective of activists in the NGO sector claim that "VOs/NGOs [working] through these social movements try to reform society, institutions and governance and act as harbingers of social change."[8] Anecdotal evidence and some recent work, however, points to a more complicated relationship between the two. The roles and activities of some movement organizations[9] and selected NGOs intersect, particularly in the spheres of fundraising, outside support, and organizing practice. Just as with NGO–state relations, this seems to suggest that, based on the location and scale of the NGO and the social movement (in physical and political space), a range of relationships from closely supportive to openly hostile provides a more robust explanation than the stark, antagonistic categories currently proposed.

SITUATING NGOS AND THE STATE

The tradition for papers, articles, and books on NGOs is to start by defining the object of their study.[10] The NGOs this chapter is concerned with work on development issues that in some manner reduce poverty and have an impact on the livelihoods of the poor and marginalized. It is estimated that there are between twenty and thirty thousand NGOs in India, "the NGO capital of the world."[11] Some of these are voluntary in nature, others are membership-based, but most have employed staff. They work in many (and often across) programmatic sectors, and with particular groups. This, together with their basic orientation towards the economic and political spheres, shapes their work practices and program, as well as the projects they undertake.[12]

Much of the polemical and image-building literature on NGOs, regardless of which end of the political spectrum it comes from, legitimizes NGO activity on two axes, the economic and the political: not only are NGOs better and more efficient at providing relief and social services than the state or the market but they are also engaged in value-driven, community-based practice that initiates and supports political and social change. Beyond the image-building literature, considerable work is being done to evaluate NGO claims of efficiency and effectiveness in both the economic and political spheres. The burgeoning critical literature reveals a complicated, messy picture of organizations adjacent to, between, and intersected by state, donor, market, and civil society actors, with complex networks and relationships that span boundaries. Studies have shown that NGO claims to economic efficiency need to be tempered: they are not as cost-efficient or innovative, lack broadness of reach, rarely target as deeply as presumed or claimed, and tend not to work in areas of highest poverty.[13] Political claims of supporting social justice and democratization are as difficult to pin down. In organizations that achieve some measure of success—however defined—a complex picture emerges of participatory management and organizational practices in the context of progressive legislation and a strong engaged state.[14] As important are issues of NGO capability, representativeness, and accountability and how these in turn shape an organization's ability to effectively reach and work with people, in particular, the poor.

In contrast to theorizing on NGOs, which is still in its early phases, the Indian state, towering as it does over society, has been theorized and understood in many ways. To NGOs the state would seem to be a multi-headed, multi-armed giant that asserts authority even as it often loses track of what its various entities are doing. Understanding the ways and nature of the state is, however, crucial to NGO effectiveness in any sphere. As a regulator the state seeks to control NGOs and make them accountable to it; as a funder it seeks to selectively collaborate with groups that can elicit people's participation and make government programs more efficient and effective. In political space, however, a strong community-based NGO is a potential threat to the local power structure and can expect to have a contentious relationship with both a cadre-based political party and other state functionaries.

The state regulates NGOs by requiring them to register, particularly if they seek state or foreign funding, and report their activities at regular intervals. The Societies Registration Act of 1860, related state acts, the Indian Trust Act of 1882, and the Charitable and Religious Act of 1920, are the primary mechanisms for registration.[15] None of these forms of registration (NGOs may also be registered as trade unions, cooperatives, or partnerships and even as companies) are appropriate to the range of NGO activity, and one result is that NGOs often stretch given definitions, leading to conflict and misunderstandings between the NGO and administrators responsible for implementing registration. Another piece of legislation with huge implications for understanding the regulatory capacity of the state is the Foreign Contribution Regulation Act (FCRA) of 1976, which was originally designed to prevent the flow of foreign funds to political parties.[16] The Act was amended in 1984 to more closely monitor the flow of funds to the Voluntary Sector. Yet another way of controlling NGOs is Commissions of Enquiry, state appointed bodies that look into allegations against NGOs. Often employed as an intimidatory tactic, the most famous among them is the Kudal Commission, which in a process that dragged on for six years (1981–1987) attempted to eviscerate Gandhian NGOs that had actively supported the opposition during Emergency rule. While the state's regulatory framework has proved to be a heavy burden for NGOs, particularly small, community-based rural groups,[17] its expanding role as a funder has changed the ways in which the 15,445 NGOs (as of February 2004) that receive state aid interact with various agencies at the district, State and Central levels.[18]

The state's role as a funder dates back to the grants-in-aid program that was started in 1956 to disburse funds to support welfare activities through the Central Social Welfare Board (CSWB). The active promotion of NGOs and the expansion of the state's role as funder began with the Sixth Plan (1980–1985), formulated by the Janata Party, which came to power after the Emergency. In every subsequent plan, the state has called for increased professionalization of NGOs and increased its allocations to NGOs through various ministries at the Central and state levels.[19] This funding has continued to expand as the state attempts to withdraw and increasingly rely on market based mechanisms to promote development. Various institutional initiatives have also been taken to simplify state funding of NGOs. In 1986, for example, the Ministry of Rural Development took the radical step of combining two existing funding units to create a trust, Council for Advancement of People's Action and Rural Technology (CAPART), to fund and support NGOs. The growth of state funding is exemplified by the growth in CAPART's funding portfolio from over Rs. 545 million for about 4,000 NGOs in 1993–1994 to about Rs. 3 billion to fund over 10,000 NGOs in 2002–2003.[20]

Even as the state seeks to control NGOs through its regulatory and funding regimes, NGO–state relations are mediated through the ideological optic of the political party in power at both the Central and the state levels. The early alliance between Gandhian NGOs and the congress fractured as the crisis of deinstitutionalization grew, and many NGOs allied instead with the Janata Party. At the same time, legislation was passed that enforced the separation between NGOs and party politics; by law registered NGOs may not be actively involved in party politics or have any of its members stand for election. Even as newer, professional, and avowedly apolitical NGOs began to occupy the public eye, the Constitutional Amendment of 1993 that brought back Panchayati Raj (PR) changed the relationship of NGOs to political spaces at the local level. In this context, the question of where NGOs stand vis-à-vis political parties becomes even more important.

The clearest position is that of the CPI(M), Communist Party of India (Marxist), that has been in power continuously in West Bengal and sporadically in Kerala for the last thirty years. In a 1988 book, *Foreign Funding and the Philosophy of Voluntary Organizations,* Prakash Karat, a respected CPI(M) adherent, explains the proliferation of NGOs from the party perspective.[21] The book attacks advocates of "non-party political groups" for social transformation, and asks that the government tighten controls on NGOs and stop foreign funds from coming into the country. The relationship between NGOs and the CPI(M) has been described as mutually distrustful and antagonistic.[22] Despite this, there is an active NGO sector in Kerala and Marxist controlled West Bengal when compared to other parts of the country, leading some researchers to point to the ways in which the pro-poor reform orientation of Left Front governments has created political opportunities for particular forms of community-based NGOs.[23]

Whether NGOs are used by political parties or party functionaries to raise funds for political activity is another issue that is constantly under debate. The rise of Hindu nationalism in general and in particular the riots and pogroms directed at Muslims in BJP-controlled Gujarat, have highlighted the relationship between NGOs and political parties. The "saffron dollar"— signifying funds raised by expatriate South Asians through U.S.- and U.K.- based nonprofits and charities and disbursed through Indian NGOs allied with the Sangh Parivar—is one issue over which allegations and counterallegations have surfaced.[24]

While NGOs may not actively associate with political parties by law, the implementation of Panchayati Raj has changed the nature of NGO involvement with elected representatives at the local level. Many NGOs support their members' attempts to contest Panchayat elections,[25] just as they use funds from state and foreign donors to conduct training programs in Panchayati Raj procedures, rules, and responsibilities, for the communities they work with, and for elected representatives, particularly women who hold 33 percent of all seats as a result of state-imposed quotas.

The dominance of the Centre in the Indian state allows overarching patterns in NGO–state relations to be traced across the country as state–society relationships have changed in post-independent India. NGOs have moved from a pro-state position as partners in consolidating nationalist development in the *first phase* (1947–1966) when the Nehruvian master frame dominated, towards a contentious antagonistic relationship with the state as the crisis of deinstitutionalization deepened through the *second phase* (1966–1988). This tumultuous period, particularly the early 1970s, saw a surge in the numbers of NGOs as agitations for change and regional autonomy gained ground. Empowerment-oriented NGOs, which opposed the state in direct and indirect ways, emerged in the first half of this phase; while the numbers of economic development-oriented NGOs increased in the latter half. In the second phase, the imposition of Emergency by Indira Gandhi in 1975 marks a deep rupture that is pivotal to understanding both the development of the NGO sector and NGO–state relations. The *third phase* (1989 to the present) is a period of active involvement of the state in the rhetoric (and reality) of promoting "partnership" with the NGO sector, mainly through increases in state funding for NGOs. This is under pressure to be economically viable both from within and from foreign donors, a pressure that also leads to NGOs being professionalized and increasingly constituted in response to the needs of the state and foreign donors. NGO responses to the state now cover the range from strongly oppositional to closely collaborative, with the majority keeping an uneasy, sometimes reluctant, but pragmatic and often sophisticated partnership with the Indian state in its various forms.

Equally important here is the role that NGOs play in poverty reduction and alleviation in each of these three phases. Academic and policy understandings of the structural causes of poverty as well as the formulation of associated strategies for eradicating poverty are produced and disseminated by a global complex of donors, international agencies, and national states under the shadow of shifting ideological positions. NGO actions respond to both national imperatives and these global understandings of how to deal with poverty. The state shifted from implementing capital-intensive growth policies in the first phase to populist antipoverty programs in the second. NGOs responded by moving from mitigating the effects of poverty by providing welfare and relief services in the first phase to claiming to attack the root causes of poverty and inequality, which the state was clearly failing to do, in the second phase. By the early 1990s as the state moved towards reducing its role, and stimulating development through macroeconomic reform and global linkages, NGOs were talking about the need to "scale-up" their activities through sustainable strategies if they wished to make a substantive impact on poverty. Four approaches to scaling up (that resonate with the Indian experience in the post-emergency period) were synthesized by Michael Edwards and David Hulme in 1992 and soon became commonly held belief. They helped shape NGO strategies for poverty alleviation in the third phase: first, working with states to spread innovative methods and change state policy; second, incorporating lobbying and advocacy efforts into NGO work; third, expanding operations and targeting deeper; and fourth, building and strengthening NGO networks.[26] The dominant conceptualization is of an uneasy partnership between NGOs and the state, with NGOs collaborating selectively with the state even as they work to hold the state accountable to its poorest and most marginalized citizens.

240
Neema Kudva

GROWTH AND DEVELOPMENT OF THE NGO SECTOR

There is a sizeable literature on the development and functioning of the voluntary sector in India.[27] Most researchers trace the development of modern voluntarism to reformist movements of the late nineteenth century. These movements, the work of Christian missionaries, who in their zeal to recruit converts brought health care and education to poor, isolated rural areas, as well as Gandhian and other community development experiments in the early twentieth century, structured the subsequent growth of the NGO sector.[28] Of these, Gandhi's massive "constructive work" program of rural development (launched in Wardha, Maharashtra, from 1922 to 1928) played a major role in influencing the voluntary sector as it shifted the focus of voluntarism from issue-based action, particularly social and religious reform, to political content aimed at nation-building.

While there is broad agreement on the ways in which various events and movements, people, and public figures have shaped and influenced the voluntary sector, the impact of specific influences changes from one region and state to another. The Gandhian movement has had a deeper impact on the voluntary sector in Gujarat, Uttar Pradesh, and Bihar, while the Left has been a strong influence in West Bengal, Kerala, and parts of Andhra Pradesh and Maharashtra. Similarly, the church has played an important role in some southern states, the northeastern states and in other areas with heavy concentrations of Adivasi and Dalit populations, while the spread of development NGOs across the nation in the 1970s can be understood only in the context of a renewed socialist movement led by Jai Prakash Narayan (JP). The variation in the implementation of decentralization reforms is another factor to consider when understanding NGO roles at the local level. These differences need to be kept in mind as we follow the general trajectory of NGO development through three phases.

THE FIRST PHASE, 1947–1966:
SILENT PARTNERS OF THE DEVELOPMENTALIST STATE

During the years after independence in which Nehru's visions of state-led capital-intensive development and poverty reduction gained precedence, NGOs largely served to provide *welfare and relief*. As Raka Ray and Mary Fainsod Katzenstein have described in their introduction, organized groups, social actors, and even those who opposed the state took their ideological cues from the Nehruvian state; NGOs and other organizations in the voluntary sector were no different.

In the years after independence, the Central state sought to reinforce its command over the rural sector even as community development projects and experiments in extension service of the 1950s failed, as did Panchayati Raj, which started in 1959 and was subsequently phased out. In this period, most NGOs remained silent partners of the state, aiding its developmental role by assisting in welfare and relief related activities. NGO practices mostly aimed to mitigate the impacts of poverty by providing a safety net for the people with whom they worked in rural areas. Many secular, non-Gandhian NGOs (including branches of international NGOs) worked to provide relief to refugees and victims of floods, famines, and other natural disasters, and health and nutrition to the marginalized. Some Gandhian NGOs were active in training government extension workers for programs initiated by the Ministry of Health and the Ministry of Community Development. In this same period church-led groups continued to work mostly in tribal belts in the North-East and the South, concentrating on education and health related issues.

The state promoted and supported NGOs through different grant-in-aid programs that were channeled through the Central Social Welfare Board (CSWB, set up in 1953) and State Social Welfare Advisory Boards (SSWAB) that were set up a year later. CSWB grants supported Gandhian NGOs that worked with extension services in agricultural and livestock programs, health, and education, and set up *khadi* and village industries and cooperatives. Social Welfare Board grants were also aimed at organizations that could assist state agencies in setting up crèches, short-stay homes, and homes for the disabled, aged, and destitute. Funding increased incrementally, from Rs. 70 million (Rs. 956 million or U.S. $51 million in 1990) for 2,128 organizations in the First Five Year Plan (1951–1956) to Rs. 233 million for about 6,000 organizations in the Second Plan (1956–1961). By the Third Plan, the state, besieged by wars with China and Pakistan, a major drought in Bihar, and an economic recession, had shrunk the welfare budget and only 5,000 organizations were funded.

THE SECOND PHASE, 1966 TO 1989: PROLIFERATION AND DIVERSIFICATION OF THE NGO SECTOR

By the mid-1960s, caught in a dual crisis of economic stagnation and political instability, the Indian state had entered a crisis of deinstitutionalization. Poverty and inequalities had grown between and within regions as the state, led by Nehru's congress, had failed to deliver on its promise of development and change. This phase—particularly in the 1970s—saw a phenomenal growth of NGOs even as the state initially became more repressive and sought to control NGOs through new legislation and regulatory mechanisms. Informed by the analysis of the causes of rural poverty and strategies that could address breaking poverty cycles, this phase also saw the rise of the technocratic, managerial NGO, in specific contrast to but alongside the awareness-oriented NGO that positioned itself in an oppositional role vis-à-vis the state. Towards the end of this phase, the issue of NGOs needing to scaleup their efforts through active lobbying, advocacy, and networking had also become important. This combined with the fact that, starting in the 1980s, the state had begun to take a more pro-market stance resulted in another shift in NGO-state relations.

The general feeling of disillusionment with the state that marks this phase took various forms of expression, as Ray and Katzenstein have described in their introduction. A number of social movements emerged even as student unrest increased on campuses across the country, trade unions grew in strength to challenge state power, and radical Left initiatives took the form of the Naxalite Movement, which sent thousands of their cadres into rural areas to organize peasants and the landless for direct action against their oppressors. Equally important, particularly in terms of understanding the dynamics of the NGO sector, was the rise of JP, a well known Gandhian, who emerged from self-imposed political exile to become one of Indira Gandhi's strongest and most vocal critics. JP urged constructive Gandhian workers, students, trade unionists, and extremists to become part of a nonviolent struggle against the government and raised the slogan of "Sampurna Kranti" (total revolution). As student activists, many of whom were young middle-class urban youth, and others from the Naxal movement and JP's grassroots socialism moved into NGOs in the 1970s, the new generation of NGOs sought to differentiate themselves from the charity and relief orientation of earlier NGOs.

The strategies that NGOs adopted responded to new understandings of the dynamics of poverty, and the context-specific nature of its production. One approach was to focus on fighting poverty by securing livelihoods and generating resources through supporting people's claims to land, income generation projects, and the design of appropriate technology strategies for sustainable development.[29] Another approach—inspired in part by Paolo Freire's *Pedagogy of the Oppressed*—was to refocus attention on education, awareness building, and conscientization as a tool for social transformation, with the expectation that mobilized communities are better able to fight for their rights. This was aided by the alliance between progressive bishops, theologians and Christian intellectuals who set up "laity centers,"[30] and the work of radical protestant priests who began working with marginalized communities. These shifts towards conscientization activities of small grassroots groups were initially supported by European protestant donor agencies.[31] The catchwords became appropriate technology, awareness building, and empowerment.

During this phase, associations and networks of NGOs also began to form with the intent of scaling up NGO influence. The Association of Voluntary Agencies for Rural Development (AVARD) set up in 1958 with the aim of creating a national platform for voluntary agencies became a dynamic presence under the leadership of JP. By the early 1970s it had brought together about three hundred Gandhian organizations and was vocal in its opposition of the Emergency. A contrasting example of an apolitical federation that since its inception worked closely with the state is the Voluntary Health Association of India (VHAI). VHAI began in 1969 as the Coordinating Agency for Health Planning (CAHP) when twenty-five leaders of Christian hospitals across the country met to discuss the problem of delivering health care to millions of rural people. By 1974, VHAI had emerged as a federation of State Voluntary Health Associations that was geared towards promoting the community health movement.

In 1975, under siege from grassroots movements all across the country and threatened by the development of the progressive alliance of popular political parties, Indira Gandhi announced the imposition of Emergency. A number of senior political leaders, political activists, and leaders of grassroots NGOs were imprisoned. The state sought more information and control over NGOs, especially those that had foreign donor support and were not directly dependent on the government for their operations. It was especially threatened by NGOs that were experimenting with conscientization and people's organization-building activities. In some areas there was direct intimidation and NGOs went underground or camouflaged their work. The state also passed FCRA, the Foreign Contribution Regulation Act, in 1976, arguing that this was necessary to guard against foreign interventions and manipulations that could destabilize the country.

While the two years of Emergency rule severely constrained the activities of NGOs across the country,[32] the situation changed dramatically with the Janata Party (a coalition of interests that were committed to ending Emergency and restoring a pluralistic, socialistic democracy) coming into power in 1977. After the election, the Janata Party set up a group within the planning commission to see how NGOs could participate in the process of rural development. Successful NGO experiments began to be integrated into national programs.[33] The Sixth Five Year Plan (1980–1985) formulated during the Janata regime was the first to explicitly earmark funding for NGOs under various ministries (Rs. 500 million, about $30 million in 1990). The Janata government also sought to encourage private support of NGOs and added Section 35 CCA to the Income Tax Act of 1961. This allowed corporations to deduct donations to NGOs from their taxable income. The Janata Party fell in January 1980, a victim to internal squabbling, and with it disappeared much of the political space that had opened up for NGOs.

NGOs viewed Indira Gandhi's return to power with apprehension. Her government immediately took steps to increase oversight into NGO activities by changing the terms of FCRA in 1984 and by establishing a Commission of Enquiry in 1981 under Justice P. D. Kudal to investigate misuses of funds and activities of several NGOs, including the Gandhi Peace Foundation and

AVARD, both of which had actively opposed Indira Gandhi's government. The Kudal Commission recommended regulatory and punitive measures to control wayward NGOs and is cited by many NGO activists as the single event that played the largest role in generating hostility and suspicion between them and the government.

Interestingly, even as the Centre sought to control and repress NGOs, in 1982, state governments were instructed to work with and fund grassroots development NGOs to elicit people's participation in implementing schemes under Indira Gandhi's populist Twenty Point Development Program. Consultative groups with members from various state agencies and NGO representatives were set up under a Development Commissioner or the Chief Secretary of the State.[34] Many NGOs seized these regional initiatives, and along with increased foreign donor funds for issues relating to women and the environment, the sector continued to expand. The early 1980s also saw a number of support NGOs come up like PRIA in New Delhi, and SEARCH in Bangalore that provided technical, training, and managerial expertise to grassroots groups and other NGOs, which were both professionalizing in response to donor (both state and foreign) reporting and assessment requirements even as they were often trying to scale up their activities.

Following Indira Gandhi's assassination, her son Rajiv Gandhi became the prime minister. By then, in the words of a senior bureaucrat in Gandhi's circle of advisors, "we had realized that India was ungovernable from the Centre."[35] The rise of regional political parties across India, and the phenomenal expansion of the Bharatiya Janata Party (BJP) had eroded the power of the congress substantially, and the state was failing on economic, political, and administrative fronts. Senior bureaucrats and others in Gandhi's inner circle of advisors were sympathetic to the voluntary sector as they saw in it an answer to the state's problems of reaching its citizens. A number of changes that impacted the voluntary sector substantially were being carried out at the same time: most importantly, Panchayati Raj was being reinvoked. Given these events, it is difficult to establish what exactly drove the state to actively seek partnerships with NGOs: Was it the urgency of establishing effective governance in the context of regions spiraling out of Central control, or was it in anticipation of the need for public service contractors who could provide various services given the first moves towards liberalizing the economy and pulling back the state? This dual focus of state imperatives is crucial to understanding the possibilities that emerged for NGO action in the 1990s and beyond.

Around the same time allocations for the Seventh Plan (1985–1990) were announced. It included an entire section on the voluntary sector with a budget allocation that was reported to be five times larger than the assistance provided in the earlier plan.[36] Assistance from the state to the voluntary sector focused mainly on the areas of family planning, the environment, and women's development, with clear rules and eligibility criteria being laid down for NGOs seeking funding.[37] As one observer put it, "voluntary agencies [had] now *officially* arrived."

THE THIRD PHASE, 1989 TO THE PRESENT: UNEASY PARTNERSHIPS

The factors that helped the NGO sector grow in the second phase, particularly the expansion of state and foreign donor funding in the 1980s, accelerated in the 1990s as the state lurched towards a market dominated economy. Increased diversification was also seen among NGOs, reflecting their understanding of the multi-layered structural as well as policy processes that the remediation of poverty seemed to require. One study captured this complex understanding:

> There are very many processes, relationships and socio-economic structures underlying rural peoples' poverty: landlessness, low wages, political powerlessness, occupancy of vulnerable biophysical environments, imperfect markets, adverse macroeconomic policy environments, and elite controlled policy processes are but a few. To expect NGOs to address all (or any) of these is naïve; but for an NGO, one implication is that if the organization is to have a sustainable impact on poverty, then at least some of these underlying causes must receive systematic attention.[38]

As liberalization gathered steam in the 1990s,[39] there was a simultaneous stepping up of state initiatives to partner with NGOs. At the same time, decentralization too was moving ahead, and the 73rd Amendment to the Constitution was finally passed in 1993, resulting in the re-creation of Panchayati Raj (PR) institutions across the country. The variation in the implementation of PR across the country has further highlighted regional differences in NGO–state relations.

The state, clearly interested in closer collaboration with NGOs, engaged in discussions to streamline procedural problems that blocked effective NGO–state collaboration and encourage the formation of a national level federation.[40] The planning commission brought together NGO and central and state level ministry representatives in all-India conferences in 1992, 1994, and 2002. By 2000, when deliberations on the tenth Five Year Plan (2002–2007) had started, the Planning Commission had been appointed the nodal agency for all NGO–state interactions and within it; the Voluntary Action Cell (previously the NGO Coordination Cell) had assumed greater responsibilities including initiating meetings with NGOs, setting up a steering committee with NGO representation for drafting the approach paper for the

Tenth Plan document, and maintaining a searchable web-based database on all organizations funded through state agencies.

Starting in the early 1990s, significant state funding agencies like the Social Welfare Boards had also began to move away from funding only charity and relief services. By the late 1990s, a third of CSWB's grants were allocated for "non-traditional" awareness and education programs for women. Other ministries had also begun to actively solicit NGO collaboration by setting up NGO Coordination Cells, though none followed the example of the Ministry of Rural Development in setting up a separate funding agency. In all, the various ministries had about two hundred centrally sponsored programs with an NGO component to them in place by the mid-1990s.[41] While exact and reliable figures on funding amounts for each year are hard to pull together, it was estimated recently that the central government had spent about Rs. 10 billion in 2001 to fund over fourteen thousand NGOs.[42] NGO input into state programs however, seems mostly to be limited to implementation of government schemes to tight specifications. Despite a couple of well-publicized examples of state-initiated NGO inspired and assisted schemes such as Mahila Samakhya or the National Literacy Mission, there seems to have been little flexibility or scope for innovation.

The clustering of NGOs was, however, apparent, and in 1994 it was estimated that about 60 percent of organizations funded by the state through CAPART, CSWB, and other ministries were in four states, three of which were performing relatively well on poverty alleviation measures: West Bengal, Tamil Nadu, Maharashtra and Uttar Pradesh (UP).[43] This clustering was a cause for concern, especially since studies were showing the widening gap between regions and states in terms of the prevalence and depth of poverty and the structural conditions that led to it. The state initiated a series of efforts to spread NGO funding into the northern states where poverty is particularly pernicious and into the northeastern states where separatist violence has negatively impacted economic development. Agencies like CAPART decentralized and set up eight regional offices between 1995 and 1999, each of which was responsible for sanctioning projects with annual budgets up to Rs. 200,000, monitoring and evaluation of all projects in their respective region, training, state–NGO liaison, and promoting small informal groups. By February 2004, only 35.6 percent of all organizations funded were from West Bengal, Tamil Nadu, Maharashtra and Uttar Pradesh; the northern states (Bihar, Chattisgarh, Jharkhand, Madhya Pradesh, Orissa, and Rajasthan, not including UP) had 23 percent of all funded organizations, and the northeast had another 16 percent of all state-funded NGOs.

The amount of overseas funding to Indian NGOs from donors—northern NGOs, foreign governments through bilateral agencies, and multilateral agencies—also increased. While international donor NGO aid continued to grow, the 1990s saw an important development in the increasing percentage of bilateral and multilateral aid (aimed at rural development, health, family planning, environment, and women's development issues) being routed to NGOs through various ministries and state agencies.[44] Twenty-two donor countries including progressive funders from Northern Europe like Norway, Sweden, the Netherlands, and Denmark, together provided about $600 million of India's $2 billion–$2.5 billion in annual aid income, estimated to be about 6 percent of the state's capital investment budget.[45] The Government of India's announcement in June 2003 to stop accepting bilateral aid from all but six donor countries, routing it instead through other institutions, projects, and NGOs after "prior clearances and annual consultations between the government and bilateral partners," will thus have a significant impact on NGO work in particular regions and programmatic sectors.[46] The impact of this decision is unclear since the mechanisms for regulation have yet to be clarified. Will the bilaterals continue to provide crucial support for progressive initiatives in participatory planning, governance, and the environment without state guarantees? Alternatively, will they seek out and continue to fund the larger, better-established NGOs, which will grow even larger and more established and move either to become a countervailing force or large public service contractors to the state?[47]

Funding from northern NGO donors, which had increased substantially in the 1980s, has continued to grow at an average annual rate of 13.63 percent between 1991 and 2000, though funding focus is different from that of the state. The number of funded organizations has, however, increased at only about 5 percent annually over the same period. A study of funding under FCRA classification for the period 1996–2000 shows that activities broadly falling under the rubric of "welfare" account for a little over a quarter of all receipts. Relief funds varied by year, based on when major disasters like cyclones or earthquakes hit, while rural development activities account for about 15 percent and building construction activity between 11 and 14 percent in the same period.[48] This is in contrast to state funding, 42 percent of which went to rural development followed by 19 percent for social justice and empowerment work, and another 13 percent for activities related to human resource development, like education.[49]

The funding patterns of international donor NGOs did, however, undergo some shifts in the 1990s. At a global level, an increasing amount of donor resources were being channeled towards Africa and Eastern Europe in the early to mid-1990s, and toward Afghanistan and the Middle East in the 2000s. At a national level within India, some secular international donor NGOs like ActionAid and Oxfam that have increased their India budgets between 20 and 24 percent for the period 1996–2000 have begun, like the state, to move away from areas with established NGO presence like southern India, Maharashtra, or Gujarat and started funding groups in the northern and the northeastern regions.[50] Others like EZE, a German Protestant NGO that remains one of the largest donors in India, have seen little growth in disbursements mainly focused on tribal, dalit, and women's development, while organizations like Bread for the World have cut back. This shift in donor focus has impacted Indian NGOs in different ways. A few individual activists and some of the larger NGOs have moved into the newly funded areas; in areas where funding is being phased out, small and large groups that had relied on foreign funds have begun to actively explore ways to raise money from domestic sources, particularly industries and trusts set up by corporations.[51] Most importantly, many NGOs are actively seeking and entering into closer funding relationships with the state.

Another trend, evident for some time, but yet to be reflected in the available funding data, is the increasing attention being given to urban poverty, which until recently had been considered less pervasive. NGOs have always worked with the homeless and in low-income settlements around the issues of shelter, service provision, waste collection, and income generation; a focus on participatory and effective governance, and on the needs of lower and middle-class communities is becoming more common.

NGOs are clearly continuing to proliferate, though the sector still exists on the periphery of the development arena. There are, however, noticeable changes in the NGO sector in the 1990s post-liberalization third phase. Older divisions based on ideological differences are becoming even less visible as most NGOs seem to accept the rhetoric of empowerment and sustainable development being espoused from all ends of the political spectrum. The traditional divide between the NGO whose main aim is to create social change through awareness creation and group organizing and the techno-managerial NGO that concentrates on effective service delivery and income generation by eliciting people's participation continues to exist. It is not uncommon, however, to find NGOs accepting funding and contracts from one state agency as they actively organize to oppose another.[52] NGOs can thus claim to do both empowerment and economic development, though most established larger NGOs are firmly tied to funding sources and to project-oriented development work. The shift of foreign aid to service delivery oriented groups and the increasing amount of government funding being channeled through these groups also buttress this trend. The movement from a "commitment culture to a competence culture" seems to be gaining ground.[53]

The broad patterns and trends in NGO–state relations and the emergence and proliferation of NGOs underscores the ways in which NGOs are continually (re)constituted by the state, primarily, and by donors. The picture that emerges is drawn in the context of a federal state where tensions between the Centre and states has increased, and will continue to grow as PR reforms are implemented and consolidated. It focuses much needed attention on the extent to which the state defines the arena—at all scales—within which

NGOs function and the ways in which NGOs are constituted as institutional actors in civil society.

The everyday reality of NGO work, though circumscribed by these broad trends, is as much a result of local level politics and social relations, often in a select number of villages in a district, in several districts of a state, or occasionally across state lines in a broadly defined region. To fully understand NGO abilities to be effective in poverty alleviation, then, it is necessary to pay attention to the diversity of local conditions. The next section of this chapter will take the case of three NGOs working with a particular *target beneficiary group*, women, in the states of Karnataka, Tamil Nadu, and West Bengal, to explore the conditions under which NGOs working with communities of women function in the context of PR reforms, illustrating in the process the importance of organizational practice, progressive legislation and a strong state as conditions for NGO effectiveness (or not) in combating poverty. These cases also illustrate how NGOs can seize openings created at the local level by the twin imperatives of the central state to move towards markets even as it devolves powers to regions through decentralization reforms.

NGO–STATE RELATIONS AT THE LOCAL LEVEL

The previous section pointed to the important ways in which NGO growth is tied to donors, to the experience of associational life, and most importantly, to the role of the state as funder, regulator, and development agent. What it did less well is show how NGO programs and tactics evolve at the local level, as strategies for poverty alleviation are circumscribed by the parameters of state discourses. Even as the larger debate on the NGO sector hews close to the widespread imagining of NGOs as junior partners—more, less, or not at all important—that will deal with the poor and the marginalized in the task of nation-building, some NGOs hold to the idea of transformation through political change and social transformation. The result of these intersections—of the simultaneous move towards the market and decentralization, as well as the imagined role of junior partner—is that opportunities do open up for NGOs that are interested in political change. The final section of this chapter will focus on the work of three NGOs: SHARE in Tamil Nadu, Mahila Samakhya in Karnataka, and Nari Bikash Samithi in West Bengal to illustrate the contrast among the challenges NGOs working in tandem with the state claim to meet but sidestep, and the challenges that NGOs claiming to support discourses of poverty alleviation and social justice face.

The three states include Karnataka, a demographically progressive "middle-order" state,[54] which has wide inter-district variations.[55] Unlike Tamil

Nadu or West Bengal, Karnataka has not seen political mobilization on the basis of class or mass movements on a large scale, though caste politics play an important role in state politics. The state was ruled by the Congress Party until 1982, after which the Janata Party, the Janata Dal, and the Congress have been in and out of power. The BJP has made strong inroads into state politics in the 2004 Lok Sabha elections. Karnataka also has a strong civil service tradition that it inherited from Mysore State and reconstituted Panchayati Raj Institutions in 1982, pioneering a system of gender quotas that have since been implemented across the country. Tamil Nadu, in contrast, is generally regarded as a relatively advanced state with a well-developed and diversified economy. Non-Brahmin movements centered around the revitalization of Tamil identity, which started in 1926 and later developed into two regional political parties, the Dravida Kazhagam (1944) and the Dravida Munnetra Kazagham (1949) and which have dominated state politics. The third state, West Bengal, one of India's smallest but most densely populated, was India's industrial powerhouse at the time of independence. Since then industrial production has lagged behind and the state's economy has stagnated. West Bengal is, however, distinctive in that it has made significant inroads in poverty alleviation under the longest elected Left Front government in India, which is still in power after having first won elections after the Emergency in 1977.

All three states have active, diverse NGO sectors. In Karnataka and Tamil Nadu the majority of NGOs work in rural development, closely followed by NGOs that have a focus on health and women and children's issues.[56] In contrast, a recent survey of the voluntary sector in West Bengal showed a large number of voluntary organizations active in recreation, sports, and culture, followed by religious activity and education; conspicuously absent were NGOs that work in rural development, an arena for concerted state action.[57] Yet, the state heavily funds rural development NGOs in West Bengal (57 percent of all state-funded NGOs in West Bengal work in rural development compared to 42 percent nationwide in 2004). Given that the Planning Commission database is weighted towards the Centre, this opens up two questions: Does this indicate—in some small way—the use of Central funds to counteract the Left Front's position in the countryside? Or is it reflective of sophisticated NGO tactics at the local level, where NGOs become adept at playing off one state agency against the other?

The poverty scenarios across these three states also vary. V. M. Rao has pointed out that the southern states—Karnataka and Tamil Nadu, along with Andhra Pradesh—have several distinct characteristics. Although these States have on average been more successful at implementing antipoverty programs, poverty persists. An important factor in the persistence of poverty is the presence of active, organized non-poor groups that form alliances (including with upper layers of poor groups) to block the mobilization of the poor or those who organize on their behalf. For Rao, the only antidote is the "countervailing mobilization of the poor [which] would have to occur at the regional and higher levels where diverse groups interact and influence policy making."[58] The experience of West Bengal is once again instructive, where the Left Front used their political clout to "skillfully combine radical rhetoric with pragmatic compromises," allowing the poor to obtain a certain degree of autonomy from dominant classes even as it allowed the same dominant classes certain economic and social gains.[59] It emphasizes the importance of both a long-term institutional strategy aimed at changing the structural conditions of poverty and the large scale mobilization of poor groups in political space across existing divisions to influence policymaking at higher levels. In this perspective, the state partners with the poor not with NGOs who have little impact on poverty alleviation due to their "small number, limited area of operation, liberal foreign funding and trips, hierarchy within organizations, and lack of any system of accountability."[60]

While Rao emphasizes the structural conditions of poverty and the mobilization of the poor, a process in which he sees NGOs as playing a minor role, others like Murthy and Rao point to both tangible and intangible dimensions of deprivation, arguing that states tend to focus on and respond only to tangible dimensions of deprivation such as lack of growth, income generation, and productive employment and not on intangible dimensions such as powerlessness, vulnerability, and isolation. For them, NGOs have an important role as intermediaries who should work to enhance the bargaining power of the poor vis-à-vis other groups and the state, even as they help enhance the bargaining power of the state itself vis-à-vis mainstream international institutions.[61] The difficulty of mobilizing poor people, given the diversity of their institutional conditions based on gender, caste, the nature of work, agricultural conditions, social relations and power structures, should rest not on skills and capacity-building alone but on changing institutional structures to combat the intangible dimensions of being in poverty. The two perspectives, though not completely dissimilar, nevertheless have very different conceptualizations of the role for NGOs in poverty alleviation.

Just as important are the state's current policy responses to poverty alleviation through a patchwork of strategies, most of which aim to increase capital endowment of the poor by focusing on building their entrepreneurial skills and capabilities. One example of a heavily favored blueprint strategy— by the state, donors, and NGOs, including the three cases in this chapter— that aims to do this is microfinancing, which proposes to lift people out of poverty through financially self-sustaining income generation schemes. The claims made by proponents of microfinancing for both women's empowerment and impacts on deep poverty are, however, questionable.[62]

The important question here is: How do these different articulations of combating poverty play out in the strategies and tactics adopted by NGOs at the local level? The stories of SHARE, Mahila Samakhya, and Nari Bikash Samithi will help unpack these questions.

SHARE is an NGO working with four thousand poor women from landless and marginal land owning households in twenty-seven villages in a drought-prone area in Tamil Nadu. The area has been studied and mapped intensively and presents a picture, much like the rest of India, of a region where poverty has become more diverse and complex as a result of the state's agricultural policies.[63] The ability to mobilize people is also complicated in the absence of a politics of poverty where politics at the state and local level is dominated by identity and patronage structures, alliances between poor groups is non-existent and riven with caste, gender, and religious structures, and poverty alleviation policies largely follow the blueprint of the capital endowment model outlined above. In this context, following Rajasekhar's argument, the strategies adopted by SHARE, which started with income generation activities in craft production for national and international markets, then adding awareness and microfinancing programs to finally having members contest Panchayat seats, have had a limited impact on poverty alleviation in the area.

The villages that SHARE works in were caste- and occupation-segregated, and well and tank irrigation was used to cultivate staple food grains and pulses. Agriculture was the main economic sector, but the general standards of health and well-being at the local level were regarded as good. In the late 1950s and the 1960s, following drought and aided by state subsidies, well irrigation with diesel pumps became the norm. Cropping intensity and production increased and other employment opportunities opened up. Significant changes occurred in the area as agricultural technologies such as high-yielding seeds, fertilizers, support and credit to purchase inputs, and subsidies for electricity to run pumpsets were adopted. Some groups among the lower cultivator castes prospered, even as employment opportunities declined with the onset of mechanization, and wages between men and women continued to diverge, especially in nonagricultural sectors. As water tables fell and tanks silted over, higher investments were needed to deepen wells, resulting in deeper divisions between farmers, with smaller farmers who lacked necessary capital shifting away from paddy, which had become the major crop after the spread of irrigation, to less water-intensive crops such as groundnut and bananas. In the 1980s and 1990s non-farm employment rose as villagers commuted to nearby towns to participate in the informal sector or worked in local quarries, rolled bidis, and worked in construction and other sectors. Surveys conducted over this period show that the disparities between groups had grown: nutritional intake in better-off households had improved while landless and marginal farmers were much worse off with shifts in crop patterns; health, too, had declined as a result of changing consumption patterns and worsening sanitation. The availability of non-farm work and an active dalit movement had however, resulted in some important social transformations such as the removal of untoucha-bility and entry to temples, but had left other glass ceilings intact, which restricted dalit entry into capital-intensive farming and other profitable employment venues.

While this provides a general picture of the region, wealth-ranking exercises conducted in selected villages where SHARE works revealed further important differences between the poor and the very poor. The poor had access to a range of employment opportunities in non-farm sectors, and often one working household member with a salaried position ensured regular wages through all seasonal cycles. The very poor, in contrast, lacked stable incomes across all seasons. Non-farm employment opportunities varied greatly across villages and this combined with the gendered nature of work (women were more likely to work as agricultural labor or in bidi-rolling and palm leaf mat–making, while men worked in higher-wage jobs such as construction, quarrying, leather work, and so on) resulted in differences in severity of poverty across households. Religion, too, played a role; unmarried Muslim women and young girls in purdah tended to be clustered in home-based work such as bidi-rolling and mat-making, and the very poor tended to borrow to cover costs during festival and rainy months.

In the decades since independence, the diversity of the poor had clearly increased and was impacted by improvements in agricultural technology and mechanization, the availability of agricultural and non-farm employment opportunities across seasons, by gender, by caste, by nutritional and health status, and by inequities of wages across sectors and between men and women. Widespread corruption in line departments and PR institutions that provide jobs, and important services such as water supply, subsidies for housing or old age pensions, and the unwillingness of banks to extend loans to poor people who lacked collateral such as land or jewelry further exacerbated the situation.

SHARE was set up in this area in 1992, when most of these problems were already evident. The basis of its "intervention strategy" that aimed to facilitate poverty alleviation through economic development was to set up craft centers and income generation opportunities for poor women. The palm-leaf, sisal-fiber, and *korai* mats were marketed by the NGO in both international and national markets. Most of the women that SHARE worked with belonged to dalit or Muslim communities. SHARE also provided inputs, training, as well as education and support services such as childcare, safe drinking water, and evening study centers for members and their children. Craft incomes, though low and unstable, did play a role in making the lives of some poor women more secure. However, it soon became apparent that there were problems with the income generation approach: training was costly, craft was a low-status occupation, and older women preferred to continue to work as agricultural labor. This was also a time when donors were encouraging NGOs to move toward setting up self-help women's groups (SHGs) and sustainable microfinancing strategies with the aim of enhancing impact, building capacity and skills to enable entrepreneurial poor women to break through persistent poverty cycles. With donor funding SHARE started SHGs where members learned of their rights and entitlements, contributed savings, and finally contested *Grama Panchayat* elections. In 1995, thirteen women stood for elections, and five won. The SHGs however, were unable to reach the poorest and most vulnerable women.

Was SHARE successful in poverty alleviation? In organizational maps drawn by villagers, the NGO is rated lower than the public distribution system (PDS), schools, and water supply as being important to people's living conditions but higher than banks or cooperatives. Its members are more inclined to rank it higher. Conspicuously absent from any understanding of poverty was the possibility of elected representatives and state agents making any substantive impact by improving conditions for small and marginal farmers by improving the water table, de-silting tanks, setting equitable wage standards, or undertaking employment-oriented public works. Poor villagers, regardless of whether they were SHARE members or not, did not challenge the state at the local level, and neither did the NGO engage in any policy level work through a larger NGO network. The result as analyzed by Rajasekhar is a limited set of impacts. He writes:

> The constraints are deficiencies in its technical and political capacity. The obstacles are wider socio-economic and political processes and a lack of pro-poor attitudes in other local organizations. Given that NGOs alone cannot reduce poverty and that local organizations are not pro-poor in their nature, poverty reduction remains an outstanding problem.[64]

SHARE thus presents the case of an NGO that started to work with poor women through income–generating activities, and continued to use prescribed poverty alleviation strategies such as microfinancing and awareness raising, in the context of a state that did not have strong pro-poor, progressive legislation. In contrast, Mahila Samakhya (MS) Karnataka, started in 1987, was an innovative government-initiated NGO experiment that had nonformal education and awareness building as its basic mandate.[65] Did this difference in mandate and organizational practices impact MS's ability to be effective?

The main objective of MS "is to reverse the processes responsible for the subordination of women by empowering them with self-esteem and the knowledge with which to determine their own destinies."[66] This rhetoric is backed by an organizational structure of trained women activists, the *Sahayoginis,* who work in ten villages to initiate and support *Mahila Sanghas* in each village, and help train members to become *Sahayakis* (leaders). A

District Implementation Unit with resource people, and administrative support forms a core support team. MS works mostly with dalit and tribal women, who are among the poorest people in Karnataka. The diversification of poverty due to the agricultural and other capital-intensive development policies followed by the state, noted in detail in the area where SHARE works, is also evident in the regions where MS works. Karnataka had, however, in contrast to Tamil Nadu, committed itself to implementing PR early on and pioneered gender quotas. It has held three PR elections in 1987, 1993, and 2000, and the numbers of elected women's representatives (EWRs) is currently higher than what quotas guarantee. MS strategies for *sangha* formation and growth are deliberate and closely monitored. Though the *sanghas* initially focused on carving out time and space for poor women to reflect on their lives, over time they became a forum for women's issues through which women act to obtain rights—social, political, and economic—promised by the state, open up new avenues for access to the state, and use state guaranteed rights to contest power relations in political space through PR institutions.

MS now focuses its attention on the intersection of the *sanghas* with PR institutions. It trains *sangha* members to contest elections, supports EWRs to be effective, and works on establishing a wider political role for the *sanghas*. Every *sangha* has a *Panchayat* committee consisting of women who have contested (and lost) elections or who have interacted with the *Panchayats* in some way. This committee works on voter lists, canvassing, and most importantly on monitoring *grama sabha* activities and supporting their elected women representatives. A recent evaluation of the effectiveness of 194 *sangha* members who are EWRs shows that only 7 percent of *sangha* women fell into the category of a "surrogate member" who was represented by her husband or a male relative, a problem that is pervasive, particularly with upper-caste EWRs. In districts where poverty is more widely prevalent and caste divisions deep, *sangha* women tend to be less articulate and effective and less able to challenge corruption or existing social norms. About 80 percent of EWRs have, however, helped their *sanghas* get house sites, documents, assistance for building the *sangha* mane (main house), and assistance for *sangha* members from state programs and various poverty alleviation schemes. MS also noted that 87 EWRs, 44.8 percent, were exceptionally articulate, aware, and willing to challenge corruption by male *Panchayat* members and other state agents. *Sangha* membership and three PR elections are slowly beginning to have an impact.

There are however, some important challenges that highlight the difficulty of implementing poverty alleviation strategies. Keeping committed, trained workers is a problem. More importantly, MS has found that *sanghas*, which are encouraged to create and follow their own programs, tend to become exclusionary and not allow other poor women to join, particularly if the *sangha* is engaged in economic development activity like microfinancing or has acquired some resources. The entrenched nature of anti-poor alliances across state and civil society is also difficult to combat, though one tactic that MS has started to use is to form *taluk* level federations to take up issues with elected representatives at the district and state levels. Despite these challenges, Narayanan writes, "sangha EWRs are reversing, in small but important ways, the corrupt and inefficient working of the schemes meant for the poor."[67] The work of MS-Karnataka thus highlights the importance of empowerment strategies aimed to allow women better access the state, and through that to engage in redistributive politics at the local level.

A primary challenge to MS comes from the structural condition of entrenched anti-poor alliances, which cross the lines between state and civil society actors to form barriers that are difficult to break. The third case, the Nari Bikash Samiti (NBS) in Bankura, West Bengal, which is an apex body for a group of twenty-two silkworm cooperatives focuses on the issue of how a pro-poor state can break these alliances, allowing the organization to be more effective. The NBS was initiated and continues to be supported by an NGO, the Centre for Women in Development Studies (CWDS) that is based in New Delhi. The area where NBS started is in the dry and hilly "jungles." Almost two-thirds of the population are poor *adivasi,* who have traditionally served as the labor reserve for the development of coal mines in the nineteenth century, and later, as the forest deteriorated, for the Green Revolution–inspired paddy fields. Seasonal migrations are the survival strategy that *Adivasi* households have adopted in the face of extreme deprivation. The forests, however, remain their home and their point of reference.[68]

In 1977, a little before NBS was established, the Left Front came to power with the support of the rural poor in West Bengal. The early period of their rule was marked by a sharply conflictual, often violent agrarian politics along with broad-based state initiatives such as registering sharecroppers, implementing land reform and minimum wage levels, and securing access to credit, in an effort to radically transform local agrarian relations. In 1978, the Left Front reinstituted Panchayati Raj to implement their agrarian redistributionist policies, and this proved crucial in changing political space at the local level. By 1985, PR institutions had been brought into development planning and the CPI(M), the dominant member of the Left Front, was encouraging party members to monitor and direct *Panchayats* in order to have a less corrupt, transparent, accountable local government. Four PR elections have followed since then, and the tradition of accountable local government that is pro-poor is well established.

It is in this context that the success of NBS needs to be understood. Its genesis was in the cooperative movement in the area, which began in the early 1980s to help *adivasi* women avoid seasonal migration to work in the paddy fields of Hindu farmers in the *namal,* the fertile plains further east. The cooperatives were a limited success in economic terms, typically earning their members a reduction in the number of seasonal migrations from four to two, and also reducing the number of family members that needed to leave. More important was

> the belief, openly articulated, that it has been an achievement by them [the women] against others—men in the household, men in the village, forestry officials, government officers, party representatives, Hindu farmers in the *namal* upon whom they are no longer so dependent for work, and so on.[69]

By 1997, the NBS working with CWDS had expanded its role and secured benefits from *Panchayats* through various state programs for childcare, health, and literacy. They had also actively engaged in sharing their stories, discussing and learning through NGO networks, traveling both nationally and internationally to do so. Finally, they had, through their engagement in Forest Protection Committees (FPCs), taken the political skills they had learned through NBS into another arena, which offered further possibilities of securing their forest-based livelihoods.

In 1988, a new National Forest Policy was announced that sought the collaboration of local communities to jointly manage forests with the state. Two years later the Forestry Department (which is located under the Centre with a few responsibilities to the state government) was asked to set up "Joint Forest Management Committees" consisting of representatives from local government and communities. The sixty-eight FPCs set up in Bankura District were to both protect and rehabilitate degraded forest lands. The *Adivasi* women from NBS were active in the FPCs in their areas and insisted that a third of all members of the executive committee be women, based on the fact that women were the primary collectors of forest produce and were therefore central to sustainable use and protection of forests. The policy spread to all FPCs in Bankura district. Over time the formal recognition of the role of communities in forest management has reduced the tensions and antagonism between the villagers and the Forest Department. By 1997, CWDS had helped NBS organize the 68 FPCs into another apex body, which could enter into negotiations and make claims on behalf on the villagers to the Forest Department and other local agencies. As Neil Webster wrote, "[T]he result has been that the women of the cooperatives have begun to assert a presence beyond the local that in turn has impacted the local."[70]

The three cases together tell a story of when NGOs can be effective. SHARE's inability to read and respond to the context and determinants of poverty through its organizational practices and strategies led to a limited impact on poverty alleviation. MS was able to step up its impact despite local conditions that were decidedly anti-poor due to its clear mandates and strong organizational practices. It did so in a state environment that was both market- and decentralization-friendly, with the state offering an important opening for MS to contest poverty through strong *sangha* structures at the local level. Finally, NBS successes can be seen in its being both a strong NGO using participatory, innovative practices in the context of a strong pro-poor state with effective institutions at the local level. The cases also suggest that NGOs, despite their limited impact, can play an intermediary role between communities and the state. The issue is not as much about whether NGOs can precipitate change or not as it is about recognizing that it is the relationship between NGOs and the state that has the possibility of stimulating reiterative processes that require both strong states and strong NGOs to enable change.

STRONG STATES, STRONG NGOS

This chapter has laid out two arguments: first, that broad patterns in the growth of the NGO sector across three phases are primarily a result of changing NGO–state relations. Second, that the impact of NGOs in the context of the uneasy partnerships of the third phase can be positive for poverty alleviation under certain conditions at the local level: strong NGO organizational practices, and a strong state with pro-poor policies, progressive legislation, and effective PR institutions. Together the two arguments lay out the complex relationship between NGOs and the state in poverty alleviation in the overwhelmingly poor, yet diverse and vibrant "noisy polity" that is India.

The first argument outlined the parameters for NGO action: changing state-society relations; the role of the state as regulator, funder, and development agent that actively supports NGOs; and the role of foreign donors. Accordingly, in the first phase, NGOs were silent partners of the state who provided a limited safety net. In the second phase they moved from actively opposing the state and initiating poverty alleviation through political or economic development strategies to engaging with the state to deliver services, enhance capacity, and through this to mobilize communities to fight for their rights. Important openings were created, however, both by the hierarchical nature of the state and by the tensions that were a result of the simultaneous movement of the state towards the market and political decentralization. In the third phase, the diversification of the NGO sector continues as macroeconomic reform, market-based development policies, state withdrawal, and religious nationalism gain ground. An uneasy partnership between NGOs and the state seems to be the norm with a number of NGOs clearly following the public service contractor model, encouraged by increased state and foreign donor funding, even as others see themselves as intermediaries with the specific aim of enhancing the bargaining power of their constituents vis-à-vis the state and other groups in society.

This chapter makes the point that NGOs—under certain conditions—can have an impact on poverty alleviation, even though it is most likely to be *limited*. It also makes the point that the reiterative nature of NGO work opens up possibilities for NGOs to be a countervailing force even if they are rarely as effective or able to achieve the reach of a strong progressive state. This raises the question of what role NGOs can have when the state is un-supportive, non-democratic, or non-functional. In this context, does the op-positional role of NGOs gain importance, particularly with support from the outside and expressed at various scales and in various ways from stimulating public discussion to supporting protest in various fora? Alternatively, in the face of nonfunctioning states, does the NGO's role as a service provider gain importance? While these questions are important and allow us to better un-derstand the role of NGOs, this chapter emphasizes the point that the ma-jority of Indian NGOs work within the parameters defined by the state and impact poverty in limited but important ways; their uneasy partnerships with a strong state, combined with their own agency, offer the possibility, given shrewd, patient action, for a renewed redistributive politics.

NOTES

1. Atal Bihari Vajpayee, speech, quoted in Planning Commission, Government of India, *Proceedings, All-India Conference on Role of the Voluntary Sector in National Development* (New Delhi: Voluntary Action Cell, Planning Commission, 2002), 35.

2. Nafisa Barot, speech, quoted in Planning Commission, *Proceedings*, 46–47. Barot works in Utthan, a Gujarat-based organization, and was the second NGO speaker in the plenary session of the conference that brought together 151 NGO lead-ers, 131 high-level officials from the Central and state government, and 51 staff, in-cluding members from the Planning Commission.

3. Planning Commission, *Proceedings*, 37.

4. Jennifer Wolch, "Decentering America's Nonprofit Sector: Reflections on Sala-mon's Crisis Analysis," in *Third Sector Policy at the Crossroads*, ed. Helmut K. An-heier and Jeremy Kendall (London and New York: Routledge, 2001), 58.

5. Rajesh Tandon estimated the financial outlay for the entire voluntary sector (NGOs are a subset) as being Rs. 160 billion for the year 1999–2000, by using Ministry of Home Affairs FCRA reports (Rs. 40 billion), PRIA surveys on philanthropic giving in India (Rs. 80 billion), and other estimates on total government funding to NGOs (Rs. 40 billion). Direct funding and support received through bilateral and multilateral donors are left out of this calculation. See Planning Commission, *Proceedings*, 40–41.

6. For data on state-funded NGOs, Planning Commission, Government of India, NGO Database. Also available at http://164.100.97.14/ngo/default.asp (accessed May 2004). For data on foreign funded NGOs, AccountAid, *Accountable Handbook, FCRA* (New Delhi: AccountAid, 2002). Also available at http://education.vsnl.com/accountaid/ (accessed May 2004). Large organizations with budgets of over Rs. 50 million account for about 3–5 percent of the total number of active NGOs. Budget size definitions are from CAF-India.

7. Sheldon Annis, "Can Small-Scale Development Be Large-Scale Policy?" in *Direct to the Poor: Grassroots Development in Latin America,* ed. Sheldon Annis and Peter Hakim (Boulder; London: Lynne Rienner Publishers, 1988), 209.

8. Rajesh Tandon, "Civil Society in India: An Exercise in Mapping. Innovations," *Civil Society* 1, no. 1 (2001): 2–9, quoted in Planning Commission, *Report of the Steering Committee on Voluntary Sector, for the Tenth Five Year Plan (2002–2007).* TYFP—Steering Committee Sr. No.7 /2001 (New Delhi: Planning Commission, Government of India, January 2002), 5.

9. The term "social movement organizations" is being used loosely here and includes a range of local organizations and people's organizations from user groups in agriculture, forestry and lift irrigation, women's groups, groups focusing on recreation, sports and other activities to larger movements based on struggles for peasant, dalit, or *adivasi* rights

10. Definitions have been a preoccupation of the NGO literature. On the process of categorization itself, see Anna Vakil, "Confronting the Classification Problem: Toward a Taxonomy of NGOs," *World Development* 25, no. 12 (1997): 2057–70.

11. Michael Norton, "The Voluntary Sector in India, Issues and Ideas for Its Future. A Report with Recommendations" (London: Centre for Innovation in Voluntary Action, 1995), 1. Estimates of numbers of NGOs are from D. Rajasekar, "Where Local Organizations Do Not Work: Problems of Poverty Reduction in Tamil Nadu, India," in *In the Name of the Poor: Contesting Political Space for Poverty Reduction,* ed. Neil Webster and Lars Engberg-Pedersen (London, New York: Zed Books, 2002), 184; and Rajesh Tandon's speech included in Planning Commission, *Proceedings,* 41.

12. NGO work is best understood as including issue-based action (where the issues may include poverty reduction, literacy, empowerment, infrastructure, health and welfare, advocacy, child labor, land rights, housing, and so on), often focused on target beneficiaries (women, children, *adivasis*, dalits, and so on). For many NGOs, their work also has clear spatial boundaries (watershed development, forest management, resettlement, particular villages and districts, and so on).

13. Among others, see Judith Tendler, "Whatever Happened to Poverty Alleviation?" A Report Prepared for the Mid-Decade Review of the Ford Foundation's Livelihood, Employment and Income Generation (LIEG) Programs (New York: Ford Foundation, 1987); Roger Riddell and Mark A. Robinson, "The Impact of NGO Poverty Alleviation Projects: Results of Case-Study Evaluations," Working Paper Series No. 68. (London: Overseas Development Institute, 1992); Roger Riddel, "Judging Success: Evaluating NGO Approaches to Alleviating Poverty in Developing Countries," Working Paper Series No. 37 (London: Overseas Development Institute, 1990); Mark A. Robinson, "Evaluating the Impact of NGOs in Rural Poverty Alleviation: India Country Study," Working Paper Series No. 49 (London: Overseas Development Institute, 1991); John Farrington and Anthony Bebbington with Kate Wellard and David J. Lewis, *Reluctant Partners? Non-Governmental Organizations, the State and Sustainable Agricultural Development* (London and New York: Routledge, 1993); S. Akbar Zaidi, "NGO Failure and the Need to Bring Back the State," *Journal of International Development* 11 (1999): 259–71; and Michael Edwards and David Hulme, eds., *Beyond the Magic Bullet: NGO Performance and Accountability in the Post–Cold War World* (West Hartford, Conn.: Kumarian Press, 1996).

14. Among others, see Neil Webster, "Local Organizations and Political Space in the Forests of West Bengal," in *In the Name of the Poor: Contesting Political Space for Poverty Reduction,* ed. Neil Webster and Lars Engberg-Pedersen; Neema Kudva, "Development and Democratization/A Contextual Critique of NGO Behavior and Practice through the Case of the Tribal Joint Action Committee in Karnataka, India," dissertation, Department of City and Regional Planning, University of California at Berkeley, 2001; Giles Mohan, "The Disappointments of Civil Society: The Politics of NGO Intervention in Northern Ghana," *Political Geography* 21, no. 1 (2002): 125–54; Kees Biekart, *The Politics of Civil Society Building: European Aid Agencies and Democratic Transitions in Central America* (Utrecht and Amsterdam: International Books and the Transnational Institute, 1999); and Sangeeta Kamat, *Development Hegemony: NGOs and the State in India* (New Delhi and New York: Oxford University Press, 2002).

15. These acts date back to legislation passed by the Colonial Government of India to regulate the explosion of associational activity in the late nineteenth century.

16. Other regulations that impact NGOs include the Industrial Disputes Act, which oversees employer-employee relations, and the Income Tax Act of 1961, which exempts voluntary organizations from payment of income tax, but is still grappling with how it can recognize the nonprofit nature of secular NGO activity.

17. A number of reports have explored problems created by government regulations, most recently see Manohar Mohanty and Anil Singh, *Voluntarism and Government: Policy, Programme and Assistance* (New Delhi: VANI, 2001).

18. Planning Commission, NGO Database.

19. The Government of India gives financial assistance, technical materials, and other assistance to its partner NGOs. The funding is extended through various ministries at the Central level in the form of grants-in-aid, subsidies, government loan/bank loan, stipends, honoraria, and cash awards. Depending on the nature of the project and type of activity, the GOI provides assistance for both recurring and non-recurring expenditures. Non-financial assistance is in the form of technical resource training, and goods and services.

20. Figures for 1993–1994 from CAPART 8th Annual Report 1993–94 and for 2002–2003 from Annual Report of the Ministry of Rural Development 2002–2003, Government of India, chapter 7, 49–55, also available at http://rural.nic.in/anual0203/anualreport.htm (accessed April 2004).

21. Prakash Karat, *Foreign Funding and the Philosophy of Voluntary Organisations: A Factor in Imperialist Strategy* (New Delhi: National Book Centre, 1988).

22. Gautam Vohra, *Altering Structures: Innovative Experiments at the Grassroots* (Bombay: Tata Institute of Social Sciences, 1990).

23. See Webster, "Local Organizations and Political Space," 233–54, and R. Sooryamoorthy and K. D. Gangrade, *NGOs in India: A Cross-Sectional Study* (Westport, Conn., and London: Greenwood Press).

24. For money being raised in the U.S., see the following report, Sabrang Communications, India and the South Asia Citizens Web, France. 2002. The Foreign Exchange of Hate: IDRF and the American Funding of Hindutva. Available at http://stopfunding hate.org/sacw/index.html (accessed March 2004). IDRF's reponse is available at http://www.idrf.org/dynamic/modules.php?name=Hncontent&pa=showpage&pid= 245 (accessed May 2004). For money being raised in the U.K., see the following report: AWAAZ–South Asia Watch Ltd. 2004. "In Bad Faith? British Charity and Hindu

Extremism." Available at http://www.awaazsaw.org/ibf/ibfsum.pdf (accessed May 2004). Sewa International's response is available at http://www.sewainternational .com/awaaz_response.htm (accessed May 2004).

25. A few voluntary organizations, registered as unions, have actively campaigned for and encouraged their members to participate in *Panchayat* elections. The extraordinary success of the Young India Project in getting 5,620 of its union members elected to 124 *mandals* across five districts in Andhra Pradesh in 1995 speaks to the influence NGOs can have at the village level (D. Rajasekhar, "Winning Panchayati Raj Elections the YIP Way," *Exchanges*, no. 10 [September 1995], Bangalore: ActionAid India).

26. Michael Edwards and David Hulme, eds., *Making a Difference: NGOs and Development in a Changing World* (London: Earthscan Publications, 1992).

27. This section draws heavily on Neema Kudva, "Uneasy Partnerships? Government–NGO Relations in India," Working Paper No. 673 (Berkeley: Institute of Urban and Regional Development, University of California, 1996).

28. For more details on the development of the voluntary sector, see Siddhartha Sen, "Defining the Nonprofit Sector: India," Working Papers of the Johns Hopkins Comparative Nonprofit Sector Project, No. 12 (Baltimore: The Johns Hopkins Institute for Policy Studies, 1993); PRIA, *Voluntary Development Organizations in India: A Study of History, Roles and Future Challenges* (New Delhi: PRIA, Society for Participatory Research in Asia, 1991); K. K. Mukherjee, *Emerging Societal Changes and Voluntary Organisations: Challenges and Responses* (Ghaziabad: Gram Niyojan Kendra, 1994); and AVARD, *Role of NGOs in Development: A Study of the Situation in India* (New Delhi: AVARD, Association of Voluntary Agencies for Rural Development, 1991).

29. For examples, see PRIA, *Voluntary Development Organisations*, 1991.

30. For more information on laity centers, the influence of Christian thinkers in educational institutions, and Christian student movements like the Student Christian Movement (SCM) and All India Catholic University Federation (AICUF), see F. Stephen, *NGOs—Hope of the Last Decade of This Century* (Bangalore: SEARCH, 1992); and Neema Kudva, *Uneasy Partnerships?*

31. A meeting of Gandhian groups with Protestant resource agencies is credited to have started this transformation.

32. See Seminar, *Voices from the Field, A Symposium on People's Experiences with the Development Process,* no. 431 (July 1995).

33. Examples include Community Health Worker Program, adult education programs, use of bio-gas, and so on.

34. This 1982 initiative is also seen as a shrewd response by Indira Gandhi to the visit of World Bank president McNamara, who had by then become a proponent of people's participation in development projects. See Karat, *Foreign Funding and the Philosophy of Voluntary Organisations.*

35. Interview, New Delhi, October 1995.

36. The Estimates Committee of Parliament later reported that for the year 1989 alone, government sources had provided about Rs. 2.5 billion in funds to the NGO sector. See Mohanty and Singh, *Voluntarism and Government*, 43–44.

37. For recent rules and eligibility criteria, see Mohanty and Singh, *Voluntarism and Government*, 50–62.

38. Farrington and Bebbington with Wellard and Lewis, *Reluctant Partners,* 94.

39. The recent debate on when exactly the Indian economy began to get "re-

formed" (Dani Rodrik and Arvind Subraminian, "From 'Hindu Growth' to Productivity Surge: The Mystery of the Indian Growth Transition," NBER Working Paper No. 10376, 2004; Arvind Panagariya, "India in the 1980s and 1990s: A Triumph of Reforms," IMF Working Paper No. WP/04/43, 2004) has some bearing on understanding increases in state funding and state support for NGOs. Clearly, the state began to open up to NGOs in the early and mid-1980s, part perhaps of the stealthier reforms under the Gandhis before the first waves of reform hit in 1991.

40. In 1985, Bunker Roy, a prominent NGO activist who had been appointed to the Planning Commission, attempted to set up a national level coordinating agency and a "Code of Conduct" that NGOs could voluntarily adopt. NGOs overwhelmingly rejected the overture, seeing it as a subtle form of repression.

41. Planning Commission. *Directory of Centrally Sponsored Schemes for Voluntary Agencies* (New Delhi: Government of India, 1993).

42. Mohanty and Singh, *Voluntarism and Government,* 44.

43. Planning Commission, *Proceedings,* 40, citing the Economic Census 1994.

44. There are no aggregate figures available to support this, since bilateral and multilateral aid giving is not under the purview of FCRA. Most people I interviewed present this perspective. This trend further strengthened the role of the state as patron.

45. *The Economist,* "No More Aid Please" (June 21–27, 2003): 35.

46. Government of India Press Release, "Finance Ministry to formulate new guidelines for bilateral aid in consultation with development partners," June 3, 2003, available at http://www.indianet.nl/pb030603.html (accessed October 2003). See also Rajya Sabha Starred Question No. 132 answered on July 29, 2003, http://164.100.24.219/rsq/quest.asp?qref=84466 (accessed October 2003).

47. For a study on the effects of bilateral aid on two large NGOs, see Alnoor Ebrahim, *NGOs and Organizational Change: Discourse, Reporting, and Learning* (Cambridge, U.K.: Cambridge University Press, 2002).

48. About one-third of all funds received were difficult to categorize under FCRA rules. For all figures, AccountAid, *FCRA,* 1–8

49. Percentages calculated on the basis of data available in the Planning Commission's NGO database.

50. For instance, NOVIB, the Dutch bilateral, shifted in 1995 to the northern belt and withdrew funding from 37 of the 45 NGOs it worked with in the early 1990s in South India. See Narasimha Reddy and D. Rajasekhar, *Development Programmes and NGOs: A Guide on Central Government Programmes for NGOs in India,* Bangalore: Bangalore Consultancy Office and NOVIB, 1996, 9.

51. For details on how NGOs are thinking about funding, see M. K. Bhat, Anita Cheria and Steve Edwin, *The Future Is Here, Sustainability of Interventions and Withdrawal: The Concept, Need and Implications* (Bangalore: Bangalore Consultancy Office and NOVIB, 1998).

52. The case of a mid-sized NGO that works with tribal communities in southern Karnataka offers a good example: the NGO has fought a long struggle to obtain land from the revenue department; it operates *balwadis,* a free lunch program, and a nonformal education program with support from two ministries at the Central and state level, even as it opposes Forest Department Policies, and, along with the people's groups that it supports, has joined the struggle for tribal self-rule that was a result, in

part, of the Bhuria Commission's findings of the applicability of the 73rd Constitutional Amendment to tribal majority areas. See Kudva, *Development and Democratization,* for more details.

53. Norton, *The Voluntary Sector in India.* The phrase comes from a staff person in a prominent Support NGO that focuses on training issues.

54. Vinod Vyasalu, "Management of Poverty Alleviation Programmes in Karnataka: An Overview," *Economic and Political Weekly* 30, nos. 41 and 42 (1995): 2635–50.

55. The two extremes within which all other districts fall are Bidar, which can be compared to Rajasthan (the northern districts resemble the Hindi heartland), and Dakshina Kannada, which is close to the same developmental level as Kerala.

56. For the NGO sector in Karnataka, see George Joseph, "Social Action Groups and Their Activists," dissertation, School of Social Work, Roshni Nilaya, Mangalore, Karnataka, India (1995), and Kudva, *Uneasy Partnerships.* For the NGO sector in Tamil Nadu, see PRIA and Anjaneya Associates in collaboration with the Center for Civil Society Studies, Johns Hopkins University, "Exploring the Non Profit Sector in India: Some Glimpses from Tamil Nadu," Working Paper No. 4 (New Delhi: PRIA, Society for Participatory Research in Asia, October 2002).

57. PRIA and Society for Socio-Economic Studies and Services in collaboration with the Center for Civil Society Studies, Johns Hopkins University, "Exploring the Non Profit Sector in India, Some Glimpses from West Bengal," Working Paper Number 6 (New Delhi: PRIA, Society for Participatory Research in Asia, December 2002).

58. V. M. Rao, *The Poor in a Hostile Society, Glimpses of Changing Poverty Scenario in India* (New Delhi: Vikas Publishing House Pvt. Ltd., 1998), 21.

59. Particularly in terms of dominating Panchayati Raj Institutions (up to 70 percent of all seats belong to lower-income groups) through which half the state's budget is directed.

60. Rao, *The Poor in a Hostile Society,* 26, quoting S. Iyengar and Praveen Visaria, Voluntary Agencies, the Banks and the Rural Poor: Six Case Studies.

61. Ranjani Murthy and Nitya Rao, *Addressing Poverty, Indian NGOs and Capacity Enhancement in the 1990s* (New Delhi: Friedrich Ebert Stiftung, 1997), 4–9.

62. For a study questioning assumptions of women's empowerment through microfinancing, see Naila Kabeer, "Conflicts over Credit: Re-Evaluating the Empowerment Potential of Loans to Women in Rural Bangladesh," *World Development* 29, no. 1 (2001): 63–84; on how credit is utilized, and on the difficulty of working with the very poor, see Paul Mosely and David Hulme, "Microenterprise Finance: Is There a Conflict between Growth and Poverty Alleviation?" *World Development* 26, no. 5 (1998): 783–90; and Shantana Halder and Paul Mosely, "Working with the Ultra-Poor: Learning from BRAC Experiences," *Journal of International Development* 16 (2004): 387–406.

63. Various researchers, including John Harris, Barbara Harris-White, and S. Janakarajan surveyed the area in 1973–1974, the mid-1980s, the mid-1990s, and the late 1990s. The case description draws on D. Rajasekhar, "Where Local Organizations Do Not Work," 183–207.

64. Rajasekhar, "Where Local Organizations Do Not Work," 205.

65. This case draws on Srilatha Batliwala, "Transforming of Political Culture: The Mahila Samakhya Experience," *Economic and Political Weekly* 31, no. 21 (1996):

1248–51; Revathi Narayanan, "Grassroots, Gender and Governance: Panchayati Raj Experiences from Mahila Samakhya Karnataka," in *The Violence of Development: The Politics of Identity, Gender and Social Inequalities in India,* ed. Karin Kapadia (New Delhi: Kali for Women, 2002), 295–351; and Kudva, *Uneasy Partnerships.* MS is a registered society, currently running in eight states across India. It is funded and run by the Department of Education, Ministry of Human Resources Development. MS-Karnataka works in six districts, five of which are in the poorer northern belt.

66. Narayanan, "Grassroots, Gender and Governance," 299.

67. Narayanan, "Grassroots, Gender and Governance," 341.

68. This case draws on Webster, "Local Organizations and Political Space in the Forests of West Bengal," 233–54; and Neil Webster, "Tribal Women's Co-operatives in Bankura, West Bengal," *European Journal of Development Studies* 6, no. 2 (1994): 95–103.

69. Webster, "Local Organizations and Political Space," 247.

70. Webster, "Local Organizations and Political Space," 246.

Archival Abbreviations

DSR	Department of State Records, U.S. National Archives
JNSW	Jawaharlal Nehru Selected Works
NAI	National Archives of India
NMML	Nehru Memorial Museum and Library
QIMSD	Quit India Movement—British Secret Documents
PT	Purshottamdas Thakurdas Papers

Bibliography

AccountAid. *Accountable Handbook, FCRA.* New Delhi: AccountAid, 2002. http://education.vsnl.com/accountaid/ (May 2004).

Agarwal, Anil. "Human–Nature Interactions in a Third World Country." *The Environmentalist* 6, no. 3 (1987): 167.

Agarwal, Bina. "The Gender and Environment Debate: Lessons from India." *Feminist Studies* 18, no. 1 (1992): 119–58.

——. "Women, Poverty and Agricultural Growth in India." *Journal of Peasant Studies* 13, no. 4 (1986): 165–220.

Agnihotri, Indu, and Vina Mazumdar. "Changing Terms of Political Discourse: Women's Movement in India." *Economic and Political Weekly* 30, no. 29 (1995): 1869–1878.

Agrawal, Arun. *Community in Conservation: Beyond Enchantment and Disenchantment.* CDF Discussion Paper. Florida: Conservation and Development Forum (1997).

Ahluwalia, Montek S. "Economic Performance of States in Post-Reforms Period." *Economic and Political Weekly,* May 6, 2000, 1637–48.

Akerlof, George. "The Theory of Social Customs of which Unemployment May Be One Consequence." *Quarterly Journal of Economics* 94, no. 4 (June 1980).

——. "The Economics of Caste and of Rat Race and Other Woeful Tales." *Quarterly Journal of Economics* 90, no. 4 (November 1976).

Alvares, Claude. "The Peasants Rehearse the Uprising." *Illustrated Weekly* (February 24, 1985).

Ambedkar, B. R. "Untouchables, or the Children of India's Ghetto." In *Writings and Speeches,* vol. 5, compiled by Vasant Moon, 115–16. Bombay: Government of Maharashtra, 1989.

Anandhi, S. "Interlocking Patriarchies and Women in Governance: A Case Study of Panchayati Raj Institutions in Tamil Nadu." In *The Violence of Development: The Politics of Identity, Gender and Social Inequalities in India,* edited by Karin Kapadia, 425–58. New Delhi: Kali for Women, 2002.

————. *Land to the Dalits: Panchama Land Struggle in Tamil Nadu.* Bangalore: Indian Social Institute, 2000.

Anderson, Walter K., and Shridar D. Damle. *The Brotherhood in Saffron: The Rashtriya Swayamsevak Sangh and Hindu Revivalism.* Boulder, Colo.: Westview Press, 1987.

"Angry Farmer." *India Today,* January 16–31, 1981.

Annis, Sheldon. "Can Small-Scale Development Be Large-Scale Policy?" In *Direct to the Poor: Grassroots Development in Latin America,* edited by Sheldon Annis and Peter Hakim, 209–18. Boulder; London: Lynne Rienner Publishers, 1988.

Anveshi. "Reworking Gender Relations, Redefining Politics: Nellore Village Women against Arrack." *Economic and Political Weekly* 28, nos. 3–4 (January 16–23, 1993): 87–90.

Appadurai, Arjun. *Modernity at Large: Cultural Dimensions of Globalization.* Minneapolis: University of Minnesota Press, 1996.

Assadi, Muzaffar. "'Khadi Curtain,' 'Weak Capitalism' and 'Operation Ryot': Some Ambiguities in Farmers' Discourse, Karnataka and Maharashtra 1980–95." In *New Farmers' Movements in India,* edited by Tom Brass. London: Frank Cass, 1995.

————. *Peasant Movement in Karnataka, 1980–94.* Delhi: Shipra, 1997.

AVARD. *Role of NGOs in Development: A Study of the Situation in India.* New Delhi: AVARD, Association of Voluntary Agencies for Rural Development, 1991 (mimeo).

Avery, Dennis T. "Biotech Foods . . . Safe, Tested and Ready for the World," *Global Food Quarterly.* Churchville, Va.: Hudson Institute, Center for Global Food Issues, 1999.

Aziz, Abdul. *Decentralized Planning: The Karnataka Experiment.* New Delhi: Sage Publications, 1993.

Baiocchi, Gianpaolo. "Participation, Activism, and Politics: The Porto Alegre Experiment." In *Deepening Democracy: Institutional Innovations in Empowered Participatory Governance,* edited by A. Fung and E. O. Wright. London: Verso, 2003.

Banerjee, Nirmala. "How Real is the Bogey of Feminization?" *The Indian Journal of Labour Economics* 40, no. 3 (1997): 427–38.

————. "Whatever Happened to the Dreams of Modernity? The Nehruvian Era and Women's Position." *Economic and Political Weekly* 28, no. 17, May 1, 1998, WS-2–7.

Banerjee, Sumanta. *India's Simmering Revolution: The Naxalite Uprising.* London: Zed Press, 1984.

————. *In the Wake of Naxalbari: A History of the Naxalite Movement in India.* Calcutta: Subarnarekha Publications, 1980.

Banik, Nilanjan, and Saurabh Bandopadhyay. "Cotton Textile Industry in India in the Wake of MFA Phase-Out." New Delhi: Rajiv Gandhi Institute for Contemporary Studies, Working Paper No. 9, 2000.

Bardhan, Pranab. "Decentralization of Governance and Development." *Journal of Economic Perspectives* (2002).

————. *The Political Economy of Development in India.* New York: Basil Blackwell, Inc., 1984.

————. "Sharing the Spoils: Group Equity, Development, and Democracy." In *The Success of India's Democracy,* edited by Atul Kohli, 226–41. Cambridge: Cambridge University Press, 2001.

————. "Sharing the Spoils: Group Equity, Development, and Democracy." Unpublished paper, University of California, Berkeley, 1997.

Barot, Nafisa. Speech, quoted in Planning Commission, *Proceedings, All-India Conference on Role of the Voluntary Sector in National Development*. New Delhi: Voluntary Action Cell, Planning Commission, 2002. http://planningcommission.nic.in/data/ngo/vac_prced.pdf (January 2004), 46–47.

Basu, Amrita. *Two Faces of Protest: Contrasting Modes of Women's Activism in India*. Berkeley: University of California Press and Delhi: Oxford University Press, 1992.

Basu, Aparna, and Bharati Ray. *Women's Struggle: A History of the All India Women's Conference, 1927–1990*. New Delhi: Manohar, 1990.

Basu, Kaushik. "Has Poverty in India Declined?" *Business Standard* (January 23, 2003).

Basu, Tapan, Pradip Datta, Sumit Sarkar, Tanika Sarkar, and Sambuddha Sen. *Khaki Shorts and Saffron Flags: A Critique of the Hindu Right*. Delhi: Tracts for the Times, Orient Longman, 1993.

Batliwala, Srilatha. "Transforming of Political Culture: The Mahila Samakhya Experience." *Economic and Political Weekly* 31, no. 21 (1996): 1248–51.

Batliwala, Srilatha, B. K. Anita, Anita Gurumurthy, and S. Chandana Wali. *Status of Rural Women in Karnataka*. Bangalore: National Institute of Advanced Studies, 1998.

Bautista, Romeo M., and Alberto Valdes. *The Bias Against Agriculture: Trade and Macroeconomic Policies in Developing Countries*. San Francisco: International Center for Economic Growth and International Food Policy Research Institute, 1993.

Baviskar, Amita. "Between Violence and Desire: Space, Power and Identity in the Making of Metropolitan Delhi." *International Social Science Journal* 175 (2003): 89–98.

———. "The Fate of the Forest: Conservation and Tribal Rights." *Economic and Political Weekly* 29, no. 38 (1994): 2493–2501.

———. *In the Belly of the River: Tribal Conflicts over Development in the Narmada Valley*. Delhi: Oxford University Press, 1995.

———. "The Politics of the City." *Seminar* 516 (2002): 40–42.

———. "Tribal Politics and Discourses of Environmentalism." *Contributions to Indian Sociology* 31, no. 2 (1997): 195–223.

———. "Vanishing Forests, Sacred Trees: A Hindu Perspective on Eco-consciousness." *Asian Geographer* 18, nos.1–2 (1999): 21–31.

———. "Who Speaks for the Victims?" *Seminar* 451 (1997): 59–61.

———. "Written on the Body, Written on the Land: Violence and Environmental Struggles in Central India." In *Violent Environments*, edited by Nancy Peluso and Michael Watts. Ithaca, N.Y.: Cornell University Press, 2001.

Baviskar, B. S. "Dairy Cooperatives and Rural Development in Gujarat." in *Who Shares? Cooperatives and Rural Development*, edited by D. W. Attwood and B. S. Baviskar. Delhi: Oxford University Press, 1998.

Bhagat, Rashida. "The Spectre of Starvation." *Frontline*, October 13–26, 2001.

Bhalla, Surjit. "Recounting the Poor: Poverty in India, 1983–99." *Economic and Political Weekly*, January 25, 2003.

Bharathan, Geeta. "Bt-Cotton in India: Anatomy of a Controversy." *Current Science* 79, no. 8 (October 25, 2000): 1067–75.

Bhat, M. K., Anita Cheria, and Steve Edwin, *The Future Is Here, Sustainability of Interventions and Withdrawal: The Concept, Need and Implications*. Bangalore: Bangalore Consultancy Office and NOVIB, 1998.

Bhatt, Chetan. *Hindu Nationalism: Origins, Ideologies and Modern Myths.* Oxford and New York: Berg, 2001.

Bhatt, Ela. "Doosri Azadi: SEWA's Perspectives on the early years of Independence." *Economic and Political Weekly,* April 15–May 1, 1998, WS 25–27.

Bhishikar, C. P. *Keshub Sanohnirmata.* Pune, 1979. Hindi translation, Delhi, 1980.

———. *Pandit Deen Dayal Upadhyaya: Ideology and Perception,* Part V. Delhi: Suruchi Prakashan, 1991.

Bidwai, Praful. "Class Conflict May Sharpen" and "Era of Defiance Ushered In." *Times of India* 19 (January 11, 1982).

Biekart, Kees. *The Politics of Civil Society Building: European Aid Agencies and Democratic Transitions in Central America.* Utrecht and Amsterdam: International Books and the Transnational Institute, 1999.

Birasal, N. R. "Haveri Farmers Will Resist KRRS Destruction Trial." *Times of India,* December 5, 1998.

Bourdieu, Pierre. *Distinction: A Social Critique of the Judgement of Taste.* Translated by Richard Nice. London: Routledge, 1986.

Bowles, Samuel, and Herbert Gintis. *Democracy and Capitalism: Property, Community and the Contradictions of Modern Social Thought.* London: Routledge and Kegan Paul, 1986.

Brass, Tom. "Moral Economists, Subalterns, New Social Movements, and the (Re-)Emergence of a (Post-)Modernised (Middle) Peasant." *Journal of Peasant Studies* 18, no. 2 (1991): 173–205.

———. "The Politics of Gender, Nature and Nation in the Discourse of the New Farmers' Movements" and "Introduction." In *New Farmers' Movements in India,* edited by Tom Brass. London: Frank Cass, 1995.

Breman, Jan. *Wage Hunters and Gatherers: Search for Work in the Urban and Rural Economy of South Gujarat.* Delhi: Oxford University Press, 1994.

Brosius, J. Peter. "Analyses and Interventions: Anthropological Engagements with Environmentalism." *Current Anthropology* 40, no. 3 (1999): 277–88.

Brown, David L., and Rajesh Tandon. *Strengthening the Grass-Roots: Nature and Role of Support Organisations.* New Delhi: Society for Participatory Research in Asia, PRIA, 1990.

Buch, Nirmala "Women's Experience in New Panchayats: The Emerging Leadership of Rural Women." Centre for Women's Development Studies, New Delhi, Occasional Paper No. 35, 2000.

Bunsha, Dionne. "A Can of Bollworms." *Frontline* 18, Issue 24 (November 24–December 7, 2001).

Byres, Terence J. "Introduction." In *The State, Development Planning and Liberalization in India,* edited by Terence J. Byres. New Delhi: Oxford University Press, 1998.

Carr, Marilyn, Martha Chen, and Renana Jhabvala, eds. *Speaking Out: Women's Economic Empowerment in South Asia.* New Delhi: Vistaar, 1997.

Carroll, Thomas F. *Intermediary NGOs: The Supporting Link in Grassroots Development.* West Hartford: Kumarian Press, 1992.

Castells, Manuel. *The Power of Identity.* Oxford: Blackwell Publishers, 1997.

Centre for Environmental Studies Warangal. *Citizens' Report: Gathering Agrarian Crisis—Farmers' Suicides in Warangal District (A.P.) India.* Kishanpura, 1998.

Chakrabarty, Dipesh. *Rethinking Working-Class History: Bengal 1890–1940*. Delhi: Oxford University Press, 1989.

Chakravarty, Sukhamoy. *Development Planning: The Indian Experience*. New Delhi: Oxford University Press, 1987.

"Challenge of the Times." In *Bunch of Thoughts*, 3rd ed., edited by M. S. Golwalkar, 24–26. Bangalore: Jagarana Prakashna, 1960.

Chandra, Kanchan. "The Ethnification of the Party System in Uttar Pradesh and Its Consequences." In *Indian Politics and the 1998 Election*, edited by Ramashray Roy and Paul Wallace, 55–104. New Delhi: Sage Publications, 1999.

———. "The Transformation of Ethnic Politics in India: The Decline of Congress and the Rise of the Bahujan Samaj Party in Hoshiarpur." *Journal of Asian Studies* 59, no. 1 (2000): 26–61.

Chang, Ha-Joon. *Kicking Away the Ladder: Development Strategy in Historical Perspective*. London: Anthem Press, 2002.

Charles, Dan. *Lords of the Harvest: Biotech, Big Money, and the Future of Food*. Cambridge, Mass.: Perseus Publishing, 2001.

Chatterjee, Partha. "The Nationalist Resolution of the Women's Question." In *Recasting Women: Essays in Colonial Colonial History*, edited by Kumkum Sanghari and Sudesh Vaid. New Delhi: Kali for Women, 1989.

Chattopadhyay, Raghabendra. "The Idea of Planning in India, 1930–1950." Ph.D. Dissertation, Australian National University, 1985.

Chaudhuri, Indrani. "Women and Environment in the Development Process: A Case Study of the Chipko Movement in Uttarakhand." M.Phil. Sociology dissertation, University of Delhi, 1996.

Chaudhuri, Shubham, K. N. Harilal, and Patrick Heller. "Does Decentralization Make a Difference? The People Campaign for Decentralized Planning in the India State of Kerala." New Delhi, Report submitted to the Ford Foundation, 2004.

Chaudhuri, Shubham, and Patrick Heller. "The Plasticity of Participation." Working paper, Columbia University, 2002.

Chaun, Surajmal. *Gehu Ki Roti*.

Chibber, Vivek. *Locked in Place: State-Building and Late Industrialization in India, 1940–1970*. Princeton, N.J.: Princeton University Press, 2003.

Chopra, P. N., ed. *Quit India Movement: British Secret Documents, Vol. II*. Delhi: Interprint Publishers, 1990.

Chowdry, Kamla. "The Frontyards and Backyards of Development: Dissent and the Voluntary Sector." in *A Common Cause: NGOs & Civil Society*, edited by Anuradha Maharishi and Rasna Dhillon. New Delhi: National Foundation for India, 2002.

Clark, John. *Democratizing Development: The Role of Voluntary Organizations*. West Hartford, Conn.: Kumarian Press, 1991.

Cleaver, Harry. "Food, Famine and the International Crisis." *Zerowork* 2 (1977).

"CMP Rejects 'Hire and Fire' Labour Policy." *Deccan Herald*, May 28, 2004.

Cohn, Bernard S. *Colonialism and Its Forms of Knowledge: The British in India*. Princeton, N.J.: Princeton University Press, 1996.

Confederation of Indian Industry. *Biotechnology on the Fast Track*. Unpublished conference proceedings, New Delhi, 2001.

Conway, Gordon. *The Doubly Green Revolution: Food for All in the 21st Century*. New York: Penguin Books, 1997.

Crouch, Harold. *The Indian Trade Union Movement.* Bombay: Asia Publishing House, 1966.

CSE (Centre for Science and Environment). *State of India's Environment: The Citizens' Fifth Report.* New Delhi: CSE, 1999.

——. *The State of India's Environment: A Citizens' Report.* New Delhi: CSE, 1982.

Curran, J. A. *Militant Hinduism in Indian Politics: A Study of the RSS.* New York: Institute of Pacific Relations, 1951.

Custers, Peter. *Women in the Tebhaga Uprising. Rural Poor Women and Revolutionary Leadership (1946–47).* Calcutta: Naya Prokash XII, 235 S., 1987.

Dahrendorf, Ralf. "Liberalism." In *The New Palgrave: The Invisible Hand,* edited by John Eatwell, Murray Milgate, and Peter Newman. New York: W.W. Norton, 1987.

Dangle, Arjun. ed. *Poison Bread.* New Delhi: Orient Longman, 1983.

Das, Maitreyi. *The Women's Development Programme in Rajasthan: A Case Study in Group Formation for Women's Development.* Washington, D.C: World Bank, 1991.

Das, Veena. "The Anthropological Discourse on India: Reason and Its Other." In *Critical Events: An Anthropological Perspective on Contemporary India,* edited by Veena Das. Delhi: Oxford University Press, 1995.

Das Gupta, Jyotirindra. *Language Conflict and National Development; Group Politics and National Language Policy in India.* Berkeley: University of California Press, 1970.

Das Gupta, Monica, and P. N. Mari Bhatt. "Intensified Gender Bias in India: A Consequence of Fertility Decline." In *Gender, Population and Development,* edited by Maithreyi Krishnaraj, Ratna M. Sudarshan, and Abusaleh Shariff, 73–93. Delhi: Oxford University Press, 1998.

Das Gupta, Monica, Lincoln Chen, and J. N. Krishnan. *Women's Health in India: Risks and Vulnerabilities.* Delhi: Oxford University Press, 1995.

Datt, Gaurav, Valerie Kozel, and Martin Ravallion. "A Model-Based Assessment of India's Progress in Reducing Poverty in the 1990s." *Economic and Political Weekly,* January 25, 2003.

Datt, Gaurav, and Martin Ravallion. "Why Have Some Indian States Done Better Than Others at Reducing Poverty?" Policy Research Working Paper No. 1594, World Bank, Washington, D.C., 1996.

Datta, Bisakha, ed. *And Who Will Make the Chapatis? A Study of All Women Panchayats in Maharashtra.* Calcutta: Stree, 1998.

Datta, Pradip K. *Carving Blocs: Communal Ideology in Early Twentieth Century Bengal.* Delhi: Oxford University Press, 1999.

Dawkins, Kristin. *Gene Wars: The Politics Of Biotechnology.* New York: Seven Stories Press (Open Media Pamphlet Series), 1997.

Debroy, Bibek, Laveesh Bhandari, and Nilanjan Banik. "How Are the States Doing." Rajiv Gandhi Institute for Contemporary Studies and Confederation of Indian Industry, 2000.

Deccan Herald. "Operation Cremate Monsanto: Raitha Sangha to Burn Bollgard Cotton in Bellary." Bangalore, December 2, 1998.

Department of Agriculture and Cooperation, Ministry of Agriculture, Government of India. *Report of the Study Group on Distress Caused by Indebtedness of Farmers in Andhra Pradesh.* New Delhi, September 1998.

Department of Biotechnology, Ministry of Science and Technology, Government of India. *Annual Report,* 2002.

——. *Biotech News* 2, Issue 2 (November 2001).

———. *Biotechnology: A Vision.* New Delhi, 2001.

———. *Revised Guidelines for Research in Transgenic Plants and Guidelines for Toxicity and Allergenicity Evaluation of Transgenic Seeds, Plants and Plant Parts.* New Delhi, August l996.

Desai, Darshan, and Sonu Jain. "Government Gets Cotton Farmers to Pay for Its Incompetence." *Indian Express,* October 21, 2001.

Desai, Neera. "From Articulation to Accommodation: Women's Movement in India." In *Visibility and Power: Essays on Women in Society and Development,* edited by Leela Dube, Eleanor Leacock, and Shirley Ardener, 287–99. Delhi: Oxford University Press, 1986.

Deshpande, Satish. "From Development to Adjustment: Economic Ideologies, the Middle Class and 50 Years of Independence." *Review of Development and Change* II, no. 2 (July–December 1997): 294–318.

———. "Hegemonic Spatial Strategies: The Nation-Space and Hindu Communalism in Twentieth-Century India." *Public Culture* 10, no. 2 (1998): 249–83.

Dev, S. Mahendra. "Economic Liberalisation and Employment in South Asia." *Economic and Political Weekly,* January 8 and 15, 2000.

———. "Economic Reforms, Poverty, Income Distribution and Employment." *Economic and Political Weekly,* March 4, 2000.

Devi, Mahasweta. "Contract Labor or Bonded Labor?" *Economic and Political Weekly* 16, no. 23 (June 6, 1981): 1010–13.

———. *Outcaste: Four Stories.* Translated by Sarmistha Datta Gupta. Calcutta: Seagull Books Pvt. Ltd., 2002.

Dirks, Nicholas B. *Castes of Mind: Colonialism and the Making of Modern India.* Princeton, N.J.: Princeton University Press, 2001.

D'Monte, Darryl. "Gandhi's Disputed Heritage." *UNESCO Courier* (2000): 1–4.

Drabek, Anne Gordon, ed. "Development Alternatives: The Challenge for NGOs." *World Development,* Special Issue, Supplement to Vol. 15 (1987).

Drèze, Jean, and Amartya Sen. *India: Economic Development and Social Opportunity.* Delhi: Oxford University Press, 1995.

———. *Hunger and Public Action.* Oxford: Clarendon Press, 1989.

Dryzek, John. *The Politics of the Earth.* New York: Oxford University Press, 1997.

Dube, Siddharth. *In the Land of Poverty: Memoirs of an Indian Family 1947–97.* New York: Zed Books Ltd., 1998.

Dutt, Gaurav. "Has Poverty Declined Since Economic Reforms: Statistical Data Analysis." *Economic and Political Weekly,* December 11, 1999.

Dutta, Pradip Kumar. *Carving Blocks: Communal Ideology in Early Twentieth Century Bengal.* Delhi: Oxford University Press, 1999.

Ebrahim, Alnoor. *NGOs and Organizational Change: Discourse, Reporting, and Learning.* Cambridge, U.K.: Cambridge University Press, 2002.

Economist, The. "No More Aid Please." London, June 21–27, 2003.

Edelman, Murray. *Politics As Symbolic Action.* Champaign/Urbana: University of Illinois Press, 1962.

Edwards, Michael, and David Hulme, eds. *Beyond the Magic Bullet: NGO Performance and Accountability in the Post–Cold War World.* West Hartford, Conn.: Kumarian Press, 1996.

———, eds. *Making a Difference: NGOs and Development in a Changing World.* London: Earthscan Publications, 1992.

Elliott, Carolyn M. "Decline of a Patrimonial Regime: the Telengana Rebellion in India, 1946–51." *Journal of Asian Studies* 34, no. 1 (1974): 27–47.

Escobar, Arturo. *Encountering Development: The Making and Unmaking of the Third World.* Princeton, N.J.: Princeton University Press, 1995.

Evans, Peter. "Looking for Agents of Urban Livability in a Globalized Political Economy." In *Livable Cities? The Politics of Urban Livelihood and Sustainability,* edited by Peter Evans. Berkeley: University of California Press, 2002.

"Farmer Suicides Lead to GM Moratorium Call." *The Times of India,* September 26, 2000.

Farrington, John, and Anthony Bebbington, with Kate Wellard and David J. Lewis. *Reluctant Partners? Non-Governmental Organizations, the State and Sustainable Agricultural Development.* London and New York: Routledge, 1993.

Farrington, John, and David J. Lewis, with S. Satish and Aurea Miclat-Teves, eds. *Non-Governmental Organizations and the State in Asia: Rethinking Roles in Sustainable Agricultural Development.* London and New York: Routledge, 1993.

FEVORD-K. *Voluntarism Vis-à-vis the State: A Collection of Articles and Statements in Response to Proposals for Establishment of National and State Councils of Rural Voluntary Agencies and a "Code of Conduct" for Non-Governmental Organizations.* Bangalore: FEVORD-K, 1985.

Forbes, Geraldine. *Women in Modern India.* Cambridge: Cambridge University Press, 1996.

Forgacs, David, ed. *An Antonio Gramsci Reader: Selected Writings, 1916–1935.* New York: Schocken Books Inc., 1988.

Fowler, Alan. "Capacity Building and NGOs: A Case of Strengthening Ladles for the Global Soup Kitchen?" *Institutional Development* 1, no. 1 (1995): 18–24.

———. *Striking a Balance.* London: Earthscan, 1998.

Frankel, Francine. *India's Political Economy, 1947–1977: The Gradual Revolution.* Princeton, N.J.: Princeton University Press, 1978.

Fung, A., and E. O. Wright. *Deepening Democracy: Institutional Innovations in Empowered Participatory Governance.* London: Verso, 2003.

Gadgil, Madhav, and Ramachandra Guha. *Ecology and Equity: The Use and Abuse of Nature in Contemporary India.* New Delhi: Penguin, 1995.

———. *This Fissured Land: An Ecological History of India.* New Delhi: Oxford, 1992.

Gandhi, M. K. *Hind Swaraj or Indian Home Rule.* Ahmedabad: Navjivan Publishing House, 1938.

Gandhi, Nandita, and Nandita Shah. *The Issues at Stake: Theory and Practice in the Contemporary Women's Movement in India.* New Delhi: Kali for Women, 1992.

Gang, Ira N., Kunal Sen, and Myeong-Su Yun. "Caste, Ethnicity, and Poverty in Rural India." Department of Economics, Rutgers University, School of Development Studies, University of East Anglia and the Department of Economics, Tulane, February 2004, http://oll.temple.edu/economics/Seminars/GangSenYun-IndiaPovertyCaste.pdf.

George, Shanti. "Cooperatives and Indian Dairy Policy: More Anand than Pattern." In *Who Shares? Cooperatives and Rural Development,* edited by D. W. Attwood and B. S. Baviskar. Delhi: Oxford University Press, 1988.

Ghosh, Jayati. "Perceptions of Difference: The Economic Underpinnings." In *The Concerned Indian's Guide to Communalism,* edited by K. N. Panikkar. Delhi: Viking, 1999.

Ghosh, Partha. *BJP and the Evolution of Hindu Nationalism: From Periphery to Centre.* New Delhi: Manohar, 1999.

Gilbert, Virginia Baldwin, and Thomas Lee. "Genetically Altered Cotton Transforms Farming in South Africa." *St. Louis Post-Dispatch,* November 26, 2001.

Goffman, Erving. *Frame Analysis.* New York: Harper Colophon, 1974.

Gold, Ann Grodzins. "Vanishing: Seeds' Cyclicality." *Journal of Material Culture* 8, no. 3 (2003): 255–72.

Golwalkar, M. S. *We or Our Nationhood Defined.* Nagpur: Bharat Publication, 1939.

Gopal, Sarvepalli, ed. *Anatomy of a Confrontation: The Babri Masjid-Ramjanambhoomi Issue.* Delhi: Penguin, 1991.

———, ed. *Selected Works of Jawaharlal Nehru,* Vol. 3. New Delhi: Orient Longmans, 1972.

Government of India. *Draft National Population Policy,* New Delhi, Ministry of Health and Family Welfare, 1994.

Government of India. *National Population Policy,* New Delhi. Ministry of Health and Family Welfare, 2000.

Government of India, Department of Social Welfare. *Towards Equality,* Report of the Committee on the Status of Women in India. December 1974.

Government of India, Ministry of Environment and Forests. *Rajya Sabha: Unstarred questions,* various volumes.

Government of Kerala (GOK). *People's Planning: Towards a Handbook.* Kerala State Planning Board, 1999.

Government of Kerola. Committee on Decentralisation of Powers: Final Report: V. 1, parts A and B. December 23, 1997.

Government of Madhya Pradesh. *The Bhopal Document: Charting a New Course for Dalits in the 21st Century* (draft by Chandra Bhan Prasad). Bhopal, 2001.

Graham, Bruce. *Hindu Nationalism and Indian Politics: The Origins and Development of the Bharatiya Jana Sangh.* Cambridge and New York: Cambridge University Press, 1993.

Greenpeace–India. "Bt Cotton Saga Takes a Ludicrous Turn." *Greenpeace Newsletter* 11. New Delhi, December 2001.

Guha, Ramachandra. *Environmentalism: A Global History.* Delhi: Oxford University Press, 2000.

———. "The Environmentalism of the Poor." In *Between Resistance and Revolution: Cultural Politics and Social Protest,* edited by Richard G. Fox and Orin Starn, 17–40. New Brunswick, N.J.: Rutgers University Press, 1997.

———. "The Malign Encounter: The Chipko Movement and Competing Visions of Nature." In *Who Will Save the Forests? Knowledge, Power and Environmental Destruction,* edited by Tariq Banuri and Fredrique Apffel Marglin. London: Zed Books, 1993.

———. *The Unquiet Woods: Ecological Change and Peasant Resistance in the Himalaya.* Delhi: Oxford University Press, 1989.

Guha, Ramachandra, and Juan Martinez-Alier. *Varieties of Environmentalism: Essays North and South.* Delhi: Oxford University Press, 1998.

Guha, Ranajit. *Elementary Aspects of Peasant Insurgency.* Delhi: Oxford University Press, l983.

Gulati, Ashok, and Seema Bathla. "Capital Formation in Indian Agriculture: Re-Visiting the Debate." *Economic and Political Weekly,* May 19, 2001.

Gulati, Ashok, Rajesh Mehta, and Sudha Narayanan. "From Marrakesh to Seattle: Indian Agriculture in a Globalising World." *Economic and Political Weekly,* October 9, 1999, 2931–42.

278   *Bibliography*

Gulati, Ashok, and C. N. Hanumantha Rao. "Indian Agriculture; Emerging Perspectives and Policy Issues." *Economic and Political Weekly*, December 31, 1994.

Gulati, Ashok, and Anil Sharma. "Agriculture under GATT: What It Holds for India." *Economic and Political Weekly*, July 16, 1994.

———. "Subsidising Agriculture: A Cross-Country View." *Economic and Political Weekly*, September 26, 1992.

Gulhati, Ravi, and Kaval Gulhati, with Ajay Mehra and Janaki Rajan. *Strengthening Voluntary Action in India: Health—Family Planning, the Environment and Women's Development*. New Delhi: Centre for Policy Research and Konark Publishers Pvt. Ltd., 1995.

Gupta, Akhil. *Postcolonial Developments: Agriculture in the Making of Modern India*. Durham, N.C.: Duke University Press, 1998.

Gupta, Anil. "Rewarding Local Communities for Conserving Biodiversity: The Case of the Honey Bee." In *Protection of Global Biodiversity: Converging Strategies,* edited by Lakshman D. Guruswamy and Jeffrey A. McNeely, 180–89. Durham, N.C.: Duke University Press, 1998.

Gupta, Dipankar. *Rivalry and Brotherhood: Politics in the Life of Farmers in Northern India*. Delhi: Oxford University Press, 1997.

Gupta, S. P. "Economic Reform and Its Impact on the Poor." *Economic and Political Weekly,* June 3, 1995.

Guru, Gopal. "Education as Baby-Sitting." *The Hindu,* May 27, 2000.

———. "The Language of Dalit-Bahujan Political Discourse." In *Dalit Identity and Politics,* edited by Ghanshyam Shah. New Delhi: Sage Publications India Pvt. Ltd., 2001.

Guruswamy, Lakshman D., and Jeffrey A. McNeely, eds. *Protection of Global Biodiversity: Converging Strategies*. Durham: Duke University Press, 1988.

Halder, Shantana, and Paul Mosely, "Working with the Ultra-Poor: Learning from BRAC Experiences," *Journal of International Development* 16 (2004): 387–406.

Hansen, Thomas Blom. *The Saffron Wave: Democracy and Hindu Nationalism in Modern India*. Princeton, N.J.: Princeton University Press, 1999.

Hansen, Thomas Blom, and Christophe Jaffrelot, eds. *The BJP and the Compulsions of Politics in India*. Delhi: Oxford University Press, 1998.

Hanumantha Rao, C. H. "Economic Reforms, Agricultural Growth and Rural Poverty: Reflections on Relevance of East and Southeast Asian Experience for India." *Mainstream,* April 13, 1996.

Hardgrave, Robert L., Jr., and Stanley A. Kochanek. *India: Government and Politics in a Developing Nation,* 5th ed. Forth Worth, Tex.: Harcourt Brace College Publishers, 1993.

Harilal, K. N., and K. J. Joseph. "Stagnation and Revival of Kerala Economy: An Open Economy Perspective." Working Paper No. 305, Centre for Development Studies, Trivandrum, 2000.

Harriss, John. "Do Political Regimes Matter: Poverty Reduction and Regime Differences Across India." In *Changing Paths,* edited by Peter Houtzager and Mick Moore. Ann Arbor: University of Michigan Press, 2003.

———. "The Limitations of HYV Technology in North Arcot District: the View from a Village." In *Green Revolution? Technology and Change in Rice Growing Areas of Tamil Nadu and Sri Lanka,* edited by B. H. Farmer. Boulder, Colo.: Westview Press, 1977.

Harriss-White, Barbara. "Gender Cleansing: The Paradox of Development and Deteriorating Female Life Chances in Tamil Nadu." In *Signposts: Gender Issues in Post-Independence India,* edited by Rajeswari Sunder Rajan, 124–53. New Delhi: Kali for Women, 1999.

Harriss-White, Barbara, and S. Janakarajan. "From Green Revolution to Rural Industrial Revolution in South India." *Economic and Political Weekly* 32, no. 25 (1997).

Hasan, Zoya. *Dominance and Mobilisation: Rural Politics in Western Uttar Pradesh, 1930–1980.* New Delhi: Sage, 1989.

———, ed. *Politics and the State in India.* New Delhi: Sage, 2000.

Hawley, John Stratton, ed. *Sati, The Blessing and the Curse: The Burning of Wives in India.* New York: Oxford University Press, 1993.

Haynes, Douglas, and Gyan Prakash. *Contesting Power: Resistance and Everyday Social Relations in South Asia.* Berkeley: University of California Press, 1992.

Hazell, Peter B. R., and C. Ramaswamy, with contributions by P. K. Aiyasamy. *The Green Revolution Reconsidered: The Impact of High Yielding Rice Varieties in South India.* Baltimore: Johns Hopkins University Press, 1991.

Healthwatch Update. Issue 11, September/December 2000.

Heller, Patrick. "Degrees of Democracy: Some Comparative Lessons from India." *World Politics* 52 (July 2000): 484–519.

———. *The Labor of Development: Workers in the Transformation of Capitalism in Kerala, India.* Ithaca, N.Y.: Cornell University Press, 1999.

———. "Moving the State: The Politics of Decentralization in Kerala, South Africa and Porto Alegre." *Politics and Society* 29, no. 1 (2001): 131–63.

Hensman, Rohini. "Globalisation, Women and Work." *Economic and Political Weekly,* March 6, 2004, 1030–34.

———. "World Trade and Workers' Rights." *Economic and Political Weekly,* April 8–14, 2000, 1247–54.

Herring, Ronald J. "Authority and Scale in Political Ecology: Some Cautions on Localism." In *Biological Diversity: Balancing Interests through Adaptive Collaborative Management,* edited by Louise Buck et al., 187–205. Boca Raton, La.: CRC Press, 2000.

———. *Land to the Tiller: The Political Economy of Agrarian Reform in South Asia.* New Haven, Conn.: Yale University Press, 1983.

———. "Political Conditions for Agrarian Reform and Poverty Alleviation." Institute for Development Studies Discussion Paper 375, University of Sussex, Brighton, U.K., June 2000.

———. "The Political Impossibility Theorem of Agrarian Reform: Path Dependence and Terms of Inclusion." In *Changing Paths: The New Politics of Inclusion,* edited by Mick Moore and Peter Houtzager. Ann Arbor: University of Michigan Press, 2003.

———. Review of Varshney. *American Political Science Review* (Fall 2000).

———. "State Property in Nature." In *Land, Property and the Environment,* edited by John F. Richards. Oakland, Calif.: Institute for Contemporary Studies, 2002.

Hilgartner, Stephen. "Acceptable Intellectual Property." *Journal of Molecular Biology* (2002): 319, 943–46.

The Hindu, March 4, 2001.

Horsch, Robert B., and Robert T. Fraley. "Biotechnology Can Help Reduce the Loss of Biodiversity." In *Protection of Global Biodiversity: Converging Strategies,* edited by Lakshman D. Guruswamy and Jeffrey A. McNeely. Durham, N.C.: Duke University Press, 1998.

Hulme, David, and Michael Edwards, eds. *NGOs, States and Donors: Too Close for Comfort?* New York: St. Martin's Press, 1997.

Human Rights Watch. "Broken People: Caste Violence against India's Untouchables." New York, March 1999.

Institute of Social Sciences. *Women and Political Empowerment: Proceedings.* New Delhi: The Institute, 1995.

Ismael, Yousouf, Richard Bennett, and Steven Morse. "Biotechnology in Africa: The Adoption and Economic Impacts of Bt Cotton in the Makhathini Flats, Republic of South Africa." Paper presented for AfricaBio Biotechnology Conference for Sub-Saharan Africa, Johannesburg, South Africa, September 26–27, 2001.

Iyengar, S., and Praveen Visaria. "Voluntary Agencies, Banks and the Rural Poor: Six Case Studies." Ahmedabad: Gujarat Institute of Area Planning, 1989 (mimeo).

Jaffrelot, Christophe. *The Hindu Nationalist Movement and Indian Politics.* New York: Columbia University Press, 1998.

———. *The Hindu Nationalist Movement and Indian Politics, 1925 to the 1990s: Strategies of Nation Building, Implementation and Mobilisation.* London: Hurst Press, 1996.

———. *India's Silent Revolution: The Rise of the Lower Castes in North India.* New York: Columbia University Press, 2003.

Jagajeevan, N., and N. Ramakanthan. "Grama Sabhas: A Democratic Structure for Development Planning." Paper presented at the International Conference on Democratic Decentralisation, Thiruvananthapuram, May 23–27, 2000.

Jain, Devaki. *Panchayat Raj: Women Changing Governance.* Gender in Development Monograph Series No. 5. New York: UNDP, 1996.

Jain, Devaki, and Nirmala Banerjee, eds. *The Tyranny of the Household: Investigative Essays into Women's Work.* New Delhi: Shakti Books, 1985.

Jain, L. C. *Grass without Roots.* New Delhi: Sage Publications, 1985.

———. *Women Entering Panchayats: A Promising Start.* Bangalore: ISST, 1992.

Jain, L. C., and Karen Coelho. *In the Wake of Freedom: India's Tryst with Co-operatives.* New Delhi: Concept, 1996.

Jain, Sonu. "Bt in Bt Cotton means Blocking the Seed, Trashing the Fact." *Indian Express,* October 27, 2001.

James, Clive. *Global Review of Transgenic Crops: 2001 Feature: Bt Cotton.* ISAAA Briefs No. 26. Ithaca, N.Y.: ISAAA, 2002.

Jayaraman, K. S. "Illegal Bt Cotton in India Haunts Regulators." *Nature Biotechnology* 19, no. 12 (December 2001): 1090.

———. "Illicit GM Cotton Sparks Corporate Fury." http://www.poptel.org.uk/panap/latest/btindia2.htm (October 13, 2001).

———. "India Produces Homegrown GM Cotton." *Nature Biotechnology* 22, no. 3 (March 2004): 255–56.

Jenkins, Rob. *Democratic Politics and Economic Reform in India.* Cambridge: Cambridge University Press, 1999.

Jha, Srinand. "Seeds of Death, GMO Cotton, India." www.tompaine.com (May 30, 2001).

Jhabvala, Renana, and R. K. A. Subrahmanya, eds. *The Unorganised Sector: Work Security and Social Protection.* New Delhi: Sage, 2000.

John, Mary E. "Gender and Development in India, 1970s–1990s: Some Reflections on the Constitutive Role of Contexts." *Economic and Political Weekly,* November 23, 1996, 3071–77.

———. "Globalisation, Sexuality and the Visual Field: Issues and Non-issues for Cultural Critique." In *A Question of Silence? The Sexual Economies of Modern India,* edited by Mary E. John and Janaki Nair, 368–96. New Delhi: Kali for Women, 1998.

John, Mary E. (with K. Lalita). *Background Report on Gender Issues in India.* Sussex: Bridge, IDS and ODA, U.K. 1995.

Johnson, D. Gale. "Agriculture in the Liberalization Process." In *Liberalization in the Process of Economic Development,* edited by Lawrence B. Kruse and Kim Kihwan, 283–391. Berkeley: University of California Press, 1991.

Joseph, George. "Social Action Groups and Their Activists." Dissertation, School of Social Work, Roshni Nilaya, Mangalore, Karnataka, India, 1995.

Joshi, Barbara, ed. *Untouchable! Voices of the Dalit Liberation Movement.* London: Zed Books, 1986.

Joshi, Sharad. "Effects of GATT on Indian Agriculture." *Agri-India,* 1997.

———. *Swatantra ka Nasle?* [What Went Wrong with Independence?]. Parbhani: Renuka Prakashan; draft translation by Gail Omvedt, 1998.

———. "Unquiet on the Western Front." *The Hindu,* Business Line, December 19, 2001.

Kabeer, Naila. "Conflicts over Credit: Re-Evaluating the Empowerment Potential of Loans to Women in Rural Bangladesh," *World Development* 29, no.1 (2001): 63–84.

Kakuta, Eri. "Hindu Nationalist Views on Rural Development: A Case Study of the Deendayal Research Institute's Chitrakoot Project." *The Journal of the Japanese Association for South Asian Studies* 15 (2003).

Kamat, Sangeeta. *Development Hegemony: NGOs and the State in India.* New Delhi and New York: Oxford University Press, 2002.

Kannan, K. P. *Of Rural Proletarian Struggles: Mobilization and Organization of Rural Workers in South-West India.* Delhi: Oxford University Press, 1988.

———. "Poverty Alleviation as Advancing Basic Human Capabilities: Kerala's Achievements Compared." Working Paper No. 294, Centre for Development Studies, Trivandrum, 1999.

Kannan, K. P., K. R. Thankappan, V. Raman Kutty, and K. P. Arvindan. *Health and Development in Rural Kerala.* Trivandrum: Kerala Sastra Sahitya Prishad, 1991.

Kapur, Devesh, and Pratap Mehta. "India in 1998: The Travails of Political Fragmentation." *Asian Survey* 39, no. 1 (January/February 1999).

Karat, Prakash. *Foreign Funding and the Philosophy of Voluntary Organisations: A Factor in Imperialist Strategy.* New Delhi: National Book Centre, 1988.

Kaushik, Susheela. *Participation of Women in Panchayati Raj in India: A Stock Taking; A Study of Six States.* New Delhi: National Commission for Women, Government of India, 1998.

———. *Women and Panchayati Raj.* New Delhi: Har-Anand, 1993.

Kaviraj, Sudipta. "Critique of the Passive Revolution." In *State and Politics in India,* edited by Partha Chaterjee. Delhi: Oxford University Press, 1998.

———. "The Modern State in India." In *Politics and the State in India,* edited by Zoya Hasan. Sage, 2000.

———. *Politics in India.* New Delhi: Oxford University Press, 1997.

Keck, Margaret, and Kathryn Sikkink. *Activists Beyond Borders: Advocacy Networks in International Politics.* Ithaca, N.Y.: Cornell University Press, 1998.

King, Robert D. *Nehru and the Language Politics of India.* Delhi, New York: Oxford University Press, 1997.

Kishwar, Madhu. "Laws, Liberty and Livelihood: Towards a Bottom-Up, Woman Friendly Agenda of Economic Reforms." *Manushi,* no. 122 (January–February 2001): 8–12.

Kishwar, Madhu, and Ruth Vanita, eds. *In Search of Answers: Voices from Manushi.* London: Zed Press, 1987.

Kohli, Atul. *Democracy and Discontent; India's Growing Crisis of Governability.* Cambridge: Cambridge University Press, 1990.

———. *The State and Poverty in India.* Cambridge: Cambridge University Press, 1987.

———, ed. *The Success of India's Democracy.* Cambridge: Cambridge University Press, 2001.

Korten, David. *Getting to the 21st Century: Voluntary Action and the Global Agenda.* West Hartford, Conn.: Kumarian Press, 1990.

Kothari, Rajni. "The Congress 'System' in India, Party System and Election Studies." Occasional Papers of the Centre for Developing Societies, No. 1. Bombay: Allied Publishers, 1967.

———. *Growing Amnesia: An Essay on Poverty and the Human Consciousness.* New Delhi: Viking, 1993.

———. "NGOs, the State and World Capitalism." *Economic and Political Weekly* 21, no. 50 (1986): 2177–82.

———. "The Non-Party Political Process." *Economic and Political Weekly* 19, no. 5 (1984): 219.

Kothari, Smitu, and Michelle Chawla, ed. *UN DeePer in the Techno-Corporate Mire.* New Delhi: Kalpavriksh, Lokayan et al., 2002.

Kozel, Valerie, and Barbara Parker. "A Profile and Diagnostic of Poverty in Uttar Pradesh." *Economic and Political Weekly,* January 25, 2003.

Krishna, Anirudh. "What Is Happening to Caste? A View from Some North Indian Villages." *Journal of Asian Studies* 62, no. 4 (November 2003): 1171–93.

Krishnakumar, Asha. "Biotechnology: Bt cotton, again." *Frontline* 21, no. 10, May 8–21, 2004.

Krishnamurthy, J., ed. *Women in Colonial India: Essays on Survival, Work and the State.* Delhi: Oxford University Press, 1989.

Krueger, Anne O., Maurice Schiff, and Alberto Valdes. *The Political Economy of Agricultural Pricing Policy, Volume 2: Asia, A World Bank Comparative Study.* Baltimore and London: Johns Hopkins University Press, 1991.

Kudva, Neema. "Development and Democratization/A Contextual Critique of NGO Behavior and Practice through the Case of the Tribal Joint Action Committee in Karnataka, India." Dissertation, Department of City and Regional Planning, University of California at Berkeley, 2001.

———. "Engineering Elections: The Experiences of Women in Panchayati Raj in Karnataka, India." *International Journal of Politics, Culture and Society* 16, no. 3 (2003): 445–64.

———. "Uneasy Partnerships? Government-NGO Relations in India." Working Paper No. 673. Berkeley: Institute of Urban and Regional Development, University of California, 1996.

Kumar, Radha. *A History of Doing: An Illustrated Account of Movements for Women's Rights and Feminism in India, 1800–1990.* New Delhi: Kali for Women, 1993.

Kumar, Vijendra. *Rise of Dalit Power in India.* Jaipur: ABD Publishers, 2001.

Kumar, Vivek, and Uday Sinha. *Dalit Assertion and the Bahujan Samaj Party: A Perspective from Below.* Lucknow: Bahujan Sahitya Sansthan, 2001.

Lal, Deepak, ed. *"Hindu Equilibrium," Cultural Stability and Economic Stagnation,* vol.1. Oxford: Clarendon Press, 1988.

Lal, Deepak, Rakesh Mohan, and I. Natarajan. "Economic Reforms and Poverty Alleviation: A Tale of Two Surveys." *Economic and Political Weekly,* March 24, 2001.

Lalita, K. "Women in Revolt: A Historical Analysis of the Progressive Organisation of Women in Andhra Pradesh." In *Women's Struggles and Strategies,* edited by Saskia Wieringa, 54–68. Aldershot: Gower, 1988.

Leissinger, K. M. "Ethical Challenges of Agricultural Biotechnology for Developing Countries." In *Agricultural Biotechnology and the Poor,* edited by G. J. Persley and M. M. Lantin. Washington, D.C.: Consultative Group on International Agricultural Research, 2000.

Li, Tania Murray. "Articulating Indigenous Identity in Indonesia: Resource Politics and the Tribal Slot." *Comparative Studies in Society and History* 42, no. 1 (2000): 149–79.

———. "Images of Community: Discourse and Strategy in Property Relations." *Development and Change* 27, no. 3 (1996): 501–27.

Lieten, George. *Development, Devolution and Democracy: Village Discourse in West Bengal.* New Delhi: Sage Publications, 1996.

Lindberg, Staffan. "Farmers' Movements and Agricultural Development in India." In *Social Movements in Development: The Challenge of Globalization and Democratization,* edited by Staffan Lindberg and Ani Sverrisson. New York: Macmillan Ltd., 1997.

———. "New Farmers' Movements in India as Structural Response and Collective Identity Formation: The Cases of the Shetkari Sanghatana and the BKU." In *New Farmers' Movements in India,* edited by Tom Brass. London: Frank Cass, 1995.

Lindberg, Staffan, and Stig Toft Madsen. "Farmers' Movements in South Asia: Contemporary Trends in a Historical Context." *Cambridge Review of International Affairs,* forthcoming.

Liptak, Adam. "Saving Seeds Subjects Farmers to Suits Over Patent." *New York Times,* November 2, 2003, 18.

Lipton, Michael, with Richard Longhurst. *New Seeds and Poor People.* Baltimore: Johns Hopkins University Press, 1989.

Liu, Mannie. "Venture Capital, Growth and Poverty." Presentation at Seminar on Profiles of Poverty and Networks of Power, Madurai, February 14–16, 2001.

Low, D. A. *Rearguard Action: Selected Essays on Late Colonial Indian History.* New Delhi: Sterling Publishers, 1996.

Ludden, David, ed. *Making India Hindu: Community, Conflict and the Politics of Democracy.* New Delhi: Oxford University Press, 1996.

Madan, T. N. *Modern Myths, Locked Minds: Secularism and Fundamentalism in India.* New Delhi: Oxford University Press, 1997.

Madsen, Stig Toft. "Post Festum: The Lotus and the Mud in an Indo-Global Context." Paper for the Conference on Globalization and Democratic Developments in Asia, Department of Political Science, Lund University, Sweden, May 18–20, 2000.

———. "The View from Vevey." *Economic and Political Weekly,* September 29, 2001, 3733–42.

Maheswari, Uma. "Anti-arrack Movement, Prohibition and After: *Eenadu*'s Strategic Support and Silence." *Journal of Arts and Ideas, Special Issue on Gender, Media and the Rhetorics of Liberalization,* nos. 22–23 (1999): 73–86.

Majumdar, Asok. *Peasant Protest in Indian Politics. Tebhaga Movement in Bengal.* New Delhi: NIB Publishers, 1993.

Malik, Balji. "There Is Still Hope." *Illustrated Weekly,* April 29, 1984.

Malik, Yogendra K., and V. B. Singh. *Hindu Nationalists in India. The Rise of the Bharatiya Janata Party.* Boulder, Colo.: Westview Press, 1994.

Mallick, Ross. *Development Policy of a Communist Government: West Bengal since 1977.* Cambridge: Cambridge University Press, 1993.

Mandal, Rabindra Nath. *The Tebhaga Movement in Kakdwip.* Kolkata: Ratna Prakashan, 2001.

Manjula, B. "Voices From the Spiral of Silence: A Case Study of Samatha Self Help Groups of Ulloor." Paper presented at the International Conference on Democratic Decentralisation, Thiruvananthapuram, May 23–27, 2000.

Mansbridge, Jane. "What Is the Feminist Movement?" In *Feminist Organizations: Harvest of the Women's Movement,* edited by Myra Marx Ferree and Patricia Yancey Martin. Philadelphia: Temple University Press, 1995.

Markovits, Claude. *Indian Business and Nationalist Politics, 1931–1939.* Cambridge: Cambridge University Press, 1985.

Marx, Karl. *The Eighteenth Brumaire of Louis Bonaparte.* Moscow: Progress Publishers, 1852.

Mathew, George. *Panchayati Raj from Legislation to Movement.* New Delhi: Concept Publishing, 1994.

Mathew, Vinod. "India's GM Cotton Story Gets Bigger—'Uproot & Destroy' Begins on Gujarat Farms." *The Hindu* Business Line, October 20, 2001.

Mathias, Edward. *Panchayati Raj Institutions and Role of NGOs: The Experiences in Mysore and Tumkur Districts of Karnataka (1993–1999).* New Delhi: Indian Social Institute, 2000.

McHughen, Alan. *Pandora's Picnic Basket: The Potential and Hazards of Genetically Modified Foods.* Oxford: Oxford University Press, 2000.

McKean, Lise. *Divine Enterprise: Gurus and the Hindu Nationalist Movement.* Chicago: Chicago University Press, 1996.

Mehra, Rekha. "Rural Development Programmes: Neglect of Women." In *Women and Rural Transformation—Two Studies,* edited by Rekha Mehra and K. Saradamoni, 3–31. New Delhi: Concept, 1983.

Mehta, Pratap. "India: Fragmentation Amid Consensus." *Journal of Democracy* 8, no. 1 (1997): 56–69.

Mendelsohn, Oliver, and Marika Vicziany. *The Untouchables: Subordination, Poverty and the State in Modern India.* Cambridge: Cambridge University Press, 1998.

Menon, Dilip. *Caste, Nationalism and Communism in South India: Malabar 1900–1948.* New Delhi: Cambridge University Press, 1994.

Menon, Nivedita, ed. *Gender and Politics in India.* Delhi: Oxford University Press, 1999.

Menon, Parvathi. "Waking Up to GM Cotton." *Frontline* 18, Issue 23, November 10–23, 2001.

Merkl, Peter, and Kay Lawson, eds. *When Parties Fail.* Princeton, N.J.: Princeton University Press, 1988.

Misra, V. N. "Price and Non-Price Determinants of Rural Poverty: A Critique." *Economic and Political Weekly*, March 4, 2000.

Mistry, Sharad. "Terminator Gene a Figment of Imagination: Monsanto Chief." *Indian Express*, December 4, 1998.

Mitra, Asok. "Implications of Declining Sex Ratio in India." Reprinted in *Enduring Conundrum: India's Sex Ratio; Essays in Honour of Asok Mitra*, edited by Vina Mazumdar and N. Krishnaji, 143–98. New Delhi: Rainbow, 2001.

Mohan, Giles. "The Disappointments of Civil Society: The Politics of NGO Intervention in Northern Ghana." *Political Geography* 21, no. 1 (2002): 125–54.

Mohanty, Manohar, and Anil Singh. *Voluntarism and Government: Policy, Programme and Assistance.* New Delhi: Voluntary Action Network India, VANI, 2001.

Mosely, Paul, and David Hulme. "Microenterprise Finance: Is There a Conflict between Growth and Poverty Alleviation?" *World Development* 26, no. 5 (1998): 783–90.

Mukherjee, K. K. *Emerging Societal Changes and Voluntary Organisations: Challenges and Responses.* Ghaziabad: Gram Niyojan Kendra, 1994.

Mukherjee, Vanita. "Democratic Decentralisation and Associative Patterns." Unpublished paper, Trivandrum, 2002.

———. "Gender Matters." in *Beyond Numbers: A Symposium on Population Planning and Advocacy, Seminar*, no. 511 (2002): 67–75.

Mukta, Parita, and Chetan Bhatt, eds. "Hindutva Movements in the West: Resurgent Hinduism and the Politics of Diaspora." *Ethnic and Racial Studies* 23, no. 3 (May 2000, Special Issue).

Murthy, Ranjani, and Nitya Rao. *Addressing Poverty, Indian NGOs and Capacity Enhancement in the 1990s.* New Delhi: Friedrich Ebert Stiftung, 1997.

Murugkar, Lata. *Dalit Panther Movement in Maharashtra: A Sociological Appraisal.* Bombay: Popular Prakashan, 1991.

Nadkarni, M. V. *Farmers' Movements in India.* Allied Publishers, 1987.

Nadkarni, M. V., assisted by K. H. Vedisa. "Accelerating Commercialisation of Agriculture: Dynamic Agriculture and Stagnating Peasants?" *Economic and Political Weekly*, June 29, 1996.

Nagaraj, D. R. *The Flaming Feet: A Study of the Dalit Movement in India.* Bangalore: South Forum Press and ICRA, 1993.

Nagaraj, K. "Decentralisation in Kerala: A Note." Discussion Paper No. 2, Kerala Research Programme on Local Level Development, Centre for Development Studies, Thiruvananthapuram, June 1999.

Namboodiripad, E. M. S. "Caste, Classes and Parties in Modern Political Development." *Social Scientist*, November 1977.

Nanda, B. R., ed. *Indian Women from Purdah to Modernity.* New Delhi: Vikas, 1976.

Nandy, Ashis. "An Anti Secularist Manifesto." *Seminar* 314 (October 1985): 1–12.

———. "The Political Culture of the Indian State." in *Politics and the State in India; Readings in Indian Government and Politics—3,* edited by Zoya Hasan. New Delhi: Sage Publications, 2000.

———. *Science, Hegemony, and Violence.* New Delhi: Oxford University Press, 1990.

Nanjundaswamy, M. D. "Statement of Professor Nanjundaswamy at the Demonstration Against the World Economic Summit, Cologne, June 19th 1999." GreenFiles, WWF-I, New Delhi.

Narayanan, Revathi. "Grassroots, Gender and Governance: Panchayati Raj Experiences from Mahila Samakhya Karnataka." In *The Violence of Development: The Politics of Identity, Gender and Social Inequalities in India,* edited by Karin Kapadia, 295–351. New Delhi: Kali for Women, 2002.

National Commission to Review the Working of the Constitution. Chair: Justice Dr. K. Ramaswamy. A Consultation Paper on the Pace of Socio-Economic Change under the Constitution, chapter 9, 5. May 11, 2001. http://lawmin.nic.in/ncrwc/final report/v2b1–4.htm.

National Commission of Women. *The Sathin as an Agent of Women's Development.* New Delhi: Government of India, 1996.

National Council of Educational Research and Training (NCERT). *Guidelines and Syllabi for Primary Stage,* New Delhi, 2001.

Nayar, Raj. "The Limits of Economic Nationalism in India: Economic Reforms under the BJP-led Government." *Asian Survey* 40, no. 5 (2000): 792–815.

Nehru, Jawaharlal. *India's Freedom.* London: Allen and Unwin, 1962.

Nielsen, A. C. "Nationwide Survey by A. C. Nielsen ORG-MARG Underscores Benefits of Bollgard™ Cotton. Press Release." A. C. Nielsen ORG-MARG, Mumbai, 2004.

"No More Aid Please." *The Economist,* June 21–27, 2003.

Noonan, Rita K. "Women against the State: Political Opportunities and Collective Action Frames in Chile's Transition to Democracy." *Sociological Forum* 10 (1995): 81–111.

Noronha, Frederick. "India's High Court Stops Field Trials of Biotech Cotton." *Environmental News Service,* February 23, 1999.

Norton, Michael. "The Voluntary Sector in India, Issues and Ideas for Its Future." A Report with Recommendations. London: Centre for Innovation in Voluntary Action, 1995 (mimeo).

Offe, Claus. *Disorganized Capitalism.* Cambridge, Mass.: MIT Press, 1985.

Omvedt, Gail. "Agrarian Transformation, Agrarian Struggles and Marxist Analysis of the Peasantry (Review Article)." *Bulletin of Concerned Asian Scholars* 26, no. 3 (July–September 1994).

———. "Brahmanic Socialism." *The Hindu,* January 27, 1998.

———. *Dalit Visions: The Anti-Caste Movement and the Construction of an Indian Identity.* New Delhi: Orient Longman, 1995.

———. *Dalits and the Democratic Revolution: Dr. Ambedkar and the Dalit Movement in Colonial India.* New Delhi: Sage Publications India Pvt. Ltd., 1994.

———. "Ideology and Organization in the Farmers' Movement: Shetkari Sanghatana from 'Remunerative Prices' to 'Farmers for Freedom.'" Paper for Farmers' Movement Organization project, Copenhagen, Denmark: Nordic Institute for Asian Studies, June 2000.

———. "India's Green Movements." *Race and Class* 28, no. 4 (1987).

———. *Reinventing Revolution: New Social Movements and the Socialist Tradition in India.* New York: M. E. Sharpe, Inc., 1993.

———. "The Restaurant-and-Bar Economy." *The Hindu*, May 7 and 8, 2001.

———. "Struggle against Dams or Struggle for Water? Environmental Movements and the State." In *Indian Democracy, Meanings and Practices*, edited by Rajendra Vora and Suhas Palshikar. New Delhi: Sage, 2003.

———. "'We Want the Return for Our Sweat': The New Peasant Movement in India and the Formation of a National Agricultural Policy." In *New Farmers' Movements in India*, edited by Tom Brass. London: Frank Cass, 1994.

———. *We Will Smash This Prison! Indian Women in Struggle*. London: Zed Books, 1980.

Omvedt, Gail, and Chetna Gala. "The New Economic Policy and Women: A Rural Perspective." *Economic Review* (October 1993): 8–18.

Organiser, May 1, 1994.

Organiser, August 26, 1996.

Paarlberg, Robert L. *The Politics of Precaution: Genetically Modified Crops in Developing Countries*. Baltimore: Johns Hopkins University Press, 2001.

Padmanabhan, Mukund. "The Dilemmas over Illicit GM Cotton." Editorial, *The Hindu*, October 30, 2001.

Pai, Sudha. *Dalit Assertion and the Unfinished Democratic Revolution: The Bahujan Samaj Party in Uttar Pradesh*. New Delhi: Sage Publications India Pvt. Ltd., 2002.

Palekar, Shreekant. *Real Wages in India, 1939–1950*. London: Asia Publishing House, 1962.

Palit, Chittaroopa. "The Historian as Gatekeeper." *Frontline*, January 5, 2001.

Palmer-Jones, Richard, and Kunal Sen. "On India's Poverty Puzzles and Statistics of Poverty." *Economic and Political Weekly*, January 20, 2001.

Panagariya, Arvind. "India in the 1980s and 1990s: A Triumph of Reforms." IMF Working Paper No. WP/04/43 (2004).

Pandey, Gyan. *The Construction of Communalism in North India*. Delhi: Oxford University Press, 1990.

Parameswaran, M. P. "From Voters to Actors: People's Planning Campaign and Participatory Democracy in Kerala." Kerala Sastra Sahitya Parishad, Trichur, 2001.

———. "Role of the Kerala Sastra Sahitya Parishad in the Movement for Democratic Decentralisation." Paper presented at the International Conference on Democratic Decentralisation, Thiruvananthapuram, May 23–27, 2000.

Parthasarthy, G. "Public Intervention and Rural Poverty: Case of Non-Sustainable Reduction in Andhra Pradesh." *Economic and Political Weekly*, October 14–21, 1995.

Peluso, Nancy, and Michael Watts. *Violent Environments*. Ithaca, N.Y.: Cornell University Press, 2001.

Persley, G. J., and M. M. Lantin, eds. *Agricultural Biotechnology and the Poor*. Washington, D.C., Consultative Group on International Agricultural Research, 2000.

Peters, Julie Stone, and Andrea Wolper, eds. *Women's Rights, Human Rights: International Feminist Perspectives*. New York: Routledge, 1995.

Pinstrup-Anderson, Per, and Ebbe Schioler. *Seeds of Contention: World Hunger and the Global Controversy over GM Crops*. Baltimore: Johns Hopkins University Press, 2000.

Planning Commission, Government of India. *Directory of Centrally Sponsored Schemes for Voluntary Agencies*. New Delhi: Government of India, 1994.

———. NGO Database. http://164.100.97.14/ngo/default.asp (May 2004).

———. *Ninth Five Year Plan 1997–2002. Volume I: Development Goals, Strategies and Policies,* New Delhi, 1999.

———. *Ninth Five Year Plan 1997–2002. Volume II: Thematic Issues and Sectoral Programmes.* New Delhi, 1999.

———. *Proceedings, All-India Conference on Role of the Voluntary Sector in National Development.* New Delhi: Voluntary Action Cell, Planning Commission, 2002. http://planningcommission.nic.in/data/ngo/vac_prced.pdf (January 2004).

———. *Report of the Steering Committee on Voluntary Sector, for the Tenth Five Year Plan (2002–2007).* TYFP—Steering Committee Sr. No. 7 /2001. New Delhi: Planning Commission, Government of India, January 2002. http://planningcommission.nic.in/aboutus/committee/strgrp/stgp_vol.pdf (January 2004).

———. *Report of the Task Force on Self-Managed Institutions for Integrated Development.* New Delhi: Planning Commission, 1991 (mimeo).

Plotkin, Sarah. "A Nation Up in Arms vs. A Nation Shrouded in Silence: Great Britain vs. the United States on Genetically Modified Organisms." Cornell University, April 2000.

Pollan, Michael. *The Botany of Desire: A Plant's Eye View of the World.* New York: Random House, 2001.

Pradhan, Basanta K., P. K. Roy, M. R. Saluja, and Shanta Venkatram. "Rural-Urban Disparities: Income Distribution, Expenditure Patterns and Social Sector." *Economic and Political Weekly,* July 15, 2000.

PRIA. *Voluntary Development Organizations in India: a Study of History, Roles and Future Challenges.* New Delhi: PRIA, Society for Participatory Research in Asia, 1991.

PRIA and Anjaneya Associates in collaboration with the Center for Civil Society Studies, Johns Hopkins University. "Dimensions of Giving and Volunteering in Tamil Nadu: Some Glimpses from Tamil Nadu." Working Paper Number 5. New Delhi: PRIA, Society for Participatory Research in Asia, November 2002.

———. "Exploring the Non Profit Sector in India, Some Glimpses from Tamil Nadu." Working Paper Number 4. New Delhi: PRIA, Society for Participatory Research in Asia, October 2002.

PRIA and Society for Socio-Economic Studies and Services in collaboration with the Center for Civil Society Studies, Johns Hopkins University. "Dimensions of Giving and Volunteering in West Bengal, Some Glimpses from West Bengal." Working Paper Number 5. New Delhi: PRIA, Society for Participatory Research in Asia, March 2003.

———. "Exploring the Non Profit Sector in India, Some Glimpses from West Bengal." Working Paper Number 6. New Delhi: PRIA, Society for Participatory Research in Asia, December 2002.

Prakash, C. S. "The Biotech Miracle." *Indian Express,* Letters to the Editor, 5 November 2001.

Purushothaman, Sangeetha, Padma Anil Kumar, and Simone Purohit. *Engendering Local Governance: The Karnataka Experience.* Bangalore: Best Practices Foundation in collaboration with The Hunger Project, 2000.

Qadeer, Imrana. "Maternal Health in India." In *Gender, Population and Development in India,* edited by Maitrayi Krishnaraj, Ratna Sudarshan, and Abusaleh Shariff, 270–90. Delhi: Oxford University Press, 1998.

———. "Reproductive Health: A Public Health Perspective." *Economic and Political Weekly* 33, no. 41 (1998): 2675–84.

Qaim, Matin, and David Zilberman. "Yield Effects of Genetically Modified Crops in Developing Countries." *Science* 299 (2003): 900–902.

Raj, Ranjit Dev. "Indian Farmers Take the War to Europe." Inter Press Service, May 24, 1999.

Rajasekhar, D. "Where Local Organizations Do Not Work: Problems of Poverty Reduction in Tamil Nadu, India." In *In the Name of the Poor: Contesting Political Space for Poverty Reduction,* edited by Neil Webster and Lars Engberg-Pedersen, 183–207. London, New York: Zed Books, 2002.

———. "Winning Panchayati Raj Elections the YIP Way." *Exchanges,* no. 10 (September 1995). Bangalore: ActionAid India.

Rajshekhar, V. T. *Dalit: The Black Untouchables of India,* 3rd edition. Atlanta: Clarity Press, 1995.

Ramachandran, R. "Green Signal for Bt Cotton." *Frontline* 19, Issue 8 (April 13-26, 2002).

Ramanjaneyula, G. V., and A. Ravindra. *Terminator Logic: Monsanto, Genetic Engineering and the Future of Agriculture.* Science for People / Research Foundation for Science, Technology and Ecology, New Delhi, January 1999.

Ramaswamy, E. A. *Power and Justice: The State in Industrial Relations.* Delhi: Oxford University Press, 1984.

———. *Worker Consciousness and Trade Union Response.* Delhi: Oxford University Press, 1988.

Ramesh, Jairam. "A New Round of Controversy." *India Today,* October 30, 2000.

———. "Poverty of Numbers." *India Today,* March 20, 2000.

———. "Reforms and the Poor." *India Today,* July 27, 1998.

Ramoo, S. K. "Karnataka Farmers' Organisation Splits." *The Hindu,* November 16, 2000.

Ranadive, B. T. *Caste, Class and Property Relations.* Calcutta: National Book Agency, 1982.

Rangan, Haripriya. *Of Myths and Movements: Rewriting Chipko into Himalayan History.* Delhi: Oxford University Press, 2000.

Rangarajan, Mahesh. "The Politics of Ecology: The Debate on Wildlife and People in India, 1970–95." *Economic and Political Weekly* 31, nos. 35–37 (1996): 2391–2409.

Rao, Mohan. "Population Policies: States Approve Coercive Measures." *Economic and Political Weekly* 36, no. 29 (21 July 2001): 2739–41.

Rao, Narasimha. *The Insider.* New Delhi: Viking (Penguin Books India), 1998.

Rao, V. M. *The Poor in a Hostile Society: Glimpses of Changing Poverty Scenario in India.* New Delhi: Vikas Publishing House Pvt. Ltd., 1998.

Ravallion, Martin. "Food Prices and Rural Poverty." *Economic and Political Weekly* 33, no. 28 (11 July 1998): 1870–71.

———. "On Reform, Food Prices, and Poverty in India." *Economic and Political Weekly* 33, nos. 1–2 (10 January 1998): 29–36.

———. "What Is Needed for a More Pro-Poor Growth Process in India." *Economic and Political Weekly* 35, no. 13 (March 25, 2000): 1089–93.

Ravallion, Martin, and Gaurav Dutt. "India's Checkered History in Fight Against Poverty." *Economic and Political Weekly* 31 (1996): 2479–86.

Ravindran, T. K. Sundari. "Women and the Politics of Population and Development in India." *Reproductive Health Matters,* no. 1 (1993): 26–38.

Ray, Bharati, ed. *From the Seams of History: Essays on Indian Women.* Delhi: Oxford University Press, 1995.

Ray, Raka. *Fields of Protest: Women's Movements in India*. Minneapolis: University of Minnesota Press and New Delhi: Kali for Women, 1999.

Reddy, Narasimha N. L., and D. Rajasekhar. *Development Programmes and NGOs: A Guide on Central Government Programmes for NGOs in India*. Bangalore: Bangalore Consultancy Office and NOVIB, 1996.

Rediff.com. "Bt Cotton Will Kill Farmers, Financially and Literally." An Interview with Devinder Sharma, December 12, 2001.

Regini, Marino. *Uncertain Boundaries: The Social and Political Construction of European Economies*. New York: Cambridge University Press, 1995.

Reid, Walter V. "Gene Co-Ops and the Biotrade: Translating Genetic Resource Rights into Sustainable Development." *Journal of Ethno-pharmacology* 51 (1996): 75–92.

Revri, Chamanlal. *The Indian Trade Union Movement: An Historical Outline 1880–1947*. New Delhi: Orient Longman, 1972.

Riddell, Roger. "Judging Success: Evaluating NGO Approaches to Alleviating Poverty in Developing Countries." Working Paper Series No. 37. London: Overseas Development Institute, 1990.

Riddell, Roger, and Mark A. Robinson. "The Impact of NGO Poverty Alleviation Projects: Results of Case-Study Evaluations." Working Paper Series No. 68. London: Overseas Development Institute, 1992.

Robinson, Mark A. "Evaluating the Impact of NGOs in Rural Poverty Alleviation: India Country Study." Working Paper Series No. 49. London: Overseas Development Institute, 1991.

Rodrik, Dani, and Arvind Subraminian. "From 'Hindu Growth' to Productivity Surge: The Mystery of the Indian Growth Transition." NBER Working Paper No. 10376 (2004).

Roy, Aruna. "Democracy, Ethics and the Right to Information." Department of Education, Delhi University, December 19, 2000.

Roy, Arundhati. *The Greater Common Good*. Bombay: IndiaBook Distributors, 1999.

Rudolph, Lloyd I., and Susan Hoeber Rudolph. *In Pursuit of Lakshmi: The Political Economy of the Indian State*. Chicago: University of Chicago Press, 1987.

Rudra, Ashok. "The Emergence of the Intelligentsia as a Ruling Class in India." *Economic and Political Weekly* 24, no. 3 (1989): 142–50.

Rustagi, Preet. "Identifying Gender Backward Districts using Selected Indicators." *Economic and Political Weekly*, November 25, 2000, 4276–86.

Sadgopal, Anil, and Shyam Bahadur Namra. *Sangharsh aur Nirmaan: Shankar Guha Niyogi aur unka Naye Bharat ka Sapna* [Struggle and Construction: Shankar Guha Niyogi and His Dream of a New India]. New Delhi: Rajkamal Prakashan, 1993.

Sahai, Suman. "Bt Cotton: Confusion Prevails." EPW Commentary, *Economic and Political Weekly*, May 25, 2002 (also posted on AgBioIndia Mailing List June 19, 2002).

———. "An Open Letter to the WTO Chief Mr. Ruggiero." Gene Campaign, New Delhi.

Sahrasabudhe, Sunil. "Peasant Movement and the Quest for Development." In *Peasant and Peasant Protest in India*, edited by M. N. Karna. New Delhi: Intellectual Publishing House, 1989.

Sainath, P. *Everybody Loves a Good Drought*. New Delhi: Penguin Publications, 1996.

———. *The Hindu*, June 1, 2004.

Sangari, Kumkum, and Sudesh Vaid, eds. *Recasting Women: Essays on Colonial India*. New Delhi: Kali for Women, 1989.

Sanghatana, Stree Shakti. *"We Were Making History"* . . . *Life Stories of Women in the Telangana People's Struggle.* New Delhi: Kali for Women, 1989.

Sanyal, Bishwapriya. *Cooperative Autonomy: The Dialectic of State–NGOs Relationship in Developing Countries.* Geneva: International Institute for Labour Studies, ILO, 1994.

Sarkar, Sumit. "The Fascism of the Sangh Parivar." *Economic and Political Weekly,* January 30, 1993.

———. *Modern India: 1880–1947.* Delhi and London: Macmillan, 1983.

Sarkar, Tanika. "Educating the Children of the Hindurashtra: Notes on RSS Schools." In *Religion, Religiosity and Communalism,* edited by Praful Bidwai, Harbans Mukhia, and Achin Vanaik. Delhi: Manohar, 1996.

———. "The Gender Predicament of the Hindu Right." In *The Concerned Indian's Guide to Communalism,* edited by K. N. Panikkar. Delhi: Viking Press, 1999.

Sarkar, Tanika, and Urvashi Butalia, eds. *Women and the Hindu Right.* Delhi: Kali for Women, 1995.

Sathin Karamchari Sangh. "The Sathin Issue: A Collective Strategy: The Need of the Hour." Unpublished pamphlet.

Savarkar, V. D. *Hindutva: Who Is a Hindu?* 6th ed. Delhi: Bharti Sahitya Sadan, 1989.

Scholte, Jan Aart. *Globalization: A Critical Introduction.* New York: Palgrave, 2000.

Schultz, Theodore W. "Economic Growth from Traditional Agriculture." In *Chicago Essays in Economic Development,* edited by David Bell, 3–22. Chicago and London: University of Chicago Press, 1972.

Scoones, Ian. "Regulatory Manoeuvres: The Bt Cotton Controversy in India." IDS Working Paper No. 197, Brighton, U.K., August 2003.

Scott, James C. *The Moral Economy of the Peasant.* New Haven, Conn.: Yale University Press, 1976.

———. *Seeing Like a State: How Certain Schemes to Improve the Human Condition Have Failed.* New Haven, Conn.: Yale University Press, 1998.

Seema, T. N., and Vanitha Mukherjee. "Gender Governance and Citizenship in Decentralised Planning." Paper presented at the International Conference on Democratic Decentralisation, Thiruvananthapuram, May 23–27, 2000.

Seidman, Gay. *Manufacturing Militance: Workers' Movements in Brazil and South Africa, 1970–1985.* Berkeley: University of California Press, 1994.

Seminar. *Voices from the Field: A Symposium on People's Experiences with the Development Process,* no. 431 (July 1995).

Sen, Abhijit. "Estimates of Consumer Expenditure and Its Distribution: Statistical Priorities after NSS 55th Round." *Economic and Political Weekly,* December 16, 2000.

Sen, Amartya. "Hunger: Old Torments, New Blunders." *The Little Magazine* 2, no. 6 (2001). Internet edition: http://www.littlemag.com/hunger/aks.html.

Sen, Amartya, and Jean Drèze. *India: Economic Development and Social Opportunity.* Delhi: Oxford University Press, 1995.

Sen, Gita, Adrian Germaine, and Lincoln Chen, eds. *Population Policies Reconsidered: Health, Empowerment and Rights.* Cambridge, Mass.: Harvard University Press, 1994.

Sen, Ilina, ed. *A Space within the Struggle: Women's Participation in People's Movements.* New Delhi: Kali for Women, 1990.

Sen, Siddhartha. "Defining the Nonprofit Sector: India." Working Papers of the Johns Hopkins Comparative Nonprofit Sector Project, No. 12. Baltimore: The Johns Hopkins Institute for Policy Studies, 1993.

Sethi, Harsh. "Micro-struggles, NGOs and the State." *People's Rights: Social Movements and the State in the Third World,* edited by Manoranjan Mohanty and Partha Nath Mukherji, with Olle Tornquist. New Delhi, Thousand Oaks, and London: Sage Publications, 1998.

———. "Movements and Mediators." *Economic and Political Weekly* 36, no. 4 (2001): 268–70.

Shah, Ghanshyam. *Dalit Land Struggle in India.* Mumbai: Vikas Adhyayan Kendra, 2001.

———. *Social Movements in India; A Review of the Literature.* New Delhi: Sage Publications, 1990.

Shah, Ghanshyam, ed. *Social Movements and the State.* Delhi: Sage Publications, 2002.

Shah, Nandita, Sujata Gothoskar, et al. "Feminisation of Labour Force and Organisational Strategies." *Economic and Political Weekly,* April 30, 1994, WS 39–48.

Shaik, Sajid. "Farmers Decide to Defend Their Bt Gene Cotton Crops." *The Times of India,* October 31, 2001.

Sharma, Devinder. "The Introduction of Transgenic Cotton in India." *Biotechnology and Development Monitor,* no. 44 (March 2001): 10–13.

Sharma, H. R. "Land Distribution in Rural India, 1982–1992: A Comparative Study of Scheduled Caste, Scheduled Tribe and Non-scheduled Caste and Tribe." Paper for National Seminar on Employment and Poverty of Social Groups in Context of New Economic Policy." Center for the Study of Regional Development, Jawaharlal Nehru University, April 3–5, 1997.

Sharma, Jyotirmaya. *Hindutva: Exploring the Idea of Hindu Nationalism.* New Delhi: Penguin, 2003.

Sharma, Kumud. "Power vs. Representation: Feminist Dilemmas, Ambivalent State and the Debate on Reservation for Women in India." Occasional Paper No. 28. New Delhi: Centre for Women's Development Studies, 1998.

———. "Shared Aspirations, Fragmented Realities: Contemporary Women's Movement in India, its Dialectics and Dilemmas." New Delhi: Centre for Women's Development Studies, Occasional Paper No. 12, 1989.

Sharma, Mukul. "Saffronising Green." *Seminar* 516 (2002): 26–31.

Sheshadri, H. V., K. S. Sudarshan, K. Surya Narayan Rao, and Balraj Madhok. *Why Hindu Rashtra?* Delhi: Suruchi Prakashan, 1990.

Sheth, D. L. "Alternative Development as Political Practice." *Alternatives* 12, no. 2 (1987): 155–71.

———. "The Changing Terms of Elite Discourse: The Case of Reservation for 'Other Backward Classes.'" In *Politics and the State in India,* edited by Zoya Hasan. New Delhi: Sage, 2000.

———. "Globalisation and New Politics of Micro-movements." *Economic and Political Weekly,* January 3–9, 2004, 45–58.

———. "Secularization of Caste and Making of New Middle Class." *Economic and Political Weekly* 34, nos. 34–35 (1999): 2502–10.

Sheth, D. L., and Harsh Sethi. "The NGO Sector In India: Historical Context and Current Discourse." *Voluntas* 2 (1991): 49–68.

Shiva, Vandana. *Biopiracy: The Plunder of Nature and Knowledge.* Cambridge, Mass.: South End Press, 1997.

———. "Ecological Balance in an Era of Globalization." In *Global Ethics and Environment*, edited by Nicholas Low, 47–69. London: Routledge, 1999.

———. *Globalisation of Agriculture, Food Security and Sustainability*. New Delhi: Research Foundation for Science, Technology and Ecology, 1998.

———. "Monocultures, Monopolies, Myths and Masculinization of Agriculture." Paper prepared for the International Conference on Women and Agriculture, 1998.

———. *Patents: Myths and Reality*. Delhi: Penguin, 2001.

———. *Staying Alive: Women, Ecology and Survival in India*. New Delhi: Kali for Women, 1988.

———. *Stolen Harvest: The Hijacking of the Global Food Supply*. Cambridge, Mass.: South End Press, 2000.

Shiva, Vandana, Afsar H. Jafri, Ashok Emani, and Manish Pande. *Seeds of Suicide: The Ecological and Human Costs of Globalization of Agriculture*. Delhi: Research Foundation for Science, Technology and Ecology, 2000.

Simpson, David R., Roger A. Sedjo, and John W. Reid. "Valuing Biodiversity for Use in Pharmaceutical Research." *Journal of Political Economy* 104, no. 1 (1996): 163–85.

Singh, Jagpal. *Capitalism and Dependence: Agrarian Relations and Politics in Western Uttar Pradesh, 1951–1991*. New Delhi: Manohar, 1992.

Sinha, Mrinalini. "Refashioning Mother India: Feminism and Nationalism in Late-Colonial India." *Feminist Studies* 26, no. 3 (Fall 2000): 623–44.

Sinha, Sanjay. "Profile of the Poorest among Poor." *The Administrator* XLII (January–March 1997): 173–83.

Sinha, Subir, Shubhra Gururani, and Brian Greenberg. "The 'New Traditionalist' Discourse of Indian Environmentalism." *The Journal of Peasant Studies* 24, no. 3 (1997): 65–99.

Snow, David, and Robert D. Benford. "Ideology, Frame Resonance, and Participant Mobilization." In *International Social Movement Research*, vol. 1, 197–217. Greenwich, Conn.: JAI Press, 1988.

———. "Master Frames and Cycles of Protest." In *Frontiers of Social Movement Theory*, edited by Aldon Morris and Carol Mueller, 138. New Haven, Conn.: Yale University Press, 1992.

Sooryamoorthy, R., and K. D. Gangrade. *NGOs in India: A Cross-Sectional Study*. Westport, Conn., and London: Greenwood Press.

South Commission. *The Challenge to the South: Report of the South Commission*. Delhi: Oxford University Press, 1992.

Srivastava, Kavita, and Jaya Sharma. "Training Rural Women for Literacy." Institute of Development Studies, Jaipur, 1991.

Stephen, F. *NGOs—Hope of the Last Decade of This Century*. Bangalore: SEARCH, 1992.

Stone, Glenn Davis. "Biotechnology and Suicide in India." *Anthropology News*, May 2002.

Stree Shakti Sanghatana. *"We Were Making History": Women and the Telengana Uprising*. London: Zed Books, 1989.

Subramanian, K. N. *Labour-Management Relations in India*. Bombay: Asia Publishing House, 1967.

Sundar, Nandini. "Caste as Census Category: Implications for Sociology." *Current Sociology* 48, no. 3 (July 2000).

Sundaram, K. "Employment and Poverty in 1990s: A Postscript." *Economic and Political Weekly*, August 25, 2001.

———. "Employment and Poverty in 1990s: Further Results from NSS 55th Round Employment-Unemployment Survey, 1999–2000." *Economic and Political Weekly*, August 11, 2001.

———. "Employment-Unemployment Situation in the Nineties: Some Results from NSS 55th Round Survey." *Economic and Political Weekly*, March 17, 2001.

Sundaram, K., and Suresh D. Tendulkar. "Poverty in India in the 1990s: Revised Results for All-India and 15 Major States for 1993–94." *Economic and Political Weekly*, November 15, 2003.

Suresh, V. "Dalit Movement in India." In *Region, Religion, Caste, Gender and Culture in Contemporary India*, vol. 3, edited by T. V. Satyamurthy. New Delhi: Oxford University Press, 1996.

Survey, Narayan. *Sanad.* Mumbai: Granthali, 1987.

Suryanarayana, M.H. "How Real Is the Secular Decline in Rural Poverty?" *Economic and Political Weekly*, June 17, 2000.

Svarstad, Hanne, and Shivcharn S. Dhillion, eds. *Responding to Bioprospecting.* Oslo: Spartacus Forlag AS, 2000.

Swaminathan, M. S. "GM to Do Good to Agri and Food Security." *Economic Times*, 13 November 2001.

Tandon, Rajesh, and David Brown. "The Evolution of the Development Sector in India: An Overview Report." New Delhi: Society for Participatory Research in Asia, PRIA, 1990 (mimeo).

Tangraj. *Dalit in India.* Mumbai: Vikas Adhyayan Kendra.

Tanksley, Steven D., and Susan R. McCouch. "Seed Banks and Molecular Maps: Unlocking Genetic Potential from the Wild." *Science* 277 (22 August 1997): 1063–66.

Tansakul, Reungchai, and Peter Burt. "People Power vs. the Gene Giants." *Bangkok Post*, August 1, 1999.

Tellis, Olga. "Nasik's Farmers Demand Justice." *Sunday*, December 15, 1980.

Tendler, Judith. *Good Government in the Tropics.* Baltimore: Johns Hopkins University Press, 1997.

———. "Turning Private Voluntary Agencies into Development Agencies: Questions for Evaluation." AID Program Evaluation Discussion Paper No. 12. Washington, D.C.: U.S. Agency for International Development, 1982.

———. "Whatever Happened to Poverty Alleviation?" A Report Prepared for the Mid-Decade Review of the Ford Foundation's Livelihood, Employment and Income Generation (LIEG) Programs. New York: Ford Foundation, 1987 (mimeo).

Tendulkar, Suresh D. "Economic Reforms and Poverty." *Economic and Political Weekly*, July 10, 1995.

Tendulkar, Suresh D., and L. R. Jain. "Economic Reforms and Poverty." *Economic and Political Weekly*, June 10, 1995.

"Terminator Technology Not Terminated." Agra/Industrial Biotechnology Legal Letter 1, No. 1 (2000), 4.

Thakore, Dilip. "Why Bharat Has Declared War on India." *Business World*, June 6, 1985.

Tharu, Susie, and K. Lalita, eds. *Women Writing in India: From 600 B.C. to the Present.* 2 vols. New York: The Feminist Press and Delhi: Oxford University Press, 1991 and 1993.

Tharu, Susie, and Tejaswini Niranjana. "Problems for a Contemporary Theory of Gender." In *Subaltern Studies IX: Writings on South Asian History and Society,* edited by Shahid Amin and Dipesh Chakrabarty, 232–60. Delhi: Oxford University Press, 1996.

Thirumalai, I. "Peasant Class Assertions in Nalgonda and Warangal Districts of Telengana, 1930–1946." *Indian Economic and Social History Review* 31, no. 2 (1994): 217–38.

Thomas Isaac, T. M., and Richard Franke. *Local Democracy and Development: People's Campaign for Decentralised Planning.* New Delhi: LeftWord Books, 2000.

Thomas Isaac, T. M., Richard Franke, and M. P. Parameswaran. "From Anti-Feudalism to Sustainable Development: The Kerala People's Science Movement." *Bulletin of Concerned Asian Scholars* 29, no. 3 (1997).

Thomas Isaac, T. M., and Patrick Heller. "Democracy and Development: Decentralized Planning in Kerala." In *Deepening Democracy: Institutional Innovations in Empowered Participatory Governance,* edited by A. Fung and E. O. Wright. London: Verso, 2003.

Thorat, S. K., and R. S. Deshpande. "Caste System and Economic Inequality: Economic Theory and Evidence." In *Dalit Identity and Politics,* edited by Ghanshyam Shah. New Delhi: Sage Publications India Pvt. Ltd., 2001.

Timmer, C. Peter. *Getting Prices Right: The Scope and Limits of Agricultural Price Policy.* Ithaca and London: Cornell University Press, 1986.

Tornquist, Olle. "Making Democratisation Work: From Civil Society and Social Capital to Political Inclusion and Politicisation; Theoretical Reflections on Concrete Cases in Indonesia, Kerala, and the Philippines." Research Programme on Popular Movements, Development and Democratisation, University of Oslo, 1997.

Tsing, Anna Lowenhaupt. "Becoming a Tribal Elder, and Other Green Development Fantasies." In *Transforming the Indonesian Uplands: Marginality, Power and Production,* edited by Tania M. Li. Amsterdam: Harwood, 1999.

United Nations Development Programme. *Human Development Report: Making Technologies Work for Human Development.* New York: Oxford University Press, 2001.

United Nations Food and Agriculture Organization (UNFAO). "The State of Food and Agriculture 2004: Agricultural Biotechnology—Meeting the Needs of the Poor?" Rome, 2004.

Unni, Jeemoi. "Non-Agricultural Employment and Poverty in Rural India." *Economic and Political Weekly,* March 29, 1998.

Vachani, Lalit. *The Boy in the Branch,* Channel Four, 1991.

Vaidyanathan, A. "Poverty and Development Policy." *Economic and Political Weekly,* May 26, 2001, 1807–22.

Vajpayee, Atal Bihari. Speech, quoted in Planning Commission, Government of India, *Proceedings, All-India Conference on Role of the Voluntary Sector in National Development.* New Delhi: Voluntary Action Cell, Planning Commission, 2002, 35.

Vakil, Anna C. "Confronting the Classification Problem: Toward a Taxonomy of NGOs." *World Development* 25, no. 12 (1997): 2057–70.

Vanaik, Achin. "The Enemy Within." *The Times of India Sunday Review,* December 16, 1990.

———. *The Furies of Indian Communalism: Religion, Modernity and Secularisation.* London: Verso Press, 1997.

———. *The Painful Transition: Bourgeois Democracy in Indias.* London: Verso Press, 1990.

VANI. *Report of the Task-Force to Review and Simplify Acts, Rules, Procedures affecting Voluntary Organisations.* New Delhi: Voluntary Action Network India, VANI, 1994.

Varshney, Ashutosh. "Democracy and Poverty." Conference on World Development Report. 1999.

———. *Democracy, Development and the Countryside: Urban Rural Struggles in India.* Cambridge: Cambridge University Press, 1995.

Vasavi, A. R. "Agrarian Distress in Bidar: Market, State and Suicides." *Economic and Political Weekly,* August 7, 1999, 2263–68.

———. *Harbingers of Rain: Land and Life in South India.* Delhi: Oxford University Press, 1999.

Vasavi, A. R., and Catherine P. Kingfisher. "Poor Women as Economic Agents: The Neo-Liberal State and Gender in India and the U.S." *Indian Journal of Gender Studies* 10, no. 1 (January–April 2003): 1–24.

Verma, Prashanjan. "Divided Colours of Cotton." *Down to Earth* (2001): 7–15.

Véron, R. "The 'New' Kerala Model: Lessons for Sustainable Development." *World Development* 29, no. 4 (2001): 601–17.

Vijayanand, S. M. "Issues Related to Administrative Decentralisation and the Administering of Decentralisation." Paper presented at the Workshop on Decentralisation, organized by the Institute for Social and Economic Change at Bangalore, May 31 and June 1, 2001.

Visaria, Pravin M. "The Sex Ratio of the Population of India." *Census of India 1961,* vol. 1. Monograph no. 10, 1969.

Visvanathan, Shiv, and Chandrika Parmer. "A Biotechnology Story: Notes from India." *Economic and Political Weekly,* July 6, 2002, 2714–24.

Viswanath, Vanita. *NGOs and Women's Development in Rural South India: A Comparative Analysis.* Boulder, Colo.: Westview Press, 1991.

Vohra, Gautam. *Altering Structures: Innovative Experiments at the Grassroots.* Bombay: Tata Institute of Social Sciences, 1990.

Vyas, V. S., and Pradeep Bhargava. "Public Intervention for Poverty Alleviation: An Overview." *Economic and Political Weekly,* October 14–21, 1995.

Vyasulu, Poornima, and Vinod Vyasulu. "Women in the Panchayati Raj: Grassroots Democracy in India." in *Women's Political Participation and Good Governance: 21st Century Challenge,* edited by UNDP. New York: UNDP, 2000.

Vyasulu, Vinod. "Management of Poverty Alleviation Programmes in Karnataka: An Overview." *Economic and Political Weekly* 30, nos. 41 and 42 (1995): 2635–50.

Wade, R. "The Market for Public Office: Why the Indian State Is Not Better at Development." *World Development* 13, no. 4 (1995): 467–97.

Webster, Neil. "Local Organizations and Political Space in the Forests of West Bengal." In *In the Name of the Poor: Contesting Political Space for Poverty Reduction,* edited by Neil Webster and Lars Engberg-Pedersen, 233–54. London and New York: Zed Books, 2002.

———. "The Role of NGDOs in Indian Rural Development: Some Lessons from West Bengal and Karnataka." *The European Journal of Development Research* 25, no. 2 (1995): 407–33.

———. "Tribal Women's Co-operatives in Bankura, West Bengal." *European Journal of Development Studies* 6, no. 2 (1994): 95–103.

Webster, Neil, and Lars Engberg-Pedersen, eds. *In the Name of the Poor: Contesting Political Space for Poverty Reduction.* London, New York: Zed Books, 2002.

Weiner, Myron. "The Struggle for Equality: Caste in Indian Politics." In *The Success of India's Democracy,* edited by Atul Kohli. Cambridge: Cambridge University Press, 2001.

Weiss, Charles, and Thomas Eisner. "Partnerships for Value-Added through Bioprospecting." *Technology in Society* 20 (1998), 481–98.

Winston, Mark L. *Travels in the Genetically Modified Zone.* Cambridge: Harvard University Press, 2002.

Wolch, Jennifer. "Decentering America's Nonprofit Sector: Reflections on Salamon's Crisis Analysis." In *Third Sector Policy at the Crossroads,* edited by Helmut K. Anheier and Jeremy Kendall, 51–60. London and New York: Routledge, 2001.

"Women's Role in Planned Economy." Report of the Subcommittee. Bombay: Vora and Co., 1947.

World Bank. *Gender and Poverty in India.* Washington, D.C.: The World Bank, 1991.

———. "India Shows Mixed Progress in the War against Poverty." News Release No. 98/1449SAS. 1997.

———. "Volume I: Overview of Rural Decentralization in India" and "Volume II: Approaches to Rural Decentralization in Seven States." September 27, 2000.

Wright, Erik Olin. "Worker's Organization and Capitalist Class Interests." *American Journal of Sociology* (March 2000).

Zaidi, A. M., ed. *The Annual Register of Indian Political Parties: Proceedings and Fundamental Texts.* New Delhi: S. Chand, 1980.

Zaidi, S. Akbar. "NGO Failure and the Need to Bring Back the State." *Journal of International Development* 11 (1999): 259–71.

Zelliot, Eleanor. *From Untouchable to Dalit: Essays on the Ambedkar Movement.* New Delhi: Manohar Publications, 1992.

Index

grain surpluses, 218
Gramsci, Antonio, 147
Green Revolution, 193, 194, 195, 218, 219
Guha, Ramachandra, 11, 24, 83, 162–64, 167, 174
Guha, Ranajit, 215
Gujarat, 62
Gurusabha, 70
Guruswamy (labor leader), 49

Hardgrave, Robert, 8
Hasiru Sene, 208
Hegdewar, Dr., 67
Hegel, G. W. F., 83
Heller, Patrick, 56
Hensman, Rohini, 122–23
Hindu nationalism. *See* Hindu Right; religious nationalism
Hindu Right, 62–76; backlash of, 5; environmental movements and, 177n23; global investors and, 62–63, 74–75; not an ideology, 181; Left critique of, 65–66; multiple facets of, 62, 66; women's movement and, 111. *See also* Bharatiya Janata Party (BJP); Rashtriya Swayamsevak Sangh (RSS)
Hindurashtra, 10
Hindutva. *See* Hindu Right
HMSS, 38
Hulme, David, 239

identity politics, 142–46
IFL. *See* Indian Federation of Labor
imperialism, 179
India, self-perception of, 74–75
India Shining, 72, 134n53, 198
Indian Association of Women's Studies, 121
Indian Cooperative Union, 14
Indian Farmers Federation, Andhra Pradesh, 214
Indian Farmers Petition, 216
Indian Federation of Labor (IFL), 38
Indian Merchants Chamber, 47
Indian National Congress. *See* Congress Party

Indian National Trade Union Congress (INTUC), 43, 49, 50, 55
Indian Trust Act (1882), 236
Industrial Disputes Act (1947), 42, 49
Industrial Employment (Standing Orders) Act, 42
Industrial Truce Conference, 39–41, 43–44, 53
informal sector, dalits in, 138
insulin, 204–5
Integrated Child Development Scheme (ICDS), 114–15
intellectual property, 221
Inter-Continental Caravan, 216–17
International Dalit Solidarity Network, 153
International Rivers Network, 168
INTUC. *See* Indian National Trade Union Congress
irrigation, 192–93
Isaac, Thomas, 94
Iyer, V. R. Krishna, 209

Jagmohan, Shri, 170
Jain, Devaki, 111
Jain, L. C., 14
Jan Sangh, 16–17
Janakeeya Aasoothranam, 93
Janata Party, 237, 243
Jhabvala, Renana, 123–24
Jharkhand Mukti Morcha, 18
Jhaveri, Jharna, 168
Joshi, N. M., 36, 49
Joshi, Sharad, 184–90, 192–94, 197, 212–13
JP, 242–43

Kamath, M. V., 73
Kanwar, Roop, 2
Karat, Prakash, 238
Karnataka, 249–50; Mahila Samakhya in, 254–56; NGOs in, 250
Karnataka Rajya Rayatu Sangha (KRRS), 185, 187–88, 190, 193–94, 196, 206–10, 216, 217
Kaviraj, Sudipta, 5, 88
Kentucky Fried Chicken, 206

Uttar Pradesh (UP), 150, 166
Uttaranchal, 166, 173

Vajpayee, Atal Bihari, 204, 233
Varshney, Ashutosh, 4, 214
Vasavi, A. R., 193
Ventakatachaliah, Justice, 119
VHP. *See* Vishwa Hindu Parishad
Via Campesina, 207
Visaria, Pravin, 110
Vishwa Hindu Parishad (VHP), 64, 72–73, 166
voluntarism. *See* nongovernmental organizations (NGOs)
Voluntary Action Cell, 245
Voluntary Health Association of India (VHAI), 243
Voluntary Technical Corps, Kerala, 98
Vyavasayigal Sangham, 185

wages: business versus labor on, 50–51; minimum, 52
Warrangal farmer suicides, 205–6, 207
WDP. *See* Women's Development Programme
Webster, Neil, 257
Weiner, Myron, 139
welfare, dismantling of, 9
West Bengal, 250–51; land reform in, 2; Nari Bikash Samiti in, 256–57; NGOs in, 238, 250
women: female/male ratio, 127–28, 134n59; NGOs and, 249–58; in

politics, 125–26, 254, 255. *See also* women's movement
Women's Development Programme (WDP), 113–15
Women's Indian Association (WIA), 108
women's movement, 107–28; anti-arrack agitation, 115–17; development and, 109–12; developments in, 19; future of, 128; history of, 108–9; inequalities not gender-based and, 126; liberalization and, 120–23, 192; middle and upper class emphasis of, 110–11; multiple facets of, 110–11, 120–21; in Nehruvian state, 14–15; politics and, 125–26; population control and, 117–20; poverty and, 184; SEWA and, 123–24; Women's Development Programme, 113–15
Women's Role in a Planned Economy, sub-committee on, 108–9
Women's Voice, 152
working class movements, 180
World Bank, 9, 114, 124, 168, 170
World Conference against Racism, 153
World Council of Churches, 153
World Trade Organization (WTO), 180, 187

Yadav, Mulayam Singh, 150

Zamindara Union, 185

About the Contributors

Amita Baviskar has taught sociology at the University of Delhi and is currently a Ciriacy-Wantrup Fellow at the University of California, Berkeley. Her research focuses on the cultural politics of environment and development. Her publications include the monograph *In the Belly of the River: Tribal Conflicts over Development in the Narmada Valley* (Oxford University Press, 1995) and the edited volumes *Waterlines: The Penguin Book of River Writings* (Penguin, 2003) and *Waterscapes: The Cultural Politics of a Natural Resource* (Permanent Black, forthcoming).

Anuradha Chakravarty earned her bachelor's degree in political science from Presidency College, Calcutta, and her master's degree in international relations from Jawaharlal Nehru University, New Delhi. A student of comparative politics, her research interests center on issues of identity, nationalism, social movements, political transitions, and social change. For many years, she has researched the role of grass roots actors in the peace process in Nagaland in northeast India. Currently a PhD candidate in the Department of Government at Cornell University (Ithaca, N.Y.), she is on a grant conducting dissertation fieldwork in Rwanda on the topic of justice and reconciliation in postgenocide Rwanda, focusing on conflict management.

Vivek Chibber received his PhD at the University of Wisconsin and is assistant professor of sociology at New York University. He is author of *Locked in Place: State-Building and Late Industrialization in India* (Princeton University Press, 2003). He is currently studying the developmental state in Latin America and the Middle East and has also started a project on the onset of liberalization in the developing world.

Gopal Guru is professor of political science at the Centre for Political Studies, Jawaharlal Nehru University, New Delhi. He has worked extensively on dalit culture and politics. He is at present editing a book on humiliation.

Patrick Heller is an associate professor of sociology at Brown University. He is the author of *The Labor of Development: Workers and the Transformation of Capitalism in Kerala, India* (Cornell University Press, 1999) and has written on a range of topics on India, including democratic consolidation, the politics of economic transformation, social capital, and social movements. He is currently engaged in a long-term project exploring the dynamics of democratic deepening in India, Brazil, and South Africa.

Ronald J. Herring has long been involved in issues of property, poverty, and agriculture in the subcontinent. He is currently editing a special issue of the *Journal of Development Studies,* entitled "Transgenics and the Poor," examining the ways in which new technologies interact with agrarian systems and public policy in terms of life chances of the poor. His earliest academic interests were with land relations and poverty; *Land to the Tiller: The Political Economy of Agrarian Reform in South Asia* (Yale University Press/Oxford University Press) won the Edgar Graham Prize (London 1986). His political writings have appeared in *Frontline, Times of India, Financial Express* and other publications. Herring is currently director/convener of the Program on Nature and Development at Cornell University.

Mary E. John is associate professor and deputy director of the Women's Studies Programme in Jawaharlal Nehru University, New Delhi. She has published widely in the fields of women's studies and feminist theory. Her publications include *Discrepant Dislocations: Feminism, Theory, and Post Colonial Histories* (University of California Press, 1996), *A Question of Silence? The Sexual Economies of Modern India* coedited with Janaki Nair, (Zed Books, 1998), and a coedited book, *French Feminism: An Indian Anthology* (Sage Publications, 2003).

Mary Fainsod Katzenstein is professor of government and faculty member of the feminist, gender, and sexuality studies (FGSS) program at Cornell. Her books and articles address issues of gender and race in the United States; the women's movements in Europe, the United States, and India; and issues about equality, ethnicity, and social movements in India. Her book, *Faithful and Fearless; Moving Feminist Protest Inside the Church and Military* (Princeton University Press, 1998) won the Victoria Schuck prize from the American Political Science Association. In the last several years, her work has focused on prison reform activism in the United States.

Neema Kudva is assistant professor of city and regional planning at Cornell University. Her research examines the institutional basis for planning, development and change through the work of nongovernmental and community-based organizations and through the ways in which local governments respond to increasingly diverse communities in the United States. She is also interested in the diversity of urbanization patterns as well as the development of intermediate cities in India, an overlooked topic critical to understanding contemporary urbanism. She is currently working on an edited volume of original essays on intermediate urbanization across the world.

Gail Omvedt is a sociologist working on issues of caste and social stratification and currently a senior fellow at the Nehru Memorial Museum and Library, New Delhi. Recent books include *Ambedkar: Towards an Enlightened India* (Penguin India, 2004); *Buddhism in India: Challenging Brahmanism and Caste* (Sage India, 2003); translation of *Growing Up Untouchable in India: A Dalit Autobiography* (Rowman & Littlefield, 2002). She has worked as an activist with women's movements and farmers' movements in India.

Raka Ray is associate professor of sociology and South and Southeast Asia studies and chair of the Center for South Asia Studies at the University of California, Berkeley. Her areas of specialization are gender and feminist theory, social movements, and relations between dominant and subaltern groups in India. Publications include *Fields of Protest: Women's Movements in India* (University of Minnesota, 1999; Kali for Women, 2000), "Masculinity, Femininity And Servitude: Domestic Workers in Calcutta in the Late Twentieth Century" in *Feminist Studies* (26:3), and (with Seemin Qayum) "Grappling with Modernity: Calcutta's Respectable Classes and the Culture of Domestic Servitude" in *Ethnography* (4:4, 2003). She is an editor of *Feminist Studies*.

Tanika Sarkar is professor at the Centre for Historical Studies, Jawaharlal Nehru University in New Delhi. She is the author of *Bengal 1928-1934: The Politics of Protest* (Oxford University Press, 1987), *Words to Win: The Making of Amar Jiban, A Modern Autobiography* (Kali for Women, 1999) and *Hindu Wife, Hindu Nation: Community, Religion, and Cultural Nationalism* (Permanent Black, 2001). She has also coauthored, along with Basu, et al., *Khaki Shorts and Saffron Flags: A Critique of Hindutva* (Orient Longman, 1993); and, coedited with Urvashi Butalia, *Women and the Hindu Right* (Kali, 1995).